BASIC READING SKILLS HANDBOOK

Sixth Edition

Instructor's Annotated Edition

HARVEY S. WIENER

Marymount Manhattan College

CHARLES BAZERMAN

University of California, Santa Barbara

New York San Francisco Boston
London Toronto Sydney Tokyo Singapore Madrid
Mexico City Munich Paris Cape Town Hong Kong Montreal

Senior Acquisitions Editor: Susan Kunchandy
Development Editor: Janice Wiggins-Clarke
Senior Marketing Manager: Melanie Craig
Senior Supplements Editor: Donna Campion
Production Manager: Stacey Kulig
Project Coordination, Text Design, and Electronic Page Makeup: Electronic Publishing Services Inc., NYC
Cover Design Manager: Wendy Ann Fredericks
Cover Designer: Joseph DePinho
Photo Researcher: Photosearch, Inc.
Manufacturing Buyer: Roy Pickering
Printer and Binder: R. R. Donnelly and Sons Company
Cover Printer: Coral Graphics Services, Inc.

For permission to use copyrighted material, grateful acknowledgment is made to the copyright holders on pp. 513–518 which are hereby made part of this copyright page.

Library of Congress Cataloging-in-Publication Data

Wiener, Harvey S.
Basic reading skills handbook / Harvey S. Wiener, Charles Bazerman. -- 6th ed.
p. cm.
Includes bibliographical references and index.
ISBN 0-321-19887-5
1. Reading (Higher education)--Handbooks, manuals, etc. 2. Reading comprehension—Handbooks, manuals, etc. 3. Vocabulary—Handbooks, manuals, etc. I. Bazerman, Charles. II. Title.
LB2395.3.W446 2006
428.4'071'1—dc22

2005013278

Visit us at http://www.ablongman.com.

ISBN 0-321-19887-5
Annotated Instructor's Edition ISBN 0-321-32889-2

1 2 3 4 5 6 7 8 9 10—DOC—08 07 06 05

Contents

Unit Two USING AIDS TO READING 51

Unit Three UNDERSTANDING MAIN IDEAS 135

Preface

Basic Reading Skills Handbook, Sixth Edition, has the good fortune of a new publisher, Pearson Education, Inc. As in the previous editions, this book is written specifically for the first-level college reading course. Following the successful approach and format of the next-level companion text, *Reading Skills Handbook*, this text focuses on more basic college reading, study, and literal comprehension skills. Important pedagogical features include:

- A handbook of reading skills with exercises keyed to the skills.
- An anthology of high-interest reading selections with extensive exercises that refer back to the handbook chapters.
- Special attention to using contextual clues and to learning multiple meanings of words.
- Chapters on prereading warm-ups, visual aids, and SQ3R.
- Material on the visual organization of Web pages.
- Extensive practice in comprehension skills such as finding the main idea, sorting out major and minor details, and inference skills.
- A "Cultural Exchange" glossary for each chapter and reading selection to explain references to cultural traditions and the languages and customs of the diverse peoples of the United States.
- A "Writing to Read" unit with chapters on underlining, listing, and summarizing, and on personalizing, where students learn to draw connections between their readings and their personal experiences, knowledge, and beliefs.
- "Critical Thinking and Writing" activities in the handbook and "Writing Practice" activities for each anthology reading.
- Internet resources and activities for each anthology selection.
- Lively readings on a wide range of topics, extracted from textbooks, magazines, and newspapers.
- Tests for self-assessment for each chapter, and review tests for each unit.

Organization

The text is divided into two main parts. The *Handbook* provides instruction in the essential reading skills, integrated with examples and extensive practice exercises. The *Reading Selections* include twelve long reading passages accompanied by prereading, comprehension, interpreting, vocabulary, and writing exercises that are coordinated and cross-referenced with the skills taught in the *Handbook*. If students have difficulty answering a question, they can easily find and review the material that covers that particular skill. Thus, a **7** after a question means that a review of Chapter 7, "Using Visual Aids," will help the student recall the techniques readers use to interpret visual material.

The anthology now also ends with a casebook of selections on a single theme: Romance, Love, and Marriage. The casebook readings are presented with discussion and writing questions. In this way, students can practice and integrate all their reading skills in a holistic way. The teacher may guide the discussion and activities as they fit for the class needs and interests.

In this book, students read a careful explanation of a specific skill and an analysis of how that skill applies to a particular passage. Then they can test their mastery of that skill by means of the many exercises designed for practice and review. This step-by-step approach allows students to move from simple skills to more complex ones with confidence. Throughout the text, students will find questions that guide their understanding and interpretation of specific passages.

The organization of the book allows teachers to adapt it to specific courses in several ways. Instructors may teach the units in the *Handbook* in the early weeks of the term, postponing the study of the *Reading Selections* until students know the essential reading skills. The brief readings in the *Handbook* allow the reinforcement of newly learned concepts, and students should be ready for the longer readings by the time they reach the *Reading Selections*. Or, instructors may choose to reinforce the skills taught in the *Handbook* by immediately assigning appropriate selections from the *Reading Selections*. In either case, chapters from the *Handbook* may be taught in any order that the instructor determines will fit the students' needs. Finally, as another alternative, instructors may begin with the *Reading Selections* and turn to key instructional units in the *Handbook* as specific needs arise in class. One of the hallmarks of the book is its flexibility of use for both teachers and students.

New to the Sixth Edition

A new chapter on critical reading helps students become better evaluators of what they read and offers specific practice on how to critically read an essay, textbook selection, and Web site.

A new section on the visual organization of web pages has been added to Chapter 7 on Using Visual Aids. This new section guides students through a number of well-known web sites (for example: The U.S. Census Bureau and The National Highway Safety Administration) and shows them how to use the various visuals on the sites to find important information.

Internet sources and activities are included with every anthology selection helping readers gain a deeper understanding of the topic presented.

A single theme casebook on romance, love, and marriage presents different perspectives on the subject along with a series of advertisements, a web site, and various articles. Throughout the section, readers encounter thought-provoking selections that stimulate and challenge their beliefs about romance, love, and marriage in the 21st century.

One-third of the readings are new to the sixth edition. Readings in both the Handbook and the Reading Selections include lively selections from books, magazines, and newspapers. We continue to emphasize materials from textbooks that students typically use during their college career.

Support for Instructors

Longman is pleased to offer a variety of support materials to help make teaching reading easier on teachers and to help students excel in their coursework. Many of our student supplements are available free or at a greatly reduced price when packaged with a Longman reading or study skills textbook. Contact your local Longman sales representative for more information on pricing and how to create a package.

Support Materials For Reading Instructors

Annotated Instructor's Edition (Instructor / 0-321-32889-2) The AIE includes all the answers to the exercises.

The Test Bank to Accompany *Basic Reading Skills Handbook* (Instructor / 0-321-19889-1) The Test Bank offers hundreds of questions specific to each chapter of the text.

Printed Test Bank for Developmental Reading (Instructor / 0-321-08596-5) Offers more than 3,000 questions in all areas of reading, including vocabulary, main idea, supporting details, patterns of organization, critical thinking, analytical reasoning, inference, point of view, visual aides, and textbook reading. (Electronic version also available; see CDs.)

Electronic Test Bank for Developmental Reading (Instructor / CD 0-321-08179-X) Offers more than 3,000 questions in all areas of reading, including vocabulary, main idea, supporting details, patterns of organization, critical thinking, analytical reasoning, inference, point of view, visual aides, and textbook reading. Instructors simply choose questions, then print out the completed test for distribution OR offer the test online.

The Longman Guide to Classroom Management (Instructor / 0-321-09246-5) This guide is designed as a helpful resource for instructors who have classroom management problems. It includes helpful strategies for dealing with disruptive students in the classroom and the "do's and don'ts" of discipline.

The Longman Guide to Community Service-Learning in the English Classroom and Beyond (Instructor / 0-321-12749-8) Written by Elizabeth Rodriguez Kessler of California State University-Northridge, this monograph provides a definition and history of service-learning, as well as an overview of how service-learning can be integrated effectively into the college classroom.

The Longman Instructor's Planner (Instructor / 0-321-09247-3) This planner includes weekly and monthly calendars, student attendance and grading rosters, space for contact information, Web references, an almanac, and blank pages for notes.

For Students:

Vocabulary Skills Study Card (Student / 0-321-31802-1) Colorful, affordable, and packed with useful information, Longman's Vocabulary Study Card is a concise, 8 page reference guide to developing key vocabulary skills, such as learning to recognize context clues, reading a dictionary entry, and recognizing key root words, suffixes, and prefixes. Laminated for durability, students can keep this Study Card for years to come and pull it out whenever they need a quick review.

Reading Skills Study Card (Student / 0-321-33833-2) Colorful, affordable, and packed with useful information, Longman's Reading Skills Study Card is a concise, 8 page reference guide to help students develop basic reading skills, such as concept skills, structural skills, language skills, and reasoning skills. Laminated for durability, students can keep this Study Card for years to come and pull it out whenever they need a quick review.

The Longman Textbook Reader, Revised Edition (with answers Student / 0-321- 11895-2 or without answers Student / 0-321-12223-2) Offers five complete chapters from our textbooks: computer science, biology, psychology, communications, and business. Each chapter includes additional comprehension quizzes, critical thinking questions, and group activities.

The Longman Reader's Portfolio and Student Planner (Student / 0-321-29610-9) This unique supplement provides students with a space to plan, think about, and present their work. The portfolio includes a diagnostic area (including a learning style questionnaire), a working area (including calendars, vocabulary logs, reading response sheets, book club tips, and other valuable materials), and a display area (including a progress chart, a final table of contents, and a final assessment), as well as a daily planner for students including daily, weekly, and monthly calendars.

The Longman Reader's Journal, by Kathleen McWhorter (Student / 0-321-08843-3) The first journal for readers, The Longman Reader's Journal offers a place for students to record their reactions to and questions about any reading.

The Longman Planner (Student / 0-321-04573-4) Ideal for organizing a busy college life! Included are hour-by-hour schedules, monthly and weekly calendars, an address book, and an almanac of tips and useful information.

10 Practices of Highly Effective Students (Student / 0-205-30769-8) This study skills supplement includes topics such as time management, test taking, reading critically, stress, and motivation.

***Newsweek* Discount Subscription Coupon (12 weeks) (Student / 0-321-08895-6)** *Newsweek* gets students reading, writing, and thinking about what's going on in the world around them. The price of the subscription is added to the cost of the book. Instructors receive weekly lesson plans, quizzes, and curriculum guides as well as a complimentary *Newsweek* subscription. The price of the subscription is .59 cents per issue (a total of $7.08 for the subscription). *Package item only.*

Interactive Guide to *Newsweek* (Student / 0-321-05528-4) Available with the 12-week subscription to *Newsweek*, this guide serves as a workbook for students who are using the magazine.

Research Navigator Guide for English, H. Eric Branscomb & Doug Gotthoffer (Student / 0-321-20277-5) Designed to teach students how to conduct high-quality online research and to document it properly, Research Navigator guides provide discipline-specific academic resources; in addition to helpful tips on the writing process, online research, and finding and citing valid sources. Research Navigator guides include an access code to Research Navigator™—providing access to thousands of academic journals and periodicals, the *New York Times* Search by Subject Archive, Link Library, Library Guides, and more.

Penguin Discount Novel Program In cooperation with Penguin Putnam, Inc., Longman is proud to offer a variety of Penguin paperbacks at a significant discount when packaged with any Longman title. Excellent additions to any developmental reading course, Penguin titles give students the opportunity to explore contemporary and classical fiction and drama. The available titles include works by authors as diverse as Toni Morrison, Julia Alvarez, Mary Shelley, and Shakespeare. To review the complete list of titles available, visit the Longman-Penguin- Putnam website: http://www.ablongman.com/penguin.

***The New American Webster Handy College Dictionary* (Student / 0-451-18166-2)** A paperback reference text with more than 100,000 entries.

***Merriam-Webster Collegiate Dictionary* (Student / 0-321-10494-3)** This hardcover comprehensive dictionary is available at a significant discount when packaged with any Longman text.

Multimedia Offerings

Interested in incorporating online materials into your course? Longman is happy to help. Our regional technology specialists provide training on all of our multimedia offerings.

MySkillsLab 2.0 (www.myskillslab.com) This exciting new website houses all the media tools any developmental English student will need to improve their reading, writing, and study skills, and all in one easy to use place. Resources for reading and study skills include:

- **Reading Roadtrip 4.0 Website.** The best selling reading software available, Reading Roadtrip takes students on a tour of 16 cities and landmarks throughout the United States, with each of the 16 modules corresponding to a reading or study skill. The topics include main idea, vocabulary, understanding patterns of organization, thinking critically, reading rate, notetaking and highlighting, graphic and visual aids, and more. Students can begin their trip by taking a brand diagnostics test that provides immediate feedback, guiding them to specific modules for additional help with reading skills.
- **Longman Vocabulary Website.** The Longman Vocabulary Website component of MySkillsLab features hundreds of exercises in ten topic areas to strengthen vocabulary skills. Students will also benefit from "100 Words That All High School Graduates Should Know," a useful resource that provides definitions for each of the words on this list, vocabulary flashcards and audio clips to help facilitate pronunciation skills.
- **Longman Study Skills Website.** This site offers hundreds of review strategies for college success, time and stress management skills, study strategies, and more. Students can take a variety of assessment tests to learn about their organizational skills and learning styles, with follow-up quizzes to reinforce the strategies they have learned.

- **Research Navigator.** In addition to providing valuable help to any college student on how to conduct high-quality online research and to document it properly, Research Navigator provides access to thousands of academic journals and periodicals (including the *New York Times* Archive), allowing reading students to practice with authentic readings from college level primary sources.

MySkillsLab 2.0 is available in Website, CourseCompass, WebCT, and Blackboard formats.

Reading Road Trip 4.0 Plus Website (www.ablongman.com/readingroadtrip) The best selling reading site available, Reading Road Trip takes students on a tour of 16 cities and landmarks throughout the United States, with each of the 16 modules corresponding to a reading or study skill. The topics include main idea, vocabulary, understanding patterns of organization, thinking critically, reading rate, notetaking and highlighting, graphics and visual aids, and more. Students can begin their trip by taking a brand new diagnostics test that provides immediate feedback, guiding them to specific modules for additional help with reading skills. The all-new Reading Road Trip 4.0 PLUS will include:

- **Longman Vocabulary Website.** This site features hundreds of exercises in ten topic areas to strengthen vocabulary skills. Students will also benefit from "100 Words That All High School Graduates Should Know," a useful resource that provides definitions for each of the words on this list, vocabulary flashcards and audio clips to help facilitate pronunciation skills.
- **Longman Study Skills Website.** This site offers hundreds of review strategies for college success, time and stress management skills, study strategies, and more. Students can take a variety of assessment tests to learn about their organizational skills and learning styles, with follow-up quizzes to reinforce the strategies they have learned.
- **Research Navigator.** In addition to providing valuable help to any college student on how to conduct high-quality online research and to document it properly, Research Navigator provides access to thousands of academic journals and periodicals (including the NY Times Archive), allowing reading students to practice with authentic readings from college level primary sources.

Reading Road Trip 4.0 PLUS *with CourseCompass* Offers all the features of Reading Road Trip 4.0 Plus with course management features—including a gradebook to record student progress automatically as they progress through the program and an electronic test bank of over 3000 questions organized by grade level.

- **The Longman Vocabulary Website** ***(http://www.ablongman.com/vocabulary)*** This unique website features hundreds of exercises in ten topic areas to strengthen vocabulary skills. Students will also benefit from "100 Words That All High School Graduates Should Know," a useful resource that provides definitions for each of the words on this list, vocabulary flashcards and audio clips to help facilitate pronunciation skills. *Open access.*
- **Longman Study Skills Website (http://www.ablongman.com/studyskills)** This site offers hundreds of review strategies for college success, time and stress management skills, study strategies, and more. Students can take a variety of assessment tests to learn about their organizational skills and learning styles, with follow-up quizzes to reinforce the strategies they have learned. *Open access.*

STATE SPECIFIC SUPPLEMENTS

For Florida Adopters:

Thinking Through the Test: A Study Guide for the Florida College Basic Skills Exit Test, by D.J. Henry FOR FLORIDA ADOPTIONS ONLY. This workbook helps students strengthen their reading skills in preparation for the Florida College Basic Skills Exit Test. It features both diagnostic tests to help assess areas that may need improvement and exit tests to help test skill mastery. Detailed explanatory answers have been provided for almost all of the questions.

Available Versions:

- Thinking Through the Test A Study Guide for the Florida College Basic Skills Exit Tests: Reading and Writing, 2/e (0-321-27660-4)
- Thinking Through the Test A Study Guide for the Florida College Basic Skills Exit Tests: Reading and Writing, w/Answers, 2/e (0-321-27756-2)
- Thinking Through the Test A Study Guide for the Florida College Basic Skills Exit Tests: Reading (0-321-27746-5)
- Thinking Through the Test A Study Guide for the Florida College Basic Skills Exit Tests: Reading, w/Answers (0-321-27751-1)

Reading Skills Summary for the Florida State Exit Exam, by D. J. Henry (Student / 0-321-08478-0) FOR FLORIDA ADOPTIONS ONLY. An excellent study tool for students preparing to take Florida College Basic Skills Exit Test for Reading, this laminated reading grid summarizes all the skills tested on the Exit Exam.

CLAST Test Package, 4/e (Instructor / Print ISBN 0-321-01950-4) These two, 40-item objective tests evaluate students' readiness for the Florida CLAST exams. Strategies for teaching CLAST preparedness are included.

For Texas Adopters

The Longman THEA Study Guide, by Jeannette Harris (Student / 0-321-27240-0) Created specifically for students in Texas, this study guide includes straightforward explanations and numerous practice exercises to help students prepare for the reading and writing sections of THEA Test. **TASP Test Package, 3/e (Instructor / Print ISBN 0-321-01959-8)** These 12 practice pre-tests and post-tests assess the same reading and writing skills covered in the Texas TASP examination.

For New York/CUNY Adopters

Preparing for the CUNY-ACT Reading and Writing Test, edited by Patricia Licklider (Student / 0-321-19608-2) This booklet, prepared by reading and writing faculty from across the CUNY system, is designed to help students prepare for the CUNY-ACT exit test. It includes test-taking tips, reading passages, typical exam questions, and sample writing prompts to help students become familiar with each portion of the test.

Correlations to Basic Reading Skills Tests

Many states require college students to demonstrate their competence in reading. In the tables below, the reading skills included in two representative state tests are correlated to the sections in *Basic Reading Skills Handbook* where the specific skills are covered.

TEXAS ACADEMIC SKILLS PROGRAM (TASP)	
Determine the Meaning of Words and Phrases	
Words with multiple meanings	1d
Unfamiliar and uncommon words and phrases	1a, 1b, 1c, 2a, 2b, 3f
Figurative language	1d, 13
Understand the Main Idea and Supporting Details in Written Material	
Stated vs. implied main idea	8c(1), 8c(2)
Supporting details	10b
Identify a Writer's Purpose, Point of View, and Intended Meaning	
Recognizing a writer's intent	12, 13
Analyze the Relationship Among Ideas in Written Material	
Organizational patterns and relationships in written materials	10b, 10c
Drawing conclusions from written material	12, 13
Use Critical Reasoning Skills to Evaluate Written Material	
Steps in critically evaluating written material	12, 13, 14

Apply Study Skills to Reading Assignments	
Summarizing, notetaking, outlining	15a, 15b, 15c
Interpreting information in graphic form	7

FLORIDA COLLEGE LEVEL ACADEMIC SKILLS TEST (CLAST)	
Reading with Literal Comprehension	
Recognizing main ideas	8, 9
Identifying supporting details	10b
Determining meaning of words on the basis of context	1c
Reading with Critical Comprehension	
Recognizing the author's purpose	14
Identifying the author's overall organizational pattern	10c
Distinguishing between statements of fact and statements of opinion	12
Detecting bias	12, 13, 14
Recognizing the author's tone	12, 13, 14
Recognizing the explicit and implicit relationships within sentences	8a
Recognizing the implicit as well as explicit relationships between sentences	8b, 8c
Recognizing valid arguments	12, 13, 14
Drawing logical inferences and conclusions	13

Handbook

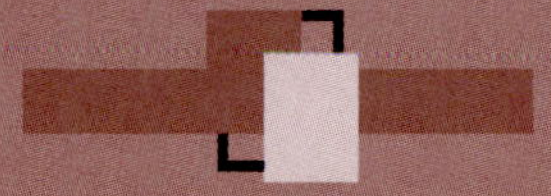

Learning to read is not learning just a single skill. It is learning many skills that work together and build on one another. Each time you improve any one skill, you strengthen all the others. As your vocabulary improves, you will be able to understand and interpret your reading. As you learn to comprehend and interpret better, you will gain more clues about the meaning of unfamiliar words.

The first part of this book teaches the basic skills of reading. Each section explains a separate skill. Exercises follow each section so you can practice each skill as you learn about it. Teachers may assign chapters for the whole class to study or may assign you sections to work on individually, depending on your needs. Also, as you find areas you want to work on personally, you can go over chapters on your own. We have included new self-tests at the end of each chapter. When you finish a test, check your answers beginning on page 505.

The skills are separated into six units: Building Vocabulary, Using Aids to Reading, Understanding Main Ideas, Finding Information, Interpreting What You Read, and Writing to Read. The detailed table of contents and index will help you locate the exact page of any skill you want to work on.

Each skill also is given a number based on the chapter and section in which it is discussed. For example, finding main ideas in paragraphs is discussed in section c of Chapter 8, "Reading for the Main Idea." The number **8c**, then, refers to the section you need to review for help in finding main ideas in paragraphs. When you are reading one section, the book may refer to another section by using the number of the other section. Your teacher may write a section number on a piece of your work to suggest you go over a particular section.

The second part of this book has reading selections with questions. Each question has a reference number that lets you know which skill is needed to answer the question. If you have problems with the question, you can look at that section in the first half of the book for help.

Finally, chapters include a section called "Cultural Exchange." This section includes a list of terms and definitions that will help you better comprehend the material in the exercises and readings in *Basic Reading Skills Handbook*. These terms, listed in the order in which they appear in the text, provide social and historical background information about American culture and the language, traditions, or customs of varied ethnic groups. "Cultural Exchange" also precedes each reading selection in the second part of this book.

UNIT ONE

Building Vocabulary

CHAPTER ONE

Recognizing Word Meanings

1a Finding Out What Words Mean

Most of us know enough vocabulary to read from the many sources of information around us. We can read newspapers, magazines, signs, posters, advertisements, credit card and job applications, instructions, and recipes, to name a few examples. The richer our vocabulary, the more sources of information are available to us. The more we read, the more our vocabulary grows. You may not be as confident about reading a textbook or a set of directions on how to work your iPOD, as you are about reading newspaper ads or signs in the supermarket. Still, adding to your usual readings with a wide variety of materials can help you expand your knowledge of words. It also can improve your reading skills.

First, you should realize that you cannot know the meaning of every word you see. Sometimes you may say to yourself, "I sort of know what this means" or "I can get by without figuring this one out." Often, however, you need to find out exactly what an unfamiliar word means. In the short run, not paying attention to words you don't know may save you some work. In the long run, not paying attention to words means you just won't know as much as you should.

Here are some ways to find the meanings of difficult words:

- Learn to use the context—that is, the clues that surrounding words and sentences give about the meanings of new words.
- Learn to use visual clues, such as pictures, drawings, signs, and symbols, that can help you figure out meanings. Often a picture starts you thinking about an unfamiliar word on the page, and you can work out a usable definition.

- Look for familiar parts within a word you don't know; you might know what the parts mean. For example, if you know the meaning of *art*, you might be able to guess at the meaning of *artistic* or *artful*.
- Learn the difference between what a word means and what a word suggests or makes you feel. Even words that have the same meaning can suggest different things to different people. Although *happy* and *joyous* both suggest good feelings, *joyous* is a much stronger word; it creates a feeling of powerful happiness.
- Be aware that one word can have many meanings. The word *check*, for example, has more than thirty separate meanings! We check our facts, write a check to pay bills, get a checkup at the doctor's, and put a check next to a correct answer, just to name a few.
- Learn to use a dictionary so you can find meanings easily. Dictionaries help you in many ways, not only for finding the meanings of words but also for finding how to pronounce the words, how to spell them, how to use them correctly, and how to change their forms, among many other uses.
- Keep a list of words that you want to add to your vocabulary. By writing down new words and trying to learn them, you can improve your vocabulary.

1b Remembering New Words

Once you've learned a new word and you think you understand it, try to make sure you don't forget it. To remember new words, do the following:

- Write the word and its definition often, just for practice.
- Say the word. Learn to pronounce it correctly by using the pronunciation clues in your dictionary.
- Use the word when you talk—in class, with friends, at home. Make sure you pronounce the word correctly.
- Try to learn the word and its meaning the first time you see it.
- Use index cards to study vocabulary. Write the word on one side of a card and its definition on the other side.
- Make up a sentence you can understand using the word.

- Change the ending of the word: Try to make it plural; try to change the tense; try to add *ly*.
- Use the word whenever you can in your writing assignments.
- Say the word and its meaning over and over again in your mind.
- Don't try to learn long lists of new words. Study just a few words each day for several days so you can learn by repeating.

1c Using Context Clues

An important part of building your reading skills is learning how to guess what unfamiliar words mean. Very often a word you have never seen before appears in a sentence. Perhaps it is a word you *have* seen before, but you don't remember its meaning. Maybe it is a word whose meaning you thought you knew, but the meaning doesn't make sense in the sentence you're reading.

All readers, even the best and most experienced, come across such words from time to time. You see a word and it stumps you. You don't know its meaning quickly. But don't reach for the dictionary right away! (Use your dictionary when nothing else works.) Often you can figure out what a word means from clues in the sentence in which it appears or in surrounding sentences. These clues are *context clues. Context* here means surrounding words, phrases, sentences, and paragraphs that help you find out meanings.

Sentences give clues that help a reader guess at definitions of unfamiliar words. Try to use clues to figure out the meaning of the word *pillory* from the sentences below.

(1) An early form of punishment in America was the pillory. (2) A wooden framework with holes for the hands and head, the pillory stood in a central place for everyone to see. (3) A person who committed a crime was locked in the structure so that people could make fun of the criminal. (4) Even now, when we say that a person is *pilloried*, we are saying that the person is exposed to scorn or ridicule.

What is a pillory?

Student responses will vary.
____

____

You probably wrote something like this: *A pillory is a wooden structure used for punishing criminals in America many years ago. The criminal's head and hands were locked in the pillory, and he or she was put in a public place for everyone to make fun of.*

How did you figure out the meaning? You didn't stop reading when you saw the word *pillory* even though you might not have known its meaning right away. You knew from the first sentence that pillory was a form of punishment in early times in our country. Later sentences gave you other clues. You saw from sentence 2 that a pillory was a structure made of wood and that it had holes for people's hands and heads. You saw, too, that criminals were placed in these wooden traps so others could make fun of them. Sentence 4 explains how we use the word *pillory* today.

Words you think you don't know may be words you can figure out. Use the words and the sentences around the unfamiliar word to guess at the meaning. Of course, not every unfamiliar word is made clear by surrounding sentences. Sometimes context gives you no help at all. In many cases, however, you can come up with definitions from sentence clues.

The following chart names kinds of context clues, gives examples, and explains how to use the clues to find word meanings.

Using Sentence Clues to Find Word Meanings

Clue	*Example*	*Explanation*
Some sentences set off the definition for a difficult word by means of punctuation.	The *principal*—the money he put in his savings account to earn interest—was safe even though the bank was closed by the police.	The pair of dashes sets off the definition of *principal*, here used to mean "sum of money." Other punctuation that can set off meaning includes commas,, parentheses (), and brackets [].
Sometimes helping words, along with punctuation, introduce important clues to meaning.	Carlos looked *dazed*, that is, stunned, as if someone had shocked him with bad news or with a heavy blow to the head.	Helping words: *that is, meaning, such as, or, is called*.

Clue	*Example*	*Explanation*
Some sentences tell the opposite of what a new word means. From its opposite, you can figure out the meaning of the word.	During office hours, he looks very *tense*, but on weekends he is quite relaxed.	The word *but* helps you understand that *relaxed* is the opposite of *tense*. If you know that *relaxed* means "at ease," you can figure out that *tense* means "tight" or "at attention."
Sometimes you can use your own experience to figure out the definition of a word.	Martha's husband and mother died within a month of each other. She cried often at her terrible *sorrows*.	You know that family tragedy would fill a person with "great sadness," the meaning of *sorrows*.
Sentences before or after a sentence that contain a difficult word sometimes explain the meaning of the word.	The lovely wooden tray had grown *brittle*. It was dry and hard, and it cracked easily.	Anything dry, hard, and easily cracked can be called *brittle*.
Some sentences provide exact definitions of difficult words—words readers need to know to understand what they are reading.	She wanted baked clams for her *appetizer*. An appetizer is the first course of a meal.	The second sentence defines the word *appetizer* exactly.
Some sentences give examples for a new word, on which you can build a definition.	*Legumes*, such as string beans, lima beans, and green peas, are important in your diet.	The sentence doesn't say that *legume* is a name for a group of vegetables with pods, but you can figure out some of that meaning from the examples.
Some sentences use a word you do know to help explain a word you don't know.	The mayor wanted *privacy* because she knew that being alone would help her solve her problems.	You can tell from the sentence clues that *privacy* means "being alone."

EXERCISES

1.1 Sentence Clues

The words in italics (slanted type) may not be familiar to you. Try to use the hints in each sentence to make up a definition for the italic word. Then select the letter of the word you feel is closest to the meaning. Write the letter in the blank space. Finally, on a separate sheet of paper, identify the clues that helped you determine the meaning of the word in italics. Student responses will vary concerning clues.

__b__ 1. After staying up all night studying for finals, the students' faces looked *haggard*.
Haggard means
a. intelligent.
b. tired.
c. angry.
d. confused.

__c__ 2. We were not pleased about returning to school after the long summer *hiatus*.
Hiatus means
a. party.
b. days.
c. break.
d. work.

__d__ 3. The schoolyard bully was the *nemesis* of the smallest boy in the class. Every day at recess, the bully beat him up.
Nemesis means
a. brother.
b. equal.
c. protector.
d. enemy.

__a__ 4. The climate of the desert is hot and *arid*.
Arid means
a. dry.
b. dusty.
c. misty.
d. rainy.

__d__ 5. While she was waiting in the doctor's office, she *perused* a news magazine.
Perused means

a. stole.
b. tore up.
c. picked up.
d. looked at.

b 6. In the courtroom, the relationship between the prosecutor and the defense attorney in a murder case is *adversarial*. Outside of the courtroom, they may be friends.
Adversarial means
a. trusting.
b. in opposition.
c. polite.
d. comic.

d 7. If you complain about everything, you might gain a reputation as a *malcontent*.
Malcontent means
a. flatterer.
b. leader.
c. talker.
d. fault-finder.

d 8. The young child thinks lima beans taste *loathsome*. She refuses to eat them.
Loathsome means
a. fresh.
b. spicy.
c. sweet.
d. horrible.

a 9. Viewing women as wives and mothers only is *anachronistic*. Today women are doctors, lawyers, and CEOs.
Anachronistic means
a. out of proper time.
b. out of proper place.
c. not polite.
d. in a bad mood.

b 10. She fell asleep with her history book on her pillow and hoped she would learn the material through *osmosis*.
Osmosis means
a. reading.
b. absorption.
c. repetition.
d. friends.

___c___ 11. He wanted to be a chef, so he went to *culinary* school.
Culinary means
a. trade.
b. high.
c. cooking.
d. night.

___a___ 12. He wondered if his mother was *omniscient* because she seemed to know everything he did, even when she was not there.
Omniscient means
a. all-knowing.
b. fast.
c. ignorant.
d. all-powerful.

___c___ 13. The teacher graded down the student's essay because it was written in a *colloquial*, rather than a formal, style.
Colloquial means
a. fancy.
b. comic.
c. everyday.
d. misspelled.

___b___ 14. The cats who live in the park are *feral*. You can feed them, but don't try to pet them or pick them up.
Feral means
a. tame.
b. wild.
c. large.
d. peculiar.

___d___ 15. If you tell your teacher your dog ate your homework, she will question the *veracity* of your statement.
Veracity means
a. owner.
b. color.
c. logic.
d. truth.

1.2 Meanings in Your Own Words

Use whatever context clues you can to find the meaning for each word in italics. Write the definition in your own words. Do *not* use a dictionary.

1. I was extremely *apologetic* for being late to the party.

   Apologetic means expressing regrets.

2. The jury's verdict led to civil *strife*. There was so much rioting and looting that a dawn-to-dusk curfew was imposed.

   Strife means conflict.

3. The word bombshell *literally* means a bomb, but the word usually refers to anything that is a shock or a surprise. Sometimes the word even refers to people.

   Literally means precisely, according to exact meaning.

4. She spoke so softly her answer was almost *inaudible*.

   Inaudible means impossible to hear.

5. My room was in a state of *disarray*. Books and papers were piled up on the desk, clothes were all over the floor, and the bed had not been made in a week.

   Disarray means mess.

6. He kept *scrupulous* records. He balanced his checking account every month, kept receipts for all expenditures, and filed all important papers alphabetically.

   Scrupulous means careful; detailed and neat.

7. The car was equipped with all the *accessories* available: air conditioning, CD and DVD players, sunroof, electric windows, remote-control door locks, and satellite-guided direction system.

   Accessories means additional equipment.

8. His inability to pay attention to details was an *impediment* to success in school.

   Impediment means obstacle.

9. My name was written in *indelible* ink on the inside of my leather jacket.

   Indelible means permanent; not erasable.

10. She is an *altruistic* person. She gives money to the Red Cross and UNICEF, and on the weekends she works at the local shelter for battered women.

    Altruistic means selfless.

11. My grandmother taught me the importance of *decorum*. Whenever I receive a gift, I write a thank-you note.

    Decorum means appropriate behavior.

12. Most people (and other animals) are *repelled* by the odor a skunk emits when it is frightened.

    Repelled means driven away.

13. He was *frazzled* because he was trying to do three tasks at the same time.

    Frazzled means having worn-out nerves.

14. Washing your face, brushing your teeth, and combing your hair are *mundane*, but necessary, activities.

    Mundane means ordinary; unexciting.

15. The arrest of the suspect was *premature*. Later, someone else confessed to the crime.

    Premature means too early.

1.3 Word Meanings from Textbooks

Using context clues, determine the meaning of the italicized word in the textbook sentences. Select the correct definition from the choices given and write the letter of the correct answer in the blank.

c 1. Related to power and politics in organizational life is conflict. In its simplest form, *conflict* is disagreement among parties.

—*Management*

Conflict means
a. the organizational power of the controlling party.
b. office politics.

c. opposing views among different groups.
d. a violent fight.

__a__ 2. The problem of limited resources in the world results in a *scarcity* of available resources to meet all the wants of a group of people. Scarcity is a lack of something that can be used to satisfy all the wants of a group of people.

—*Economics*

Scarcity means
a. a lack of something.
b. available resources.
c. satisfying people's wants.
d. an environmental problem.

__d__ 3. Some computer systems use *cryptography* (secret writing) to protect information. Such systems store information in the computer in coded or scrambled form.

—*Computer science*

Cryptography means
a. protected information.
b. computer systems.
c. stored information.
d. secret writing.

__a__ 4. The source of the sun's energy is a process known as *fusion*. In this process, hydrogen atoms combine to form helium atoms. The sun contains plenty of hydrogen fuel.

—*Chemistry*

Fusion means
a. the process by which hydrogen atoms combine to become atoms of helium.
b. confusion among atoms of the sun.
c. the process by which the sun develops new hydrogen fuel.
d. sunrise.

__d__ 5. Presidents have occasionally refused to spend the money Congress has authorized. This practice is called *impoundment*.

—*Government*

Impoundment means
a. the national budget.
b. spending federal funds.
c. Congress's refusing funds that a president requests.
d. the President's not spending funds approved by Congress.

1.4 More Word Meanings from Textbooks

Each example contains one or more words in italics. Clues in the sentences will help you figure out the meaning of the italicized words. Write their definitions in the space provided. Do *not* use a dictionary.

1. When you make a reasonable guess that explains how or why something happened, you are making a hypothesis. A *hypothesis* is a possible explanation that can be tested. It is based on what you already know. You are not sure that your hypothesis is correct. You can often make more than one hypothesis for a situation.

   —*Life science*

   Hypothesis means a possible explanation that can be tested.

2. History books usually present events in *chronological* order—that is, they start with the earliest events and end with the most recent ones. Chronological order is order based on time.

   —*History*

   Chronological means time order.

3. *Hypnotism* is the process of *inducing* a state of relaxation in which people seem to behave in ways they may not do otherwise. People who have been hypnotized often report that their actions are *involuntary*—things that are happening to them, not things they are doing.

   The key to hypnotism is *suggestion*, the odd sort of communication used by hypnotists. Instead of issuing a command—"Raise your arm!"—a hypnotist might say, "When I count to three, your arm will rise" or "Your arm is getting very light." In responding to hypnotic suggestions, subjects adopt a curiously *passive* attitude toward their own actions, lifting their arm without feeling they are in fact responsible for the movement.

   —*Psychology*

   Hypnotism means process of inducing a special state of relaxation.

   Inducing means bringing about.

   Involuntary means not under a person's control.

   Suggestion means an indirect command.

   Passive means not under a person's control.

4. The most important crop in South China is rice. If you could fly over South China during certain times of the year, you might think you were looking down into a giant mirror. What you saw would not be glass, however. Instead, it would be thousands of water-covered fields called *paddies*. Those are the fields where rice is grown. Fields are *flooded* with about fifteen centimeters (six inches) of water, and rice seedlings are planted. While the rice grows, farmers work hard to keep the fields free of weeds. Just before the harvest, the water is *drained* from the fields. The rice is then *harvested*, tied into bundles, and dried in the sun for about a week. Finally, farmers *thresh* the rice, separating the grains from the stalks.

—*Geography*

Paddies means water-covered fields.

Flooded means overrun with water.

Drained means liquids removed.

Harvested means gathered, as a crop.

Thresh means separate into parts.

5. A *set* is a collection of objects. The objects are called the *members*, or *elements*, of the set. You use *braces*, { }, to indicate that a set is being named. Within the braces, you separate the members of the set by commas. For example, to indicate "the set whose members are 1, 3, 5, and 7," you write

$$\{1, 3, 5, 7\}.$$

To indicate that 5 is a member of this set, you use the symbol $\in$, is a member of, and write

$$5 \in \{1, 3, 5, 7\}.$$

If you wish to indicate that 9 is not a member of this set, you use the symbol $\notin$, is not a member of, and write

$$9 \notin \{1, 3, 5, 7\}.$$

Sets that contain exactly the same members are called *equal sets*. You use the symbol $=$, is equal to, to indicate that sets are equal. The order in which you list the members of a set does not matter, and so

$$\{1, 3, 5, 7\} = \{3, 1, 7, 5\}.$$

On the other hand, the sets $\{1, 3, 5, 7\}$ and $\{1, 3, 5, 9\}$ do *not* contain exactly the same members. Therefore, you use the symbol ≠, does not equal, and write

$$\{1, 3, 5, 7\} \neq \{1, 3, 5, 9\}.$$

—*Algebra*

Set means a collection of objects.

Members means objects in a set.

Elements means objects in a set.

Braces means curly brackets { }.

∈ means is a member of.

∉ means is not a member of.

Equal sets means sets that contain exactly the same members.

≠ means does not equal.

1.5 Context Clues from Your Textbooks

Using one of your textbooks from another course, locate ten sentences that give clues for words with which you are not familiar. On a separate sheet of paper, copy each of the sentences and underline the word you do not know. Circle the clues that help you figure out the meaning. Then write your own definition of the word.

1d Considering Multiple Meanings

Some words have many meanings. Did you know, for example, that the word *light* has more than thirty definitions? Among those meanings are that which makes things visible, daytime, not heavy, pale in color, a gleam or sparkle in the eyes, and to set on fire. Look at the uses of the word in the following sentences. What does *light* mean in each case?

1. Please *light* the fire in the fireplace.
2. Esteban wore a *light* jacket despite the cold.
3. I painted my room a *light* blue.

4. We didn't know about his criminal record; only today has it come to *light*.
5. The wall cuts off our *light*.

If you had just one definition of the word *light* in mind when you read, you would not get the meanings in every case above. You have to consider the multiple definitions—multiple means "many"—of a word before making a decision about its meaning in a sentence.

How do you decide? Of course you want to start with what you believe the word means, based on your own experience and knowledge. Then, and this is very important, *test the meaning in the sentence*.

Let's look at sentence 2 above. Suppose you knew that the word *light* often meant "not dark." Suppose, too, you did not consider other possible meanings. You would think *light* referred to the color of the jacket. But you'd be wrong. If you looked at the surrounding words, however, you'd soon figure out what *light* meant.

The words *despite the cold* in sentence 2 tell you the jacket Esteban wore was not one the writer thought he should wear that day. The sentence tells you the weather was cold. In cold weather, you expect people to wear heavy jackets. But the word *despite* here says this jacket was not what you might expect. *Despite the cold* is a context clue that tells you the jacket was not heavy. The weather was cold, the sentence says, but Esteban wore an unexpected kind of jacket. You could pretty much guess at the meaning of the word *light*, then, as the opposite of *heavy*. You can see how far off base the meaning "not dark" would be.

Here again, context clues **(1c)** are very important. Don't decide on a meaning until you see how nearby words and sentences affect it.

EXERCISES

1.6 One Word, Many Meanings

Three familiar words—*free*, *tip*, and *dash*—appear below with many of their meanings. Next to each meaning is a letter. For each sentence that uses the word defined, select the letter of the definition that works best.

1. *free*
   a. at liberty
   b. costing nothing
   c. liberal or generous
   d. without restriction
   e. unoccupied

e 1. He circled the parking lot until he found a *free* space.

b 2. I have a coupon for a *free* hamburger when I buy one at the regular price.

d 3. The students had *free* choice on which book to read for their next report.

a 4. The criminal paid his debt to society, and now he is *free*.

c 5. She is so *free* with her money you might think she has a million dollars.

2. *tip*
   a. give a small sum of money for services rendered
   b. strike gently
   c. give advance or inside information
   d. tilt or lean
   e. touch or raise in greeting

e 1. The gentleman *tipped* his hat as I approached him.

b 2. The batter *tipped* the ball down the third-base line.

d 3. The lampshade was *tipped* slightly to one side, so I reached over and straightened it.

c 4. The robber was *tipped* off that the police were about to arrive.

a 5. I *tipped* the porter for carrying my bags to the cab.

3. *dash*
   a. strike or break with violence
   b. apply roughly, as if splashing
   c. a short line used as punctuation
   d. a small amount of something mixed in with other things
   e. ruin something
   f. a short race
   g. write something quickly

f 1. Miranda won the fifty-yard *dash* for the second year in a row.

e 2. The low score I got on my final exam *dashed* my hopes for an A in history.

a 3. He *dashed* the picture to the ground in a fit of anger.

b 4. The heat and the dust so weakened him that even the cold water he *dashed* across his face did not make him feel better.

d 5. Use a *dash* of hot pepper sauce to spice up the gravy.

c 6. Use a *dash* to show a sudden pause or break in a written sentence.

g 7. Jack *dashed* off a memo requesting new figures.

1.7 Many Meanings for Words You Know

You should know several meanings for each of the following words. On a separate paper, copy the words and then write at least two definitions for each. If you need help, use a dictionary **(2)**. Student responses will vary.

1. resort
2. desert
3. scale
4. fair
5. mean

1.8 Sentence Clues for Correct Meanings

For each word in italics, choose the letter of the correct meaning. Be careful! All the choices offer correct definitions for the word. However, only one definition works right in the sentence. Read carefully and use the context clues before choosing.

b 1. Karen asked Fran to *spot* her while she practiced gymnastics.
   a. make a stain
   b. pay attention
   c. situate precisely
   d. detect

d 2. After being caught taking bribes, the official was asked to *tender* his resignation.
   a. a rail car behind the engine
   b. easily crushed or bruised
   c. gentle and loving
   d. offer or hand in

d 3. He dried the *lip* carefully after he poured acid from the jar.
   a. the fleshy, outer part of the mouth
   b. words that are insincere
   c. the rim at the end of a pipe
   d. the edge of a container

d 4. When day *breaks*, you can see rays of brilliant sunlight over the Blue Ridge Mountains.
   a. divides into parts
   b. fractures
   c. discontinues
   d. dawns

a 5. He *engaged* her attention with tales of travel through Africa's national parks.
   a. occupied
   b. planned to marry
   c. entered into conflict
   d. pledged

CULTURAL Exchange

bully	an individual who is cruel or threatening, especially to smaller or weaker people (page 10)
CEO	a business term meaning Chief Executive Officer of a business firm or organization (page 11)
"My dog ate my homework."	a flippant answer to the question, "Where is your homework?"; an excuse given to a teacher when a student does not have the homework assignment done for class (page 12)

UNICEF	The United Nations Childrens Fund, an international nonprofit organization devoted to improving the health, education and quality of lives of children in all countries (page 14)
shelter for battered women	a safe place for women who are physically or sexually abused by their spouse or by any man in their lives (father, brother, son, etc.) (page 14)
pro-choice	a position relating to abortion, supporting a woman's right to have one if she so chooses and believing it is solely her choice (page 25)

Chapter 1 SELF-TEST
Recognizing Word Meanings

Use whatever information you can—context clues, word part clues, or multiple meanings—to figure out the meaning of each italicized word. Write your definition in the space provided. Count five points for each correct answer.

1. After many years, Betty Chan *encountered* her old friend on the street in a joyous, tearful meeting.

   Encountered means met.

2. The window was absolutely *transparent* or clear.

   Transparent means crystal clear.

3. Penny considered honesty an *axiom* or rule she would never betray.

   Axiom means basic principle; rule.

4. No eating, no chewing gum, no talking: Darius hated the *prohibitions* in his sixth-grade class.

   Prohibitions means forbidden acts.

5. Ricardo kept *embroidering* the story with unbelievable details so it sounded like fiction instead of fact.

   Embroidering means adding details to.

6. At *intervals*, the lost climbers lit candles, but the periods of time they had light grew shorter and shorter as their supplies ran low.

   Intervals means periods of time.

7. We knew we could count on support from the *clergy*. All the local priests, nuns, and rabbis joined in the effort to raise money for the needy after the earthquake in Mexico.

   Clergy means leaders of organized religions.

8. We had hoped for sun, but the sky remained *overcast* all day.

   Overcast means dark; gloomy.

9. It's a mistake to *rehash* that idea because you wrote about it twice before, and your teacher will see that it's just an old point in a new form.

   Rehash means go over again.

10. No wonder she refused to sell you her car; you offered such a *meager* sum in payment.

    Meager means insignificant.

11. The wind was *intense*—that is, strong and extreme—and we clung to the walls along the alleys so we wouldn't be blown away.

    Intense means strong and extreme.

12. *Nomads*—people who wander in tribes from place to place according to the food supply—often travel in the deserts of Asia and Africa.

    Nomads means wandering people.

13. Charlene was an active, busy, and lively child. Maureen, on the other hand, was quite *passive*.

    Passive means not given to action.

14. Latoya needed help unloading her car when she moved to her new apartment. But *inhospitable* neighbors showed no signs of friendship.

    Inhospitable means unfriendly.

15. Despite all his jokes, flattery, and sweet talk, Fred was not able to *cajole* his parents into buying him a car.

    Cajole means coax.

16. As a supporter of strict gun control laws and pro-choice measures, Juanita Sanchez is a leading *proponent* of liberal causes in the state.

    Proponent means supporter; advocate.

17. It was a horrible sight—with one powerful paw, the cat had *mauled* the sparrow, which lay bruised on the ground.

    Mauled means beaten up; injured badly.

18. The hotel manager called his name many times over the microphone, but he never answered the *page*.

    Page means announced call.

19. Bill didn't need his wool coat any longer, so he *donated* it to charity.

    Donated means gave.

20. They started their law careers together. Kwan's rise to success was *meteoric*, but her brother David's was slow and not particularly brilliant.

    Meteoric means quick and brilliant.

Score: __________ correct × 5 points each = ______

CHAPTER TWO

Using Word Part Clues

2a Compound Words

Occasionally, two words may be put together to form a new word called a *compound word*. If you look at each word part, you sometimes can recognize the new word. Then you can try to understand the meaning. For example, look at the following words:

bookmark	(book + mark)
landlocked	(land + locked)
openminded	(open + minded)
undercut	(under + cut)
broomstick	(broom + stick)
paperwork	(paper + work)
upstart	(up + start)

EXERCISES

2.1 Two Words in One

Each of the following words contains two or more words joined together to form a new word. Try to figure out the meaning of the new word by looking at the words that make it up. Write a definition in your own words in the space provided. Check your answer in a dictionary.

1. handspring a gymnastic feat
2. breakneck recklessly rapid
3. steelhead a kind of trout

4. mainstay a reliable support
5. doorstop a wedge for holding a door
6. laptop a light portable computer
7. chickpea a kind of small vegetable
8. spaceship vehicle for traveling outside the earth's atmosphere
9. toehold a small place to rest the foot
10. gatekeeper a person who decides who may enter

2.2 New Words

Choose a word from column A and combine it with a word in column B to form a new word that makes sense. (You may use some words in column B twice.) Write twelve new words and their definitions on a separate sheet of paper. Use a dictionary if you need help. Student responses will vary.

A	B
base	stream
wind	storm
sand	board
care	shooter
frame	bag
arrow	stain
fog	line
jet	head
brain	giver
sharp	horn
waist	chime
blood	work

Examples:

windbag a talkative person who says little
baseline starting point

2b Prefixes, Suffixes, and Roots

Words new to you may contain certain groups of letters that have meanings you can learn. If you don't know what a word itself means, these groups of letters may help you define it.

- When a group of letters with a special meaning appears in front of a word, it is called a *prefix*.
- When a group of letters with a special meaning appears at the end of a word, it is called a *suffix*.

You've probably seen the word *emotion*. It means "feeling." Now look at the word *unemotional*.

- The prefix *un* means "not" or "lack of."
- The suffix *al* means "related to."

When you break down the meaning of the parts of the word *unemotional*, you get "related to a lack of feelings." Knowing the prefix and suffix helps you figure out what the word means. You might not have to use a dictionary.

The *root* (or stem) is the basic part of the word. We add prefixes and suffixes to some roots and create new words. In the example above, *emotion* is the stem. You knew that word and could build meanings for words made by adding prefixes and suffixes to the stem.

Now look at a word whose root you might not know: *transcription*.

The prefix *trans* means "across."

The suffix *tion* means "state of."

The root *script* means "to write."

The word *transcription* means "the state of writing across." When you transcribe something, you change it from one form to a written form—that is, you "write across." Many spoken interviews are turned into transcriptions so you can read what was said.

It's not always easy to figure out the exact meanings for words from prefixes, suffixes, and roots. But knowing these word parts can help you gain at least some idea of the meanings of many words without having to look them up in a dictionary.

Important Prefixes

Prefixes meaning "no" or "not":

Prefix	*Meaning*	*Example*
a	not; without	amoral
anti	against	antisocial

Prefix	*Meaning*	*Example*
dis	not	disfavor
il	not	illegal
im	not	immobile
in	not	inexact
ir	not	irresponsible
mal	badly	malformed
mis	wrongly	mislead
non	not	nonreturnable
un	not	unknown

Prefixes dealing with time:

Prefix	*Meaning*	*Example*
pre	before	predate
post	after	postwar

Prefixes dealing with numbers, one or more than one:

Prefix	*Meaning*	*Example*
auto	self	autograph
bi	two	bicycle
mono	one	monologue
multi	many	multicolored
poly	many	polygon
tri	three	tripod
uni	one	unicycle

Prefixes dealing with placement:

Prefix	*Meaning*	*Example*
ab	away from	abnormal
circum	around	circumscribe
com, con	with; together	committee
de	down from	deceit
dis	away	discharge
ex	out of	exconvict
in	into; within	inborn
inter	among	intermix
mid	in the middle	midpoint
pro	forward; in favor of	pro-American
re	again	recall
sub	under	submarine
super	above	superior
trans	across	transition

Important Suffixes

Suffix	*Meaning*	*Example*
able ible	able to be	manageable defensible
al ance ence	related to	regal resistance independence
hood ic ion ism ity ment	state of; quality of	brotherhood patriotic union Catholicism legality puzzlement
er ite or	one who	writer Mennonite investor
ful y	full of	wishful soapy

Important Roots

Root	*Meaning*	*Example*
cred	believe	credence
duc, duct	lead; make; fashion; shape	deduct
equ	equal	equate
fac, fact, fic	do; make	factory
graph	written	monograph
log	speech	monologue
mis, mit	send	missile
mor, mort	die	mortify
nom, nomen	name	nominal
port	carry	portable
pos	place	position
scrip, scrib	write	describe
spic, spec	look	spectator
tang	touch	tangible
ten, tin, tain	have; hold	detain
tend, tens, tent	stretch	extend
vid, vis	see	vision
voc	call	evoke

EXERCISES

2.3 Prefixes, Suffixes, and Roots

For each word, draw one line under the prefix, two lines under the suffix, and a circle around the root. Leave the spaces below the words blank until you do Exercise 2.9 on page 35.

1. *multivocal*

   having several voices

   expressing multiple opinions

2. *reposition*

   movement again

   move from its original place or orientation to another

3. *polygraphic*

   having several written parts

   relating to a device that determines truth-telling

4. *nonmaintenance*

   not keeping in place

   not taking care of

5. *extension*

   holding out

   being straightened or stretched out

2.4 Word Parts in Words You Know

Think of the many words you know and use regularly. Do you recognize prefixes and suffixes in those words? Make a list of the words you know that have the following prefixes and suffixes. Write the words with their definitions on a separate sheet of paper. Student responses will vary.

1. Three words that begin with the prefix *multi*
2. Three words that begin with the prefix *post*

3. Three words that begin with the prefix *trans*
4. Three words that begin with the prefix *dis*
5. Three words that end with the suffix *ance* or *ence*
6. Three words that end with the suffix *ity*
7. Three words that end with the suffix *ment*
8. Three words that end with the suffix *able* or *ible*

2.5 Meanings and Prefixes

Define each word using what you know about prefixes. In the blank space, write the meaning of each word.

1. prehistoric before written record
2. remainder leftover material
3. dysfunctional not working
4. mistaken in error
5. apolitical not interested in politics
6. disintegration falling apart
7. antimanagement against those in charge
8. illogical not following reason
9. automatic operating by itself
10. translate change from one language to another
11. disgusting repellent to the taste
12. unpredictable cannot be determined ahead of time
13. circumlocution talking around a subject
14. prejudge decide before having facts
15. bilingual having two languages

2.6 Meanings and Suffixes

In each word, the suffix is in italics. In the second column, write what each suffix means. In the third column, write the meaning of the complete word.

Word	*Meaning of Suffix*	*Meaning of Word*
1. matur*ity*	state of	state of being fully grown

	Word	Meaning of Suffix	Meaning of Word
2.	president*ial*	related to	related to the chief leader
3.	ed*ible*	able to be	able to be eaten
4.	national*ism*	quality of	belief in one's country
5.	wonder*ful*	full of	full of awe, wonder
6.	medita*tion*	state of	state of contemplation
7.	pli*able*	able to be	able to be bent or flexed
8.	monumen*tal*	related to	of grand size
9.	neighbor*hood*	state of	area where people live together
10.	crusad*er*	one who	one who fights moral battles

2.7 Prefixes and Suffixes Together

Use what you know about prefixes and suffixes to figure out the meaning of each word. Do *not* use a dictionary.

1. autobiographical relating to one's own life story
2. subterranean beneath the earth
3. preparedness degree of being ready
4. immaterial not of substance
5. antagonistic in opposition
6. posttraumatic after a painful experience
7. nonjudgmental not evaluating
8. unreasonable illogical
9. disrespectful contemptuous
10. intangible not able to be touched

2.8 Meanings and Roots

The words in each group have the same root. Circle the root in each case. Then try to figure out the meaning of each word and write the definition in the blank space. Use a dictionary only to check your answer.

1. description a statement describing something
   mistranscribe copy wrongly

2. transportation act of carrying from place to place
   report a detailed account
   deported expelled from a country
3. invisible not able to be seen
   revision a looking over; a correction
   supervisor a person who looks over someone else
4. tension the process of stretching
   extensive large in range or amount
   retentive having the ability to retain
5. spectacle a public performance or display
   spectator an observer of an event
   introspection self-examination

2.9 Prefixes, Suffixes, and Roots

Go back to Exercise 2.3 on page 132. On the first blank line under each word, write your own definition of the word, using what you know about prefixes, suffixes, and roots. Then look up the word in a dictionary. On the second blank line, write a definition based on your dictionary's explanation.

2.10 Related Words in Groups

The words in each of the following groups are related. Write a definition for each of the words in italics. Use a dictionary if you need one. Then, from what you know about prefixes and suffixes, write definitions for all the words beneath the word in italics. Check a dictionary only after you try to figure out the meaning on your own.

1. *creed* belief
   credible believable
   credence trust
   discredit show as untrustworthy
2. *claim* state as true
   disclaim deny
   claimant person who makes a statement
   reclaim regain possession

3. *vocal* having to do with the voice
   irrevocable not capable of being called back
   invoke mention; bring in
   subvocal below the sound of the voice
   vociferous loud; outspoken
4. *sign* symbol
   signify make known
   resign quit
   insignia a symbol of rank
   insignificant not worth noting
   signature a person's name written by himself or herself
5. *repeat* state again
   repetition the act of repeating
   repeated occurring again and again
   repeatedly over and over again
   unrepeated not repeated
   repeater one who repeats

Chapter 2 SELF-TEST
Word Part Clues

Break each of the words in List A below into word parts, and then write the letter of the appropriate definition from List B. Score five points for identifying the word parts of each correctly and five points for identifying the appropriate meaning. (perfect score = 100)

List A	*Word parts*	*Meaning*
1. malaise	mal/aise	b
2. indescribable	in/de/scrib/able	h
3. interethnic	inter/ethn/ic	i
4. distended	dis/tended	e
5. prefabricate	pre/fab/ric/ate or pre/fabric/ate	c
6. circumspection	circum/spec/tion	j
7. inequality	in/equal/ity	d
8. fieldwork	field/work	f
9. deportation	de/port/ation	g
10. truehearted	true/hearted	a

List B

a. loyal, faithful
b. a vague ill feeling
c. to make ahead of time
d. a difference of rights, values or meanings
e. swollen
f. data gathering outside the laboratory
g. sending someone out of a country
h. cannot be presented in words
i. between culture groups
j. caution, examining different possibilities before acting

Score: ______ correct × 5 points each = ______

CHAPTER THREE

Using a Dictionary

A dictionary is an important tool to help you build your reading skills. You can find the following in most dictionaries:

- The meanings of a word
- The spelling of a word
- Whether or not a word is capitalized
- The word broken into syllables
- The pronunciation of a word
- The part of speech of a word: verb, noun, adjective, and so forth
- The spelling of a special plural or verb form of a word, or the abbreviation of a word
- A sentence or expression that uses a word correctly
- The meaning of important prefixes and suffixes
- The special usage of a word
- A word that means the same as a word you look up (*synonym*)
- A word that means the opposite of a word you look up (*antonym*)
- The history of a word
- Words made from a main word

Look at the page from *New American Webster Handy College Dictionary, Third Edition*, on page 40. The important features are labeled and explained for you.

3a The Guide Words

All the words in a dictionary are arranged in alphabetical order. Two words appear at the top of each page. These *guide words* tell you what words to expect on that page. The guide word on the left tells you the first word on the page; the guide word on the right tells you the last word on the page. If you wanted to look up *niche*, for example, on the sample dictionary page, the left guide word *news* is a hint that your word is here because *nic* comes after *ne* The right guide word is *nidus*. Because *nic* comes before *nid*, you know your word must appear between these two guide words.

3b The Main Entry

The word itself first appears in heavy black letters. (This kind of type is called *boldface type*.) In the main entry, centered dots show where to put a hyphen in case you have to break the word at the end of a line of writing. The main entry gives the correct spelling.

3c The Pronunciation Key

The groups of letters, which come right after the main entry, tell you how to say the word. The letters stand for special sounds. To know what sound a letter makes, check the pronunciation key at the bottom of the page.

Check the key at the bottom of the entry on the sample page. Notice that the *e* in *news* sounds like the *oo* in the word *tool.*

You also learn from the accent marks just which syllable to stress when you say the word. In *nick′el (nik′el)*, the heavy mark (′) after the *k* tells you that the first syllable gets the most stress when you say the word.

3d The Parts of Speech

The part of speech tells you how the word works in the system of English grammar. The *n.* after the pronouncing letters of *news* means "noun." *Adj.* after *newsy* means "adjective." Sometimes a word has different meanings based on the part of speech it is. *Nick* as a noun means "a notch." As a verb, the word *nick* means "to make a notch."

You're not expected to know what all the abbreviations or symbols mean (*n., adv., adj., v.t., v.i.*). Just check the special section in the front or the back of your dictionary whenever you need help.

news — guide words — 458 — nidus

main entries

news (nooz) *n.sing.* **1,** tidings, esp. of recent public events. **2,** the reports published in a newspaper. **3,** (*Informal*) a matter not previously known. —**newsboy″, news′girl″,** *n.* a boy or girl who sells or delivers newspapers. —**news′cast″,** *n.* a radio or TV broadcast of current news. —**news′deal″er,** *n.* a person who sells newspapers. —**news′man″, news′wom″an,** *n.* a person who writes, edits, reports, etc., the news. —**news′pa″per,** *n.* a printed publication giving chiefly news. —**news′-print″,** *n.* a cheap paper used in newspapers. —**news′reel″,** *n.* motion pictures of current events. —**news′stand″,** *n.* a stand where newspapers are sold.

news′let″ter *n.* a periodical news bulletin, usu. for a particular special interest group.

news′mon″ger *n.* a gossip.

new′speak″ *n.* the intentional use of ambiguous and misleading language.

history of the word

newspeak
↔ Coined by novelist George Orwell in his novel 1984.

pronunciation

news′wor″thy *adj.* worthy of being reported as news; of general interest.

news′y (noo′zė) *adj.* full of news; informative. —**news′i′•ness,** *n.*

newt (noot) *n.* a small, semiaquatic salamander.

newt
↔ A misdivision of the Middle English phrase *an ewte*, an eft.

special forms and spelling

New Testament the books of the Holy Bible relating to Jesus Christ or Christianity.

New Year a year just beginning. —**New Year's Day,** Jan. 1. —**New Year's Eve,** Dec. 31.

next (nekst) *adj. & adv.* **1,** nearest. **2,** immediately following in time, place, order, etc. —*prep.* nearest to.

nex′us (nek′səs) *n.* [*pl.* **nex′us**] **1,** a tie; link. **2,** a connected series.

ni′a•cin (nī′ə-sin) *n.* nicotinic acid.

nib *n.* **1,** the point of anything, esp. of a pen. **2,** a bird's beak.

meaning

nib′ble (nib′əl) *v.i. & l.* bite off small pieces (of). —*n.* **1,** a small bite. **2,** in computers, half a byte.

nib′lick (nib′lik) *n.* a golf club for high lofting shots; no. 9 iron.

nibs (nibz) *n.* (*Informal*) an important person, as *his nibs* or *her nibs*.

nice (nīs) *adj.* **1,** requiring precision or tact. **2,** subtle, as a distinction. **3,** delicately sensitive; minutely accurate. **4,** fastidious; refined; discriminating. **5,** (*Informal*) pleasing or pleasant; attractive; kind. —**nice′ness,** *n.*

nice
↔ The source of this word is Latin *nescius*, ignorant; only by a very tortuous path did it reach its present sense of pleasant.

nice-″nel′ly•ism (-nel′ė-iz-əm) *n.* a euphemism.

ni′ce•ty (nī′sə-tė) *n.* **1,** precision; accuracy. **2,** a minute distinction or detail. **3,** something choice. **4,** (usu. *pl.*) refinement.

niche (nich) *n.* **1,** a recess in a wall, as for a vase, statue, etc. **2,** a suitable place or position.

Ni′chrome (nik′rōm) *n.* (*T.N.*) an alloy of nickel, chromium, and iron.

nick (nik) *n.* **1,** a notch. **2,** a slightly chipped place, as on a dish. **3,** the exact moment (of time). —*v.i.* **1,** make a notch in; chip. **2,** (*Slang*) steal: shoplift.

nick′el (nik′əl) *n.* **1,** a hard silvery-white metallic element much used in alloys, no. 28, symbol Ni. **2,** a U.S. five-cent coin. —**nickel** or **German silver,** an alloy of nickel, copper, and zinc, used for tableware, etc.

nickel
↔ Coined by a Swedish mineralogist from German *Kupfernickel*, lit., copper-demon, used by miners as a term for nickel-bearing ore.

nick″el•o′de•on (nik″ə-lō′dė-ən) *n.* **1,** a movie theater with an admission price of five cents. **2,** a jukebox.

nick′er (nik′ər) *v.i.* **1,** neigh. **2,** laugh; snicker. —*n.* a neigh; a vulgar laugh.

nick′name″ (nik′nam″) *n.* an additional or substitute name.

nickname
↔ The result of the improper division of Middle English *an ekename*, an added name.

nic′o•tine″ (nik′ə-tēn″) *n.* a poisonous, colorless, oily liquid extracted from tobacco. —**nic′o•tin″ic acid,** a B vitamin derived from nicotine; niacin.

nicotine
↔ From Jacques *Nicot*, the French ambassador to Lisbon, Portugal, who supposedly introduced tobacco to France.

ni′dus (nī′dəs) *n.* [*pl.* **-di** (-di)] **1,** a nest,

pronunciation key — fat, fāte, fär, fãre, fâll, ȧsk; met, hē, hẽr, maybē; pin, pīne; not, nōte, ôr, tool

3e Special Forms and Special Spellings

The word newscast is made from the word *news*. Therefore, newscast is included as part of the entry for *news* instead of as a main entry itself. Because not everyone knows that the plural of *nexus* is *nexus*, the dictionary shows that word, too. Only specially formed plurals appear.

3f The Meanings of the Word

Meanings of words are numbered in boldface print. Because words often have more than one meaning, many meanings can appear. Numbers help separate them. Usually the most important definitions come first.

Some Dictionary Pointers

- Review your skill with alphabetical order. Can you arrange words correctly?
- Use the guide words. They save you time.
- Check all abbreviations and symbols in the special section.
- If you look up a word and it's not where you expect it to be, don't think it's not in your dictionary! Check under several possible spellings. If you couldn't spell the word *crime*, for example, the sound of the word might suggest these spellings:

  cryme krime
  kryme krhyme
  criem crhyme
- If you couldn't spell the word, you might have to check all the spellings before you found *crime*.
- Test the *meaning* you find for the word in the sentence in which the word appears. You may not have picked a definition that works for the word as it is being used.
- Try to say the word aloud after you look at the pronunciation key.

3g The History of the Word

Sometimes dictionaries tell the way a word has developed in the English language, sometimes called *etymology*. Many words have origins in foreign languages such as Latin or Greek. In this dictionary, the history of words is presented in boxes, as after *nicotine*. This box informs us that *nicotine* is named after James Nicot, who introduced tobacco to France.

Before you begin the following exercises, review "Some Dictionary Pointers" on page 41.

EXERCISES

3.1 Order of the Alphabet

Put the words in this list in correct alphabetical order. Rewrite them on the blank lines.

1. split ______ spineless
2. splatter ______ splashboard
3. squander ______ splatter
4. split-level ______ splinter
5. splinter ______ split
6. squalid ______ split-level
7. spool ______ spool
8. splashboard ______ squad
9. squad ______ squalid
10. spineless ______ squander

3.2 Guide Words

If the guide words at the top of a dictionary page are *embellish* and *emend*, circle the words you would expect to find on that page. Put an *X* before any words that would not appear on the page.

X	emerald		(embryo)		(embrace)
	(embroider)	X	embed		(emboss)
X	emote	X	emergence	X	elusive
X	embarrass	X	embark		(emblem)

3.3 One Word, Several Meanings

Each italicized word in the following list has several meanings. Look up each word in a dictionary and write two definitions for it. After each definition, write a sentence that uses the word correctly. Student responses will vary.

Example: book

a. Definition: a written work for reading

Sentence: I read the *book* titled *Sissy* by John Williams.

b. Definition: to engage a performer for a show

Sentence: David Merrick *booked* a Russian dance group for a U.S. tour.

1. *cut*

Definition: __________

Sentence: __________

Definition: __________

Sentence: __________

2. *warm*

Definition: __________

Sentence: __________

Definition: __________

Sentence: __________

3. *pound*

Definition: __________

Sentence: __________

Definition: __________

Sentence: __________

4. *iron*

Definition: __________

Sentence: __________

Definition: __________

Sentence: __________

5. *partial*
   Definition: ______
   Sentence: ______
   Definition: ______
   Sentence: ______

3.4 Practice in Dictionary Skills

Using a good dictionary, find the answer to each question.

1. What is the plural of *elf*? elves
2. What parts of speech can the word *toy* be? noun, verb, and adjective
3. What language does the word *burro* come from? Spanish
4. What do the following words mean?
   a. claptrap nonsense
   b. calico a coarse cloth with bright designs
   c. faction a small cohesive political group
   d. factotum an assistant who does everything
   e. intrepid fearless
5. How do you pronounce the following words?
   nuclear nōō'klē-ər
   bogie bō'gē
   boogie bŏŏg'ē
   buggy bŭg'ē
   bonsai bōn-sī

CULTURAL Exchange

contribution plate a container, such as a basket or plate, passed around at church into which people put money for the support of the church (page 48)

to paddle to spank with a paddle, especially as a punishment; to give someone a paddling (page 50)

Chapter 3 SELF-TEST
Using a Dictionary

Use the sample dictionary page (found on page 40) to answer each of the following questions. Count ten points for each correct answer. Give yourself the appropriate partial score if you got only part of the answer correct.

1. What is the plural of nidus? nidi
2. What is the origin of the word nickname? from the middle English for an added name
3. Which three words or phrases begin with a capital letter? New Testament, New Year, Nichrome
4. Circle the words whose *i* sound is the same as the *i* sound in *pin*.

   nice (nickel) (niche) nidus (nick)

5. What is a *nexus*? a tie, link
6. What language does the word *nice* come from? Latin
7. What did the origin word of *nice* mean? ignorant
8. List five words that build on the word *news*. newsboy, newsgirl, newsblast, newspaper, newsreel, etc.
9. What does niceness mean? It appears under the word *nice*. However, niceness is not defined. Why not? *Niceness* is the quality of being *nice*. Knowing that the suffix *ness* turns the word into a noun describing a quality helps us know the meaning.

10. The symbol ə is a *schwa*. A schwa stands for a vowel sound in a syllable that is not accented. List three words in which schwas are used to show pronunciation.

    Possible answers include nibble, nicety, nickel, nicotine, nexus

Score: ______ correct × 10 points each = ______

UNIT 1 REVIEW TEST

Select the best meaning of each word in italics and write the letter of the correct answer in the blank space provided.

__b__ 1. "Sean calls out all the time," his teacher said to the child's mother. "He hits the other children and will not stay in his seat. Such behavior is highly *undesirable* for a student in a third-grade classroom."
a. wild
b. not wanted
c. lively
d. evil

__c__ 2. Recent floods in Texas are just another *episode* in the history of nature's attacks on the Lone Star state.
a. climate
b. overflow
c. related incident
d. embarrassment

__d__ 3. Her effort was almost *ceaseless*. She woke up early, worked hard all day, took little time to rest, and was ready to start again at five the next morning.
a. lazy
b. tiring
c. done without much thought
d. done without stop

__a__ 4. For his hard work on her campaign, the new mayor kissed her manager and gave him her *heartfelt* thanks.
a. deeply felt
b. hardly felt
c. politically active
d. joyful

__c__ 5. In 1960, Jane Goodall *pioneered* a study of chimpanzees. She was one of the first people to observe the animals close up in the wild.
a. traveled across the country
b. carried out

c. was one of the first to do
d. photographed

___c___ 6. The smallest blood vessels branch into tiny *capillaries*, which can be seen only with a microscope. Capillaries are blood vessels with very thin walls.
a. small hatlike structures
b. veins
c. thin-walled blood vessels
d. large branches

___b___ 7. Small trees and shrubs created a dense *underbrush* in the forest.
a. problem
b. ground cover
c. garden
d. home

___b___ 8. When she starts her diet for losing weight, tacos and hot-fudge sundaes are *unmentionable* in her presence.
a. fattening
b. not to be spoken of
c. not to be eaten
d. desirable

___b___ 9. To everyone's surprise, the monkey had *treed* the lion cub, who howled noisily from the topmost branches.
a. frightened
b. forced to climb a tree
c. made tired by running
d. bitten

___b___ 10. In the fifteenth century, da Vinci's careful drawings and illustrations *prefigured* our modern airplanes.
a. looked nothing like
b. suggested with an early model
c. designed fully and completely
d. painted simply

___c___ 11. Although he could afford much more, he put only ten cents in the contribution plate. What a *paltry* amount!
a. generous
b. religious
c. insignificant
d. charitable

__b__ 12. Will allowing citizens to carry concealed weapons *deter* (or prevent) more crimes in America?
a. create
b. stop from happening
c. make more attractive
d. replace

__a__ 13. The people who wanted America to stretch from the Atlantic to the Pacific were called *expansionists* because they tried to expand U.S. territory.
a. people who wanted to expand land holdings
b. politicians
c. people who wanted to sail from the Atlantic to the Pacific
d. landowners in the West

__d__ 14. The children enjoyed colorful beads, bits of glass, cheap rings and necklaces, mirrors, and other *trinkets*.
a. Native Americans
b. valuable items
c. money
d. small, fancy items of little worth

__b__ 15. Every time her mother spoke, Karen said the same words her mother did. She copied every action of her mother's, too, coughing and clearing her throat each time, just after her mother did. Finally, Karen's mother said angrily, "I wish you wouldn't *parrot* me like that. It's very annoying!"
a. squawk like a bird
b. copy
c. annoy
d. attach

__a__ 16. Her aides wanted to keep the discussion on the new law going; the mayor, on the other hand, insisted on *closure*. "We've talked enough," she said.
a. ending
b. continuing
c. eating
d. going out

__c__ 17. Mr. Gomez gave many tests and papers in his chemistry course, and everyone worked very hard for this *taskmaster*.
a. smart man
b. mean teacher

c. someone who makes people work hard
d. someone who makes people dislike him

__a__ 18. *Torrential* rains swept across the roadways, burying the cars in water.
a. wild
b. cool
c. warm
d. delayed

__a__ 19. A *sullen* child is always gloomy and resists cheering up.
a. sad and moody
b. bad and lively
c. tired and quiet
d. strange and helpful

__d__ 20. Teachers in Alabama now can paddle students without worry; a new state law gives teachers legal *immunity* for paddling.
a. help
b. criticism
c. expenses
d. protection

UNIT TWO

Using Aids to Reading

CHAPTER FOUR

Previewing the Parts of a Book

Even before you begin reading a book, you can learn about its subject by previewing. *Previewing*—viewing in advance—means looking ahead and checking for information. Previewing gives you a general idea of a work before you actually read it. Knowing about a book in advance helps you understand a little about its content and about its special features. Before reading your textbooks in biology, math, and business, for example, look them over carefully.

Use the following steps to help you preview a book:

- *Look at the title of the book.* A history book called *America: The Glorious Republic* will be much different from a history book called *Urban America: A History*. The title can tell you a great deal about a book. Before you read, take time to think about what the book's title means.
- *Look at the table of contents.* The table of contents appears at the front of the book. It is a list of the names of the chapters and the pages on which they begin. Sometimes chapter subheadings are listed too. If the book is divided into parts, that information also appears in the table of contents. Study the names of the chapters and subheadings to get an idea of what each section of the book deals with and how the topics relate to one another.
- *Look at the preface.* The preface, which also appears in the front of the book, is a brief essay in which the author gives reasons for writing the book. Not every book has a preface. Authors who write them are sending a personal message to the reader. In the preface you get an idea of

    1. the kind of reader for whom the author is writing.
    2. the goals of the book.

3. what the author expects you to learn as a result of reading the book.
4. the topics in the book and the best approaches to understanding those topics.

- *Look briefly at the index.* An index appears at the end of the book. It is an alphabetical list of the topics, subjects, ideas, and names mentioned in the book. A quick look at the index tells you the main points in the book.
- *Look at the following special features that sometimes appear in books:*
  1. At the end of a book a writer sometimes provides a glossary. A *glossary* is a list of difficult words or terms that appear in the book. The words are listed in alphabetical order with their definitions.
  2. An *appendix* (plural is *appendixes* or *appendices*) at the end of the book adds information to the book. However, the book is complete without the appendix; the information there is extra. An appendix may include charts and graphs, special letters or documents, or facts about the lives of the people mentioned in the book. It may give information to explain something the author felt needed more attention. A look at the appendix, if the book has one, indicates how a writer deals with special issues.
- *Read the introduction.* Often the first chapter of the book is an introduction. The introduction states the basic idea, issue, or problem the author addresses. It gives background information about or discusses the history of the topic. It may summarize what others have said about the subject. It may even explain research the author did. Sometimes someone other than the author writes the introduction. This kind of introduction often explains the book to the readers, pointing out key ideas.
- *Look at the bibliography.* At the back of the book, an author sometimes gives a bibliography. A *bibliography* is a list, in alphabetical order, of some or all of the sources (such as books and magazine articles) the author used to write the book. The bibliography gives full publishing information about all sources referred to directly in the book.

EXERCISES

4.1 A Table of Contents

Look at the brief table of contents that appears on page 56 from a book called *The Media in Your Life: An Introduction to Mass Communication*. Figure out as much information as you can about the book. Then answer each question.

1. In which parts of the book would you expect to find information that relates to all media?

   Parts one and three

2. In which part would you find information about specific industries?

   Part two

3. In which chapter would you look to find out about the film industry?

   Chapter 8

4. In which chapter would you find out about the impact of the World Wide Web?

   Chapter 12

5. What information would you expect to find in Chapter 14?

   How government controls media

4.2 An Index

Look at the excerpt from a book index on page 57. Then answer the following questions.

c 1. This book is probably about
   a. psychology
   b. American history
   c. studying and writing about history
   d. gender

BRIEF CONTENTS

INDEX

2. On what pages would you find
   a. discussion of diplomatic history? 17–19
   b. ideas about using art in a history course? 21–24, 66
   c. guidelines for footnotes and endnotes? 186–190
   d. suggestions for reading analytically? 87–93
   e. advice for writing essay questions? 155–166
   f. advice for organizing answers to essay questions? 161
   g. advice about answering hypothetical questions? 163–165

4.3 A Preface

Read the preface on page 59 from *Careers as a Rock Musician* by Del Hopkins. Then answer these questions.

1. What choice did Del Hopkins face as he neared high school graduation? Why wouldn't college postpone that choice?
   He had to decide what kind of work to do. College still meant thinking about a career.

2. What did he think of the work that he had been doing?
   His work was fun and fulfilling.

3. What had been his attitude toward music in high school?
   It was a social activity.

4. What advice could he get on musical careers from adults and libraries? Why wasn't that information useful?
   The information was only about classical music careers, which are very different from popular music careers.

5. Where did he find out about rock-and-roll careers?
   friends, questionable experts, trial and error

PREFACE

Perhaps you are now where I once was as a high school student. Graduation was approaching, and also my last free meal at home. There were hints that I ought to be making up my mind about what kind of work I wanted to do. It was expected of me to pitch in like everyone else to make a living. College was the only choice besides a job, but that, too, required a career focus. There was no way to avoid it—I had to start thinking about work.

I had been working all along, but it was so much fun and so fulfilling that I never considered it drudgery, which is what I thought work meant in those days. By the time I became a senior. I had played in several rock bands, spent most of my evenings practicing with a group, and had performed in gigs for money.

My classmates seemed to like me for my music, which was fine because I wasn't exactly on the principal's list for good grades, nor was I a star quarterback. Up to then my life in music had been more like a high school social activity; but now, with all the pressure for a career, I began to think otherwise. I looked everywhere for information on how to get ahead in the rock business.

The school library was no help at all. There were books on music careers leading to opera or symphony, but none leading to popular music forms such as rock, country, or jazz. The differences are too great to make comparisons between the two career paths. If I had been interested in academic music, I would have stayed in the school band and planned on attending college. So, with no guidance available from the adult world, I relied on the advice of friends and questionable experts. My journey of trial and error through the real world of rock has given me one certainty—it's not like high school. If you are considering a career in the rock business, please read on.

The purpose of this book is to provide an inside view of the music business behind the glitter of rock concerts and compact discs. I shall also tell some true-life experiences about work as a rock musician so that you will not have to rely on speculation. Such a book would have been of immeasurable help during my eighteen years to date as a professional musician.

6. What is the purpose of this book?

   to provide an inside view of the rock music business

7. How did the author's experiences prepare him to write this book?

   His experiences taught him about the business.

8. Who do you think would find this book most useful?

   Student responses will vary.

4.4 The Parts of a Book

Select one of your textbooks or a book from the library. Locate the parts of the book. On a separate sheet of paper, write what you can find out about each of the parts listed below. Also write if the book does not have one of the parts. Student responses will vary.

1. title and author
2. title page
3. table of contents
4. preface
5. introduction or first chapter
6. glossary
7. bibliography
8. index
9. appendix

Cultural Exchange

to pitch in	to get busy and help with something (page 59)
gig	a musician's job or performance at a particular club or city [informal] (page 59)
quarterback	in American football, the player who gets the ball at the beginning of every play and tries to move it along the field by carrying it, throwing it, or handing it over to another teammate (page 59)
glitter	the excitement, splendor, lights, colors, or sounds of an event (page 59)

Chapter 4 SELF-TEST

Previewing the Parts of a Book

Look at the table of contents at the beginning of this book and the two indexes at the end. Then answer the following questions, count five points for each correct answer.

1. How many units does this book have? six
2. What is the subject of the fourth unit? Finding Information
3. Which unit would help you most with learning new words?
   Unit One
4. In what chapter would you expect to learn about SQ3R?
   Chapter 11
5. In what chapter would you find out how to write a journal?
   Chapter 16
6. How many subsections are there in Chapter 6? four
7. What is the last subsection of Chapter 6? Freewriting
8. In what subsection would you find out about place order?
   subsection 10 c(2)
9. On what page would you find the selection "Teachings of Confucius"?
   365
10. Who wrote "Blending Music to Make Rock 'n' Roll"?
    Jean Folkerts and Stephen Lacy
11. What is the title of the first reading selection?
    "Climates in the United States and Canada"

12. What is the difference between the two indexes? What would you find in each? The subject index lists the various topics covered in the book. The author index lists who wrote the selections.

13. On what pages would you find information about graphs? 96–100

14. On what pages would you find information about summarizing? 65, 328–336

15. What are the subtopics you can find out about relating to paragraphs? first paragraphs, first sentences, inferences from, main ideas in, stated and implied main ideas, time order, place order, order of importance, summarizing, topic sentences, topics, patterns

16. If you are looking for information on details, what other headings should you check?
major details; minor details

17. On what page can you find a cartoon? 291

18. On what page can you find a selection by John Irving? 450

19. On what pages can you find a selection by Mel Lazarus?
382–392

20. On how many different pages can you find selections by Richard J. Hardy? four

Score: ______ correct × 5 points each = ______

CHAPTER FIVE

Previewing Individual Selections

Previewing a reading selection, such as a chapter or an essay, before you read it can give you important information. Like previewing longer works (4), previewing a reading selection prepares you for the material and helps you get your mind ready to receive new facts, ideas, and opinions.

Previewing a Reading Selection: Tips and Pointers

- *Look at the title.* Titles often give the main idea of a selection. Does the title tell what you will be reading about? If so, you can then set a purpose for your reading.
- *Look for subtitles or headings.* Essays, newspaper articles, and other longer readings sometimes have subtitles or headings. Appearing below titles in boldface print or in italics, subtitles suggest the kind of information you will find in a portion of the reading.
- *Look at lists of goals or objectives.* Sometimes the author lists chapter objectives. Here, the writer tells you what you should get out of the chapter. Check the objectives before you read so you know what to read for.
- *Look at the pictures, charts, or drawings.* Often an illustration helps you figure out in advance what you will be reading about.
- *Look at the first sentence of each paragraph.* This gives you a quick idea of what the reading involves before you begin to read carefully.
- *Look at the first paragraph.* The first paragraph usually tells just what the reading will be about. Read it, and then try to say

in your own words what you think you will be reading about.

- *Look at any questions that appear after the reading.* If you look at the questions before you read anything, you will then have an idea of what is important. Questions tell you what to expect from a passage. When you know the questions in advance, you know what kind of information to look for.
- *Look for key words in different print.* Sometimes boldface letters, italics, or even colored ink call your attention to important words or ideas. Titles of books, for example, appear in italics. Noticing these in advance can give you important information.
- *Look for a summary.* At the end of a piece, a writer sometimes summarizes the main points. Look at the summary before you read a selection. The summary can help you see more clearly what the selection deals with.

EXERCISE

5.1 A Textbook Excerpt

Part of a chapter from a textbook on study skills appears on pages 66–72. Before you read the selection, preview it by answering each of the following questions.

1. Read the chapter title. What does it tell you about the contents of the selection?

   The selection tells how to improve your memory.

2. Look at the bulleted list at the end of the opening paragraph. What four points does it suggest will be made in the chapter?

   It is normal to forget.

   You can remember more and for longer than you think.

   A few memory aids may help you.

   The best memory techniques are the ones you create or adapt for

   for your own learning style.

3. Look at the major section heading after the first paragraph. What does this heading say the first section will be about?

   How memory works

4. What does Figure 11.1 show? How does what it shows relate to the subheadings in the section?

   It shows the three R's of memory.

   They are the same as the subheadings.

5. Each subheading has a bulleted list. What kind of information is in these lists?

   tips to improve that skill

6. What kind of information is presented in the four paragraphs printed in italics?

   a case study of one student

7. What does the photograph show, and how does it relate to the section?

   It shows an attentive student who is working on remembering.

8. What kind of information is asked for in the exercise questions at the end of the selection?

   four truths about memory

   the three R's of memory

   tips for improving memory

CHAPTER 11

BUILDING A POWERFUL MEMORY

Much has been written about how memory works. In fact, a whole technical vocabulary has been developed to describe the brain and its functions. Experts from fields as diverse as business, psychology, and education have advocated specific methods and aids to increase the power of memory. Go to any bookstore and find the self-help section. You'll see a variety of books packed with tips, tricks, and techniques for improving your memory. The purpose of this chapter is to cut through all the fancy language to some simple truths about memory.

- **It is normal to forget.**
- **You can probably remember more and retain more for a longer period of time than you think you can.**
- **A few memory aids that many students have found useful may work for you.**
- **The best memory techniques may be those you create or adapt for yourself, that correspond to your learning style.**

How Memory Works

When you were a child, your teacher explained the multiplication tables and wrote them on the chalkboard. While you were listening to the teacher and looking at the board, you were *receiving* information about the tables through your senses of sight and sound. Then, to help you learn them, your teacher asked you to write them out on paper, and that activity engaged your sense of touch. You also recited the tables aloud. Those practices in the classroom helped you to *retain* the tables. Finally, the teacher told you to practice your tables at home because you would be tested on them. You would have to *recall* them. If your practice and memory techniques have served you well, then you have retained the tables and can recall them even now.

Memory is the process by which your mind receives information and either *discards it or stores it for later use.* Memory involves *reception* of information, *retention* of information that has been received, and *recollection* of information that has been retained. (Researchers also refer to these activities as *encoding, storage,* and *retrieval.*) As Figure 11.1 shows, reception, retention, and recollection are the three R's of memory.

Reception

Your mind receives, takes in, or processes information through your five senses. It is important for you to understand the information you receive because you can't retain or recall material that you don't understand.

Relating new information to something familiar can aid understanding and reception because it either adds to or changes what you already know. As you connect new information with what you already know, you start thinking critically about it. The information now has a *context* and is easier to remember. Suppose you have been assigned a chapter on stress in your psychology text. Before beginning, think of what stress means to you. Imagine yourself in stressful situations, and recall what you have done to overcome stress. If you have not successfully managed stress in the past, the chapter may suggest a new method to try. Read to

R eception

R etention

R ecollection

FIGURE 11.1 The three R's of memory

find out whether the writer's points about stress confirm what you already know or give you new information.

Here are some more tips to improve your reception:

- **Become more attentive and observant.** If you stay alert in class and keep your attention focused, you will be a better receiver.
- **Engage as many of your senses as possible when receiving information.** In a lecture, *look* at the speaker. *Listen* attentively to what he or she says. *Take notes* to help you remember. If you do these things, you will be making full use of your visual, auditory, and tactile senses.
- **Ask questions, as needed, to aid understanding.** Remember: *you can't recall what you don't understand.* Make sure you understand the information you receive.
- **Before you read a textbook chapter, *survey* it** to get an overview of its content and to establish a purpose for reading. This step is especially helpful when the chapter covers a topic that is new to you. Surveying is the first step in the SQ3R study system.

Retention

Your mind stores and retains, for varying lengths of time, the information it receives. Some information — your name, your birth place, your birthday — you remember for life. Such information is part of you, although you may not remember when you first learned it. You retain other information — the multiplication tables, how to ride a bicycle — through use or practice. Was it difficult for you to learn to drive a car? You probably had trouble at first, but eventually you were able to get into a car and drive without mentally reviewing each step.

When you reached that point, you had *internalized* the process of driving. You do not easily forget information you have internalized. Like your name, it has become part of you.

Anything you really want to learn is going to stay with you because you are motivated to remember it. The key to retaining academic information is to *make a conscious effort to remember.* Here are some ways to make retention an active and effective process:

- **Become an active reader.** Underline and mark your textbook while you are reading.
- **Review frequently.** The more often you review information that you hope to learn and remember, the longer it will stay in your memory.
- **Recite to improve retention.** When you repeat information to yourself that you want to remember, you are activating your auditory sense and opening another pathway into your brain. You can recite information from note cards and study guides that you make.
- **Do all homework assignments.** Homework provides practice using new information or procedures. Frequent practice helps you internalize information.
- **Find a reason to remember.** Motivating yourself to learn because you want better grades is a start, but try to get beyond grades. Really think about what you are learning and how it relates to your goals and your hopes.

Recollection

Problems with Recollection Your mind enables you to recall information you have retained. Sometimes recollection is difficult. When you are taking a test, you might know one of the answers but be unable to remember it. Later, after the test is over, you remember the elusive answer. Or perhaps you have gotten confused because two similar kinds of information were competing for your attention. That was the problem plaguing a student named Otis.

> *Otis decided to take trigonometry and statistics in the same semester. Because he had consistently made A's and B's in math courses, he didn't anticipate any difficulty. A serious student, Otis attended classes faithfully, listened and took notes, asked questions when confused, and did his homework every day. Unfortunately, his first few grades in both courses were not as good as he had expected. Otis failed his first trig test, mainly because of making careless errors. When he made a D on his statistics test, he began to wonder what he was doing wrong.*
>
> *Finally, with the help of one of his instructors, Otis realized that he was having trouble because the information from trig was conflicting with the information from statistics. He was confusing the two because the courses were similar. He found it difficult to keep their concepts and formulas separate. Also, the classes met one after the other, so he had no time to absorb the lessons from one before going to the other.*

If you make reception an *active* process by looking at the speaker, listening attentively, and taking notes, then you are more likely to understand the information you receive and be able to remember it later. © *Jean-Claude Lejeune*

Otis realized that he should have taken trig and statistics in different terms or at least on different days. Another solution might have been to take them on the same day but separate them with some free time or an entirely different type of course. He also realized that he shouldn't study the two subjects one right after the other. He should study for trig and then take a break or study something not mathematical before turning to statistics. In this way he might be able to separate trig and statistics in his mind.

Otis recognized that he was off to a very poor start in both courses and thought it would be hard to bring up his average unless he withdrew from one of them. Since he was doing better in statistics, he withdrew from trig. Because of the extra time he had to devote to statistics, he ended up passing it with a C. Otis feels that he made a sound decision. The C won't hurt him; he can take trig next semester, and he now knows how to avoid similar problems in the future.

Improving Recollection Otis had problems with recollection because he was confusing one course's information with another's. If you have this problem, or if you need to improve your recollection for other reasons, try one or more of these suggestions:

- **Before a test, organize the information you want to study** in a way that is meaningful to you. Make summaries or set up categories in which you group similar items.

- **Use your preferred sensory mode.** If you learn best visually, make diagrams, charts, or information maps of material you want to remember. Picture these in your mind while you are studying and when you are responding to test questions. If auditory modes work best for you, try reciting aloud information you want to remember. Or you could study with a partner and quiz each other orally. If you are a tactile learner, try combining recitation with a physical activity such as walking or jogging. In this way you are engaging both your auditory and tactile senses.
- **Give yourself practice tests.** Try to anticipate test questions and write some of your own. Answer them; then check yourself against your textbook and your notes.
- **Go over old tests.** Review material that gave you trouble in the past. Past mistakes are clues to information that you haven't retained and have difficulty recalling.

Exercise 11.1 Working with a partner, imagine that you will be tested on the part of this chapter that you have read so far. You need to practice organizing the information in a way that will help you study for the test. Fill in the following outline by answering the questions with information from this chapter.

1. What are four simple truths about memory?

   a. ______________________________

   b. ______________________________

   c. ______________________________

   d. ______________________________

2. What are the three R's of memory?

   a. ______________________________

   b. ______________________________

   c. ______________________________

3. What are some tips for improving memory?

   ____

   ____

   a. How can you improve reception?

      1. ______________________________

      2. ______________________________

      3. ______________________________

      4. ______________________________

b. How can you improve retention?

1. ______________________________
2. ______________________________
3. ______________________________
4. ______________________________
5. ______________________________

c. How can you improve recollection?

1. ______________________________
2. ______________________________
3. ______________________________
4. ______________________________

—*Carol C. Kanar*

CULTURAL Exchange

naturalist	someone who studies the history of plants and animal species (page 74)
bonsai	the Japanese art of growing miniature plants in artistic forms (page 76)
pampas	flat, fertile plains in Argentina (page 76)

Chapter 5 SELF-TEST
Previewing Individual Selections

Preview the chapter from a biology textbook on pages 74–80. Follow the directions and answer each question below before you read. Then read the chapter to check your answer. Count six points for each correct answer.

1. Read the chapter title. What is the chapter about?

   How Darwin came to his theory of evolution

2. Look in the margins. What three objectives are set out for you in reading the chapter?

   a. Summarize ideas influencing Darwin.

   b. Identify Darwin's key observations.

   c. Describe two points of theory.

3. What four key terms are identified in the margin?

   a. evolution

   b. adaptation

   c. descent with modification

   d. natural selection

4. Where do the key terms appear again, and where are defined?

   They appear in bold print in the main text, where they are defined.

5. Look at the three subheadings. What topics are discussed?

   a. ideas from Darwin's time

   b. the voyage of the *Beagle*

   c. Darwin's main points

6. Look at Figure 14–3. What does it show?

   A map of Darwin's journey on the *Beagle*

7. What do the photographs in the other figures show?

   a. Animals and plants

   Why are they shown?

   b. They provide evidence and examples for Darwin's theory.

8. What are Darwin's two main points in his theory?

   a. Organisms change over generations.

   b. Changes are determined by natural selection.

Score: ______ correct × 6 points each = ______

CONCEPT 14.1
Darwin developed a theory of evolution.

Objectives

- **Summarize ideas from Darwin's time that influenced his work.**
- **Identify some key observations from Darwin's voyage that led to his theory.**
- **Describe the two main points of Darwin's theory.**

Key Terms

- **evolution**
- **adaptation**
- **descent with modification**
- **natural selection**

A new view of life came into focus in 1859, when Charles Darwin published his book *The Origin of Species.* Darwin's ideas provided a framework for understanding Earth's diversity of organisms and their relationships to one another and with their environments.

Ideas From Darwin's Time

On its grandest scale, **evolution** is all of the changes that have transformed life over an immense time. In a sense, evolution is the biological history of life on Earth. Before Darwin, two ideas about life on Earth prevailed. One was that species are fixed, or permanent. In other words, they do not change. The other idea was that Earth itself is less than 10,000 years old and also relatively unchanging. These ideas were challenged as people became aware of the incredible diversity of organisms, past and present, and the nature of Earth's geologic processes.

In the mid-1700s, the study of fossils led French naturalist Georges Buffon to suggest that Earth might be much older than a few thousand years. He also observed that specific fossils and certain living animals were similar but not exactly alike. In the early 1800s, another French naturalist, Jean Baptiste Lamarck suggested an explanation of Buffon's observations. Lamarck proposed that life evolves, or changes. He recognized that species are not permanent. Lamarck explained evolution as a process of adaptation.

FIGURE 14-1 Powerful muscles in the large hind legs of a kangaroo are an adaptation that help the animal move about quickly and efficiently. The large tail provides balance when the kangaroo is leaping or sitting on the ground.

Today, biologists consider an **adaptation** to be an inherited characteristic that improves an organism's ability to survive and reproduce in a particular environment. An example of evolutionary adaptation is the massive hind legs of a kangaroo that moves about by hopping and leaping (Figure 14–1).

Today, Lamarck is unfairly remembered in large part for his mistaken explanation of how adaptations evolve. He proposed that by using or not using certain body parts, an organism develops certain characteristics. Lamarck thought that these enhanced characteristics would be passed on to the offspring. Lamarck called this idea *inheritance of acquired characteristics.* For example, Lamarck might explain that a kangaroo's powerful hind legs were the result of ancestors strengthening their legs by jumping and then passing that acquired leg strength on to offspring. However, an acquired characteristic would have to somehow modify the DNA of specific genes in order to be inherited. There is no evidence that this happens (Figure 14–2). Still, it is important to note that Lamarck proposed that evolution occurs when organisms adapt to their environments. This idea helped set the stage for Darwin.

FIGURE 14-2 A bonsai tree is "trained" to grow as a dwarf by pruning and shaping. But seeds from this tree would produce offspring that could grow to normal size.

The Voyage of the Beagle

On a cold December day in 1831, the HMS *Beagle* set sail on a voyage around the world. Figure 14–3 shows the route the ship followed. The main mission of the voyage was to chart poorly known stretches of the South American coastline for the British navy. Accompanying the captain was a 22-year-old college graduate, Charles Darwin. Darwin's main interest was to study the geology, plants, and animals encountered on the voyage. It was a tour that would greatly affect Darwin's thinking and eventually the thinking of many others.

Darwin spent most of his time on shore while the ship's crew was busy surveying. There, he observed and collected thousands of specimens of South American plants and animals from diverse environments. He studied organisms and their adaptations from places as different as the Brazilian jungle, the grasslands of the pampas, and the frigid lands near Antarctica.

Throughout the voyage and the rest, of his life, Darwin maintained extensive journals of his observations, studies, and thoughts. These journals provide a window into Darwin's thinking. His writings indicate that before the voyage he felt that the concept of fixed or unchanging species best described nature. During the voyage, he began to question this concept. Sometime after he returned to England, Darwin became convinced that species change as they adapt to their changing environments.

In 1844, Darwin wrote a 200-page essay that outlined his idea, but he didn't release it to the public. Instead, for the next several years he continued to accumulate more evidence to support his idea. He told only a few of his closest colleagues, who encouraged him to publish his work before someone else came to the same conclusions. In 1858, another British natu-

FIGURE 14-3 The route of the *Beagle* (top inset) took Darwin around the world during a five-year voyage.

ralist, Alfred Wallace, *did* come to the same conclusion. Darwin was shocked to receive a letter from Wallace that described the same basic mechanism for evolutionary change that Darwin had proposed. Within a month, some of Wallace's and Darwin's writings were jointly presented in public. Darwin published his book *The Origin of Species* about a year later.

Darwin's Two Main Points

Darwin made two main points in his book. First, he argued from evidence that the species of organisms living on Earth today descended from ancestral species. In other words, life has a history of change. Darwin proposed that the descendants of the earliest organisms spread into various habitats over millions of years. In these habitats, they accumulated different modifications, or adaptations, to diverse ways of life. Darwin called this process **descent with modification.** He saw descent with modification as a way to account for the diversity of life. Figure 14.4 shows two species of hares that are adapted to living in

FIGURE 14-4 The large ears of the jackrabbit (left) are an adaptation to the animal's hot environment. Rich with blood vessels, the ears radiate heat, which helps cool the jackrabbit's body. The white fur of the snowshoe hare (right) camouflages the animal in its environment.

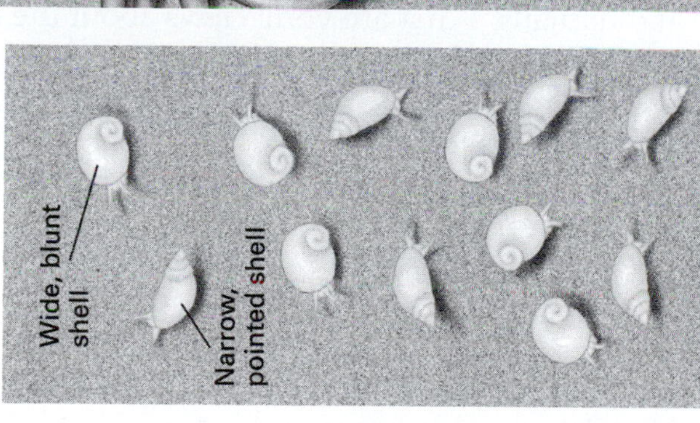

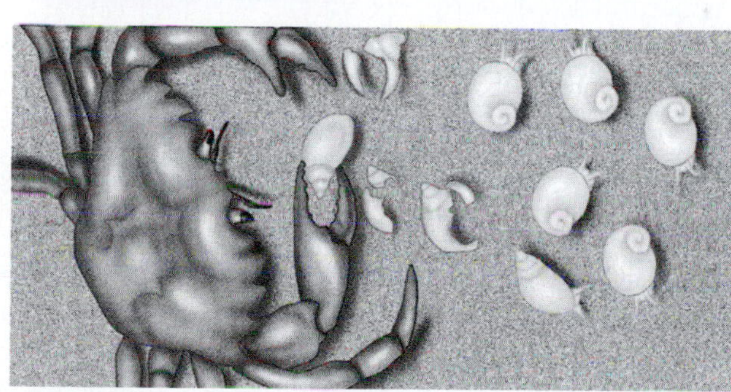

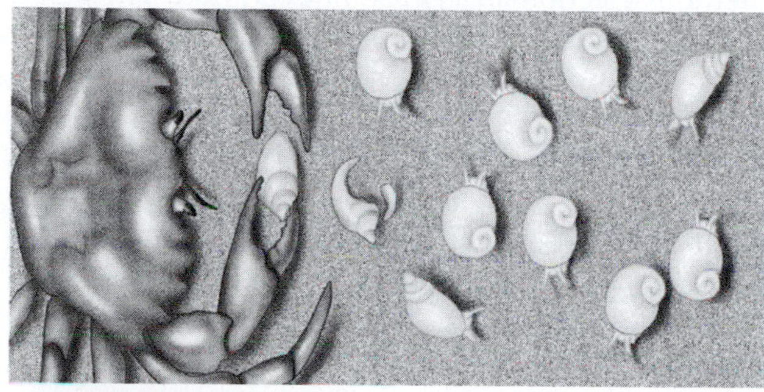

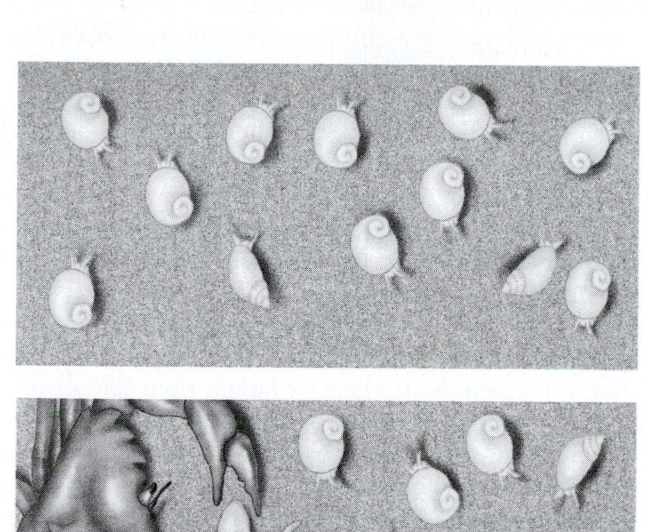

FIGURE 14-5 In this hypothetical population of snails, inherited shell variations make some snails less likely than others to be attacked by predators. Wide, blunt shells increase the chances for snails to survive and pass their traits to the next generation by reproducing.

different environments. The jackrabbit benefits from fur that blends well in the desert and ears that help cool its body. White fur provides protective camouflage in the snowy northern regions of the snowshoe hare's range.

Darwin's second main point was his argument for natural selection as the mechanism for evolution. **Natural selection** is the process by which individuals with inherited characteristics well-suited to the environment leave more offspring on average than do other individuals. Figure 14-5 models how certain inherited traits can give individuals some advantage over other individuals of the same species in the same environment. This process can cause a population to change over time. When biologists speak of "Darwin's theory of evolution," they are referring to natural selection as a cause of evolution. The result of natural selection is adaptation. This process of natural selection is another way of defining evolution. But the term *evolution* can also be used on a much broader scale to mean the history of life, from the earliest microbes to the enormous diversity of modern organisms.

Concept Check 14.1

1. How did the work of Lyell and Malthus influence Darwin as he developed his theory of evolution?
2. What characteristics of the Galapagos Islands were particularly important for Darwin?
3. What is natural selection?
4. Which of the following is an adaptation: the sharp teeth of a house cat, or a scar on the cat's ear? Explain.

Critical Thinking and Writing

Some people see a conflict between Darwin's views about the origins of plant and animal species, including humans, and what various religious scriptures say about the origins of life and humans. What are your views about the relation of Darwin's ideas and religious teachings?

CHAPTER SIX

Using Prereading Warm-Ups

Like previewing, warming up or prereading can help you before you read. (*Prereading* means "before reading.") When you warm up, you get yourself ready to do something. To warm up, runners stretch, baseball players hit balls, and golfers swing clubs. Readers can warm up, too.

You can get a general idea of what a reading selection is about from the title, the headings, the illustrations, and other features (see chapters 4 and 5). But it's also important to warm up by trying to think of whatever you know about the selection's topic before you read.

If you explore a topic by thinking about it before you read, you will understand it better when you read. For example, suppose you are ready to read an essay about dinosaurs. Before you start reading, you should think about whatever you know, remember, or imagine about those huge animals that roamed the earth millions of years ago. Force yourself to do "advance thinking." In this way, you prepare your mind to accept new information. When you read, you will understand ideas more easily because you warmed up.

Many readers like to write down their prereading warm-ups. It doesn't take very much time. Writing your thoughts down before you read lets you add to your thinking as one idea leads to another. When you do a prereading warm-up on paper, don't worry about making mistakes in spelling or grammar. Just get your ideas down.

Of the many ways to write down and organize your warm-ups, one of the following may help you:

- Making a list
- Making a word map

- Brainstorming
- Freewriting

6a Making a List

In this prereading warm-up, you simply write down in list form whatever comes to mind about the topic of your reading. Here's an example that a student prepared before reading a selection on college basketball.

lots of action
NCAA turnament
Big-name schools
TV
Betting
Scholships
under-the-table money
Getting into the pro's—Most don't, most don't even fin. college
Women's basketball—why not so popular?
How about small schools like ours?
Local league
Our women's team—better than men
Intramural
Club sports
Never on tv.
Players still have big dreams
When's our 1st game

Notice how the student put down whatever came to mind about college basketball—everything from big national teams small local teams, from betting to finding the schedule. Also notice the errors (*tournament* and *scholarships* are misspelled) and the abbreviations (*pro's, fin., 1st*). Errors and informality don't matter as the student is just trying to record ideas, and making the list helps the student explore the topic before reading.

If necessary, you can reorganize your list later by clustering related information to make it clearer and easier for you to use.

EXERCISES

6.1 Making a List

On page 84 are the title and headings of a chapter from a college textbook called *Racial and Ethnic Relations in America*, by S. Dale McLemore, Harriet D. Romo, and Susan Gonzalez Baker. After you preview (see chapter 4), use a separate sheet of paper to make a list of everything you know or think about reducing prejudice and discrimination. Student responses will vary.

6.2 Checking a List

Which items on the student's list on page 82 seem related to one another? On a separate sheet of paper, rewrite the list so the related items are close together.

6b Making a Word Map

A word map is a visual warm-up (see chapter 7). When you make a visual as a warm-up, you create a figure that links words and phrases about the topic. The visual is called a *map* because it names areas and connects them. A student made the visual on page 85 before reading a selection called "The Greatest Tightrope Walker," by Robert Kraske. As you can see, a word map links ideas with lines, boxes, circles, or arrows.

There are no rules for developing your own visual device as a prereading warm-up. You simply want to lay out the information in a kind of picture so you can see your thoughts clearly. The value of the visual is that it helps you keep related information together. Notice how all the circled thoughts connected to the word *circus* are in fact related to the circus: main acts, bicycles, nets, clowns, and jugglers. These probably refer to the student's memory of a visit she made to the circus.

14 Reducing Prejudice and Discrimination 419

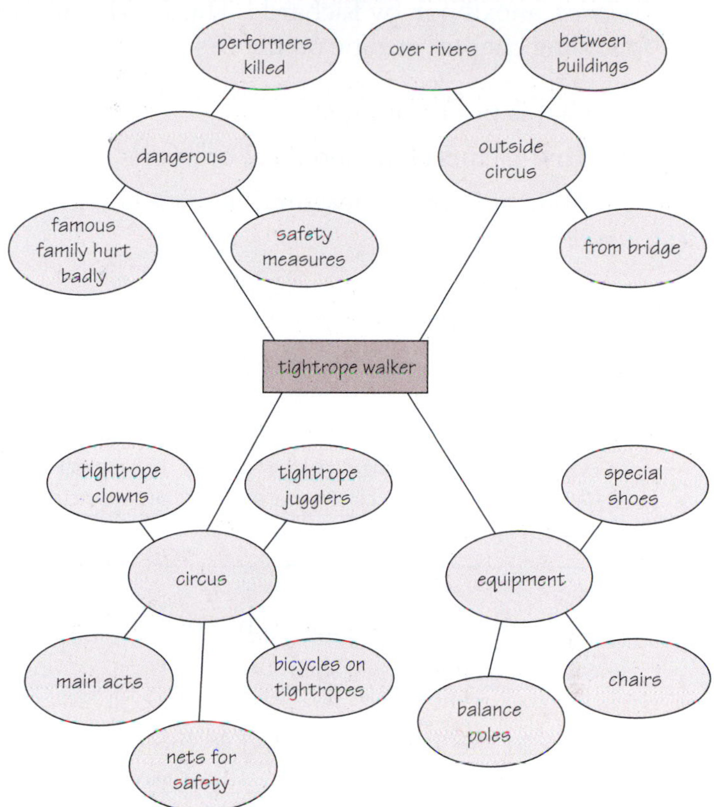

With this "thinking on paper," the student prepared herself to read. Without realizing it, she wrote down many words and ideas the story would deal with. "The Greatest Tightrope Walker" is about Blondin, a Frenchman, who walked tightropes in circuses — and across Niagara Falls in 1859.

EXERCISES

6.3 A Prereading Visual

On a separate sheet of paper, draw a word map for a chapter called "Public Opinion in American Democracy" from *Government in*

America, a textbook by Richard J. Hardy. The author provides the following chapter outline on the first page of the chapter:

1. What is public opinion?
2. Many factors shape political opinions.
3. Public opinion is measured in several ways. Student responses will vary.

6.4 A Word Map

Look at the word map on page 85. Then answer the following questions.

1. What are the four main areas mapped from the words *tightrope walker?* circus, dangerous, outside circus, equipment
2. What other main areas might you add? Student responses will vary.
3. Look at the areas connected to the main ones. How do they relate to the main group? They derive from the main heading.
4. How do the areas connected to the main ones relate to one another? Student responses will vary.

6c Brainstorming

Brainstorming is using questions to help you think, "to make a storm," in your brain. When you brainstorm as a prereading exercise, you raise as many questions as you can about a reading selection. Ask *who, what, when, why, where*, and *how*. Or ask any other useful questions.

Remember that you're brainstorming *before* you read. First use as many clues as you can from previewing (see chapter 4). Look at the title, headings, drawings, and photographs. Then make a list of questions.

Look at the brainstorming one student did before she read a chapter in her psychology book, *Developmental Psychology* (Third Edition), by Robert Biehler and Lynne M. Hudson. The chapter was called. "Two to Five: Relations with Others." There were three main headings: "Parent-Child Relationships," "The Impact of Day Care and Preschool Experience," and "Relationships with Peers." The student prepared the following questions:

Who establishes important relationships with the child?
How does the child view his or her mother at this stage?
What must the mother do or not do?
When should a parent use day care for a child?
How does day care affect the child?
How many child-abuse cases at day care are really true?
Are kids in danger at day care centers?
How do kids play together at this age?
Should parents teach kids how to read at this age?
What part do fathers play in raising kids in this age group?

The value of questions in general is that they stimulate thinking and prepare you to find answers. By brainstorming before you read, you prepare your mind to get information. You may not find all the answers to your brainstorming questions, but you'll read with much more attention.

EXERCISE

6.5 Brainstorming

Following is a chapter called "Study Techniques" from *The McGraw-Hill College Handbook* (Second Edition). On a separate sheet of paper, brainstorm on this chapter. Examine the various headings, but don't read the selection yet.

After you brainstorm, read the chapter. Which of your questions did you answer? Which did you not answer?

Study Techniques

Develop your study skills by applying techniques for improving your comprehension and retention of what you read. Learn to take useful notes when you read and when you listen to lectures. Studying is an active, continual process that requires planning, repetition, and *writing* to help you remember and use newly acquired information.

First, Plan a Reasonable Study Schedule

Examine your week's activities, and develop a realistic plan for studying. Consider all the demands on your time — eating, sleeping, attending classes, doing homework, exercising, socializing, commuting, watching TV — and set aside time for regular studying. Some students make a weekly chart of their activities so that it's easier to keep track of their hours. If you do block in regular activities and study time on a calendar, leave a number of free periods so that you have time for relaxing and for making adjustments. When exams or special projects come up, for example, you'll need blocks of time over several days, even weeks, to complete your work on time. Try to avoid cramming for tests, because the stress it produces prevents deep learning and memory. If you must cram, try to outline the major points you need to cover and concentrate on learning the central ideas and facts.

Learn and Retain Information by Reading Actively

You can improve your ability to learn and retain material by approaching your reading with a clear plan and by taking various kinds of notes.

1. *Survey your text before you read it carefully.* Surveying — looking at the text for information without reading every word — gives you an outline of the material so that you can focus on what you are about to read. When you survey a book, look for chapter titles and subtitles, headings and subheadings, charts, graphs, illustrations, and words in boldface or italics. Skim the opening and closing paragraphs of a chapter or of chapter sections. Surveying like this can give you the sense of a book very quickly.
2. *Write out questions in advance so that you can read with a purpose.* Once you have looked quickly through the reading material, jot down some questions about it. Writing will help make things stick in your mind, and your written questions will provide a good short review. It is always better to write your own questions about a text you are reading, but if questions do appear at the end of a chapter, consider them carefully before you read. Then let them guide your reading.

   Keeping specific questions in mind as you read will get you actively involved in the material at hand. Your reading then has a purpose: you are trying to find answers to your questions.

3. *Take notes on your reading.* Take notes on what you read. Learn how to make summaries. When you read, try to summarize every paragraph by composing a simple, short sentence. Be ruthless in cutting out the nonessential, and put the author's thoughts into your own words. Don't try to duplicate the style of the book or article you are reading. Putting somebody else's ideas into your own words is a good way of making sure that you truly know those ideas.

   Many students underline as they read. Underlining has several disadvantages. Obviously, you cannot underline in a library book; so if you underline material, you will have to own the book. Underlining is also a passive way of learning; it is merely a signpost to tell you that something here is worth remembering. But often, when students come back to passages they have underlined, they cannot remember why they put those lines down in the first place. Often, too, they underline too much, and too much emphasis becomes boring and confusing. Underlining is never as effective as writing down a short summary sentence for each paragraph. Writing a summary sentence ensures that you will reconsider the thoughts in the book, translate them into your own words, and put them on paper.
4. *Look up your reading topic in some reference books.* You can also aid your memory by looking for the same information or closely related information in another source. Your teacher may require you to buy one or more books for the course, and you should read these books and make notes about them. But it is also an excellent idea to check information mentioned in your reading by looking things up in some of the many reference books available in the library. Try an encyclopedia, various dictionaries, and other reference books your librarian may help you find.... When you read the same information several times, presented in slightly different ways, you will find that each source has some details that the others do not have. This seeking of variety in your learning will provide wonderful help to the mind in remembering. If you have taken careful summary notes on the various things you have read, your memory will be all the more strengthened.
5. *Learn to analyze what you read by asking questions about it.* Another skill required in study is the ability to analyze, to tell what things mean, to discover how they fit with other things you know. Here again, writing will help you to study. Many writing teachers advise students to keep a notebook in which they can jot down their notes from sources on one page and then jot down their thoughts about those notes on

a facing page. If you ask yourself questions about the things you put down, you will develop your analytical powers. Pay attention to your own feelings. Do you like a book? Make yourself set down reasons why you like it. Do you dislike a book? Again, write down the reasons for your preference. Whether you feel interested, bored, repelled, or excited, ask yourself what there is in the book (or movie or whatever else you may be studying) that rouses such feelings. Then write your reasons down. Don't think that you have to like a work of literature or art or a study in history merely because someone else does. But you should be able to justify your opinions, not merely to others but to yourself. And as you get into the habit of writing out these justifications, you will find your analytical ability improving steadily.

6. *Look up unfamiliar words, practice using them, and build them into your vocabulary.* With the aid of a dictionary ... keep a record of new words; write them on index cards or in a notebook. Include correct spelling, pronunciation clues, clear definitions that you write yourself, and a phrase or a sentence using the word properly. Arrange the words in related groups to help yourself study (business words, economics words, psychology words, literature words, and so on). Incorporate new words in your speaking and your writing vocabulary. Here is an example of a word written down for further study.

   puerile (PYOO ar il)

   juvenile in a bad sense. People who are puerile are not just children; they are *childish.* He was *puerile* when he refused to let her name appear before his on the program for the play.

7. *Review your notes and your reading assignments.* Immediately after you finish reading, and at convenient intervals thereafter, look over whatever questions, notes, summaries, or outlines you have created from your reading. Don't try to read every word of the original material in the book or article every time you review. Skim over it. You will learn better from many rapid readings than from one or two slow readings. Skimming will help you get the shape of the material in your mind, and as you study your own notes, you will recall many of the supporting details.

Use your written work to help you complete your assignments. It often helps if you close your book, put away your notes, and try to jot down from memory a rough outline of what you are studying. The more different ways you can write about material you are learning, the more effectively you will learn it.

Learn to Write Useful Notes on Your Lectures, and Compare Notes with Your Classmates

Taking good notes during a lecture is a skill that requires practice. Some students tape-record lectures so they can listen again to what the teacher has said. But even if you have a tape recorder and the teacher is willing to be recorded, writing can still help you understand and remember the lecture.

Never try to write down everything you hear in the lecture as it is going on. Unless you know shorthand, you cannot write as fast as a person speaks, and while you are struggling to get a sentence down, the lecturer will have gone on to another point. In your haste, you may garble both what has been said and what is being said.

Your best bet is to write down words, phrases, and short sentences. Use these jottings to stimulate your memory later on. As soon as possible after the lecture is over, take your notes to a quiet place and try to write down as much of the lecture as you can remember. If you do this regularly, you probably will find yourself remembering more and more of each successive lecture.

Once you have written up your notes, compare what you have with the notes taken by another member of the class. If four or five of you get together to share your notes, you will each acquire an amazingly complete set, and, in your discussions of gaps and confusions, you will further your learning.

Take Breaks

Don't try to sit for hours without a break, writing notes about your reading or your lectures. Get up every forty-five minutes or so and walk around the room and stretch. Then sit back down quickly and go to work again. Taking a break will relax your body and perhaps stimulate your mind to some new thought that you can use when you start studying again.

—Richard Marius and Harvey S. Wiener

Critical Thinking and Writing

Which of the study techniques described in the selection have you used? Which ones have you never used? How effective are the techniques you currently use?

Write a few paragraphs evaluating your current study methods, telling which new techniques you might like to try.

6d Freewriting

Your purpose with freewriting is to write freely about the subject of the piece you are going to read. Do not stop writing for any reason. Write down whatever comes into your mind about the reading selection before you read it. Don't correct words or cross them out. Just get on paper as many ideas as you can, no matter how strange or silly they seem.

A student did the following freewriting before she read an essay called "Colleges Put a Cork on College Drinking" from *Time* magazine. The article is about efforts by colleges to prevent alcohol abuse among students.

> Colleges and drinking. Drinking at college. I don't drink. My boyfriend sometimes drinks too much. Dorm parties. Tailgate parties. Too much beer. Beer. Drinking too much beer. Students need to drink. It relaxes them, takes pressure off. Can they relax in other ways? Drinking can be a serious problem. Problem. Problem. Drunk driving, of course. But you can hurt your body? In what ways? Maybe if we knew the effects of alcohol. Kids wouldn't abuse it. What can colleges do? Suspend you for drinking. Maybe give courses. My sister belongs to Students Against Drunk Driving at High School. Maybe colleges have groups like that. Just how big a problem is campus drinking?

Do you see how this student put down whatever thoughts came into her head about the selection before she read it? She was tapping her own experiences. When she reads, many points in the article will be familiar to her.

EXERCISE

6.6 Freewriting

On a separate sheet of paper, freewrite on a reading selection titled "Peer Pressure and Family Values," a chapter from *Sociology in Your Life*. Freewrite on the basis of what the title makes you think of.

CULTURAL Exchange

NCAA	National Collegiate Athletic Association — organizes and regulates college sports (page 82)
intramurial	sports played with local teams within a campus community (page 82)
pros	professional-level sporting activities (page 82)
to cram	to try to learn a lot very quickly, usually by staying up the entire night before an exam or a test (page 88)
to garble	to mix up or scramble a signal or message to such an extent as to make it misleading or incomprehensible (page 91)
tailgate party	an outdoor event, typically in the parking lot of a sports stadium, where food and drinks are served on the open tailgates of station wagons; occurs either before or after a sporting event (page 92)

Chapter 6 SELF-TEST
Using Prereading Warm-Ups

Answer the following questions in the spaces provided. Count ten points for each correct answer.

1. In what way does warming up before reading help you better understand your reading?

   By thinking about a subject, you prepare your mind to accept new information.

2. List four ways to organize your warm-up thinking.

   a. making a list

   b. making a word map

   c. brainstorming

   d. freewriting

3. How important are grammar and spelling in warm-ups?

   They are not important; don't worry about them.

4. How should you organize a warm-up list?

   Follow the ideas that come to mind about the subject of the reading.

c 5. A word map should be drawn
   a. always using long descriptive phrases.
   b. always using circles and squares connected by solid lines.
   c. following your idea of how topics relate to each other.
   d. in the order events happened.

a 6. When brainstorming, you should
   a. make up questions about the subject matter of the reading.
   b. write out why you don't like the topic of the reading.
   c. decide whether you want to read the selection.
   d. choose the ten most important words in the reading.

d 7. When freewriting,
a. stop to think about the subject.
b. put your thoughts together carefully.
c. list the facts you know about the subject of the reading.
d. write your thoughts on the subject without stopping.

Score: ______ correct × 10 points each = ______

CHAPTER SEVEN

Using Visual Aids

Information in print can appear in more than just words and sentences. Writers often use illustrations—that is, drawings, photographs, charts, graphs, and tables—as *visual aids*. (*Visual* refers to what you can see; an *aid* is a helper.) You often see sentences and visual aids used together, for example, in advertisements, cartoons, cookbooks, maps, and repair manuals. These and other print forms communicate with both words and pictures.

Why do writers use illustrations? Sometimes you can understand a difficult point more easily with a picture or a drawing. Illustrations are really helpful, for example, when you're trying to figure out how to do or make something. If you've ever put together a stereo unit, a bookcase, or a child's toy, you know how useful illustrations can be. To make the meaning of numbers visual, other aids—such as charts and graphs—can present data briefly and clearly. Using sentences and paragraphs alone might make an explanation longer and more complicated than necessary. Sometimes a cartoon or a photograph adds an element of delight or surprise that keeps readers interested and involved.

7a Reading with Visual Aids

Good readers, adults and children alike, always use visual aids to help them understand written words. As you build your reading skills, rely on photographs and drawings to fill in anything you're not sure of. Visual aids often supply important information the words alone do not supply.

Most of us probably learned to recognize words by connecting them with visual aids. Young children can read the word *STOP*, which they associate with the red-and-white eight-sided sign on the corner; the familiar shape and color of the sign help them learn the word. Similarly, children learn to read *McDonald's* because of the golden arches, *Band-Aids* because of the picture on the box, and *Coca-Cola* because of the white script letters and red can or label.

Using Visual Aids to Help You Understand What You Read

- *Carefully review visual aids.* Many inexperienced readers think pictures charts, or other illustrations are there just to make the page look good. So these readers do not look at the visual aids carefully. If you skip over an illustration, you might be skipping information that is important in understanding what you are reading.
- *Carefully read the captions, titles, or notes that help explain the illustrations.* A *caption* is an explanation in words for a picture. Often a group of words or a sentence or two tell why the illustration is important. In newspapers, photographs usually have captions that name the people in the pictures or give other information. Captions and titles for charts, graphs, and tables often highlight the main point of the visual aid in addition charts and graphs often have notes that explain what certain figures and symbols mean. Look at those notes carefully.
- *Try to connect the words you are reading with the illustrations.* You may look at a picture before you read or you may read and then study the picture. However, when an illustration appears with a selection, readers most often use the words and picture together. You read a few paragraphs, and then you examine the illustration to connect it to what you've read so far. Then you continue reading, returning now and then in the illustration. The point is to try to put the illustration and the words together. Ask yourself questions: What is this visual information showing me? What does the illustration have to do with what I'm reading? Why has the writer included the picture? What does the picture tell that the words do not?
- *State visual information in your own words.* Illustrations give information. Try to state that information in your own words. A graph, chart, or table, for example, puts information in visual terms, which makes it easier to look at lots of data quickly. From the information, you can make comparisons on your own. In fact, unless you try to state comparisons in your own words, you may miss the point of the graph, chart, or table.

Look at the following graph about estimated numbers—an *estimate* is a rough guess—of illegal aliens in America. Illegal aliens are people who are not permitted to enter a country but who go there and stay anyway. Answer the questions after you study the graph. Then check your answers in the explanation that follows the questions.

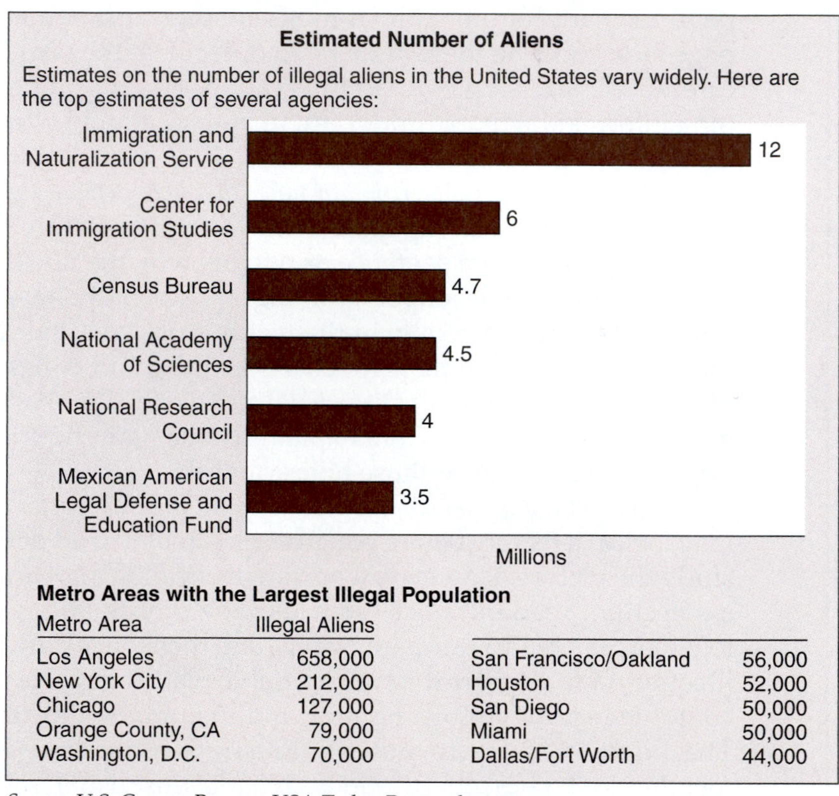

Metro Areas with the Largest Illegal Population

Metro Area	Illegal Aliens		
Los Angeles	658,000	San Francisco/Oakland	56,000
New York City	212,000	Houston	52,000
Chicago	127,000	San Diego	50,000
Orange County, CA	79,000	Miami	50,000
Washington, D.C.	70,000	Dallas/Fort Worth	44,000

Source: U.S. Census Bureau; USA Today Research

d 1. The word *agencies* that appears in line 3 probably means
   a. groups of people from another country.
   b. U.S. populations.
   c. estimates.
   d. groups that gather information or take action on behalf of others.

a 2. The shaded bars in the graph show the
   a. numbers of aliens estimated by different agencies.
   b. working conditions for aliens.

c. millions of dollars spent by agencies for aliens.
d. cities with large illegal populations.

d 3. The agency that estimates the smallest number of aliens in this country is the
a. Census Bureau.
b. National Research Council.
c. Immigration and Naturalization Service.
d. Mexican American Legal Defense and Educational Fund.

c 4. San Francisco/Oakland, Houston, San Diego, and Miami have
a. fewer illegal aliens than Dallas/Fort Worth.
b. more illegal aliens than the other cities listed in the graph.
c. between 50,000 and 60,000 illegal aliens.
d. a higher number of illegal aliens than Orange County, California.

For question 1, you should have guessed the meaning of the word *agencies* from clues in the graph. You could guess that each name appearing above a bar is the name of a group concerned with aliens. Perhaps you knew from your own experience about the work of the Census Bureau. Perhaps the word *research* in "National Research Council" told you that the group investigates data. Using these clues, you should have chosen *d* as the correct answer.

Choice *a* is wrong because the question is about *agencies* and not *aliens*. Choice *b* is incorrect; it's too broad, and there's no reason to make that choice based on the graph. Choice *c* is wrong, too. Although a form of the word *estimate* appears three times in the graph, it has nothing to do with the word *agencies*.

The only correct answer for question 2 is *a*. From the title of the graph, you know the illustration shows the estimated number of illegal aliens. To the right of each bar, you can see a number and the word *million*. These clues should tell you that each bar represents a certain number of people. The longer the bar, the higher the estimate. The shorter the bar, the lower the estimate.

If you chose answer *c* for question 2, the word *million* beside each bar tricked you into thinking about money, but the graph has nothing to do with costs or expenses. It also has nothing to do with working conditions, so choice *b* is also wrong. Finally, *d* is incorrect, too. Although a part of the graph does compare cities that have a large population of illegal aliens, the bars have nothing to do with specific cities. Only the table called "Metro Areas with Largest Illegal Population" compares cities.

For questions 3 and 4, you must use the graph to make comparisons on your own. For 3, only *d*, the Mexican American Legal Defense and Educational Fund, is correct. How do you know this group makes the smallest estimate? First, you look at the length of the bar. Then you compare its length to the lengths of the other bars. Clearly, the bar under the Mexican American Legal Defense and Educational Fund is the smallest. Your second hint is the numbers beside the bars. The 3.5 million figure is the smallest of the figures for all the agencies. The key to reaching the right answer here is making the comparison in your own mind. The graph does not say outright which group's estimates are bigger or smaller than another's. You have to make the judgment yourself.

For question 4, only *c* is correct. Looking at the numbers, you can see that each of the four cities named in the question has between 50,000 and 60,000 illegal aliens. Although the number 60,000 does not appear anywhere in the graph, you can reach that conclusion yourself. Both San Diego and Miami have 50,000 illegal aliens; Houston has 52,000; and San Francisco/Oakland has 56,000.

Answer *a* is incorrect because Dallas/Fort Worth has only 44,000 illegal aliens. Answer *b* is wrong, too, because many other cities (such as Los Angeles and New York) have higher numbers of illegal aliens than San Francisco/Oakland, Houston, San Diego, and Miami. Answer *d* is obviously incorrect, too. Orange County, California, has 79,000 illegal aliens, a much higher figure than any of the four cities named in the question.

EXERCISES

7.1 Words and Pictures for Meanings

Try to figure out the definition of each of the following words from the illustrations on pages 102 and 103. Write the letter of the correct choice in the blank space.

__a__ 1. discard

a. throw away
b. eat
c. cook
d. slice

d 2. joint
   a. bad place
   b. marijuana cigarette
   c. wing
   d. point of contact between bones

c 3. reserve
   a. throw away
   b. prepare carefully
   c. save
   d. put salt on

b 4. additional
   a. less
   b. extra
   c. fatty
   d. poor quality

b 5. expose
   a. decorate
   b. show
   c. pose
   d. make clear

a 6. sever
   a. separate by cutting off
   b. cook on high heat
   c. add spices to
   d. hit

d 7. repeat
   a. cut
   b. remove the bone
   c. remove the leg
   d. do again

a 8. incision
   a. deep cut
   b. mark
   c. line
   d. view

d 9. trim
   a. slim
   b. widen
   c. open
   d. cut away

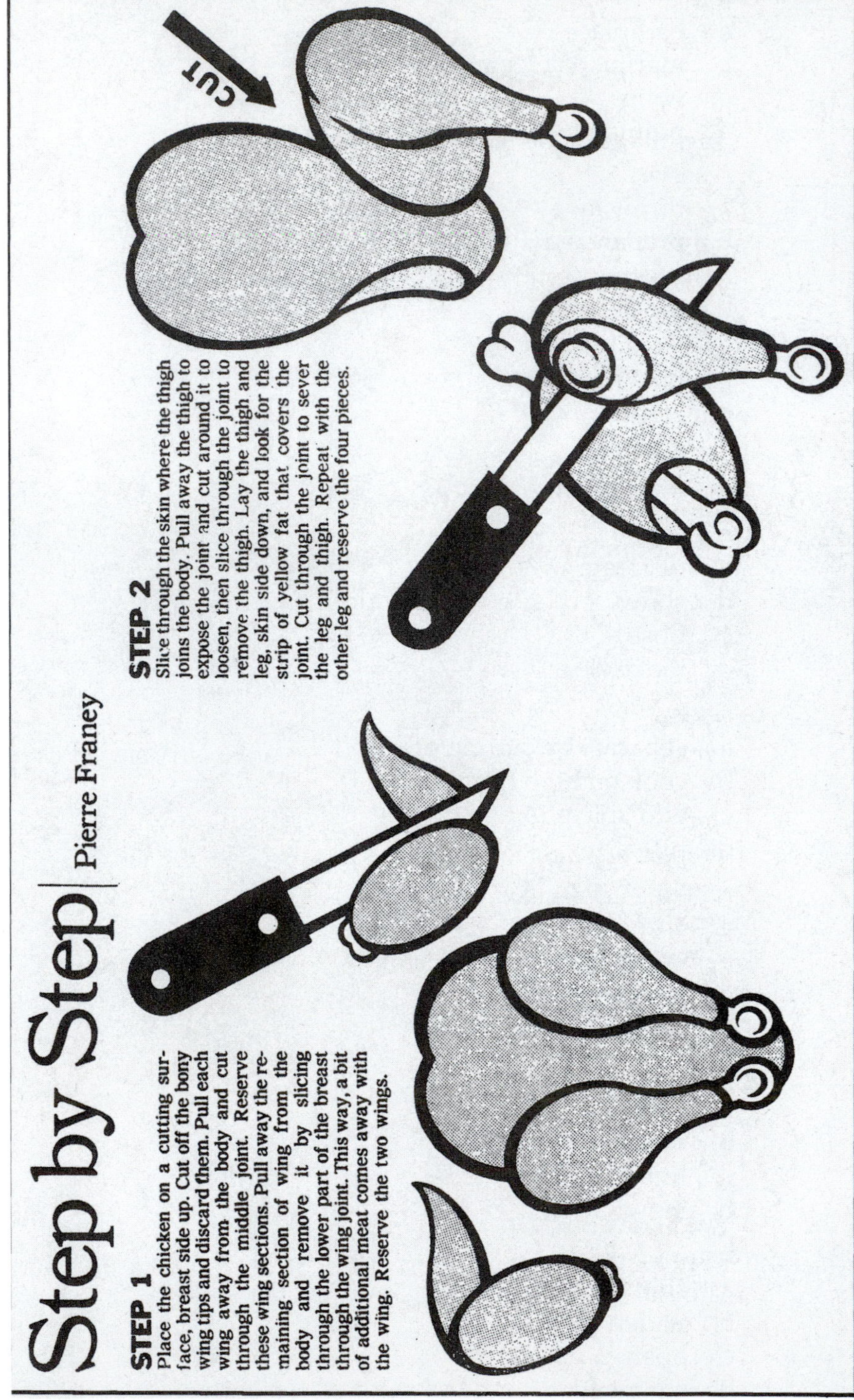

Step by Step | Pierre Franey

STEP 1
Place the chicken on a cutting surface, breast side up. Cut off the bony wing tips and discard them. Pull each wing away from the body and cut through the middle joint. Reserve these wing sections. Pull away the remaining section of wing from the body and remove it by slicing through the lower part of the breast through the wing joint. This way, a bit of additional meat comes away with the wing. Reserve the two wings.

STEP 2
Slice through the skin where the thigh joins the body. Pull away the thigh to expose the joint and cut around it to loosen, then slice through the joint to remove the thigh. Lay the thigh and leg, skin side down, and look for the strip of yellow fat that covers the joint. Cut through the joint to sever the leg and thigh. Repeat with the other leg and reserve the four pieces.

Cutting A Chicken

THIS country consumes more chicken per capita than any other kind of meat. Not only is chicken still among the most economical of foods, it is also extremely versatile. For those reasons, I have devised more recipes for chicken over the years than for anything else. Using a chicken in parts extends the cooking possiblities to include casserole dishes, such as paella, and sautéing and braising. Moreover, small pieces of chicken cook faster and more evenly than large ones.

STEP 3
Make a long incision along one side of the backbone, beginning at the neck and running to the hind section. Repeat this action until the breast meat is removed. Do the same on the other side.

CHOP THROUGH

SIDE VIEW

STEP 4
Trim excess skin and fat from the breasts. If desired, slice the breasts in half widthwise.

Drawings by Doug Taylor

Now answer these questions about the illustrations on pages 102 and 103.

__c__ 10. In the first picture, the knife is showing how to
- a. cut a chicken.
- b. remove the wing from a chicken.
- c. cut the wing at the middle joint.
- d. reserve the wing section.

__a__ 11. When you cut the wing from a chicken, you should slice through the lower part of the breast through the wing joint because
- a. extra meat comes off with the wing.
- b. the breast will be discarded.
- c. the bony tips should be reserved.
- d. the wings are too tiny.

__c__ 12. To remove the thigh and the leg, you should first
- a. cut through the joint to sever the leg and the thigh.
- b. look for the strip of yellow fat over the joint.
- c. cut the skin where the body and the thigh meet.
- d. expose the joint.

__d__ 13. You should cut along each side of the backbone from the neck to the hind section to
- a. discard the wing tips.
- b. reserve the neck.
- c. reserve the backbone.
- d. remove the breast meat.

Words and Pictures for Meanings

Answer these questions based on the instructions on page 105 for playing compact discs on a portable radio-cassette-CD player.

_____ 1. To open the compartment for the disc,

c
- a. press button 3.
- b. wait until the time elapses and the top will pop open.
- c. press the near right corner of the CD compartment.
- d. find and press the eject button.

__b__ 2. Place the CD in the compartment
- a. in any direction.
- b. with the label side up.

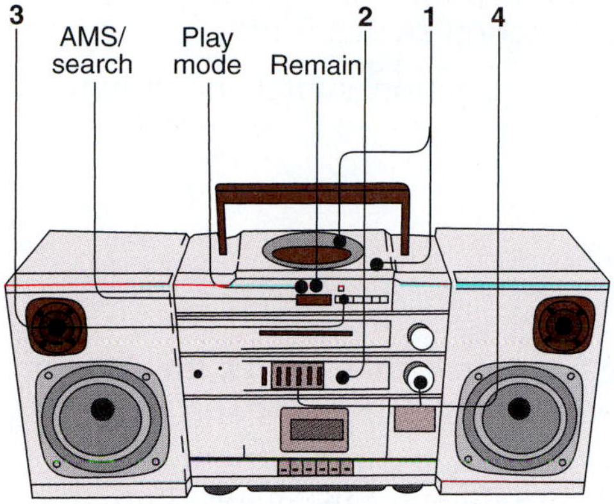

3 AMS/ search Play mode Remain 2 1 4

1

3

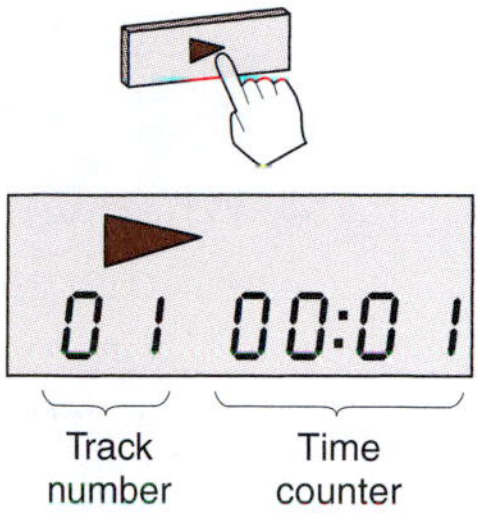

01 00:01

Track number Time counter

with the labeled surface facing upward

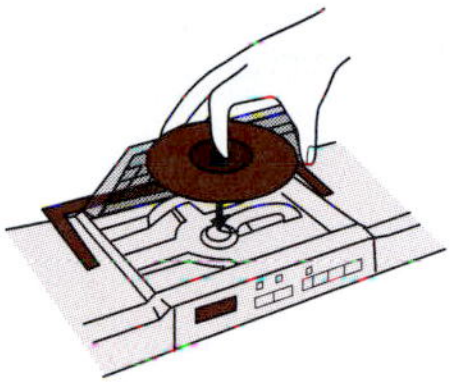

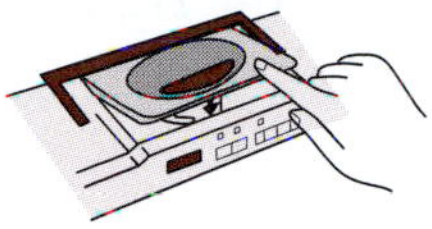

2 FUNCTION

CD
FM
AM
TAPE (CD RADIO OFF)

16 55:32

Total selection number Total playing time

How to switch the display

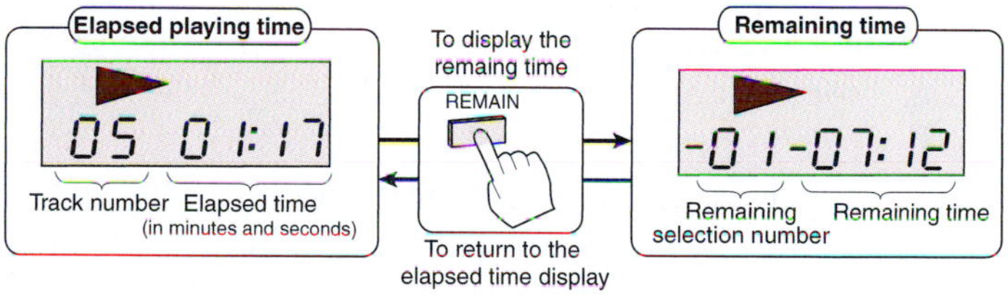

Elapsed playing time

05 01:17

Track number Elapsed time (in minutes and seconds)

To display the remaing time

REMAIN

To return to the elapsed time display

Remaining time

-01-07:12

Remaining selection number Remaining time

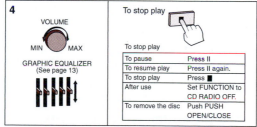

4

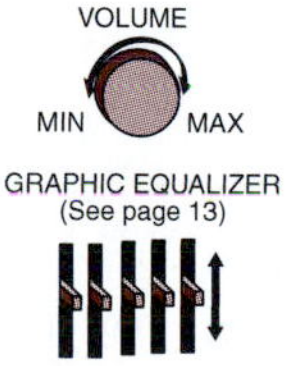

VOLUME

MIN MAX

GRAPHIC EQUALIZER (See page 13)

To stop play

To stop play

To pause	Press II
To resume play	Press II again.
To stop play	Press ■
After use	Set FUNCTION to CD RADIO OFF.
To remove the disc	Push PUSH OPEN/CLOSE

c. with the label side down.
d. only when the function switch is off.

b ______ 3. On the diagram, the function switch is shown by which number?
a. 1
b. 2
c. 3
d. 4

a ______ 4. When you set the function switch to CD, the counter
a. displays the number of selections and the total playing time of the CD inside the compartment.
b. starts at 00 : 00 and displays the elapsed time.
c. will not operate until set separately.
d. always shows 16 55 : 32.

b ______ 5. To start the CD playing,
a. press the button with the square.
b. press the button with the right-facing arrow.
c. set the counter to 01 00 : 01.
d. turn the volume switch.

b ______ 6. To make the playback louder,
a. flip the function switch.
b. turn the volume knob clockwise.
c. turn the volume knob counterclockwise.
d. flip the graphic equalizer switches down.

c ______ 7. To operate the graphic equalizer,
a. set the volume knob to MAX.
b. push button 4.
c. check page 13 of the instructions.
d. rotate the graphic equalizer switches counterclockwise.

d ______ 8. The counter displays
a. total selections and total playing time.
b. elapsed selections and playing time.
c. remaining selections and playing time.
d. a, b, or c, depending on how the machine is set.

d ______ 9. To stop the CD from playing,
a. press the button with the two vertical lines.
b. press the button with the square.
c. set the function switch to CD RADIO OFF.
d. a, b, or c.

7.3 Visuals in textbooks

The following three visuals come from textbooks in a variety of subjects. Examine each visual and the words that go with it. Then answer the questions.

1. Government

TABLE 5.1 The Political Orientation of College Freshmen

	TOTAL	MALE	FEMALE
Far left	2.9%	3.5%	2.5%
Liberal	21.7	18.8	24.1
Middle of the road	52.7	50.5	54.4
Conservative	21.0	24.6	18.0
Far right	1.7	2.5	1.0

Source: Data from Linda J. Sax, Alexander W. Astin, William S. Korn, and Kathryn M. Mahoney (1996). *The American Freshman: National Norms for Fall 1996.* Los Angeles: Higher Education Research Institute, UCLA, December 1996, pp. 28, 46, 64.

1. What does the table show?

   the political positions of college freshmen

2. What are the five kinds of political positions shown in the chart?

   far left, liberal, middle of the road, conservative, far right

3. Which is the most popular position among students?

   middle of the road, with over half of both men and women

4. Are men or women more likely to be either far left or far right?

   More men are both far left and far right.

5. Who are more liberal, men or women? Who are more conservative?

   Women are more liberal (24.1 percent to 18.8 percent) and men are more conservative (24.6 percent to 18.0 percent).

2. Psychology

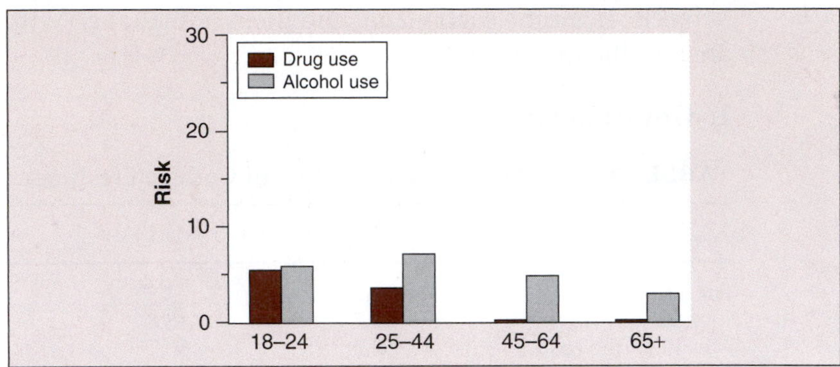

Age and Substance Abuse People between the ages of eighteen and forty-four are most prone to problem drinking and many of the other substance-abuse disorders.

6. What do the figures on the left side of the graph represent?

   the level of risk

7. What is the difference between the lighter bars and the darker bars?

   The lighter bars refer to alcohol use; the darker, to drug use.

8. Which age group has the greatest risk of drug abuse?

   18 to 24

9. Which age group has the greatest risk of alcohol abuse?

   25 to 44

10. In which age groups is alcohol abuse greater than drug abuse?

    all

11. By what age is there almost no risk of drug abuse or alcohol abuse?

    drug use: 45; alcohol use: never

Critical Thinking and Writing

The graph relating age and substance abuse suggests that people at different ages are at risk for different kinds of abuse. Have you ever known people who abused drugs or alcohol or were in danger of such abuse? Did these individuals seem to follow the patterns indicated in the graph?

After studying the graph, write a page comparing your personal knowledge of drug and alcohol abuse to the patterns shown in the graph.

3. Health

The Cerebrum

The largest and uppermost part of the brain, which regulates your thoughts and actions, is the *cerebrum* (*SER uh brum*). The cerebrum is responsible for the highly developed intelligence of human beings. As you can see in Figure 13.4, the surface of the cerebrum looks like a wrinkled walnut with many grooves. These grooves follow a pattern in normal brains. The patterns are used to identify specific regions of the brain. Some regions receive messages about what you see, hear, and smell, or how you move. Other parts control your ability to think, write, talk, and express emotions. Figure 13.4 identifies different regions of the brain.

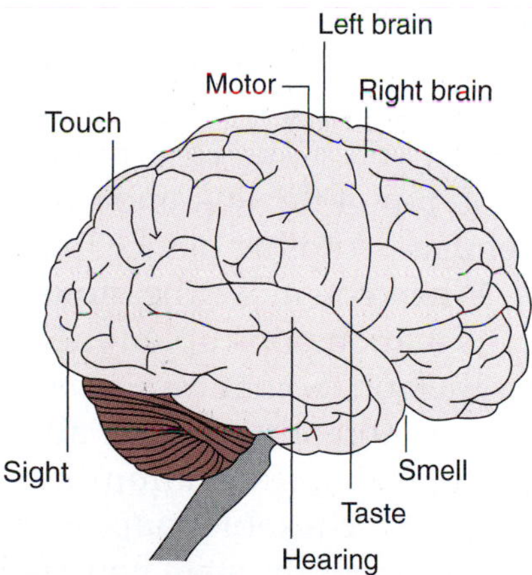

FIGURE 13.4 Control centers of the brain.

12. What does the illustration show?

    the control centers of the brain

13. Why is the illustration necessary to the paragraph?

    It helps you visualize the brain and locate the control centers.

14. What do the labels indicate?

    the different activities and their areas of control

7b Visuals on the World Wide Web

Computers, computer design and graphic tools, Internet communication, and the World Wide Web have greatly increased the use of visuals. Most webpages include at least some visual elements, whether using colors for background and lettering to get attention and set a mood or having fully interactive maps that allow you to get more information about each spot on the map. Many of the visual elements are similar to those in print, and you need only the skills you already have to understand what an illustration adds to a story or to gain information from a bar graph. But some visual elements on the Internet are different because they are interactive. *Interactive* means they change or respond when the reader does something like click on a link, roll a mouse across the picture, or enter information.

Many of the interactive parts of visual elements have to do with navigation, or going to other parts of the website or linked website. The basic navigation device is a link. A word, a picture, or a spot on a place within a picture or map may all serve as links. When you move your mouse so the arrow or other indicator is on top of the link and you then click, you are shown a new webpage. Another device to bring up new information is a *rollover*. When you move the mouse indicator over one of these, more information pops up on the screen, sometimes with more links to click on. Sometimes a picture contains many links, so you can get more information about some part of the picture. For example, an organization that has branches in each state may provide a clickable map, which will help you get to the information about the state you are interested in. Just locate the arrow over the state and click.

Sometimes pictures or texts respond to your moving your mouse around, as in a game. Others respond if you enter information in a box and then click.

In addition to links and rollovers contained in the main body of a page, most webpages show navigation bars at the top, bottom, or sides. These contain lists of links to other pages of the website so you can find your way to the areas that interest you. These navigation bars usually identify the name of the website or the organization behind it, either through a name or through a logo (identifying symbol). If you click on the name or symbol, usually it takes you back to the front page of the website. The front page of a website usually provides an introduction to or an overview of the various parts of the site. The navigation bars of more complex websites often include search functions and links to site maps that can help you find the page you are looking for.

The front page of The University of California Santa Barbara Library website serves as an example. The middle of the page has a picture of the library and links to a simpler (text only) version of the website for people who are unable to use the visual ele-

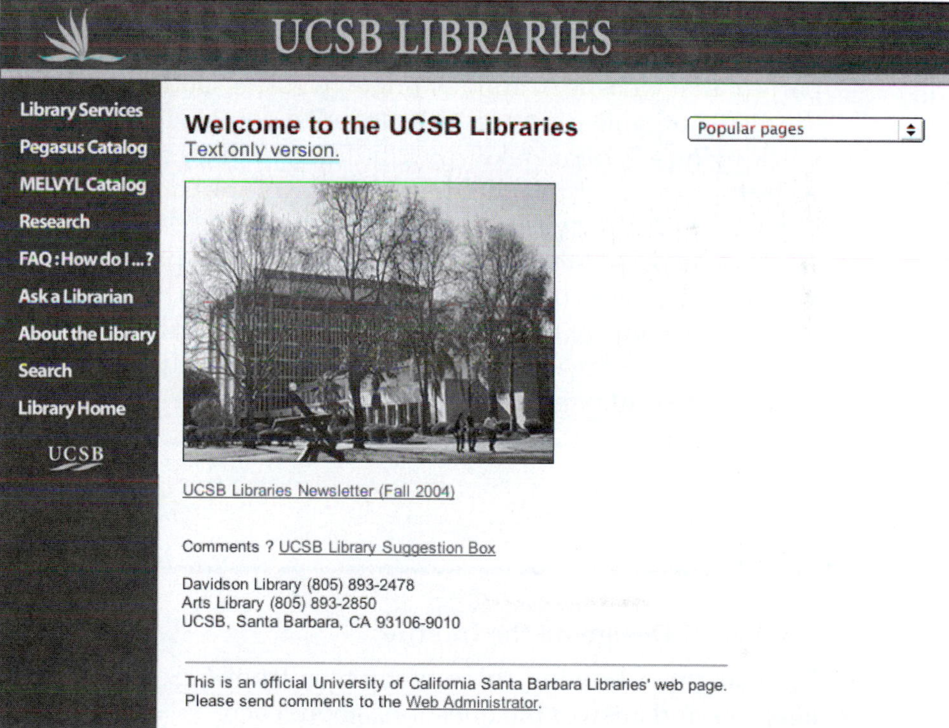

ments because of disability or computer limitations. Links also take you to a newsletter or an interactive newsletter. A link at the bottom even allows you to write an email to the person in charge of the webpage. If you click on a button on the right, you will see a list of links to the most popular pages so you can go to them directly.

Down the left-hand side is a navigation bar with links to all parts of the website. When you roll your mouse over each of these, a list of more specific links appears. At the top left corner is a logo for the library that appears on every page of this website. If you click on it, you return to this page. And at the lower left corner is a logo for the university, which takes you to the university's webpage.

Because all these features of webpages are visually arranged, you need to understand the visual organization of the website just to get around, even if most of the content is in words.

Tips for Using Visuals on the Internet

- Many visual elements on the internet are **interactive**. They change when you click or roll a mouse over the picture, or enter some information.
- Interactive visual elements help you **navigate**, or go to other parts of that website or another linked website. Understanding the visual organization of a website helps you navigate.
- **Clicking on a link** can take you to a different place on the same website or to an entirely different website. A link can be a highlighted word, a picture, or a rollover image.
- **Navigation bars** at the top, bottom, or sides of the page contain links to other pages of the website. Navigation bars also usually identify the name of the website or the organization behind it.
- Clicking on the **organization name or logo** usually takes you back to the front page of the website.

EXERCISES

7.4 Visual Design on the Internet

Look at the following three webpages from U.S. government agencies and answer the questions about each.

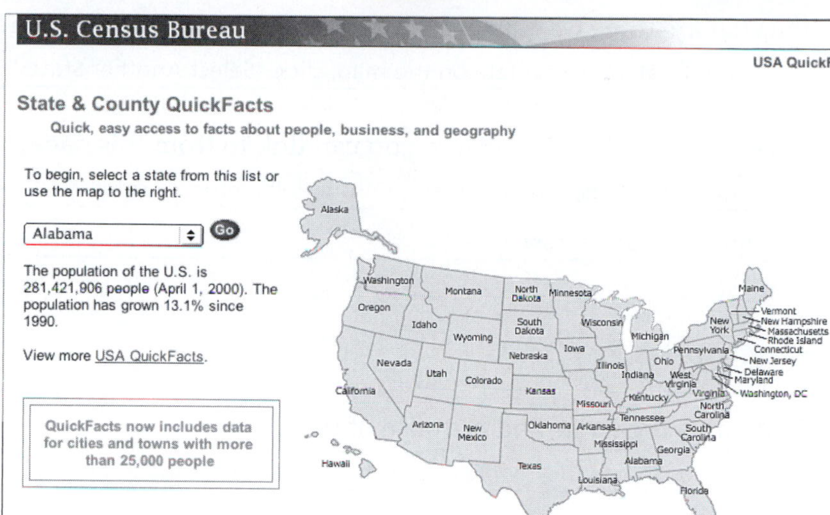

A

1. What is the purpose of this page?

   To provide census facts about the U.S. and to link to facts about each state.

2. Which government agency provides this page? And what three ways can take you to the agency home page?

   The U.S. Census Bureau

   Click the name in the top navigation bar.

   Click the name at the bottom.

   Click "Census Home" at the end of the bottom bar

3. What is the picture in the middle of the page?

   A map of the U.S.

4. What is the population of the United States, according to the last census?

   281,421,906 people

5. What are three ways to get information about a specific state?

   Use the list, click the state on the map, click "Select Another State."

6. What are some other places you can link to from this page?

   More quickfacts, thematic maps, Census 2000, product catalog, all items on bottom row.

B (see opposite page)

7. What is the name and purpose of this page?

   "Scholarship Scams," which warn students about fraud in finding and securing scholarships

8. Which government agency provides this page? And what are three ways you can get to the agency home page?

   The Federal Trade Commission, reached by clicking logo at upper left, home button right below or at bottom of page, or on www.ftc.gov in paragraph at the page bottom.

9. Where can you find statements that should warn you there is a scam?

   the first list of six bulleted items

10. What are five other pieces of information you can link to or download from this site?

    a. press release on report to Congress

    b. report to Congress

    c. advice on looking for aid

    d. a story about students being scammed

    e. an audio clip, or any of the other items in this list

11. What other language can you obtain this information in?

    Spanish

Site Map | SEARCH

HOME | CONSUMERS | BUSINESSES | NEWSROOM | FORMAL | ANTITRUST | CONGRESSIONAL | ECONOMIC | LEGAL
Privacy Policy | About FTC | Commissioners | File a Complaint | HSR | FOIA | IG Office | En Español

Need Money for College? Doesn't everybody? Unfortunately, in their efforts to pay the bills, many students and their families are falling prey to scholarship scams.

The FTC cautions students to look for tell tale lines:

- "The scholarship is guaranteed or your money back."
- "You can't get this information anywhere else."
- "I just need your credit card or bank account number to hold this scholarship."
- "We'll do all the work."
- "The scholarship will cost some money."
- "You've been selected by a 'national foundation' to receive a scholarship" or "You're a finalist" in a contest you never entered.

Information for Students and Parents

- Press Release: Federal Agencies Release First Annual Report to Congress on College Scholarship Fraud
- College Scholarship Fraud Prevention Act of 2000 - First Annual Report to Congress [PDF only]
- Looking for Student Aid
- OUCH...Students Getting Stung Trying to Find $$$ for College [PDF]
- Scholarship Scams Audio [RAM] [MP3]
- 6 $igns That Your $cholarship Is $unk
  Poster [PDF only]
  Bookmark [PDF only]
- US Department of Education
  Student Guide
  Funding Your Education
- En Español

Public Service Messages

List of Defendants in Project $cholar$cam

The FTC works for the consumer to prevent fraudulent, deceptive and unfair business practices in the marketplace and to provide information to help consumers spot, stop and avoid them. To file a complaint or to get free information on consumer issues, visit www.ftc.gov or call toll-free, 1-877-FTC-HELP (1-877-382-4357); TTY: 1-866-653-4261. The FTC enters Internet, telemarketing, identity theft and other fraud-related complaints into Consumer Sentinel, a secure, online database available to hundreds of civil and criminal law enforcement agencies in the U.S. and abroad.

12. If you have been already taken in by a scam, what will links from this page help you do?

file a complaint

CULTURAL Exchange

casserole dish	a meal prepared, cooked, and served in a covered dish or bowl; for example, macaroni and cheese, vegetables with sauce, or chicken with mushrooms and cream (page 103)
paella	a dish, Spanish in origin, consisting of rice mixed with vegetables, seafood, and chicken (page 103)
to sauté	to cook food in butter, oil, or fat over heat, usually until the food is browned (page 103)
to braise	to cook meat or vegetables slowly in a little fat and liquid in a covered pan (page 103)
census	information concerning the American population collected every ten years (page 113)
poverty level	a government-established minimum income for a household, necessary for economic well-being (page 118)

Chapter 7 SELF-TEST
Using Visual Aids

Look carefully at the four webpages (A, B, C, D) from ChildStats.gov, a U.S. government website that provides a statistical picture of how well children are doing. Many more such charts and graphs are available at <http://www.childstats.gov>. Then answer the questions. Count five points for each correct answer.

1. Which page is the home or front page for the site?

   A

2. Three pages repeat the same pictures and information in which three places?

   across the top and left-hand borders and at the bottom

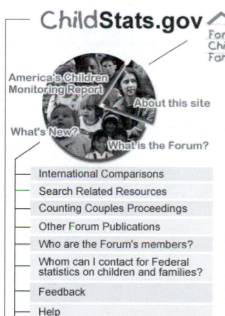

ChildStats.gov

The official Web site of the Federal Interagency Forum on Child and Family Statistics

- International Comparisons
- Search Related Resources
- Counting Couples Proceedings
- Other Forum Publications
- Who are the Forum's members?
- Whom can I contact for Federal statistics on children and families?
- Feedback
- Help
- Order Reports

JUST RELEASED! *America's Children in Brief*.

This web site offers easy access to federal and state statistics and reports on children and their families, including: population and family characteristics, economic security, health, behavior and social environment,and education. Reports of the Federal Interagency Forum on Child and Family Statistics include *America's Children: Key National Indicators of Well-Being*, the annual Federal monitoring report on the status of the Nation's children, and *Counting Couples*. The Forum fosters coordination and collaboration in the collection and reporting of Federal statistics on children and families.

PrivacyPolicy

A

ChildStats.gov **America's Children 2004**

Contents | Introduction | Press Release | Summary List | Detailed Tables | Data Sources

Population and Family Characteristics
Economic Security
Health
Behavior and Social Environment
Education
America's Children Home Page
Forum on Child and Family Statistics

Summary List of Indicators

	Previous Data Value (Year)	Most Recent Data Value (Year)	Change Between Years*
Population and Family Characteristics			
Child population			
Number of children (in millions) under age 18 in the United States	72.6 (2001)	72.9 (2002)	▲
Children as a proportion of the population			
Children under age 18 as a percentage of the U.S. population	26 (2001)	25 (2002)	▼
Racial & ethnic composition			
Percentage of children under age 18 by race and ethnic group			
White alone	76.7 (2001)	76.6 (2002)	▼
Black alone	15.6 (2001)	15.6 (2002)	NS
Asian alone	3.7 (2001)	3.8 (2002)	▲
Native Hawaiian and Other Pacific Islander alone	0.2 (2001)	0.2 (2002)	NS
American Indian and Alaska Native alone	1.2 (2001)	1.2 (2002)	NS
Two or more races	2.6 (2001)	2.6 (2002)	NS
Hispanic (of any race)	17.6 (2001)	18.0 (2002)	▲
Non-Hispanic (of any race)	82.4 (2001)	82.0 (2002)	▼
White alone, non-Hispanic	60.7 (2001)	60.1 (2002)	▼
Children of at least one foreign-born parent			
Percentage of native children under age 18 with at least one foreign-born parent	16 (2002)	16 (2003)	NS
Percentage of foreign-born children under age 18 with at least one foreign-born parent	4 (2002)	4 (2003)	NS

B

Population and Family Characteristics
Economic Security
Health
Behavior and Social Environment
Education
America's Children Home Page
Forum on Child and Family Statistics

ECON 1: Child Poverty

Percentage of related children under age 18 living below selected poverty levels by family structure, 1980-2002

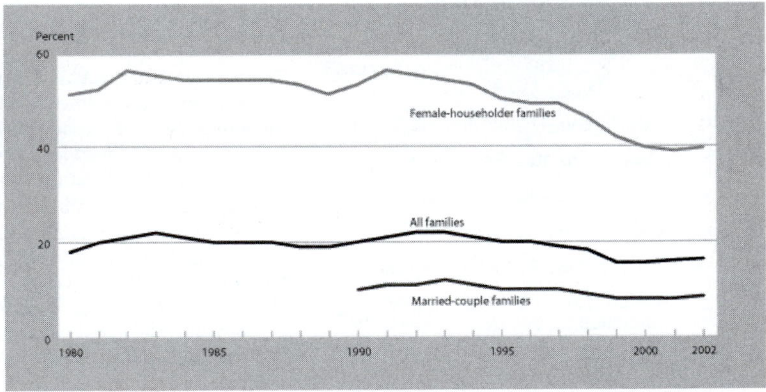

NOTE: Estimates refer to children under age 18 who are related to the householder. In 2002, the average poverty threshold for a family of four was $18,392 in annual income.

SOURCE: U.S. Census Bureau, March Current Population Survey.

Graph data can be found in Table ECON1A.

▲Top

C

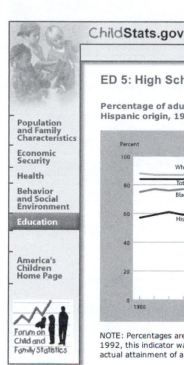

ChildStats.gov America's Children 2004

Contents | Introduction | Press Release | Summary List | Detailed Tables | Data Sources

Population and Family Characteristics

Economic Security

Health

Behavior and Social Environment

Education

America's Children Home Page

Forum on Child and Family Statistics

ED 5: High School Completion

Percentage of adults ages 18 to 24 who have completed high school by race and Hispanic origin, 1980-2001

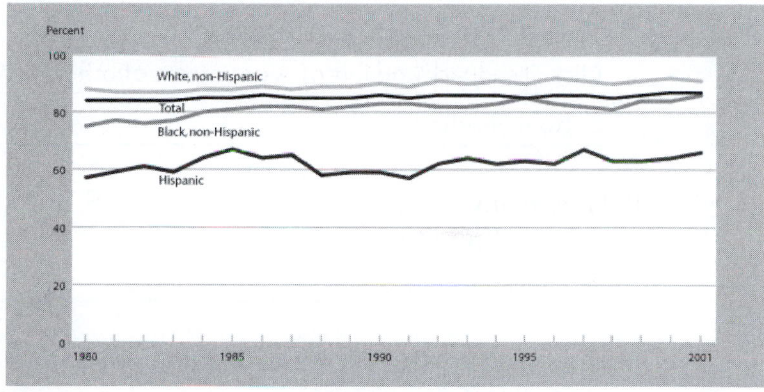

NOTE: Percentages are based only on those not currently enrolled in high school or below. Prior to 1992, this indicator was measured as completing 4 or more years of high school rather than the actual attainment of a high school diploma or equivalent.

SOURCE: U.S. Census Bureau, October Current Population Survey. Tabulated by the U.S. Department of Education, National Center for Education Statistics

Graph data can be found in Table ED5.

<<< Previous Next >>>

D

3. This information is repeated because it
provides links, is the navigation bar

4. How would you find information about children's ability to read?
Click "Education" in the left-hand column.

5. How would you find more detailed data that lie behind these charts and graphs?
Click "Detailed Tables" at the top.

6. How would you find where the website got the information?
Click "Data Sources" at the top.

7. How can you find comparisons with other countries?

   Click "International Comparisons" on list on left of A.

8. How can you find more information about this site?

   Click pie slice in page A, or at bottom of others.

9. How can you write to the agency?

   Click "Feedback" on left of A or bottom of others or "Contacts" at bottom of others.

10. How many children were there in the U.S. in 2002? What page did you find this on?

    72.9 million, page B

11. Did this increase, decrease, or remain the same from the previous year?

    increase

12. Most children are of what racial or ethnic group?

    white

13. Did that group increase, decrease, or remain the same percentage of all children between 2001 and 2002?

    decrease

14. Which ethnic or racial groups of children increased in percentage from 2001 to 2002?

    Asian and Hispanic

15. According to page C, what percentage of families with children in 2002 lived in poverty?

    between 15 and 18 percent

16. Which family arrangement has higher levels of poverty? How much higher?

    Female householder families have over twice the poverty rate of all families, over four times of married couple families

17. How do married families compare with all families with respect to poverty rate?

Married couple families with children are less than half as likely to be poor as all families with children.

18. According to page D, about what is the overall high school graduation rate?

about 85 to 90 percent

19. Which group has had the lowest graduation rate over the whole period?

Hispanic, with graduation rates ranging from 58 to 65 percent

20. During this period, what change has occurred in Black, non-Hispanic graduation rates?

They have improved from well below the overall rate to being almost the same.

Score: ______ correct × 5 points each = ______

UNIT 2 Review Test

The following selection, from an education textbook titled Understanding and Meeting the Challenge of Student Cultural Diversity, *by Eugene Garcia, discusses the diversity of students in U.S. schools. Before reading the selection, preview it, do reading warm-ups, and answer the questions that appear before the selection. After reading the selection, answer the questions that follow it.*

1. What does the title of the selection tell you about the contents?

   The selection discusses how much diversity exists among students now.

2. What are the headings of the four subsections of the selection?

   a. Immigration: The Historical Basis of Diversity

   b. Measuring Racial and Ethnic Diversity in the Population

   c. Projected Trends for U.S. Schools

   d. Indicators of Child and Family Well-Being

3. How many tables are there in the selection?

   two

4. What information do these tables provide?

   how many immigrants have come to the United States from different countries and regions in the past, how many children lived in poverty in the past and are projected to be living in poverty in the future

5. How many figures are there?

   three

6. What do Figures 1.1 and 1.2 tell you?

how many nonwhite and Hispanic students there have been and will be compared to white students

7. What information does Figure 1.3 present?

income of families headed by people under age thirty

8. What are the other clues to the content of the selection?

boxes in the margin indicating information contained in certain paragraphs

9. What kind of reading warm-up would be best to use with this selection? Why?

Student responses will vary, but they must include one of the four types: making a list, making a word map, brainstorming, or freewriting.

The Extent of Cultural Diversity Among U.S. Students Today

Immigration: The Historical Basis of Diversity

From 1981 through 1990, more than 7.3 million people immigrated to the United States, which was a 63 percent increase in immigration over the previous decade. Table 1.1 shows a detailed breakdown of immigration to the United States by country of origin. Apart from the sheer magnitude of numbers, what are the characteristics of this immigrant population? In relative terms, which are the significant countries of origin? Perhaps more importantly, what are the greatest changes in immigration patterns and emerging immigration trends?

Significant Countries of Origin Over the past two decades, Mexico has remained the country of origin for the majority of U.S. immigrants. As Table 1.1 shows, an estimated 1,655,843 Mexican citizens have emigrated here since 1981. This figure far exceeds that for any other nation of origin by over a million for the same period of time. The Philippines is ranked second with 548,764, and China (346,747), Korea (333,746), and Vietnam (280,782) follow close behind. In terms of numbers, this ranking of countries of origin has remained relatively stable since 1971, with the exception of Cuba. Immigration to the United States from Cuba declined from 264,863 in the 1970s to 144,578 in the 1980s.

Growth Rates in Immigration Comparing the past two decades, which countries of origin exhibit the greatest rate of growth in immigration to the United States? In the last ten years, more than six times as many Salvadorans have fled here from war-torn El Salvador than in the previous decade. Irish immigrants have increased 178 percent. The numbers of Iranian and Haitian immigrants have more than doubled, as have immigration figures for Eastern European countries such as Poland and Romania. The Vietnamese immigrant community in this country grew at a rate of 62 percent between 1971 and 1990. Mexico, however, shows the most significant growth trend. Immigration from Mexico has almost tripled since 1980, and this combined with the fact that Mexico ranks first in actual numbers of immigrants translates into perhaps the greatest impact on the U.S. population.

These statistics describe a U.S. immigrant population composed of vastly different peoples, which is both rapidly growing and rapidly diverging. We always have been and continue to be a nation of immigrants. As we will see, this feature of our national identity holds much significance for education.

TABLE 1.1 Immigration to the United States by Region, 1820–1990, with Special Emphasis on 1971–1980 and 1981–1990

REGION AND COUNTRY OF ORIGIN	1820–1990 (TOTAL 171 YEARS)	1971–1980	1981–1990
All Countries	**56,994,014**	**4,493,314**	**7,338,062**
Europe	**37,101,060**	**800,368**	**761,550**
Austria-Hungary	4,342,782	16,028	24,885
Austria	1,828,946	9,478	18,340
Hungary	1,667,760	6,550	6,545
Belgium	210,556	5,329	7,066
Czechoslovakia	145,801	6,023	7,227
Denmark	370,412	4,439	5,370
France	787,587	25,069	32,353
Germany	7,083,465	74,414	91,961
Greece	703,904	92,369	38,377
Ireland	4,725,133	11,490	31,969

TABLE 1.1 CONTINUED)

REGION AND COUNTRY OF ORIGIN	1820–1990 (TOTAL 171 YEARS)	1971–1980	1981–1990
Italy	5,373,108	129,368	67,254
Netherlands	374,232	10,492	12,238
Norway-Sweden	2,145,954	10,472	15,182
Norway	801,224	3,941	4,164
Sweden	1,284,475	6,531	11,018
Poland	606,336	37,234	83,252
Portugal	501,261	101,710	40,431
Romania	204,841	12,393	30,857
Soviet Union	3,443,706	38,961	57,677
Spain	285,148	39,141	20,433
Switzerland	359,439	8,235	8,849
United Kingdom	5,119,150	137,374	159,173
Yugoslavia	136,271	30,540	18,762
Other Europe	181,974	9,287	8,234
Asia	**5,019,180**	**1,588,178**	**2,738,157**
China	914,376	124,326	346,747
Hong Kong	302,230	113,467	98,215
India	455,716	164,134	250,786
Iran	176,851	45,136	116,172
Israel	137,540	37,713	44,273
Japan	462,244	49,775	47,085
Korea	642,248	267,638	333,746
Philippines	1,026,653	354,987	548,764
Turkey	412,327	13,399	23,233
Vietnam	458,277	172,820	280,782
Other Asia	1,030,718	244,783	648,354
North America	**13,067,548**	**1,982,735**	**3,615,255**
Canada and Newfoundland	4,295,585	169,939	156,938
Mexico	3,888,729	640,294	1,655,843
Caribbean	2,703,177	741,126	872,051
Cuba	748,710	264,863	144,578
Dominican Republic	510,136	148,135	252,035
Haiti	234,757	56,335	138,379
Jamaica	429,500	137,577	208,148
Other Carribean	780,074	134,216	128,911
Central America	**819,628**	**134,640**	**468,088**
El Salvador	274,667	34,436	213,539
Other Central America	544,961	100,204	254,549
South America	**1,250,303**	**295,741**	**461,847**
Argentina	131,118	29,897	27,327
Colombia	295,353	77,347	122,849
Ecuador	155,767	50,077	56,315
Other South America	668,065	138,420	255,356
Other America	110,126	995	458
Africa	**334,145**	**80,779**	**176,893**
Oceania	**204,662**	**41,242**	**45,205**
Not specified	**267,459**	**12**	**1,032**

Source: U.S. Bureau of the Census, *Historical Statistics of the United States, Colonial Times to 1970* (1975). U.S. Bureau of the Census. *Statistical Abstract of the United States, 1991* (1990). Washington, D.C.

Measuring Racial and Ethnic Diversity in the Population

In order to document the racial and ethnic heterogeneity of our country's population, the U.S. Bureau of the Census uses a set of terms that place individuals in separate exclusionary categories: white, white non-Hispanic, black, and Hispanic (the latter with some five subcategories). Unfortunately, these terms are simplistic and for the most part highly ambiguous and nonrepresentative of the true heterogeneity of the U.S. population. It is therefore important to note at the outset of this discussion that these categories are useful only as the most superficial reflection of our nation's true diversity. Given the forced-choice responses allowed them in census questionnaires, many U.S. citizens whose racial or ethnic identity crosses categories are constrained and are forced to answer inaccurately. Racially and culturally we are not "pure" stock, and any such measurement by the Census Bureau, by the Center for Educational Statistics, or by other social institutions that attempt to address the complexity of our diverse population is likely to result in only a vague sketch. [As of the 2000 census people could affiliate with more than one racial and ethnic group.]

Vulnerability for Some Populations However, once we grant the inherent restrictions on efforts to document population diversity in the United States, we must note that an examination of the available data does provide a suggestive portrait of our society. We can discern a sketchy outline of the specific circumstances of various groups within our nation's boundaries. That sketch depicts consummate social and economic vulnerability for nonwhite and Hispanic families, children, and students. On almost every indicator, nonwhite and Hispanic families, children, and students are "at-risk," meaning they are likely to fall into the lowest quartile on indicators of "well-being": family stability, family violence, family income, child health and development, and educational achievement. The census data also shows that this specific population (usually referred to as the "minority" population) has grown significantly in the last two decades and will grow substantially in the decades to come. Teachers in the U.S. schools will see increasing numbers of at-risk children in their classrooms in the years ahead.

Projected Trends for U.S. Schools

The most comprehensive report on the growing diversity of the student body in U.S. schools was published in 1991 by The College Board and the Western Interstate Commission for Higher Education. Called *The Road to College: Educational Progress by Race and Eth-*

nicity, this report indicates that the U.S. nonwhite and Hispanic student population will increase from 10.4 million in 1985–86 to 13.7 million in 1994–95. These pupils will constitute 34 percent of public elementary and secondary school enrollment in 1994–95, up from 29 percent in 1985–86. Enrollment of white students, meanwhile, will rise by only 5 percent, from 25.8 million to 27 million, and its share of the student population will drop from 71 percent to 66 percent in 1994–95.

Projections for 2026 Figures 1.1 and 1.2 graphically display this astounding shift in student demographics. Figure 1.1 presents actual nonwhite and Hispanic K–12 public school enrollments from 1976 to 1986 and projected enrollments based on changes in enrollment from 1976 to 1986 by decade through 2026. Figure 1.2 presents similar data but focuses on nonwhite and Hispanic student enrollments as a percentage of total enrollment. Each figure depicts a dramatic transformation projected for our nation's student body. Nonwhite and Hispanic student enrollments will grow from 10 million in 1976 to nearly 50 million in 2026. The percentage of those enrollments will rise from 23 percent to 70 percent of the total during this same time. Projections show that in 2026, student representation in our schools will be the exact inverse of what

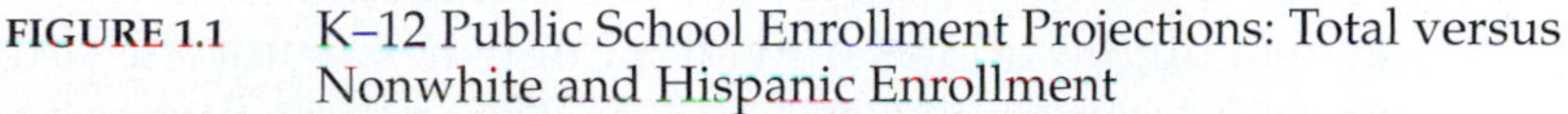

FIGURE 1.1 K–12 Public School Enrollment Projections: Total versus Nonwhite and Hispanic Enrollment

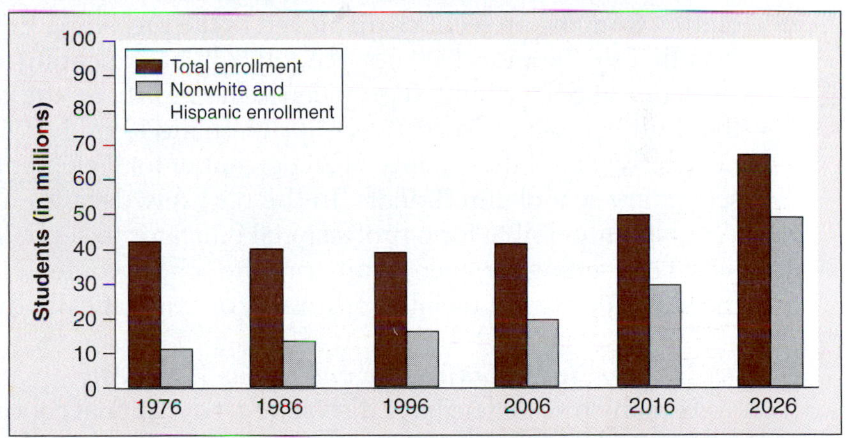

Source: U.S. Department of Education, Office for Civil Rights, Directory of Elementary and Secondary School Districts and Schools in Selected Districts: 1976–1977; and 1984–1986 Elementary and Secondary School Civil Rights Survey. As cited in U.S. Department of Education, National Center for Education Statistics, The Condition of Education, 1991, Vol. 1, p. 68, Elementary and Secondary Education. Washington, D.C.: 1991.

FIGURE 1.2 K–12 Public School Enrollment Projections: Percentage of Nonwhite and Hispanic Enrollment

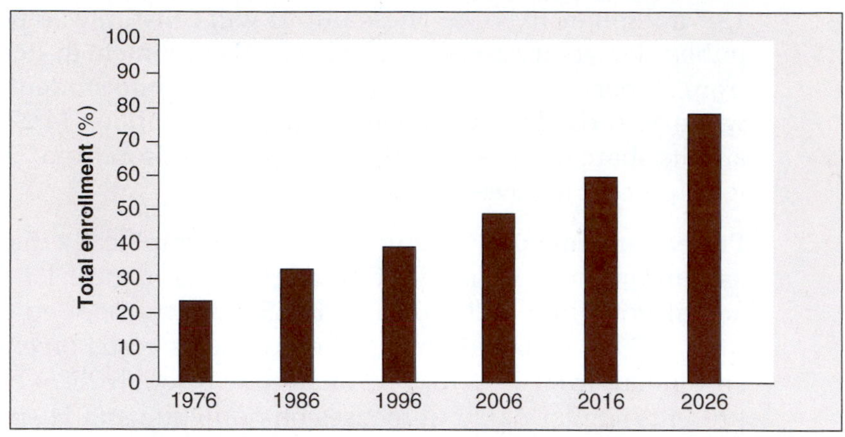

Source: U.S. Department of Education, Office for Civil Rights, Directory of Elementary and Secondary School Districts and Schools in Selected Districts: 1976–1977; and 1984–1986 Elementary and Secondary School Civil Rights Survey. As cited in U.S. Department of Education, National Center for Education Statistics, The Condition of Education, 1991, Vol. 1, p. 68, Elementary and Secondary Education. Washington, D.C.: 1991.

it was in 1990, when white students made up 70 percent of the enrolled K–12 student body.

It is of distinct educational significance that in 1986, 30 to 35 percent (3 million) of nonwhite and Hispanic students were identified as residing in homes in which English was not the primary language (August and García, 1988). Using these figures and extrapolating from the projections displayed in the preceding graphs, we find that by the year 2000 our schools will be educating 6 million students who have limited proficiency in English. By the year 2026 that number will conservatively approximate 15 million students, or somewhere in the vicinity of 25 percent of total elementary and secondary school enrollments. In the next few decades, it will be virtually impossible for a professional educator to serve in a public school setting, or even in any private school context, in which the students are not racially, culturally, or linguistically diverse.

Indicators of Child and Family Well-Being

As many researchers have discovered, educational concerns cannot be appropriately addressed without attending to related indicators of child and family well-being. Children who are healthy and who live in safe and secure social and economic environments generally do very well in today's schools. Poor students, on the other hand, are three times more likely to become dropouts than are students from the more economically advantaged homes (Children in Need, 1990). Students who reside in economically disadvantaged and socially dangerous environments are at risk for academic underachievement in today's and tomorrow's schools. Our earlier discussion of expected demographic shifts and projected trends in student enrollments is sharpened by a consideration of some economic and social realities. As noted above, family income is correlated with academic performance. Family dislocations, uncertainty, and stress associated with poverty often undermine a child's ability to concentrate and to learn. Culturally and linguistically diverse students tend to live in situations that are not always compatible with a stable educational experience. Unfortunately, on a number of related measures of child and family well-being, the circumstances are bleak for this growing body of students.

Children Living in Poverty According to the National Center for the Study of Children in Poverty in its 1990 report, *Five Million Children*, 14 million U.S. children and youth under the age of 18 resided in circumstances of poverty in 1986. This represents approximately 20 percent of the total population in this age group and was an increase of some 2 million since 1975. Of the children counted, 6.5 million, or 45 percent, were nonwhite and Hispanic. Table 1.2 presents exact numbers and percentages of children and youth in poverty for 1975 and 1986 and related projections through 2026. Projections in this table indicate that

TABLE 1.2 Children and Youth 18 Years Old and Younger in Poverty, Projected to 2026

RACE OR ETHNICITY	1975	1986	1996	2006	2016	2026
Total students in millions	**12.3**	**14.2**	**16.4**	**19.4**	**23.1**	**27.9**
White, non-Hispanic	6.7	7.8	8.8	10.1	11.6	13.2
Total Minority	**5.6**	**6.4**	**7.6**	**9.3**	**11.5**	**14.7**
Black	3.8	4.0	4.2	4.4	4.5	4.7
Hispanic	1.7	2.4	3.4	4.9	7.0	10.0
Total percent of poor children	**100.0**	**100.0**	**100.0**	**100.0**	**100.0**	100.0
White, non-Hispanic	54.8	54.4	53.6	52.1	50.0	47.2
Total Minority	**45.2**	**45.6**	**46.4**	**47.9**	**50.0**	**52.8**
Black	31.5	28.5	25.5	22.5	19.7	16.9
Hispanic	13.7	17.1	20.9	25.4	30.3	35.9

Source: U.S. Department of Commerce, Bureau of the Census, Current Population Reports, series P-60, "Poverty in the United States...," various years. As cited in the U.S. Department of Education, National Center for Educational Statistics, *The Condition of Education, 1991*, Vol. 1, pp. 200–201, Elementary and Secondary Education. Washington, D.C.: 1991.

unless poverty is checked in very direct ways, the number of children and youth in poverty will more than double by the year 2026. More than half of these children and youth living in poverty will be nonwhite and Hispanic.

Economically Vulnerable Families The overall family circumstances expected for these children over the next decades are also alarming. Most children of elementary school age presently reside in families headed by persons under the age of 30. Figure 1.3 provides evidence that these families will be economically disadvantaged. The figure shows median income from 1973 to 1986 and projected income through 2026 for families headed by persons under the age of 30. All families in this category have experienced and are projected to experience a decrease in economic capability. Again, particularly vulnerable will be families headed by persons who are nonwhite and Hispanic. By 2026 the median family income for nonwhite and Hispanic families will drop to $10,000 per year.

What are the implications for education? Children in families with income below the poverty level are nearly twice as likely to be held back a grade level as their more advantaged classmates. Young people from low-income families also tend to leave school early and enter the labor force to earn additional income for themselves or their families. While work experience during adolescence can have

FIGURE 1.3 Median Annual Income for Families Headed by Persons Under Age 30 (in 1986 Dollars), Projected to 2026

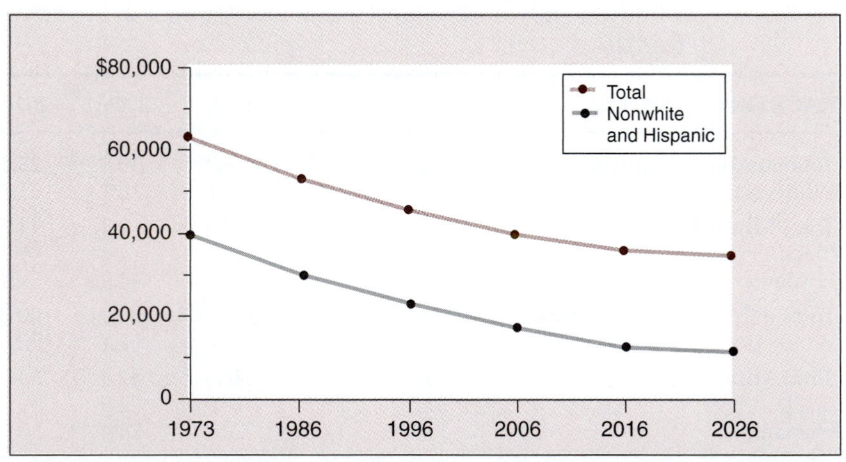

Source: Johnson, C. M.; Sum, A. M.; and Wiell, J. D. (1988), Appendix: Table 3. As cited in Five Million Children: A Statistical Profile of Our Poorest Young Citizens, National Center for Children in Poverty, School of Public Health, p. 47. New York: Columbia University, 1990.

positive effects, recent research indicates that working more than half-time during the high school years can undermine academic performance (Beyond Rhetoric, 1991). As for those students from home environments in which English is not the primary language, over 90 percent in 1984 met poverty guidelines that allowed them to receive free or reduced-price lunches (Development Associates, 1984).

Much more eloquent than any quantitative analysis of this situation are the more intense case studies that dramatically tell the disheartening educational stories of these underserved populations (Kozol, 1991; Rose, 1989; Wong-Filmore, 1991). Numerous expository in-depth studies have found that serious disruptions of individual, family, and community functioning occur when young children from nonmainstream backgrounds encounter the schooling process. There is much evidence, both in hard figures and in personal testimony, that members of culturally and linguistically diverse populations in the United States face problems socially, economically, and educationally.

10. According to Table 1.1, which region overall was the origin of most immigrants to the United States? How many immigrants came from there?

    Europe, which from 1820 to 1990 provided 37,101,060 immigrants

11. Between 1981 and 1990 which region provided the most immigrants? How many?

    North America; 3,615,255 immigrants

12. Which country provided most immigrants from 1820 to 1990? How many?

    Germany; 7,083,465 immigrants

13. Which country provided most immigrants from 1981 to 1990? How many?

    Mexico; 1,655,843 immigrants

14. Which single Asian country provided the most immigrants overall and in the decade 1981–1990? How many overall? From 1981 to 1990?

    The Philippines both overall (1,026,653) and in the decade 1981–1990 (548,764)

15. In Figure 1.1, what do the dark and light bars represent?

The dark bars represent the total number of students (in millions) in the public schools in the United States. The light bars represent the number of nonwhite and Hispanic students.

16. In Figure 1.2, what do the bars represent?

the percentage of nonwhite and Hispanic students in the public schools

17. How are Figures 1.1 and 1.2 related?

The bars in Figure 1.2 show the relation between the two kinds of bars in Figure 1.1.

18. In 1976, were there more white students or more nonwhite and Hispanic students in the public schools?

more white students (in about a 3:1 ratio)

19. In about what year are nonwhite and Hispanic students projected to be about equal in number to white students?

2006

20. In 2026, are there projected to be more white or nonwhite and Hispanic students?

more nonwhite and Hispanic students (by a ratio of about 4:1)

21. According to Table 1.2, will (or has) the number of poor students ever decrease(d)?

No, the number of children in poverty has increased since 1975 and will continue to do so into the future, from 12.3 million in 1975 to 27.9 million in 2026.

22. In 1975, which group—non-Hispanic, white, black, or Hispanic—provided the greatest percentage of children in poverty? What percentage?

white; 54.8 percent

23. In 2026, which group is projected to provide the greatest percentage of children in poverty?

    white; 47.2 percent

24. Which group is projected to provide the smallest percentage of poor children in 2006, 2016, and 2026?

    black, in all three years—decreasing from 22.5 percent in 2006 to 16.9 percent in 2026

25. Which group is projected to have the greatest numerical and percentage increase of poor children from 1975 to 2026?

    Hispanic—from 1.7 million children (13.7 percent) in 1975 to 10 million children (35.9 percent) in 2026

26. According to Figure 1.3, is the income for families headed by people under age thirty going to increase or decrease? Is there any difference between the projections for whites or nonwhites and Hispanics? If so, in what way?

    The income will decrease for both categories by about the same amount, but because the nonwhite and Hispanic families started with lower incomes than did the white families, their resulting incomes will become even lower.

27. In this selection, how are the tables and figures related to what is stated in the text?

    In the text, the statistics presented in the tables and graphs are discussed in detail, used as proof for claims, and analyzed.

UNIT THREE

Understanding Main Ideas

CHAPTER 8

Reading for the Main Idea

CHAPTER 9

Main Ideas in Long Selections

CHAPTER EIGHT

Reading for the Main Idea

A piece of writing often presents many ideas, but these ideas usually relate to one important idea. To understand how these ideas fit together, you need to spot the main idea, which gives you an overall meaning to the reading.

Ideas come in different sizes. Some are sentence-length ideas, which build a larger paragraph-length idea. A number of paragraph-length ideas build an essay, an article, or a chapter in a book.

Here we start by finding the key ideas in sentences. Then we see how sentences add up to the larger ideas in paragraphs.

8a Finding Key Ideas in Sentences

Each sentence, no matter how long it is, usually contains one key idea. The rest of the sentence simply gives more information about that key idea. The key idea is usually about one of the following:

- What a person or object is
- What a person or object does

For example, look at this sentence:

> A computer sends me bills.

Now look at this sentence:

> Every month a broken computer at the telephone company sends me outrageous bills for telephone calls I never made.

The key idea of both sentences is the same: *A computer is sending bills to someone.* The second adds details to let you know more about the computer and its bills. The key idea is important because it helps you understand the importance of all the other details. Why do you care whether or not the telephone calls were made? Because someone is being billed for them. Why is the computer "broken"? Because it sends incorrect bills. Why are the bills outrageous? Because they are being sent for calls that were never made. What happens every month? An outrageous bill is sent.

To find key ideas in sentences, do the following:

- Ask *who* or *what* the sentence is about.
- Ask *what* the person or object is doing or *what* is happening to the person or object.
- Separate the minor details that simply add information to the key idea. These details often tell *when, where, why, what kind*, and *how*. By taking away the minor details, you can see the main idea more clearly.

Look at how this method works in the following sentence:

> The old discount supermarket at the Faded Gold Shopping Center has been clean from top to bottom for a week because the Health Department threatened to close the store.

First, let's take away the minor details:

When: for a week

Where: at the Faded Gold Shopping Center

Why: because the Health Department threatened to close the store

What kind: old discount

How: from top to bottom

With those details crossed out, what is the sentence about? *The supermarket*. What happened to the supermarket? *It is clean*.

The key idea is *The supermarket is clean*. The rest of the sentence simply gives more details about this idea.

EXERCISES

8.1 Key Ideas in Sentences

In each of the following sentences, underline the words that give the key idea. Here is an example.

In today's world, <u>reading is necessary</u> for all kinds of daily jobs.

1. Even though she works forty hours per week as a cook at a restaurant, Betty Yi has to work a second job on weekends to make enough money to pay all of her bills.

2. Although thirty-two students signed up for the study-skills workshops, because a trip to an amusement park was scheduled for the same day, only eight students attended.

3. During the ten years that Rhonda has lived in this neighborhood, all of her neighbors have painted their houses and landscaped their yards.

4. After winning ten out of ten home games and eight out of ten away games during the regular season, the women's basket ball team lost the league championship game by only one point.

5. Playing computer games like Doom, Tetris, Sims, and Super Mario Brothers helps children develop important intellectual and motor skills.

8.2 Key Ideas in Newspaper Sentences

Write the key idea of each sentence in the space provided after that sentence.

1. The Irish rock band U2 called in the police after a copy of songs from their new CD disappeared while they were posing for the cover photo.

   U2 called the police.

2. Robert Barrows of Burlingame, California, has filed a patent application for a video-equipped tombstone that will display a video message from the grave's occupant.

   Barrows patented a video tombstone.

3. A few practice laps Tuesday allowed Wilson and fellow clergy members to rev up for Faster Pastor 2004, a stock-car race that pulls preachers from the pulpit to the pole at Oglethorpe Speedway Park near Savannah, Georgia.

   Clergy members compete in a stock-car race.

4. A bar of chocolate dating back 100 years and belonging to pioneering Antarctica explorers has been auctioned for £470 ($686).

   A chocolate bar was auctioned.

5. It took him two tries, but South African Philip Rabinowitz made it into the *Guinness Book of World Records* Saturday as the fastest 100-year-old to run 100 meters.

   Rabinowitz set a record.

6. The discovery of coffee plants with naturally low caffeine and high sales potential has sparked an international tug of war over their ownership, according to legal and agricultural experts.

   Coffee plants set off a struggle for ownership.

7. The huge dinosaur, which weighed an estimated 40 to 50 tons, the same as six or seven elephants, probably roamed the Spanish region up to 130 million years ago when it was a tropical "dinosaur paradise," criss-crossed with rivers and streams.

   The dinosaur roamed Spain.

8. Atmospheric experts studying clouds have observed monster-sized raindrops, the biggest recorded on Earth, up to 1 cm in size, which is bigger than a ladybug.

   Experts observed large raindrops.

8.3 Key Ideas in Textbook Sentences

Write the key idea of each of the following sentences from the textbook *Contemporary Business Communication*, by Scot Ober, in your own words on the blank lines.

1. Your message should convey the confident attitude that you have done a competent job of communicating and that the reader will do as you ask or will accept your decision.

   Your message should convey confidence.

2. Your job in writing a persuasive message is to talk your readers into something, to convince them that your point of view is right.

   Persuasive messages need to convince readers.

3. A cliché, or overused expression, lacks freshness and originality and may also send the unintended message that the writer couldn't be bothered to find language specifically geared to the reader.

   A cliché may send a message of lack of concern.

4. Words that create a positive image are more likely to help you achieve your objective than negative words; for example, you are more likely to persuade someone to do as you ask if you stress the advantages of doing so rather than the disadvantages of *not* doing so.

   Positive words are more effective than negative words.

5. It is difficult to work effectively as a group if group members do not know each other well and are not aware of each other's strengths and weaknesses, styles of working, past experiences, attitudes, and the like; thus, the first task of most new groups is to get to know one another.

   Members of groups must first get to know one another.

8b Stating Paragraph Topics

Several sentences grouped together form a paragraph. Each paragraph has a *topic*, a general point the paragraph explains. You should be able to state simply, in just a few words, the topic of a paragraph. The statement should be neither too general nor too specific. Rather, the statement should identify the chief idea that the whole paragraph develops.

Read this paragraph from an environmental science textbook. What is the topic?

Some of the best-known ideas about population growth in the past two centuries were proposed by British economist Thomas Malthus. Writing in 1798, Malthus argued that population growth was not always desirable. Malthus pointed out that populations tend to increase geometrically (1, 2, 4, 8, 16. . .) whereas the food supply tends to increase arithmetically (1, 2, 3, 4, 5. . .). The human population, therefore, has the potential to increase at a much faster rate than the food supply. Malthus believed that the tendency of the human population to outgrow its resources would lead to such conditions as famine, war, and other human suffering. To avoid

> such outcomes, Malthus advocated practices that would reduce the population growth rate, including late marriages and small families. These ideas have been widely discussed and debated ever since.
>
> —*Andrew Lapinksi, Robert Schoch, and Anne Tweed*

Did you state the topic of the paragraph as *Malthus' ideas about population growth*? The overall topic is what Malthus thought about population growth. All the sentences contribute to that topic.

You might be tempted to say that the topic of the paragraph is *Malthus* or *population*. Certainly the paragraph tells us something about each, but each is too general. We don't find out everything about Thomas Malthus, just his thinking on population growth. Similarly, the comments on population growth are only concerning Malthus' ideas on the topic. Neither would you say the topic was *food supply* or *famine*, even though those terms appear in the paragraph. They don't cover everything in the paragraph. Only the topic *Malthus' ideas about population growth* covers all there is in the paragraph without becoming so broad as to not give a clear idea of what the paragraph is about.

Look at the following paragraph from a sociology textbook. What is the topic?

> Sociologists reserve the term *small group* to refer to a group small enough for all members to interact simultaneously, that is, to talk with each other or at least be acquainted with each other. Small groups such as work groups and families are the intermediate link between the individual and the larger society. This intermediate position defines their importance in terms of attitudes, values, and behaviors. For this reason, sociologists are interested in what happens when people get together in small groups, whether it is to share gossip, reach a decision, or even play card games.
>
> *Richard T. Schaefer*

The topic here is *small groups*. The sentences in the paragraph build that topic. You wouldn't say that the topic is *the individual and society*, even though these words appear in the paragraph, because they are too general. You also wouldn't say that the topic is *sharing gossip* or *playing card games*. Those words also appear in the paragraph, but they make too narrow a point to be the topic of the paragraph.

Critical Thinking and Writing

Which small group do you belong to and value? Select a small group of which you are a member and write a few paragraphs about your group's attitudes, values, and behavior.

Read this paragraph from a book called *This Fascinating Animal World*. What is the topic of the paragraph?

To what use does a kangaroo put its great heavy tail? It leans back and props itself on it, as a man does on a shooting stick. Many lizards use their tails that way too. The original monster lizards, almost certainly, swung their tails as weapons, in a carry-over from the tail-swinging technique of fish. And today? Is it true that a crocodile uses its tail as a weapon? Yes. It can knock a man over with one wallop. Do any warm-blooded animals do the same sort of thing? Yes again. Take an ant bear. It thwacks with its tail as powerfully as a bear with its forepaw.

Alan Devoe

The topic here is *the ways some animals use their tails*. The paragraph tells us how kangaroos, lizards, crocodiles, and bears use their tails. The topic is not *animals* because that topic is too general. Yes, the paragraph deals with animals — but with only one feature of only some animals. That feature, of course, is the animals' tails and how they are used. You also couldn't say that the topic is *crocodiles' tails as weapons*. Although the paragraph mentions this idea, it is too narrow a point to be the topic of the paragraph.

Stating Paragraph Topics

- Read the sentences carefully. Ask yourself these questions: What is the paragraph about? What general point is the paragraph trying to make?
- Avoid using terms that are too general.
- Avoid terms that are too specific, or narrow.
- State the topic in a few words. Draw on the key ideas in the paragraph to state the topic in your own words.

EXERCISES

8.5 Paragraph Topics

Read each paragraph and try to determine its topic. Then look at the three choices for stating the topic. Put a *T* next to the choice that best states the topic. Put a *G* next to the choice that is too general. Put an *S* next to the choice that is too specific.

1. Children are a growing consumer market in their own right. But they are far more important to businesses as an influence on their parents' purchases. School-age children make incessant demands for toys and food. Toddlers quickly learn that they can affect their parents' behavior in stores. Even the smallest infant can cause a frazzled parent to abandon a shopping trip by throwing a tantrum in the middle of a supermarket.

—Paco Underhill

G a. Children

S b. Children's demands for toys

T c. Children's influences on parents' purchases

2. Drive-in theaters aren't the only dying corner of Americana. Instant coffee is also going by the wayside. Invented in 1906, instant coffee had the same allure that later extended to other quick-fix beverages and foods like orange-flavored drink crystals and instant puddings. It was inexpensive and fast, and it always tasted the same. But today, a new generation of coffee hounds is pushing instant coffee off the shelf. Their favorites are more expensive and less convenient, but they taste better.

—Marsha Mogelonsky

T a. People's changing coffee tastes

S b. Why people liked instant coffee

G c. Coffee

3. Coca-Cola was invented in 1886 by John Pemberton, a fifty-year-old chemist from Atlanta, Georgia. He decided to develop a syrup that would be original and thirst-quenching. Working relentlessly in the back room of his "drug store," he produced a mixture containing cola nut extract, sugar, a little caffeine, cocoa leaves with the cocaine removed, and vegetable extracts. (The syrup's exact

composition is still a closely guarded secret.) A few months later, an assistant mistakenly served a customer Coca-Cola mixed with soda water: that proved to be the little touch that made the drink a success.

To market his new drink, Pemberton formed a partnership with Frank Robertson, whose elegant handwriting was used for the Coca-Cola trademark.

In May 1985 "New" Coke was introduced and the old formula was retired. Coca-Cola drinkers were outraged and the original recipe was revived.

—*Valerie-Anne Giscard d'Estaing*

G a. Coca-Cola's history

S b. Coca-Cola's ingredients

T c. Coca-Cola's invention

8.6 Paragraph Topics

On the first blank line following each paragraph, write the topic of the paragraph in your own words. Leave blank the lines after the words *Main idea*. You'll return to use the remaining blank lines for Exercise 8.12 on page 167.

1. On the west side of Manhattan, where I live, inline skaters, or "Rollerbladers," are everywhere: on the streets, in the parks, on the sidewalks, and in the stores. Walking in my neighborhood on the weekends is like negotiating a Roller Derby. I'm sure this experience isn't unique to New York. But I'm fed up with too many adults on skates behaving like spoiled children.

   —*Joan Schmidt*

   Topic: Rollerbladers

   Main idea: Rollerbladers are everywhere in my neighborhood

2. For most kids, learning to read is just a question of practice. But an estimated 20 percent of Americans have persistent trouble converting letters on a page into sounds. Recently a brain-imaging study pinpointed where that seemingly magical conversion takes place. That was an important result: a first step toward untangling the neurological basis of why so many perfectly smart people have trouble learning to read.

   —*Sarah Richardson*

Topic: learning to read

Main idea: A study has pinpointed why so many people have trouble learning to read.

3. Being in a large earthquake is a terrifying experience. Earthquakes happen when the pressure between two tectonic plates is so intense that the plates shift their positions suddenly, causing the earth to shake. When the shaking starts, there is no way of knowing how long it will go on or how severe it will be. The longest tremor ever recorded, the Alaskan earthquake of March 27, 1964, lasted four minutes, but most quakes last less than a minute. In those brief moments, homes, stores, even entire cities are destroyed. The ground may appear to move like waves, and great cracks may open in the ground. Sometimes, despite powerful shaking, the rocks at the surface may not show any signs of the earthquake. For months after a quake people may feel unsettling aftershocks—small tremors that follow a major earthquake.

—Susan van Rose

Topic: the experience of an earthquake

Main idea: A large earthquake is a terrifying experience.

4. The booming cities of the late nineteenth century had their share of problems: crime, fires, garbage, disease. But cities also had their share of pleasures. City-dwellers were less isolated than people living in the country. City people were able to get together to share ideas, entertainment, and common creative interests. Because the large populations were necessary to support libraries, theaters, museums, and art galleries, these cultural institutions first developed as part of the trend toward urbanization.

—Beverly Armento et al.

Topic: late-nineteenth-century cities

Main idea: Although late-nineteenth-century cities had problems, they also had pleasures.

Critical Thinking and Writing

What problems and pleasures face city-dwellers today? Write a few paragraphs on your view of the city. Address the strengths and weaknesses of living in the city.

5. Crying is the most powerful way — and sometimes the only way — that babies can signal to the outside world when they need something. It is, therefore, a vital means of communication and a way for infants to establish some kind of control over their lives. Those babies whose cries of distress do bring relief apparently gain a measure of self-confidence in the knowledge that they can affect their own lives. This can be inferred from the findings that by the end of the first year, babies whose mothers respond promptly to their crying with tender, soothing care cry less. The more the mother ignores, scolds, hits, commands, and restricts the baby, the more the baby cries, frets, and acts aggressively.

   —Diane E. Papalia and Sally Wendlos Olds

   Topic: babies' crying

   Main idea: Babies' crying sends messages to other people.

6. A twenty-three-year-old Swiss, François-Louis Cailler, made the first bars of chocolate at Vevey in 1819. Small scale production of chocolate had begun in France and Italy after the Spaniards returned from South America with the recipe. At that time it was a drink prepared from roasted, crushed cocoa beans. In 1879 another Swiss, Rodolphe Lindt, built a chocolate factory in Berne. In those days blocks of chocolate were hard and had to be crunched; they also left a gritty sensation in the mouth along with a bitter aftertaste. Even when heated up, the chocolate remained thick and heavy. Because of this Lindt invented a machine that kneaded the chocolate for a long time; he then had the idea of adding cocoa butter to it. The chocolate we know today was born, and Lindt patented his invention in 1880.

   —Valerie-Anne Giscard d'Estaing

   Topic: the invention of chocolate

   Main idea: Modern chocolate was invented in two steps: first the bar; then the addition of cocoa butter.

7. The public's right to know what government does is an important element of freedom of the press. Therefore, in 1966 Congress passed the Freedom of Information Act. This act, as amended in 1974, requires the government to allow journalists and other interested persons to inspect federal records, such as budgets, records of expenses, maps, and photographs. Certain "classified" documents are not made available.

   —Richard Hardy

Topic: the Freedom of Information Act

Main idea: The Freedom of Information Act gives the press access to government records.

8. Furthermore, the federal government and many of the states have adopted sunshine laws. Sunshine laws require government agencies to open their meetings to the press and public. The Sunshine Act of 1976, for example, made public the operations of approximately fifty federal agencies, boards, and commissions. Under the law, an agency must notify the public of its meetings at least one week in advance. While some meetings may be conducted behind closed doors, the public is entitled to view the written reports of such meetings.

—Richard Hardy

Topic: sunshine laws

Main idea: Sunshine laws open government meetings to the press and public.

9. The Civil Rights Act of 1964 was one of the most far-reaching laws ever passed by Congress. Among its most important provisions, it (1) prohibited discrimination in public places such as theaters, restaurants, and hotels; (2) insisted on identical voting requirements for blacks and whites in all states; and (3) prohibited discrimination on the basis of race or sex by all employers, unions, and employment agencies engaged in interstate commerce. The new law also offered financial aid to school districts that needed help in beginning desegregation programs and required that federal funds be denied to districts practicing segregation.

—Henry F. Graff

Topic: the Civil Rights Act of 1964

Main idea: The Civil Rights Act of 1964 fought discrimination and segregation in several important ways.

10. The fish that thrive off the Antarctic coast in frigid 28° water survive the same way a car does in a North Dakota winter: with antifreeze. But a little fish antifreeze could keep your motor purring for a long time. It's 300 times as effective per molecule as the ethylene glycol in a car radiator. In the Antarctic there are almost a hundred species of fish called notothenioids, ranging from six-inch zooplankton

feeders to six-foot toothfish. They swim at all depths, from the 3,200-foot-deep bottom to the surface. Notothenioids produce their antifreeze, a glycoprotein, in the liver. They secrete it into the bloodstream, where it fills spaces around cells, says Arthur DeVries of the University of Illinois, who studies fish "freezing avoidance." Although seawater with ice crystals gets into the fish's blood, the antifreeze stops the ice from growing, and eventually it is filtered out.

—*Boris Weintraub*

Topic: antifreeze in fish

Main idea: The antifreeze in the notothenioids is extremely effective.

8c Finding Main Ideas in Paragraphs

Once you know the general topic **(8b),** you should be able to state the *main idea* of a paragraph. The main idea holds the paragraph together. Each sentence relates to the main idea and helps build the paragraph's meaning. The main idea of a paragraph is more than the general topic. To find the main idea, you start with the topic, of course, but you must figure out what the paragraph is saying about the topic.

Sometimes the main idea of a paragraph is written down directly, often at the beginning of the paragraph. So, to find the main idea, you need only find the one or two sentences that sum up the paragraph.

Some paragraphs do not state the main idea in a few direct words. Then you must put together the different parts of the idea to see what they add up to. The idea they add up to is the main idea of the paragraph.

Look again at the following paragraph, which you examined in **8b:**

Some of the best-known ideas about population growth in the past two centuries were proposed by British economist Thomas Malthus. Writing in 1798, Malthus argued that population growth was not always desirable. Malthus pointed out that populations tend to increase geometrically (1, 2, 4, 8, 16. . .) whereas the food supply tends to increase arithmetically (1, 2, 3, 4, 5. . .). The human population, therefore, has the potential to increase at a much faster rate than the food supply.

> Malthus believed that the tendency of the human population to outgrow its resources would lead to such conditions as famine, war, and other human suffering. To avoid such outcomes, Malthus advocated practices that would reduce the population growth rate, including late marriages and small families. These ideas have been widely discussed and debated ever since.

You know the overall topic is *Malthus' ideas about population growth*. But the paragraph does more than name the topic. The paragraph tells you what Malthus' ideas were. To find the main idea, ask yourself what the paragraph is saying about the topic. What does this paragraph say about Malthus' ideas on population growth? The second sentence of the paragraph tells you that *Malthus argued that population growth was not always desirable*. The second sentence gives you the main idea of the paragraph. The rest of the sentences support this main idea, explaining why Malthus thought population growth was not always desirable.

As with the topic, you should make sure your statement of the main idea is neither too specific nor too general. As you read the following paragraph from a communications textbook, think about how you might state its main idea in a way that is neither too broad nor too limited.

> When we communicate, we exchange messages and create meanings. *Meaning* is the significance we attach to messages or our translations of messages. As pointed out earlier, no two people attach the same meaning to symbols. Communication, therefore, is effective to the extent that we can maximize the overlap in the meanings communicators attach to messages. Stated differently, effective communication involves minimizing misunderstandings.
>
> *William Gudykumst et al.*

The whole paragraph is about communication, trying to define and describe it more precisely. So communication is the topic. But what does the paragraph say about communication? What does the paragraph add up to? The opening sentence does say *communication involves exchanging messages and creating meanings*, but that is too general to be the main idea because the paragraph goes on to examine effective communication. The paragraph also says about communication that *people get different meanings from messages*. This, however, is too specific, because the idea forms only a small part of the paragraph. The idea of the whole paragraph is *effective communication maximizes overlap in meanings*. Such a statement of the main idea is neither too general nor too specific. Rather, it gives an accurate picture of what the whole paragraph means.

The paragraph, in fact, makes it easy to locate the main idea by summing it up and restating it in the concluding sentence: *Effective communication involves minimizing misunderstandings*. The opening phrase of the sentence, *stated differently*, signals that the sentence will be summing up the meaning of the paragraph. Paragraphs frequently state their main ideas in single, easy-to-identify sentences, as in the two examples we have just reviewed.

8c(1) *Stated Main Ideas*

If one sentence states the main idea of a paragraph, we usually call that sentence a *topic sentence*. The topic sentence can appear almost anywhere in a paragraph — at the beginning, the middle, or the end. Most often, though, it appears at the beginning, as one of the first few sentences.

Look at the following paragraphs; in each, the topic sentence is italicized.

Main Idea at the Beginning

Preferences about what tastes good vary markedly, and many examples exist of foods that are acceptable in one culture and not in another. In China, most people think that cheese is disgusting, but in France, most people love cheese. One distinction exists between eating animals that are alive and animals that are dead. In a few cultures, consumption of live, or nearly live, creatures is considered a gourmet specialty; for example, a Philippine dish includes ready-to-be-born chicks. In many cultures where hunting and fishing are dominant ways of procuring food, people believe that the freshness of the catch is important. They consider canned meat or fish highly undesirable.

— *Barbara D. Miller*

The general topic of this paragraph is food preference. Use that topic to figure out the main idea. The main idea of the paragraph is Food preferences vary from culture to culture. All the remaining sentences in the paragraph give examples of differing food preferences in different cultures.

Main Idea in the Middle

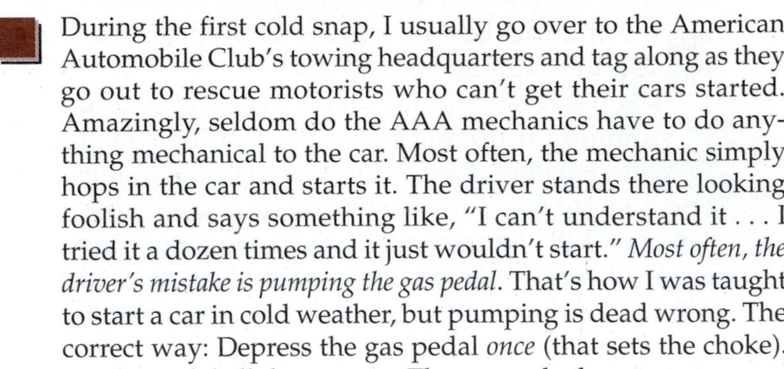

During the first cold snap, I usually go over to the American Automobile Club's towing headquarters and tag along as they go out to rescue motorists who can't get their cars started. Amazingly, seldom do the AAA mechanics have to do anything mechanical to the car. Most often, the mechanic simply hops in the car and starts it. The driver stands there looking foolish and says something like, "I can't understand it . . . I tried it a dozen times and it just wouldn't start." *Most often, the driver's mistake is pumping the gas pedal.* That's how I was taught to start a car in cold weather, but pumping is dead wrong. The correct way: Depress the gas pedal *once* (that sets the choke). Let the pedal all the way up. Then turn the key.

John Stossel

The topic of this paragraph is *problems in getting a car started in the cold*. The main idea of the paragraph is *Most often, the driver's mistake is pumping the gas pedal*. The earlier part of the paragraph lets you know about the problem this mistake causes. The latter part of the paragraph lets you know how to avoid the problem.

Main Idea at the End

We huddled together in the cool spring night, whispering in hoarse voices, thrumming with the excitement that vibrated through the crowd gathering in the parking lot outside the Ames train station. All the way home from Des Moines we had hugged each other, laughed, cried, and hugged each other again. When we passed through the small farming towns between Des Moines and Ames, we rolled down the windows of the Harbingers' station wagon and shouted down the quiet streets, "We beat Marshalltown in seven overtimes! We beat Marshalltown in seven overtimes!" It had a rhythmic beat, a chant we repeated to each other in unbelieving ecstasy. We beat Marshalltown in seven overtimes! *For the first time in ten years, Ames High School had won the state basketball championship.*

Susan Allen Toth

The topic of this paragraph is *winning a basketball game*. The main idea of this paragraph is *For the first time in ten years, Ames High School had won the state basketball championship*. All the sentences before this part of the paragraph were leading up to the main idea by explaining the excited reaction of Ames students to the basketball victory.

Main Idea in More Than One Sentence

A copyright is also a kind of protection. In this case, the protection is for authors or creators of books, plays, software, movies, and musical compositions, as well as for photographers, painters, and sculptors. This protection extends for the lifetime of the person or persons who produce the item, plus fifty years. Copyright is also a kind of right to property and a protection against persons copying what others have already made. Publishers, music recording studios, and movie studios are all examples of businesses that may be involved with copyrights.

Betty J. Brown and John E. Clow

Here, the topic is *copyrights*. The main idea is essentially the second sentence of the paragraph. But did you notice that the second sentence does not even state the word *copyright*? You have to return to the first sentence for that word. Thus, even though the second sentence states the main idea very closely, you should draw on information in the first sentence to state the main idea: *A copyright is protection for authors or creators of books, plays, software, movies, and musical compositions, as well as for photographers, painters, and sculptors.*

Finding Stated Main Ideas in Paragraphs

- Decide on the overall topic of the paragraph (see **8b**).
- Ask yourself: What is the paragraph saying about the topic?
- Make sure your main idea is neither too general nor too specific for the overall meaning of the paragraph.
- Find the sentence(s) that states what the paragraph is saying about the topic.
- Stated main ideas always appear as sentences, not as questions. Sometimes a paragraph introduces a topic by asking a question. The *answer* to that question is usually the main idea.
- Sometimes the main idea sentence uses a word such as *it* or *he* or *she*; sometimes the sentence can be made clear only by referring to another sentence in the paragraph. Feel free to use the words from other sentences when you state the main idea, even when you identify one sentence as the main idea sentence.

EXERCISES

8.7 Stated Main Ideas

For each paragraph, first write the topic in your own words in the appropriate blank. Then underline the sentence or part of the sentence that tells the main idea of the paragraph. Finally, write the main idea in your own words in the appropriate blank.

1. Recent scientific studies have demonstrated that the wolf is not particularly ferocious. Basically he is friendly and more sensitive than the dog, with a complicated and subtle social organization. Wolves do not customarily hunt in large packs. Their howling is not a hunting cry, and does not frighten other animals. Like all animals they get their food the easiest way they can, and with the least risk. Thus much of their prey is mice, squirrels, and rabbits; but also, unfortunately from man's point of view, lambs and calves. It is chiefly in winter that wolves form packs to hunt larger game. The pack is of moderate size — very often merely a family group consisting of an old couple and their mature offspring.

   —Tom Burnham

   Topic: the ferocity of the wolf

   Main idea: Wolves are not as fierce as we think.

2. Why don't buildings collapse? How can they stand with all the weight pushing down on them? The reason is the buildings push up as much as other things push down. If your feet push down on the floor, the floor pushes up on your feet. A force cannot get lost, but it must be balanced by an opposite and equal force. If the forces are not balanced, something will be pushed one way or another. And then the building may collapse.

   Topic: why buildings stand

   Main idea: Buildings stand because upward and downward forces are balanced.

3. Aristotle believed that the center for thought lies in the heart and that the brain helps cool the body. Drowsy people hang their heads, he said, because brain-created heaviness forces the head downward. We laugh now, but many experts agreed with Aristotle as recently

as the late nineteenth century. Indeed, we still know relatively little about the three pounds of flesh that makes us human.

—*Joel Swerdlow*

Topic: the purpose of the brain

Main idea: We know relatively little about the brain.

4. One thing about contemporary society is that we've lost control of the information flow our children get. In the past, parents could monitor the movies kids saw, the magazines and newspapers that came into the house. Now with TV, children get information they never would have had before. So we have to do more both to prepare them and to help them deal with what they've seen, like a body being dragged through the streets of Mogadishu on the TV, or a homeless person on the street where they walk. We should give children a healthy respect for the world out there, but focus on the good things as well as the negative ones. It's not a jungle out there; there's not someone dangerous lurking around every corner. There are lots of decent people who will help them.

—*David Elkind*

Topic: children's access to information

Main idea: We have lost control of the information children get.

5. When I was nineteen I carried a machine gun in Vietnam and lived in a village outside Da Nang. I was part of a squad of ten Marines and fifteen local villagers called a Combined Action Platoon. One night in March of 1969 we were overrun by Viet Cong. Most of my platoon was killed or wounded. A villager named Hien saved my life. I remember he had a gold front tooth, and for almost twenty-five years I've thought about Hien and some day returning to my village, returning to the origin of my pain.

—*Jack Estes*

Topic: saving the author's life

Main idea: A villager named Hien saved the author's life.

6. One approach to reading is similar to the way in which a sponge reacts to water: ABSORB IT! This commonly used approach has some clear advantages. First, it is relatively passive. The reader's job is finished after discovering what the writer said. Little thinking is required by readers who use the sponge method. Thus, reading like a sponge is quick and usually easy. The primary mental effort required is concentration and memory. Another advantage of the sponge model is that it can be a useful thinking style. If you absorb a lot of information, you have a knowledge base that can help you do more complex thinking at a later time.

   —M. Neil Browne and Stuart M. Keeley

   Topic: the sponge approach to reading

   Main idea: The sponge approach to reading has many advantages.

7. His name is in dictionaries, and his creation, the Heimlich maneuver, is known in nearly every country on earth. But Dr. Henry Heimlich has never been as famous as some of his ideas. Relatively few lay people realize that the maneuver is only one of many procedures and devices that this physician's fertile mind has produced over four decades. And there are probably thousands of people alive today who have no idea that they owe their survival to him.

   —Michael Ryan

   Topic: Henry Heimlich

   Main idea: Henry Heimlich is not as famous as his ideas.

8. The first automobile accident happened in 1769, in France. A steam carriage travelling at less than three miles an hour overturned while making a turn. Half a century later in England steam carriages would travel the roads between cities at a speed of five miles an hour. In 1885, in Germany, Gottlieb Daimler mounted a small gasoline engine on a bicycle and Karl Benz used a gasoline engine to power a three-wheeled car. The idea of using an engine to turn the wheels of a vehicle was around long before the modern automobile was invented.

   Topic: the idea of an automobile

   Main idea: Engines were used to power vehicles for over a century before the modern automobile was invented.

Critical Thinking and Writing

Write a paragraph or two about what life would be like today without the automobile.

9. "Work is a four-letter word" was a bumper sticker of the defiantly lazy in the 1960s, based on a remark attributed to the Yippie Abbie Hoffman. That illustrates the meaning of the phrase *four-letter word* as "vulgar, obscene," not for use in what used to be called *mixed company*. Of course, *work* — along with *hope, love* and thousands of other words of four letters — is not a *four-letter word*. That phrase (first used, Merriam-Webster says, in an 1897 book on flags) defines several sexually explicit or scatological terms, sometimes referred to as *barnyard epithets* or by using the first letter of the shocking term followed by the word *-word*.

   —*William Safire*

   Topic: four-letter words

   Main idea: Four-letter words are vulgar and not to be used in mixed company.

10. For centuries, Americans have classified themselves and their neighbors by the color of their skin. Belief in the reality of race is at the heart of how people traditionally perceive differences in those around them, how they define themselves and even how many scientists say humanity evolved. Today, however, a growing number of anthropologists and geneticists are convinced that the biological concept of race has become a scientific antique — like the idea that character is revealed by bumps on the head or that canals crisscross the surface of Mars. Traditional racial differences are barely skin deep, scientists say.

   —*Robert Loe Holtz*

   Topic: race

   Main idea: The traditional idea of race is out of date.

11. "Men have called me mad," wrote Edgar Allan Poe, "but the question is not yet settled, whether madness is or is not the loftiest intelligence — whether much that is glorious — whether all that is profound — does not spring from disease of thought — from moods

of mind exalted at the expense of the general intellect." Many people have long shared Poe's suspicion that genius and insanity are entwined. Indeed, history holds countless examples of "that fine madness." Scores of influential eighteenth- and nineteenth-century poets, notably William Blake, Lord Byron, and Alfred, Lord Tennyson, wrote about the extreme mood swings they endured. Modern American poets John Berryman, Randall Jarrell, Robert Lowell, Sylvia Plath, Theodore Roethke, Delmore Schwartz, and Anne Sexton were all hospitalized for either mania or depression during their lives. And many painters and composers, among them Vincent van Gogh, Georgia O'Keeffe, Charles Mingus, and Robert Schumann, have been similarly afflicted.

—*Kay Redfield Jamison*

Topic: madness

Main idea: Madness has often been associated with genius.

8.8 Stated Main Ideas in Textbooks

For each of the following textbook paragraphs, put a check mark beside the sentence or sentences that tell the main idea of the paragraph. In the blank space, write the main idea in your own words.

1. When carried to its extreme, conformity leads to groupthink. *Groupthink* is the term for situations in which a group fails to explore alternative solutions, problems, or concerns in an effort to present a united or cohesive front to outsiders. Irving Janis outlined several conditions that lead to groupthink. One is being out of touch — when a group meets for long periods of time away from its regular routines, members forget the big picture and do whatever is necessary to make the group succeed, regardless of how those actions may harm others. A second is being out of order — informal and nonstandardized decision-making procedures let a group venture into unproductive areas with no way to get back on course. A third is being overruled — when group members feel that criteria and decision-making procedures are thrust on them by a leader, they are likely to follow along without much advocacy or dissension. A fourth is being out of resources — when faced with a critical problem, a short time frame for deciding, and no reasonable alternative other than the one favored by the leader, the group falls back on groupthink.

—*Dan O'Hair and Gustav Friederich*

Main idea: Groupthink occurs when people start thinking too narrowly.

2. Reynolds, a Mormon living in Utah, was convicted of marrying two women, thus breaking a federal law. Because the Mormon church at that time approved of polygamy (having more than one spouse), Reynolds contended that the law violated his religious freedom. In this case, the Supreme Court ruled that religious freedom does have its limits. The Court held that "It was never intended that the First Amendment . . . could be invoked as protection for the punishment of acts inimical to the peace, good order, and morals of society."

—Richard J. Hardy

Main idea: Religious freedom does have limits, according to the Supreme Court.

3. Occupational choice begins when we first become aware that an occupation can help meet our needs. As we develop, we recognize that certain activities give us satisfaction whereas others are unpleasant. We tend to seek enjoyable experiences and to avoid painful ones. As we become aware of a variety of occupations, each of us gradually comes to realize that certain occupations provide experiences that are satisfying, whereas others require unpleasant activities. Some jobs attract and others repel. At this point, occupational choice actually starts for each of us.

—Bruce Shertzer

Main idea: Being aware of how jobs fill our needs helps us choose our occupations.

Critical Thinking and Writing

Which jobs attract you? Which do not appeal to you? Write a few paragraphs in which you analyze some occupations you know and how you feel about them.

4. A number of misconceptions surround suicide. One is that people who talk about it rarely do it. The facts are exactly the opposite: the majority (70 percent) of people who have attempted suicide have tried to talk about it. This means that if someone you know admits to thinking about suicide, take it seriously and help the individual

find therapeutic assistance. Another myth is that you shouldn't talk about suicide with someone who is considering it. Actually, if someone who is depressed wants to talk about suicide, it is helpful, especially if the talking leads to therapy.

—*James Laird and Nicholas Thompson*

Main idea: People have misconceptions about suicide.

5. *Sleeping.* Going without sleep for an extended period would eventually lead to insanity and even death. Common sense might say that sleep is the one natural function that is not shaped by culture, because people tend to do it every twenty-four hours, everyone shuts their eyes to do it, everyone lies down to do it, and almost everyone sleeps at night. But there are many cultural aspects to sleep, including the question of who sleeps with whom. Cross-cultural research reveals varying rules about where infants and children should sleep: with the mother, with both parents, or by themselves in a separate room. Among indigenous cultures of the Amazon, mothers and babies share the same hammock for many months, and breastfeeding occurs whenever the baby is hungry, not on a schedule. Culture also shapes the amount of time a person sleeps. In rural India, women sleep fewer hours than men since they have to get up earlier to start the fire for the morning meal. In fast-track, corporate North America, "A-type" males sleep relatively few hours and are proud of that fact—to have slept too much is to be a wimp.

—*Barbara D. Miller*

Main idea: There are many cultural aspects to sleep.

8c(2) *Implied Main Ideas*

Sometimes a writer does not tell you the main idea of a paragraph directly. Instead, the writer *implies* (suggests) the main idea through the combination of information in the paragraph. You, the reader, must draw on that information to see how it fits together. You take some words from one sentence and some words from another sentence to help you construct the main idea. When you see the overall picture of the paragraph, it is up to you to state the main idea in your own words.

The main idea you have to put together yourself is called an *implied main idea*. Here is an example from a book of consumer advice:

A lot of people assume it's nutritionally better to buy dark breads. We tend to believe that white bread has the nutrients processed out, while dark bread still has them inside. Not necessarily true. Dark bread is sometimes simply white bread, dyed dark. There's no definite data on what bread may be better for you, but consider this: Consumers Union bought thirty-three brands of bread and fed them to laboratory rats. Then they weighed and measured to see how much each rat grew or did not grow. The study found it made no difference whether the rats ate dark or white bread. It also made no difference whether the bread was "enriched." The bread companies that I called said the test was ridiculous, since no one eats only bread. Nutritionists I called said if you want a more nutritious bread, buy whole wheat. Whole wheat has more nutrients left in. The word "wheat" alone, or "health food" bread doesn't mean anything.

John Stossel

What is the topic of this paragraph? Clearly, the writer is talking about the nutritional value of breads. Knowing the topic helps you figure out the main idea. In this paragraph, however, the writer never directly tells you the main idea: *White bread is probably just as nutritious as most dark breads, except for whole wheat*. You have to figure it out from the various details the writer gives you.

Finding Implied Main Ideas

- Look at all the ideas and details in the paragraph.
- Ask if the ideas and details all relate to a single person or object. What is that topic? Then check all the sentences of the paragraph (not just the first few) to make sure they really are all about your suggested topic. If not, try to find a topic that fits all the sentences. As you have seen, all the sentences in the example on this page discuss the nutritional value of different breads.
- Ask what point all these ideas and details are making about that topic. Then write a complete sentence that (1) names the person or thing and (2) tells what that person or thing is doing.

Again, check all the sentences of the paragraph to make sure they fit your main idea sentence. If they do not, you must make your point broader so it covers everything in the paragraph. The sentence "Whole wheat bread is nutritious" does not cover the whole main idea in the paragraph.

- Be sure your implied main idea sentence is not too general. Can you make the topic more specific, or can you say something more specific about the topic and still be describing all the sentences in the paragraph? If you can, you should make your main idea sentence more specific. If your sentence covers all the details in the paragraph and cannot be made any more specific, then it is correct. "All breads have some nutrition" would be too general to be the main idea sentence. Only the sentence given — *White bread is probably just as nutritious as most dark breads, except for whole wheat* — is neither too narrow nor too general.

Reread the following paragraph, which you examined in 8b:

Sociologists reserve the term *small group* to refer to a group small enough for all members to interact simultaneously, that is, to talk with each other or at least be acquainted with each other. Small groups such as work groups and families are the intermediate link between the individual and the larger society. This intermediate position defines their importance in terms of attitudes, values, and behaviors. For this reason, sociologists are interested in what happens when people get together in small groups, whether it is to share gossip, reach a decision, or even play card games.

Richard T. Schaefer

You know that the topic here is *small groups*. But what point is the writer making about small groups? What is the main idea of the paragraph? The writer implies it; he doesn't state it directly. Using the pointers explained in the box on pages 161–162 you should be able to state the main idea in your own words. You might say: *Sociologists study small groups because they are important in understanding how people relate to one another*.

EXERCISES

8.9 Implied Main Ideas

In each paragraph below, the main idea is implied. Read each paragraph and the statements that follow. Then put a check mark next to the statement that gives the main idea most clearly. Be prepared to discuss why the other choices are not correct.

1. Oranges, as most people know, are an excellent source of vitamin C — one orange more than fulfills your daily requirement. They are also a fair source of vitamin A. Tangerines have less vitamin C than oranges, but are a better source of vitamin A. Both are good sources of potassium. Oranges provide a small amount of calcium as well. A medium-sized orange has about sixty calories, a medium-sized tangerine, about thirty-five calories.

   — *The Wellness Encyclopedia*

_______ a. Tangerines have fewer calories than oranges.

_______ b. Vitamin C is the most important nutrient in oranges, but vitamin A is the most important in tangerines.

___✓___ c. Oranges and tangerines both provide vitamins and minerals with few calories.

_______ d. Oranges and tangerines are popular citrus fruits that provide potassium and calcium.

2. Too often young women use work as a stopgap between high school and marriage. The idea is to keep themselves afloat until Mr. Right comes along. Then they can marry and have children. Being a wife and mother is a perfectly valid occupation, but no woman should allow it to cancel out her ability to be self-supporting. Life plays too many tricks. Mr. Right doesn't come along. Mr. Right doesn't earn enough to support the family and you have to work. You find housewifery boring and you want to work, but you have no skills. The marriage doesn't last and you have to go back to work. Your children grow up and don't need you so much. You must be prepared.

   — *Greta Walker*

___✓___ a. Young women should seriously prepare themselves for a career.

_______ b. Life does not always turn out as we hope.

_______ c. Being a housewife is an absolutely secure career.

_______ d. Mr. Right is bound to be a disappointment.

3. It is widely believed that if an electric chair or gas chamber should fail to operate, or the rope breaks during a hanging, the prisoner must go free because he cannot twice be put in jeopardy for the same offense. But this is a confusion between the *trial* and the *sentence*. A man cannot, under the Constitution, be tried twice for the same offense. But once he has been convicted and sentenced, then the sentence must be carried out, malfunctioning equipment or no, if the law is to be followed.

—Tom Burnham

_______ a. Electric chairs and gas chambers sometimes do not work correctly.

_______ b. If a prisoner is not executed on the first attempt, he or she should be set free.

_______ c. A trial is different from carrying out a sentence.

___✓___ d. Even if an execution attempt fails, the prisoner still must be executed.

8.10 Implied Ideas in Your Own Words

The main idea in each paragraph is implied. On the blank lines, write the main idea in your own words.

1. Breakfast is the most important meal of the day, and the most popular breakfast food is ready-to-eat (RTE) cereal. With hundreds of varieties to choose from, an American family could easily eat a different cold cereal each morning for a year. An average of two breakfast cereals are introduced each week, according to Lynn Dornblaser, publisher of *New Product News*. That number has remained steady over the past five years. Dornblaser attributes the relatively low number of new cereal products launched each year (compared with a category such as condiments, which can see over 1,000 new product introductions) to lack of shelf space.

—Marcia Mogelonsky

Main idea: People keep getting an increasing number of choices of breakfast cereals.

2. Adrian Wydeven spreads his feet, tips his head back, and howls long and low into the summer night. His mimicry is perfect — plaintive, mournful, stirring. As the last notes fade into the Wisconsin woods, he waits, listening for a reply from the wolves he knows are near. As a timber wolf biologist for Wisconsin's Department of Natural Resources (DNR), Wydeven and his colleagues trap, radio collar, and monitor wolves in remote areas of northwestern Wisconsin. During the day, they check traps and track animals by telemetry; at night, they howl.

—Scott Bestul

Main idea: Adrian Wydeven howls at night to trap wolves.

3. A Wisconsin law once required all parents to send their children to high school. This law brought protests from the Amish, a Protestant group whose centuries-old religious beliefs compel them to remain apart from modern society. In 1972, the Supreme Court declared that the state of Wisconsin could not require Amish children to attend school past the eighth grade (*Wisconsin* v. *Yoder*). The Court ruled that the law interfered with the Amish people's freedom to put their religious beliefs into practice. Similarly, in *Sherbert* v. *Verner* (1963), the Court ruled that a Seventh-Day Adventist could not be denied unemployment benefits because she refused to work on Saturday (her Sabbath day).

—Richard J. Hardy

Main idea: The Supreme Court has ruled to protect religious freedom

4. According to one sociologist, Theodore Caplow, the accident of birth often plays a large role in determining what occupation people choose. Children follow their parents' occupations: farmers are recruited from farmers' offspring, teachers from the children of teachers. The parent "passes" an occupation on to the child. Furthermore, such factors as time and place of birth, race, nationality, social class, and the expectations of parents are all accidental, that is, not planned or controlled. They all influence choice of occupation.

—Bruce Shertzer

Main idea: Accidents of birth influence occupational choice.

5. Let's consider that you want an automobile to get to work. Is it possible to get to work on the bus or with a friend while saving money for a car? Or do you need the car now? You must decide whether obtaining the car *now* is worth the extra cost of buying on credit. Thousands of decisions like this are made all the time because buying a car on installment is the most common use of credit in our economy. Appliances such as television sets, refrigerators, and washing machines are usually sold on installment. The costs of electric guitars, pianos, and other expensive musical instruments also are usually spread over a number of payments. Some of the things you buy from door-to-door salespeople are customarily bought on installment plans too. These are such items as reference book sets, vacuum cleaners, home repairs, and photography service sold to you in your home.

—Betty J. Brown and John E. Clow

Main idea: We buy many items on credit.

Critical Thinking and Writing

Many economists are critical of Americans for buying too much on credit. (When you buy on credit, you pay much more for the product because of interest charges.) Do you agree? Do Americans abuse the credit card system? What advantages and disadvantages do you see in buying on installment? Write a few paragraphs expressing your views.

8.11 Implied Main Ideas in a Short Article

On the lines after each paragraph of this short article, write the implied main idea of the paragraph. Then, on the lines at the end of the selection, write the implied main idea of the whole piece.

Oceanographer Curtis Ebbesmeyer is charmed when drifting bottles with notes in them turn up. He never thought drifting sneakers would give him the same "transforming experience" until hundreds of high tops began washing up on Pacific Ocean shores from the Queen Charlotte Islands to southern Oregon.

Curtis Ebbesmeyer found drifting sneakers as fascinating as drifting bottles with notes.

In May 1990 about 40,000 pairs of South Korean–made Nike shoes slid overboard in mid-ocean when a storm struck a ship carrying them, in airtight containers, from Pusan to Seattle. By the following January, beachcombers 2,000 miles to the east were finding sneakers. Since then, the Seattle-based Ebbesmeyer has been gathering reports, poring over computer models, and plotting where 1,300 shoes landed. He has decided that 1990 currents took the footgear farther south than they would have in a normal year. But in an El Niño year with strong southwesterly currents, shoes might have ended up farther north, in Alaska, he says.

Ebbesmeyer has gathered information on sneakers that drifted across the ocean.

Rich Hastings, transportation manager for Nike Inc., says the cargo containers probably imploded when they sank, and the sneakers floated because of an air-cushioning system in their soles. "It's like putting a life jacket on each shoe."

The sneakers floated because of their air-cushioned soles.

Whole selection: Floating sneakers reveal ocean currents

8.12 Paragraph Topics and Main Ideas

Return to Exercise 8.6 on page 145. You already have written the topic for each paragraph. Now determine the main idea of each paragraph and write it in the blanks provided. Some of the main ideas are stated directly; others are only implied. In either case, write each main idea in your own words.

8.13 Main Ideas in Paragraphs

In each of the following paragraphs, the main idea is either stated or implied. If the main idea is stated, underline the sentence that states it and then write the main idea in your own words on the blanks provided. If the main idea is implied, simply write the main idea in your own words.

1. Much as pet owners would like to believe it, animals can't predict an earthquake. Nor can tides or any of the other auguries that have been in vogue from time to time. But two Japanese research teams now say that the devastating Kobe, Japan, quake, which killed 5,000 in January, might have been signaled by changes in ground water. Analyzing bottles of commercial mineral water drawn from nearby wells at known dates in the weeks leading up to the quake, the researchers found a steady increase in certain minerals over time. Another study found an increase in radon in some wells. But other scientists have serious doubts. Much more data will be needed, they say, to prove that ground water is a reliable predictor. The studies were published in *Science* magazine.

   —*Gerald Parshall*

   Implied: Water may predict earthquakes.

2. Geothermal oddities were one of two reasons Yellowstone was carved out as a national park in 1872. The other was the abundance of wildlife: magnificent species that preoccupy my kids, and most others, for the duration of their visits. Vast herds of elk and bison share the range with mule deer and pronghorn antelope, prompting some people to call the park the Serengeti of North America. Bighorn sheep pick their way through outcroppings in the cliffs, and snow-white trumpeter swans rest in ponds. The most famous inhabitant, though, is the grizzly. While traveling in Chile once, I chatted with a fellow, trying to explain in my minimal Spanish the concept of Yellowstone's geysers. His eyes lit, and he nodded. "*Si, si,*" he said. "*Yogi y Boo Boo!*"

   —*Jim Robbins*

   Implied: Yellowstone Park was created for its geothermal oddities and its wildlife, especially the bears.

3. Why some people are fat and others are thin is a question that medical science is not yet able to answer. The old platitude that blames overweight on overeating is true, but doesn't tell the whole story about obesity. Food in the United States is plentiful, cheap, and available twenty-four hours a day, and many people not only overeat, but eat a lot of high-fat, high-calorie foods that contribute to weight gain. However, there are some people who eat anything they want and never gain weight, and studies show that obese people do not eat an inordinate amount of calories. In fact, they often eat less than

nonobese people do. Perhaps more important than overeating, far too many Americans spend their leisure time inactively — shopping, driving around, or watching television, for instance. From an environmental standpoint alone, then, it is no wonder that obesity and overweight are as prevalent as they are in this country.

— *The Wellness Encyclopedia*

We don't fully know why some people are fat and others are thin.

4. The popular notion that witches were burned in Salem is quite false. In fact, no witches were burned at any time in Salem or anywhere else in America. Nor were witches by any means all women; in fact, they were not all even human beings. Two dogs were actually put to death in Salem for "witchcraft." The means of execution in all cases, including the unfortunate dogs, was by hanging, with one exception: an old man named Giles Corey. Corey, in an instance of bravery under torture scarcely paralleled in American history, "stood mute," or refused to plead either yes or no to the charge against him. Under the law, this meant that his heirs would not be deprived of his property, which would have been sold at auction had he confessed or been found guilty. (Had he denied the charge, he would almost surely have been convicted.) Corey's death was by "pressing"; heavy stones were placed upon his chest in an attempt to force him to plead. He was crushed to death; it is said that his last defiant words were "More weight!"

—*Tom Burnham*

Implied: Witches in America were never burned; they usually were hanged.

5. It would be nice if once you have a job everything would go along perfectly. It never happens that way. Life is filled with problems, and very often they are job-related. Sometimes they loom as insoluble. This is usually because problems can create panic, and panic tends to blot out the various choices that are usually available to you. Other times you might let things slide because the difficulty doesn't seem very important. You hope that it will go away or somehow resolve itself. The opposite usually occurs — the problem gets bigger and more unwieldy. So when difficulties occur remember two things: view your problems as calmly as possible; take action immediately.

—*Greta Walker*

Implied: When job problems occur, you should face them calmly and as quickly as possible.

6. Let us face it. Nothing blows the mind more than a precise statistic. Ninety-nine and forty-four one-hundredths percent pure! That's hard to beat. But I must be honest with you. I have pulled a few classics in my time. On the average of 1.73562 times each year, a student will interrupt my lecture with a question such as: "Professor, is it true that we use only 10 percent of our brain during the course of a lifetime?" Now I ask you, how do you answer a question like that? For years, my approach has been to break down that statement. What do you mean by *use?* How does a person use his or her brain? Unless we can come up with some satisfactory definition of this word, the rest of the statement is sheer gobbledygook. Even assuming that we can agree on a definition, we're not much better off. How do we measure the proportion of the brain that gets "used" in a lifetime? Could we stick thousands of electrodes on various parts of the brain to determine whether the underlying nerve cells are firing? The question is unanswerable and any attempt to provide a statistic is a fake, no matter how well intended.

—Richard P. Runyon

Precise statistics are convincing, even if they are false.

Cultural Exchange

patent	rights to own the idea of an invention (page 139)
Clergy members	religious leaders (page 139)
Guinness Book of World Records	a book, published yearly, of extreme and unusual achievements. The book was originally published by a beer manufacturer to settle barroom bets. (page 140)
to throw a tantrum	to behave or react very angrily, especially for children who scream, cry, lie down, and kick their feet because something went wrong (page 144)
drive-in theater	an outdoor movie theater where customers remain in their cars to watch a movie (page 144)

hound	an individual who eagerly pursues something; a person who is a devotee or an enthusiast for a particular event, item, or activity (page 144)
Roller Derby	a roller-skating contest, usually indoors; skaters race round and round, sometimes pushing and knocking down their opponents (page 145)
gritty	sandy, coarse, or rough in texture (page 147)
antifreeze	a chemical substance put into water to stop it from freezing in very cold weather; it is used particularly in car engines and radiators (page 148)
Yippie Abbie Hoffman	a noted member of the Youth International Party, a left-wing group of the 1960s and 1970s that promoted the values of the counterculture movement, such as free love, marijuana, and peace (page 157)
Mormon	a member of the Mormon Church or Church of Latter-day Saints (page 159)
First Amendment	the constitutional amendment that establishes the four great liberties: freedom of the press, of speech, of religion, and of assembly (page 159)
stopgap	someone or something used as a temporary substitute while a better or more desirable solution is being sought (page 163)
Mr. Right	the man a woman would and should happily marry; one's dream mate (page 163)
Seventh-Day Adventist	a member of a religious denomination whose distinctive doctrine centers on its belief in the imminent second coming of Christ (page 165)
El Niño	a Spanish term for "the Christ Child," used to refer to a warm ocean current occurring every four to twelve years on the coasts of Ecuador and Peru during Christmastime (page 167)

augury	a sign or prediction of something coming in the future; an omen (page 168)
gobbledygook	unclear, wordy, nonsensical, or meaningless talk (page 170)
cliché	an overused expression or idea that has lost its freshness; for example, *as quick as a wink, last but not least* (page 176)

Chapter 8 SELF-TEST
Reading for the Main Idea

Read the following textbook paragraphs. (Notice that each paragraph has one italicized sentence.) Answer the questions by writing the letter of the correct response on the blank line. Count five points for each correct answer.

1. You may not think of the post office as a place to go with a consumer complaint. But anything having to do with a mail-order problem is a matter for the United States Postal Service. The mails cannot be used to cheat people. If you order by mail and do not receive your order, ask the Postal Service for help. If you have been cheated by a company, the Postal Service may take legal action to get your money back. *On this and other matters, it has a special department to help protect your rights.*

—Betty J. Brown and John E. Clow

__c__ 1. What is the key idea of the italicized sentence?
   a. The Postal Service has special departments.
   b. The Postal Service will protect your rights.
   c. The Postal Service has a special department to protect your rights.
   d. You may have rights that are not known to you.

__b__ 2. What is the main idea of the paragraph?
   a. The U.S. mail service cannot be used to cheat people.
   b. The Postal Service can help you if you are cheated.
   c. People do not know their rights.
   d. You may not know how the Postal Service can help you.

2. *Most eighteenth- and nineteenth-century earth scientists believed that the earth was very old, but proving its great age was not a simple matter.* One of the earliest attempts to date the earth was made in 1715 by an English astronomer, Edmund Halley. He assumed that the sea was originally fresh water and that it gradually became saltier as it became older. Halley knew that the salts in the sea had been dissolved from rocks on land and later carried to the sea by streams. This led him to believe that the total amount of salt in the sea might be a clue to the age of the oceans. In turn, the age of the oceans would give an estimate of the age of the earth.

—William Matthews et al.

c 3. What is the key idea of the italicized sentence?
a. Most eighteenth- and nineteenth-century earth scientists believed the earth was very old.
b. The earth is very old.
c. Proving the earth is old is difficult.
d. The great age of the earth can be proved.

a 4. What is the main idea of the paragraph?
a. Edmund Halley dated the earth by the salt in the oceans.
b. Edmund Halley made one of the earliest attempts to date the earth.
c. Edmund Halley knew a lot about the characteristics of salts in the sea.
d. Salt in the sea can help date the age of the oceans and, thus, the age of the earth.

3. To influence the conduct of the government in a significant way, citizens need organizations. Organizations are important for anyone who wishes to influence government, but they are particularly crucial for those who lack great individual resources. *By banding together and pooling their small resources, including votes, citizens who would be politically ineffectual alone can gain influence by acting jointly.* In this way, organization can be a resource that helps members of a group to compensate for their lack of individual resources.

—*Robert A. Dahl*

d 5. What is the key idea of the italicized sentence?
a. Above everything, votes can help citizens gain influence.
b. People should band together and pool their resources.
c. Citizens are politically ineffectual alone.
d. Citizens can gain influence by acting jointly.

d 6. What is the main idea of the paragraph?
a. Organizations are important for everything we do.
b. Individual citizens have small resources.
c. Citizens gain their greatest power through voting.
d. Organizations are necessary for individuals to influence government.

4. *The many forms of plant and animal life may at first glance appear chaotic, but the biologist sees in them a high degree of order.* This order is due to an elaborate system of classification. All life is first grouped into a few primary divisions called phyla; each phylum

is in turn subdivided into smaller groups called classes; each class is subdivided into orders; and so on down through the family, the genus, the species, the variety. This system brings order out of chaos, enabling the biologist to consider any plant or animal in its proper relationship to all the rest.

—*Louise E. Rorabacher*

__a__ 7. What is the key idea of the italicized sentence?
a. The biologist sees life forms as ordered.
b. Plant and animal life may at first glance appear chaotic.
c. Biologists are not easily fooled.
d. Plant and animal life have a high degree of order.

__c__ 8. What is the main idea of the paragraph?
a. All life is grouped into phyla.
b. All phyla are grouped into classes.
c. Classification gives order to the forms of life.
d. Biologists have a classification system of phyla, classes, orders, and so on.

5. The West saw many gold and silver rushes in the second half of the nineteenth century. Miners by the thousands poured into the West in search of precious metals. *Another natural resource of the region — its rich timber supply — would lure still other workers.* Meanwhile, western resources would help speed the Industrial Revolution. The gold and silver from western mines would provide capital to build industries.

—*Thomas DiBacco et al.*

__b__ 9. What is the key idea of the italicized sentence?
a. The West had more than one natural resource.
b. Timber lured workers.
c. The West had more than gold and silver; it had a rich timber supply.
d. Gold, silver, and timber attracted miners and other workers to the West.

__b__ 10. What is the main idea of the paragraph?
a. The West saw many gold and silver rushes in the second half of the nineteenth century.
b. Gold, silver, and timber attracted workers to the West.
c. Western resources speeded the Industrial Revolution.
d. Timber lured workers to the West.

6. *Always speaking in the same tone of voice, never moving or gesturing, using monotonous grammatical structure, an overly predictable pattern of speech, and lots of clichés — all these are good ways to lose an audience's attention.* Variety has motivational effects. Rosenshine (1971a) found that a lecturer's changes in the form of movement and gesturing correlate positively with student achievement. Whatever the lecturer can change fairly often, without making the change so extreme that it distracts students from the subject of the lecture, probably helps students to pay attention.

—*N. L. Gage and David C. Berliner*

__d__ 11. What is the key idea of the italicized sentence?
   a. When you speak to an audience, vary your tone of voice, your gestures, your grammar, and your speech and language patterns.
   b. Learn how to hold an audience's attention.
   c. Audience attention requires variety of tone, gestures, grammatical structure, and speech patterns.
   d. You can lose audience attention in several ways.

__b__ 12. What is the main idea of the paragraph?
   a. Most lectures are boring.
   b. Variety in a lecturer's speech and gestures helps students pay attention.
   c. Rosenshine came to many interesting conclusions while studying students' reactions to lectures.
   d. Some lecturers make such extreme changes during a lecture that students become distracted.

7. As the technology of microscopy improved, scientists obtained more accurate views of cell structure. *By 1824, sufficient observations had been made to prompt the French biologist Dutrochet to establish the first of three major principles composing the modern cell theory, namely, that all living things are composed of one or more units called cells.* The other two principles were not established fully until 1858, when, in a widely read publication, Rudolf Virchow argued forcefully, first, that cells were capable of independent existence and, second, that new cells can arise only from preexisting cells.

—*Paul B. Weisz and Richard N. Keogh*

__c__ 13. What is the key idea of the italicized sentence?
   a. Dutrochet established a major principle of modern cell theory.
   b. Modern cell theory has three major principles.

c. All living things are composed of one or more cells.
d. The first of three major principles of modern cell theory was established in 1824.

___b___ 14. What is the main idea of the paragraph?
a. Dutrochet and Virchow helped establish the major principles of modern cell theory.
b. Three major principles compose modern cell theory.
c. Improved microscopes led to new knowledge about cells.
d. New cells can arise only from preexisting cells.

8. What do you think when you hear the word *taxes?* Many people have negative feelings about taxes, because taxes take away some of their money. Realistically, we must pay income taxes to support our government and its programs. Taxes reflect the democratic ideal that the people control the government. *Nevertheless, workers often lose sight of this ideal when they see how much money is taken out of their paycheck each week or think of the complex tax forms they must fill out every year.* You may never have earned enough to fill out an income tax return, but if you have held a job, taxes were probably withheld from your paycheck.

—*Richard J. Hardy*

___c___ 15. What is the key idea of the italicized sentence?
a. Do not lose sight of why you pay taxes.
b. Workers resent money taken out of their paychecks and worry about complex yearly tax forms.
c. Workers paying taxes forget the purpose of taxes.
d. Tax forms are too complex for the average worker.

___b___ 16. What is the main idea of the paragraph?
a. Many people have negative feelings about taxes.
b. Although we do not like to pay them, taxes support our government.
c. People pay taxes even if they do not fill out income tax returns.
d. Taxes reflect the democratic ideal that the people control the government.

9. The earthworm has strong muscles under its skin and tiny bristles on its underside. When the earthworm moves, certain muscles squeeze and stretch out the front part of the body, while the rear part stays in place. Now the worm looks long and thin. The bristles on the front end stick out into the soil. Then the bristles

on the rear end let go. Other muscles squeeze and pull the rear end forward while the front end stays in place. The worm now looks short and thick. The rear bristles catch the soil and the front bristles let go. The front end is stretched out again and the motions are repeated. *In this way, the earthworm slowly tunnels through the soil.*

—*James E. McLaren, John H. Stasik, and Dale F. Levering*

__b__ 17. What is the key idea of the italicized sentence?

a. The earthworm tunnels in a particular way.
b. The earthworm tunnels.
c. The earthworm tunnels slowly through the soil in a particular way.
d. Earthworms tunnel slowly.

__a__ 18. What is the main idea of the paragraph?

a. The earthworm moves by squeezing and stretching its muscles.
b. The earthworm has strong muscles.
c. An earthworm sometimes looks long and thin, and sometimes looks short and thick.
d. An earthworm's movements are more complicated than you might think.

10. When a person wonders whether to tell the truth or tell a falsehood in order to get out of trouble, he is engaged in the process of weighing the pros and cons of each alternative action. In short, he is "deliberating." Deliberation always has to do with future actions that are within our power. We do not deliberate about the past. Nor do we deliberate about those actions about which we have no choice. Deliberation means that we are considering what we should do. Sartre speaks of the young woman who deliberates over whether to remove her hand or leave it resting in her companion's. She also deliberates about whether she wants to be involved in the actions that leaving her hand there would make possible. Deliberation means asking the question "Should I do it?" or "What ought I to do?" To a certain extent, we know in general what we want to achieve through our actions — we want to achieve a sense of well-being, of happiness. *What we deliberate over is how we shall achieve that end, or, as Aristotle says, it is "the mark of a man of practical wisdom to be able to deliberate well about what is good and expedient . . . about what sort of things conduce to the good life in general."* Certainly, deliberation has to do with action, and that is why Aristotle calls deliberation

"practical wisdom." That is what we mean when we say a person made a conscious, deliberate choice.

—*Samuel E. Stumpf*

__c__ 19. What is the key idea of the italicized sentence?

a. Aristotle discussed the good life.
b. We deliberate about how to achieve ends.
c. Wise people deliberate well about the good life.
d. We deliberate about how to achieve ends, or, as Aristotle puts it, wise men deliberate well about the good life.

__d__ 20. What is the main idea of the paragraph?

a. Deliberation has to do with the future.
b. We do not deliberate over actions about which we have no choice.
c. Deliberation always involves action.
d. Deliberation means considering what we should do.

Score: ______ correct × 5 points each = ______

CHAPTER **NINE**

Main Ideas in Long Selections

Individual paragraphs build the meaning of an entire selection. As you read the paragraphs of a long piece and consider their main ideas—whether directly stated **[8c(1)]** or implied **[8c(2)]**—you should be thinking about the main idea that all the paragraphs together are developing. Often called a *thesis*, the main idea of a long selection is the major point to which all the sentences contribute.

In some long works, the main point is clearly stated in the first paragraph, or introduction. Thus, the main idea of the first paragraph is also the main idea of the whole selection. All the other paragraphs expand and support the main idea.

In other selections, you have to develop the main idea on your own, as you do when the main idea is implied in a paragraph. To figure out the main idea of the long piece, you need to use the individual paragraph main ideas, of course. You do not simply add these points together, however; your main idea sentence would be too long and detailed. Instead, you develop a short, direct statement that includes the major points from the various paragraph main ideas.

The following is a selection from a science textbook. The main idea sentence appears beside each paragraph.

Why Is There No Life on the Moon?

1 Now that people have actually explored the surface of the moon, we have learned many things about it. One thing we knew, though, before anyone ever reached the moon, is that there's no life on it.

Paragraph 1
Main idea: ***Even before people explored the moon, we knew it had no life on it.***

2 The moon has no atmosphere, which means that there is no air around it to protect it from the sun's powerful rays. Earth's atmosphere, on the other hand, screens out dangerous radiation from the sun and still allows Earth to receive heat and light. Without that heat and light, life on Earth would not be possible.

Paragraph 2
Main idea: ***Unlike the moon, the Earth has an atmosphere that screens out the sun's harmful rays, allowing life.***

3 Because there is no atmosphere on the moon, its surface is either extremely hot or extremely cold. As the moon rotates, the side of it that is lighted up by the sun becomes very hot. The temperature there reaches more than 260 degrees Fahrenheit. That's hotter than boiling water! The hot lunar day lasts two weeks.

Paragraph 3
Main idea: ***The side of the moon lit by the sun is extremely hot.***

4 It is followed by a night that is also two weeks long. At night the temperature drops to more than 260 degrees below zero. That's more than twice as cold as temperatures reached at the Earth's South Pole!

Paragraph 4
Main idea: ***During the moon's long night, temperatures are extremely cold.***

5 Under these conditions, it's no wonder that life as we know it here on Earth could not exist on the moon.

Arkady Leokum

Paragraph 5
Main idea: ***Such extreme conditions prevent life on the moon.***

How would you state the main idea of the whole selection? First, determine the topic (see **8b**). You could state the topic like this: *why life on the moon does not exist.* The various paragraphs address this issue, and the title provides a good clue to the topic.

Next, figure out what the whole selection says about the topic. Consider the information in the individual paragraph main idea sentences. You should come up with a sentence like this: *Life cannot exist on the moon because the moon has no atmosphere to support living things.*

The main idea tells what the whole selection is about. It draws on information given in the separate sentences of the paragraphs. Yet the main idea statement does not include *all* the specifics from those separate sentences. The main idea sentence developed for the selection—clearly expressed in a few important words—makes a more general statement than the individual sentences make.

Stating Main Ideas for Long Selections

- *Define the topic.* What is the selection about? Use what you know about the topics in the individual paragraphs to state the selection topic in your own words. Often the title of a selection helps you with the topic. In the reading on pages 180–181, the title. "Why Is There No Life on the Moon?" states much of the topic neatly as a question.
- *Describe what the selection is saying about the topic.* The main idea usually asserts something about the topic; that is, the main idea expresses an opinion or a position on the topic. In the selection about the moon, the main idea asserts something about the topic, *why life on the moon does not exist.* It says that life does not exist on the moon *because the moon's harsh conditions cannot support life.*
- *Use the information you gather from the main ideas of the various paragraphs.* Notice how the individual paragraph main ideas in the selection on the moon help you develop the main idea of the whole selection. Not all the information from the separate paragraph main ideas must appear in the selection main idea. In fact only the main idea in the first two paragraphs provides the words for the selection main idea statement. Still, the main ideas of the other two paragraphs do support the selection main idea. They provide important specific details, but those details do not have to be included here. The selection main idea covers the points they make in general terms.
- *Develop a brief statement that highlights the general meaning of the selection.* There are no rules about the length of the main idea statement that you develop for a whole selection. You may choose to include more specific information in the main idea statement, and you may need more than one sentence to express the key point. For example, you might have stated the main idea for the selection "Why Is There No Life on the Moon?" in either of the following ways:
    1. Life cannot exist on the moon because the moon has no atmosphere, and its surface is either too hot or too cold to support living things.
    2. Life cannot exist on the moon because the moon's harsh atmospheric conditions cannot support living things; its surface is too hot or too cold for living things.

  You have many options in stating the main idea of the selection. However, you should aim for a relatively short statement that describes the point of the reading.

Look at this selection from a health education textbook. On the blank lines beside each paragraph, write the main idea. Then read the discussion that follows to help you determine the main idea of the whole selection.

Sleep Problems

1 Most people sleep seven to eight hours a day. The normal amount of sleep varies from person to person. The inability to sleep your usual amount is called *insomnia*. Insomnia is a problem for an estimated 75 million Americans.

Paragraph 1
Main idea: ________________________________

2 Often to get a good night's sleep, doctors advise avoiding foods or medications that keep you awake. These include many drinks that contain caffeine, such as coffee, chocolate, and cola drinks. Exercise during the day often helps people sleep better. Establish a regular bedtime and go to bed only when you are tired. If you just cannot sleep one night, get up and read a book or do work on some project. Remember that not being able to sleep well occasionally happens to everyone. Constant insomnia is serious and should be treated by a doctor. It can be a sign of a physical or mental illness.

Paragraph 2
Main idea: ________________________________

3 Some people may have problems staying awake during the day, even though they get a full night's sleep. Extreme daytime sleepiness may indicate a disorder called narcolepsy. *Narcolepsy* is a disorder in which people fall asleep suddenly even while doing something such as talking or driving. The cause of these sleep attacks is often unknown.

Paragraph 3
Main idea: ________________________________

4 *Sleep apnea* is a condition in which breathing stops periodically during sleep. It may stop because of a blockage of the upper airway or by the brain interrupting its signals to breathe. When this happens, the sleeper partly awakes, gasps for breath, and then falls back to sleep. This may happen many times during the night, leaving the person feeling very tired by day.

Bud Getchell, Rusty Pippin, and Jill Varnes

Paragraph 4
Main idea: ________________________________

Your main idea sentences for the separate paragraphs should look something like these:

Paragraph 1: Insomnia is a sleep disorder for many Americans.

Paragraph 2: People can improve the way they sleep by following some simple recommendations.

Paragraph 3: Narcolepsy is a sleep disorder in which people fall asleep suddenly during the day.

Paragraph 4: During sleep apnea, breathing stops periodically.

How would you state the main idea of the whole selection? First, determine the topic. You know from the title and from what you have read that this passage is about *sleep problems*. What is the passage asserting about sleep problems? You can tell from the various problems explained here that sleep disorders are varied and that they affect many people. The paragraph topic sentences support that point with specific information about different sleep problems. To state the main idea of the selection, you need to make a short, general statement that covers the major point expressed here.

State the whole selection's main idea in your own words on the blanks below.

____

____

____

You should have written something like this: *Various problems can affect people's normal sleeping patterns.*

Do you see how the main idea statement for the whole selection reflects the general point of the passage? It states the topic, *sleep problems*, and asserts something about the topic: These problems *can affect people's normal sleeping patterns*. Notice how the separate paragraph main ideas help you develop the main idea for the whole selection. However, few of the specific details in those paragraph main ideas appear in the selection main idea. To cover all these details, you needed to produce a general statement.

EXERCISES

9.1 Main Ideas in a Preface

The following three paragraphs from the preface to the book *The Amazing Brain* by Robert Ornstein and Richard Thompson. On the lines after each paragraph, write the main idea of the paragraph. Then, on the extra set of lines after the end of the last paragraph, write the main idea of the whole preface.

> For thousands of years, people have tried to understand the brain. The ancient Greeks thought it was like a radiator, to cool the blood. In this century, it has been compared to a switchboard, a computer, and a hologram, and no doubt it will be likened to any number of machines yet to be invented. But none of these analogies is adequate, for the brain is unique in the universe and unlike anything man has ever made.

Main idea of the first paragraph: Attempts to understand the brain by analogies are inadequate.

> Over the past few decades, great advances have taken place in the various fields of study that touch upon the brain. From evolutionary biology we have learned how and when the different parts of the brain were "built." From neuroanatomy we know how the elements of the brain are assembled, and from neurophysiology we have begun to understand how those elements and the chemicals that make them up function together. We are now beginning to understand what or "who" the brain is, but a great deal remains to be discovered in the neurosciences.

Main idea of the second paragraph: Several sciences have given us a partial understanding of the brain.

> The brain is like an old ramshackle house that has been added on to over the years in a rather disorganized fashion. In this book, we look at the architecture of that house, first by taking a tour through the various "rooms" and then by going deeper and deeper into the material with which those rooms are constructed. Later, we consider some of the mysteries of the brain and human experience. The drawings and diagrams appearing throughout will help you to visualize some of the more complex aspects of the amazing organ that is the human brain.

Main idea of the third paragraph: This book describes the complex and disorganized design of the brain.

Main idea of the entire preface: The brain is a complicated organ that we still don't understand fully.

9.2 Main Ideas in Longer Selections

Read each of the following selections from magazine stories. Then, on the lines provided, write the main idea of each paragraph and then the main idea of the entire selection.

1. *How Much Does the American Dream Cost?*

For all its allure, the American dream has always come with strings attached. The catch is that hard work and long hours on the job are part and parcel of getting ahead and making money. Family life often pays the price, of course— a bargain that makes many Americans queasy.

Bob Israel, co-owner of a motion-picture ad agency in Los Angeles, knows the feeling well. "At some point during the day, I look at my watch, and I'm faced with, 'Do I go home now and spend a little more time with my kids before they go to bed, or do I complete the work that I'm staring at?' " Mr. Israel said. "It really is a daily struggle. It sometimes causes conflict, and certainly presents conflict in my heart." Still, Mr. Israel usually stays at his desk, in the belief that long hours are necessary to take home a fatter paycheck.

Now along comes a study from the Wharton School that claws at his reasoning—and that of everyone else who buys into conventional wisdom on the work-family conflict. It found that people who placed high importance on finding the right spouse and creating a good family life actually ended up earning more money than those who were willing to sacrifice home life for their careers. "I'm sorry to hear that, because I didn't go home early," Mr. Israel said. "I'm not going to let my wife read this article."

—*Judith H. Dobryzinski*

Main idea of the first paragraph:

The American dream has often required sacrifice of family life.

Main idea of the second paragraph:

Bob Israel is daily confronted with the conflict between work and home.

Main idea of the third paragraph:

A study shows people who value family life earn more money.

Main idea of the entire selection:

Sacrificing the family for success does not, in fact, work.

Critical Thinking and Writing

When you were a child, how did your parents balance the necessity of getting ahead on the job and the desire to spend time with the family? How do you plan to balance these two in your life? Do you feel you will have to give up much to be successful in your career?

2. *The Truth about George Washington?*

Like most Americans, I learned early on the importance of honesty from the story of George Washington and the cherry tree. But it was only recently that I discovered the story's provenance, and thus its true significance—as an illustration of the market economy at work.

It first appeared in Mason Locke Weems's bestselling *The Life of Washington*, published in 1800, and reissued many times with fresh material. The author, a man of the cloth, set the story down in the fifth edition of his books as follows (we join the action at its climax):

" 'George,' his father said, 'do you know who killed that beautiful little cherry tree yonder in the garden?' This was a tough question, and George staggered under it for a moment; but quickly recovered himself; and, looking at his father, with the sweet face of youth brightened with the inexpressible charm of all-triumphant truth he bravely cried out, 'I can't tell a lie, Pa, you know I can't tell a lie, I did cut it with my little hatchet.' "

The whole thing, it turns out, is a charming fraud—as historians have long known and that you might surmise from its copious quotation of a private conversation that occurred years earlier (or from the parson's claim in the book that the story's "too true to be doubted"). Weems made it up from scratch to achieve his twin aims of enhancing the myth of Washington and attracting buyers to his new-and-improved *Life*. Thus the single most powerful American contribution to the notion of honesty illustrates a somewhat different moral: it pays to lie, if you have the knack for it. And if you lie as well as Weems you can make a lot of people happy, simply by telling them what they think they want to hear.

—*Michael Lewis*

Main idea of the first paragraph:

The story of Washington and the cherry tree illustrates the market economy.

Main idea of the second paragraph:

The story first appeared in a book originally published in 1800.

Main idea of the third paragraph:

George Washington told the truth.

Main idea of the fourth paragraph:

The story was made up by the book's author.

Main idea of the entire selection:

Lying is valuable and is part of the American tradition.

Critical Thinking and Writing

Is honesty always the best policy? Is it ever appropriate to lie? Why or why not? In what circumstances? Write a few paragraphs that explore these questions.

CULTURAL Exchange

hologram	a three-dimensional image produced on a photosensitive medium (page 185)
to come with strings attached	to have special conditions that must be fulfilled before a person can use or enjoy something (page 186)
the catch	a tricky or previously unsuspected condition or drawback to a deal or an agreement (page 186)
man of the cloth	a member of the clergy; a priest, rabbi, or minister (page 187)
from scratch	from the very beginning (page 187)
to have the knack for something	to have a specific talent for something, especially a talent or ability that is difficult to explain or teach (page 187)
hip-hop	cultural movement that began primarily among urban black American youth and has since spread around the world (page 192)
habituation	becoming accustomed to a stimulus and no longer sensitive to it (page 195)
dishabituation	becoming sensitive to a stimulus again (page 195)

Chapter 9 SELF-TEST
Main Ideas in Long Selections

Read the textbook selections below. (Notice that every paragraph in each selection is numbered.) Answer the questions by writing the letter of the correct response on the blank line.

Count eight points for correctly determining the main idea of every paragraph in the selections. Count another eight points for correctly determining the main idea of each whole selection. (Perfect score: 100)

1. *World War II Inventions*

1 World War II was the most costly and destructive conflict in history. At the same time, however, the war led to many creative inventions and new ways of doing things. Radar, invented as a weapon of war, soon made flying safer for commercial passengers. Diving became a popular sport after the invention of underwater breathing equipment used by navy divers during the war.

2 Another important wartime development was the widespread use of plastics. Soldiers carried plastic radios and telephones and used plastic chairs and tables. Wires were covered with plastic insulation, and uniforms were pressed with irons that had plastic handles.

3 After the war, Americans began to use plastics for all kinds of consumer goods. Today, Americans consume about twenty-five million tons of plastics each year for such things as dishes, furniture, toys, tools, sports equipment, and automobile parts.

—*William Jacobs*

___c___ 1. What is the main idea of paragraph 1?
   a. Radar was invented as a weapon of war.
   b. World War II was costly and destructive.
   c. World War II produced inventions.
   d. World War II was responsible for radar and underwater breathing equipment.

___b___ 2. What is the main idea of paragraph 2?
   a. Plastics were an invention of World War II.
   b. Plastics were widely used.
   c. Plastics have more uses than you would imagine.
   d. Unusual uses were made of everyday substances such as plastics.

a 3. What is the main idea of paragraph 3?
  a. Consumers use plastics for many purposes.
  b. Good things can come from a war.
  c. Plastics have some peacetime uses.
  d. The plastics industry stopped developing wartime products.

a 4. What is the main idea of the entire selection?
  a. World War II led to many inventions, including numerous new uses for plastics.
  b. Radar, underwater breathing equipment, and plastics were developed during World War II.
  c. Americans consume twenty-five million tons of plastics each year.
  d. Although World War II was costly and destructive, it led to many creative inventions.

2. *Getting the Most Out of a News Story*

1 Why do people read the newspaper? Some people read it for entertainment; they enjoy sections like the comics or the sports. Others look for things to buy or sell; they might look mostly at the advertisements. Most people, though, read the newspaper for news!

2 The news is reported in news stories, which can be found throughout the newspaper. Unlike the comics or the advertisements, news stories report facts. In this article, you will learn some hints about how to get the most out of a news story.

3 Many news stories have the following elements: headline, by-line, dateline, and lead. The *headline*, which is above the story, tells what the story is about. The size of the headline depends on the importance of the news—important news would get a large bold-typed headline. The *by-line* tells who wrote the story. Not all news stories have by-lines. The *dateline*, which some news stories also do not have, usually names the place where the story originated or where the news happened and the date on which it happened. The *lead* is the first paragraph; it gives the most important details in the story by telling *who, where, when, why*, and *how*.

—J.M. Stanchfield and Thomas G. Gunning

b 5. What is the main idea of paragraph 1?
  a. People read the newspaper for entertainment, advertisements, and news.
  b. People read the newspaper mostly for news.

c. Not everyone reads a newspaper.
d. Most people read a newspaper.

d 6. What is the main idea of paragraph 2?
a. News stories are found throughout the newspaper.
b. Most people do not know how to get the most out of a news story.
c. News stories are important.
d. News stories report facts.

d 7. What is the main idea of paragraph 3?
a. Many news stories have the same elements.
b. The headline is very important because its size communicates the importance of the news.
c. Every news story has a headline and a lead.
d. News stories usually have a headline, a by-line, a dateline, and a lead.

c 8. What is the main idea of the entire selection?
a. You can learn how to get the most out of a news story.
b. People have many reasons for enjoying the newspaper.
c. News stories report the news following a standard format.
d. The most important feature of a newspaper is its news stories.

3. *The Commercialization and Globalization of Rap*

1 Rap music developed from its roots in African American and Jamaican music during the 1970s. It started as a protest against the treatment of African Americans and as a reflection of the hip-hop culture that spawned it. Since that time, it has evolved into a variety of forms: from the old school rap recordings of The Sugarhill Gang to the gangsta' rap of Tupac Shakur, Notorious B.I.G., and Snoop Doggy Dogg, from the playa' rap of Run D.M.C. and M.C. Hammer to the message rap of KRS-One. What started as a male-dominated music form has evolved into an equal opportunity art form with the success of Queen Latifah, Lauryn Hill, and Foxy Brown.

2 Although Run D.M.C. and M. C. Hammer popularized rap, it was the success of white rappers that made the music even more commercially acceptable. Vanilla Ice experienced brief notoriety and was followed by the Beastie Boys. These musicians were criticized either for imitating or making fun of African American rappers. The more recent emergence of white rappers such as Kid Rock and Eminem who rap about their own lives has created an even greater demand among white

teenagers. In a 1999 article, *Time* magazine reported that whites bought 70 percent of the rap albums. Rap has not remained just an American music form. It can be found throughout the world as it mutates into dozens of forms. Rappers rap in France, Italy, Germany, Japan, Korea, New Zealand, and dozens of other countries. In the book *Global Noise: Rap and Hip-Hop outside the USA*. Tony Mitchell states:

3 Hip-Hop and rap cannot be viewed simply as an expression of African American culture; it has become a vehicle for global youth affiliations and a tool for the reworking of global identity all over the world. Even as a universally recognized popular music idiom, rap continues to provoke attention to local specifics.

4 Rap has become a form of music that people all over the world use to protest their conditions and to spread the word about those conditions. Despite its global development, however, the sales of rap recordings continue to be dominated by U.S. rappers.

—*Jean Folkerts and Stephen Lacy*

__a__ 9. What is the main idea of paragraph 1?
   a. Rap music has developed and evolved since 1970.
   b. Rap music's different forms include old school, gangsta', playa' and message.
   c. Rap music shows protest.
   d. Rap was male dominated, but now has popular women performers.

__d__ 10. What is the main idea of paragraph 2?
   a. Rap music started with popular black performers.
   b. White performers made rap more commercially acceptable.
   c. Rap is performed in Europe and Asia.
   d. Rap has grown from its black roots into an American and now world music.

__b__ 11. What is the main idea of paragraph 3?
   a. Rap is global.
   b. Though globally performed, rap sales are U.S. dominated.
   c. Rap protests local conditions and spreads the word.
   d. Rap is a powerful political force in the world.

__c__ 12. What is the main idea of the entire selection?
   a. Rap has lost its soul as it has moved away from its roots.
   b. Many people copy rap and give it local flavor and local topics.

c. Rap has grown to be more global and more commercial.
d. The protest messages carried by rap are more important than its global commercial success.

Score: ______ correct × 8 points each + 4 free = ______

Critical Thinking and Writing

Do you listen to rap music? Why? Do you find the music more commercial or more political? Which performers would you categorize as better than others? Write several paragraphs about your views on rap. Be sure to include examples of performers you like or have listened to.

UNIT 3 REVIEW TEST

Read the following selection on infants' mathematical abilities from a college textbook, *Child Development: Principles and Perspectives*. Then answert the questions in the spaces provided.

Mathematical Skills in Infancy

1 Amazing but true: Researchers have found evidence that even *newborns* have rudimentary mathematical skills. Humans seem to be "born with a fundamental sense of quantity" (Geary, 1994, p. 1). For example, researchers showed newborn infants (less than one week old!) a card with two black dots (Antell & Keating, 1983). The newborns looked at the dots for a bit, then started looking away. Looking away signals boredom; in Chapter 4 we referred to this as *habituation*. When researchers then switched to a card that had three dots, the newborns regained interest in looking at the dots—they *dishabituated*. Newborns also showed dishabituation when the set size was changed from three dots to two. These patterns of habituation and dishabituation show that newborns can see the difference between two and three dots. Because the cards were exactly the same except for the number of dots, these results demonstrate that newborn infants are capable of processing something that is related to the number or quantity of dots located on the cards. In this same experiment, however, the newborns failed to distinguish between cards with four and six dots. Evidently these larger quantities were indistinguishable for newborn infants.

2 In the first months after birth, infants can already distinguish among small numbers of objects (e.g., among one, two, and three objects), whether the objects are similar or different, moving or still, or presented at the same time or in sequence. They can even match the number of objects they *see* with the number of sounds they *hear*. For example, when infants hear a sound track of two drumbeats, they prefer to look at a photo of two household objects rather than a photo of three objects. When they hear three drumbeats, however, their preference switches to the photo of three objects (Starkey,

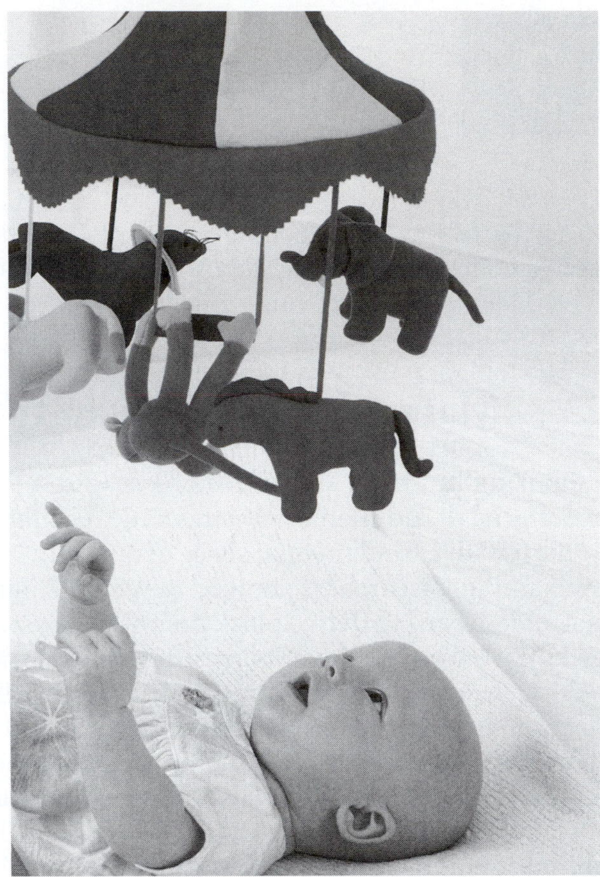

During the early months of life, what do infants understand about quantity and number? Does this infant know how many toys she is looking at?

Spelke, & Gelman, 1983, 1990). Impressive as these skills are, however, they apply only to very small sets. If researchers increase the number of objects in each set to five or more, then children don't show evidence that they recognize the quantities until they are about 3 or 4 years old (Canfield & Smith, 1996; Simon, Hespos, & Rochat, 1995; Starkey & Cooper, 1980; Strauss & Curtis, 1981; van Loosbroek & Smitsman, 1990; Wynn, 1992, 1995).

3 How are infants able to show such skills? They clearly cannot count objects. They have no experience with a number system, and they don't have the language skills they need to say the words that go with the numbers. Researchers propose that infants enumerate small sets by **subitizing**, a perceptual process that we all use to

quickly and easily determine the basic quantity in a small set of objects [without actually counting them]. To see how subitizing works, try the following experiment. Have your friend toss three or four pennies onto a table while you have your eyes closed. Now open your eyes and, as quickly as you can, look to see how many pennies there are. Most people can "see" that there are three pennies, or four pennies, without needing to actually count each penny. There is something about the visual arrangement of the pennies that lets you know immediately how many there are. Of course we can't be sure that infants are subitizing object sets exactly the way we do, but from the experimental evidence it does seem that they use a similar process. Somehow, without actually counting, they can determine that one set of objects has more items than another set, and they can match the number of things they see with the number of sounds they hear. Quite remarkable math skills for such a young age!

1. What is the topic of the sentence "Amazing but true: Researchers have found evidence that even newborns have rudimentary mathematical skills" (paragraph 1)?

   mathematical skills

2. In your own words, what is the main idea of the same sentence?

   Newborns have mathematical skills.

3. What is the topic of the sentence "In the first months after birth, infants can already distinguish among small numbers of objects (e.g., among one, two, and three objects), whether the objects are similar or different, moving or still, or presented as the same time or in sequence" (paragraph 2)?

   distinguishing numbers

4. In your own words, what is the main idea of the same sentence?

   Infants can distinguish small numbers.

5. What is the topic of the sentence "Somehow, without actually counting, they can determine that one set of objects has more items than another set, and they can match the number of

things they see with the number of the sounds they hear" (paragraph 3)?

distinguishing and matching numbers

6. In your own words, what is the main idea of the same sentence?

Infants can match numbers of sounds with numbers of objects.

7. In your own words, what is the main idea of paragraph 1?

Newborns have mathematical skills.

8. What sentence or part of a sentence best expresses the main idea of paragraph 2?

"In the first months after birth, infants can already distinguish among small numbers of objects. . . ."

9. In your own words, what is the main idea of paragraph 3?

Infants perceive numbers of objects directly by subitizing.

10. In your own words, what is the main idea of the selection "Mathematical Skills in Infancy," made up of paragraphs 1, 2, and 3?

Infants distinguish number differences and recognize number repetition.

11. Which sentence best expresses the main idea of the section "Mathematical Skills in Infancy"?

"Amazing but true: Researchers have found evidence that even newborns have rudimentary mathematical skills."

UNIT FOUR Finding Information

CHAPTER 10

Reading for Information

CHAPTER 11

Using SQ3R

CHAPTER TEN

Reading for Information

The main idea of a selection gives you an overall picture of what the writer is saying; the remaining details complete the picture. To make sense of the full picture in a paragraph, you need to do the following:

- Find the facts presented.
- Separate the major facts and details from the minor ones.
- Understand the order, or the sequence, in which the writer puts them.

Each of these steps helps you with the others.

We look at each step separately. When you actually read, you may follow a different order, or you may do several steps at the same time. All these steps, however, can help you see the details in relation to the overall meaning of your reading. Information that is just a collection of odd bits and pieces does you little good and is very hard to remember. However, information that fits in with a larger meaning makes more sense. As you come to see the whole picture, each detail fits into its own special place.

10a Finding Facts

To find and remember the facts from a reading passage, you must be an alert and active reader. Here are six ways to help you locate facts:

- *Know why you are reading.* Have a definite purpose for reading. When you read a cookbook you are thinking about buying, you check to see if the ingredients are expensive, if the dishes are easy to cook, and if the results sound tasty. When reading the same cookbook while you are cooking a particular dish, you look for the exact amounts of ingredients, the order of steps, and the cooking times and temperatures. Even if you are reading an assigned textbook to complete a homework assignment or to prepare for an exam, you will remember more if you have a definite purpose in mind. Are you reading your math book to find out how to do a particular kind of problem? Are you reading your history book to find out why the United States got into the war in Vietnam?

- *Know the overall meaning of the reading.* Read for the main idea. If you recognize the main idea, the facts that support that idea will stand out (see 8c).
- *Look for information in groups or units.* Facts often appear together in clumps.
- *Question yourself as you read.* Stop to think and let the facts sink in before you rush on to other information. Ask yourself, "What does that mean?" or "What does that information tell me?" or "Why is this information here?"
- *Use the five Ws: who, where, when, what happened, why.* These five words give you specific questions to ask about the facts.

  1. Ask yourself, "Who?" Then look for the name of someone or something.
  2. Ask yourself, "Where?" Then look for a place.
  3. Ask yourself, "When?" Then look for a date (a day, a month, or a year) or a time of day or year.
  4. Ask yourself, "What happened?" Then look for an action.
  5. Ask yourself, "Why?" Then look for an explanation.

- *Think about the questions someone might ask you about the information you have read.* Then go back over the passage to make sure you know the answers to those questions.

To see how these ways of locating facts can help you, read the following passage about an oil billionaire. The first step in helping you become an active reader and remember facts is to consider *why* you are reading. Your first reason for reading is to see how the passage serves as an example of the idea discussed in this section. That is, you will be reading to see how details help make a full picture of the man's life. You also might find that the story of how Jean Paul Getty got rich is interesting in itself. Life stories of rich people such as Getty fascinate us for many personal reasons.

Jean Paul Getty, who in 1957 sadly philosophized that "a billion dollars isn't worth what it used to be," was born in Minneapolis on December 15, 1892. His father was a lawyer who made millions on Oklahoma oil. J. Paul was educated at the University of Southern California, the University of California at Berkeley, and Oxford, from which he went to Tulsa (site of his father's Minnehoma Oil Company) in 1914, determined to make a million dollars within two years. He bought and sold oil leases with great success and—true to his resolve—was a millionaire by 1916.

After taking a few years off from the moneymaking grind to enjoy spending his earnings on women, Getty returned to Oklahoma in 1919. During the 1920s he added about $3 million to his already sizable estate. His succession of marriages and divorces (three during the 1920s, five throughout his life) so distressed his father, however, that J. Paul inherited a mere $500,000 of the $10 million the senior Getty left at his death in 1930.

Through shrewd investment during the Depression, Getty acquired Pacific Western Oil Corporation, and he began the acquisition (completed in 1953) of the Mission Corporation, which included Tidewater Oil and Skelly Oil. In 1967, the billionaire merged these holdings into Getty Oil.

His most daring business venture began in 1949, when he paid Ibn-Saud $9.5 million in cash and $1 million a year for a sixty-year concession to a tract of barren land near the border of Saudi Arabia and Kuwait. No oil had ever been discovered there, and none appeared until four years and $30 million had been spent. But from 1953 onward, Getty's gamble produced sixteen million barrels a year, which contributed greatly to the fortune that made him the richest person in the world.

He died on June 6, 1976. Getty owned the controlling interest in nearly 200 businesses, including Getty Oil, and associates put his overall wealth at between $2 billion and $4 billion.

—*David Wallechinsky and Irving Wallace*

When you considered your reasons for reading, did you read actively? Do you recall some details of Getty's life? Reading with a purpose in mind can help you remember information.

Another way to find facts is to figure out the overall meaning of the passage. This helps you see how the details support that meaning. The main theme of this piece is that Getty became rich through the clever buying and selling of oil properties. Within this framework, you can now place the various details of his oil deals.

You also can find facts if you learn to look for clumps of information. In the above passage, facts about Getty's birth and family are in the middle of the first paragraph; facts about his final wealth are at the end. In the middle are clumps of facts about his ventures.

Still another way to find facts is to ask yourself about puzzling points in the reading. For example, you may wonder why the passage begins with the remark Getty made in 1957. Why do you think the quotation is here? Why is it given a date? The quotation shows that by that time Getty was so rich he could think a billion dollars was not worth much.

The five question words—*who, where, when, what happened,* and *why*—can shed light on each paragraph.

- The *who* throughout is mainly Jean Paul Getty.
- The *where* is the oil fields of the United States and Saudi Arabia.
- The *when* is throughout his life, with different periods mentioned in each paragraph.
- The *what happened* is the gain of wealth through deals. Each paragraph gives the details of a deal.
- The *why* is to get richer, supported by specific dollar amounts given at each stage of the story.

Finally, you might ask yourself some questions to help you locate facts. In addition to the obvious questions of how Getty got rich and how rich he was, you also might ask other questions: How important was inherited money to him? Was he so busy making money that he didn't have a chance to enjoy it? Now go back over the passage with these questions in mind. Which details now seem important to answer these questions? Details about Getty's father's wealth and his inheritance now become more striking, as do the details about his romances in the second paragraph.

In these ways, you build up a much more detailed picture of this story. You learn much more than the simple fact that Jean Paul Getty was a very rich man.

EXERCISES

10.1 Finding Facts

Reread the selection on pages 202–203. Then answer each of the following questions.

1. How rich did Jean Paul Getty become?

   He had between $2 billion and $4 billion at the time of his death.

   ____

2. When and how did he make his first million dollars?

   between 1914 and 1916, by buying and selling oil leases

3. Did Jean Paul Getty do anything else besides make money?

   He spent his money on women and was married five times.

4. With what places was Getty involved?

   California; Oxford; Oklahoma; Saudi Arabia

5. Write down three of the most important facts from this selection.

   Getty did not inherit any money until he had built his own fortune.

   Getty made money through dealings with oil companies.

   Getty's largest gamble, on land in Saudi Arabia, helped make him the richest man in the world.

6. Write a question you think this passage answers.

   How did Getty build his fortune?

10.2 Finding Facts in a Textbook

Read this selection about MTV from a textbook on media. Then answer the questions that follow.

MTV: Making Money and Influencing Culture around the World

Music Television (MTV) changed the face of television in 1981 when it initiated the first twenty-four-hour music channel. The mission was simple: to capture cable viewers between the ages of twelve and thirty-five by adding video to music. The result was a form of television that spread throughout the world and continues to make money and to influence world culture.

The idea of combining video and music existed long before MTV. Rock 'n' roll joined television early with dance programs such as Dick Clark's *American Bandstand*. Later, documentaries about musicians combined video and music. Frank Zappa's 1971 movie *200 Motels* visually represented his surreal music. Short videos were used to promote music. However, MTV changed the music industry by widely distributing promotional videos through satellite and cable transmission.

Within six years, MTV began creating channels to provide music to the world outside the United States. MTV, now owned by Viacom, provides music television to Australia, Europe, Asia, and Latin America. Dozens of competing music satellite networks are available around the world.

Initially, MTV's ratings rose quickly. In 1986, however, they started to fall, and the network added nonmusic programming. The strategy worked. Even though MTV only averages about a million households at any given time, some programs, such as *Real World*, can double or triple the ratings. As a result, MTV has become the most profitable cable network and ratings were growing in the early 2000s. The greatest growth in profits came from MTV's international business.

The movement toward more nonmusic programming did not reduce MTV's influence over recording sales. *Total Request Live* has become the equivalent of the 1960s *American Bandstand* in its influence. Kid Rock, for example, commented on *TRL* to the *Los Angeles Times*: "It was like boom, overnight. Man, you hit that 'TRL,' that's the biggest thing going in music. Video is more powerful than radio these days, and who would have thought that we would ever reach that point?"

MTV exerts this type of power around the world. It has increased the flexibility of programming for various countries and cultures. This allows MTV to take advantage of music trends in the United States and other parts of the world.

Some music observers criticize the impact of video promotion, arguing that splashy, high-tech videos emphasize style over substance and that videos have increased the special effects on concert tours. This, they contend, downplays the music in favor of visuals.

Sources: Robert M. Ogles, "Music Television (MTV)," in *The Cable Networks Handbook*, Robert Picard, ed. (Riverside, CA: Carpelan, 1993), pp. 137–142; John Lannert, "Latin Notes: MTV Acts Locally; NYC Fetes Salsa." *Billboard* (September 4, 1999), via Lexis-Nexis; and Geoff Boucher, "The Listeners Are Watching: After a Lull, Music Videos Are Bigger Than Ever to a Generation

That Insists on Seeing the Hits Before Buying Them," *The Los Angeles Times* (September 4, 1999): F1.

1. What does MTV stand for?

   Music Television

2. When did MTV start?

   1981

3. What age group was it aimed at?

   twelve- to thirty-five-year-olds

4. What were some earlier models of combining music and video?

   American Bandstand; documentaries about musicians; *200 Motels*; promotional music videos

5. Where outside the United States does MTV now broadcast music?

   Australia, Europe, Asia, Latin America

6. Is MTV the only music channel?

   No, there are dozens around the world.

7. What helped MTV's ratings when they began to fall?

   nonmusic programs like *Real World*

8. Which show has most influence over recording sales?

   Total Request Live

9. Does MTV show exactly the same programs around the world?

   No, there is flexibility to follow local music trends.

10. Where did the authors of this piece get their information?

    from a book chapter by Robert Ogles, an article in *Billboard* magazine, and an article from the *Los Angeles Times*

Critical Thinking and Writing

What do you think about the values, culture, and ideas spread by MTV? Write a few paragraphs describing and evaluating MTV's message and whether it has any effect on youth in America and around the world.

10.3 Finding Facts

Read the following selection about the famous doctor Jonas Salk. Then, on a separate sheet of paper, write five questions about the facts in the selection and answer each. Student responses will vary.

One good way to assess the great figures of medicine is by how completely they make us forget what we owe them. By that measure, Dr. Jonas E. Salk ranks very high. Partly because of the vaccine he introduced in the mid-1950s, it's hard now to recall the sheer terror that was once connected to the word *polio*. The incidence of the disease had risen sharply in the early part of this century, and every year brought the threat of another outbreak. Parents were haunted by the stories of children stricken suddenly by the telltale cramps and fever. Public swimming pools were deserted for fear of contagion. And year after year polio delivered thousands of people into hospitals and wheelchairs, or into the nightmarish canisters called iron lungs. Or into the grave. In the worst year of the epidemic, 1952, when nearly 58,000 cases were reported in the United States, more than 3,000 people died.

All of that is hard to remember because, by the time of Salk's death last week, of heart failure at the age of eighty, polio was virtually gone from the United States and nearing extinction throughout the world. The beginning of the end for the virus can be dated precisely. On April 12, 1955, a Salk colleague announced that a vaccine developed by Salk and tested on more than one million schoolchildren had proved "safe, effective and potent." As a result of the nationwide effort of mass inoculation that followed, new cases in the United States dropped to fewer than 1,000 by 1962.

That triumph made Salk one of the most celebrated men of the 1950s. Streets and schools were named for him; in polls, he ranked with Gandhi and Churchill as a hero of modern history. Though his fame was expertly fostered by the public-relations machinery of the National Foundation for Infantile Paralysis and its March of Dimes campaign, which helped finance Salk's work, national adulation was still an unexpected fate for a dedicated scientist in an unglamorous field.

—*Richard Lacayo*

10b Sorting Out Major and Minor Details

As you find details and see how they are organized, you may find that your reading tells you much more than you thought—too much, in fact, to remember. When the information in your reading seems too detailed, it is time to sort out the most important details from the less important ones.

What makes a detail important? In general, a detail is important when it relates to the main idea of the reading. The detail may directly support or help explain that main idea. A *major*, or important, detail helps your basic understanding of the selection. A *minor*, or less important, detail simply helps fill out a picture already drawn. You can overlook a minor detail and still understand the reading. Minor details often help hold our attention and make the reading interesting, but we do not need to give them the attention we give to major details.

For example, in the selection about Jean Paul Getty on pages 202–203, the fact that Getty once said "a billion dollars isn't worth what it used to be" is minor. The quotation helps make the story more interesting and makes Getty's wealth seem more impressive, but his wealth is clear from a major detail at the end—that at his death his fortune was between $2 billion and $4 billion.

As you read the following paragraph from a business textbook, think about which details are more important than others for understanding the passage.

Government also protects business firms in another way. Business has special techniques, inventions, and innovations that it may wish to protect. For instance, a business may invent a machine or a process that it wants to protect. Entrepreneurs sometimes get their start in a business by inventing something. A business that develops a new manufacturing technique would like to decide who can use that technique. The United States Patent Office will grant a *patent*, a legal "right" that prevents anyone else from making the same thing for seventeen years. Sometimes a business will decide to sell its patent to other businesses if the patent is particularly valuable. Other businesses are willing to pay for the use of the patented item or idea because they need it. They cannot just steal the idea without violating the law.

Betty J. Brown and John E. Clow

As you read the paragraph, you may have noticed the following important details:

- Government protects business firms.
- Businesses may want to protect techniques, inventions, and innovations.
- A patent is a legal right that prevents anyone else from making the same thing for seventeen years.

If you understand these major details, you understand the main message of the paragraph. The other details are less important; they only help develop the major details. You can see how the minor details (the lettered items) support the major details in the following outline:

I. Government protects business firms.
II. Businesses may want to protect techniques, inventions, and innovations.
   a. A business may invent a machine or process it wants to protect.
   b. Entrepreneurs sometimes start in business by inventing something.
   c. A business would like to decide who can use its technique.
III. A patent is a legal right that prevents anyone else from making the same thing for seventeen years.
   a. The U.S. Patent Office grants patents.
   b. Sometimes a business sells its patent.
   c. Other businesses are willing to pay for the patented item or idea if they need it.
   d. Stealing the idea violates the law.

Here is how one student used underlining to separate the major details from the minor details in a textbook passage about the kinds of mental health disorders found in Americans. Before reading the passage, look at the information about separating major details and minor details in the box on page 211.

Perhaps the most thorough and comprehensive study ever conducted on the incidence of mental disorders in the U.S. adult population indicates that almost <u>one adult in five</u> (29.4 million) <u>suffers from a mental disorder (*Archives of Gen-*</u>

— **Main idea:** ***National Institute of Mental Health study shows one adult in five has a mental disorder.***

eral Psychiatry, October 1984). The study, sponsored by the National Institute of Mental Health, is still in progress and will eventually include about 20,000 subjects. Some of the preliminary results are fascinating. For example, researchers found that men and women are equally likely to suffer from mental disorders, but that they differ in the kinds of disorders they experience: Women are more likely to suffer anxieties, depression, and phobias. Men are more likely to exhibit substance abuse and antisocial personality.

With regard to incidence, anxiety disorders are the most common (8.3 percent or 13.1 million Americans), followed by drug, and alcohol abuse (6.4 percent or 10 million Americans). Schizophrenia, often one of the most severe mental disturbances, afflicts 1 percent of the population, or about 1.4 million Americans.

In the National Institute study, an individual who is not in need of professional help is considered not to be afflicted by a mental disorder.

Separating Major Details and Minor Details

- State the main idea in your own words.
- Look for the information that directly supports that main idea.
- Look for signal words that emphasize information, such as *most important, the facts are, in support, finally, in fact, certainly,* and *necessarily*. Look for signal words that suggest minor details, such as *incidentally, less important, as an aside*, and *a minor point*.
- Underline the major details as you locate them.
- Look for punctuation such as parentheses or brackets, which often signal minor details.

By determining the main idea and writing it down, the student can spot the details that help explain the main idea. The main idea here is that according to an important National Institute of Mental Health study, one of five adults suffers from a mental disorder. The most important details, then, are those that show the results of the study. Men and women suffer equally, but from different disorders. The kinds of disorders are important, as is the incidence, or frequency, of the disorders.

The student passes over other things that are not as important, the details that are interesting but not essential to understanding the main idea. You can understand the piece without knowing the name of the journal that reported the study, *Archives of General Psychiatry*, or the date it was published. Notice that those details appear in parentheses. Other minor details reinforce or explain statements already made. The references to numbers of people are minor because they only reinforce the percentage given in the sentences. The information about the severity of schizophrenia is minor here too. The point being made is that compared with other mental illnesses, schizophrenia afflicts only 1 percent of the population.

Keep in mind that not all details are equal in importance. Remember not to let minor details throw you off the track of the main idea. When you think about what you read, don't make a minor detail more important than it is.

EXERCISES

10.4 Major Details

Read the following paragraph about the invention of the potato chip. Then answer each question.

> Potato chips were originally called *Saratoga chips* after the site of their discovery. In the late nineteenth century a Native American named George Crumb worked as chef for Moon's Lake House in Saratoga Springs, New York, where a fashionable crowd convened to take the waters of the spa. A persnickety guest reportedly disliked the cut of his French fries one night, and kept sending the oversized potato strips back to the kitchen for a more refined look. Crumb, finally exasperated by the guest's unreasonable persistence, decided to cut the potatoes just as skinny as he could. He boiled the slices in fat and presented them to the complaining diner, who was delighted and didn't think twice about the indecorous crunching and lip smacking and greasy fingers that accompanied their consumption. From this elegant dining room, the new and scarcely

wholesome potatoes traveled throughout the nation, becoming one of the largest-selling snack foods in America.

—*Caroline Sutton*

__a__ 1. What is the main idea of the paragraph?
   a. Potato chips were invented to satisfy a restaurant guest who liked his French fries thin.
   b. Potato chips have become the largest-selling snack food in the United States.
   c. Potato chips are made by cutting potatoes as thin as possible and then boiling them in oil.
   d. Potato chips should really be called *Saratoga chips*.

2. Place a check mark next to each major detail from the paragraph. (There are two.)

____ a. The story took place in Moon's Lake House.

____ b. Saratoga Springs has a spa.

__✓__ c. A guest sent his oversized potatoes back to the kitchen.

____ d. The chips made the customer's fingers greasy.

__✓__ e. The customer found the chips delicious.

3. Place a check mark next to each minor detail from the paragraph. (There are two.)

____ a. The chef cut the potatoes as skinny as he could.

__✓__ b. The chef was exasperated.

____ c. The chef boiled the potato slices in fat.

__✓__ d. The customers were visiting a spa.

10.5 Major Details and Minor Details in a Textbook Selection

Read this selection from an economics textbook describing how people react to standing in lines and how businesses try to decrease the time people have to spend in lines. Then answer the questions that follow.

The Opportunity Cost of Waiting

Standing in line has never been a popular activity, but today it seems that Americans are likely to be more impatient about waiting in line than they have been in twenty years. According to a recent Louis Harris survey, Americans' leisure time has shrunk by 37 percent in the last two decades. With leisure time more valuable, the opportunity cost of waiting in lines is much higher.

Businesses recognize that people choose their products on the basis of the full opportunity cost, not just the price of the good or service. By keeping customers waiting, businesses may be losing customers. They are finding that people will choose one establishment over another because of shorter lines. As a result, businesses are focusing their marketing efforts on what marketers call time utility—providing products and services in ways that do not consume valuable time or providing values to offset the time losses. When the multipleline approach is used in banks and stores, people get frustrated because they often find themselves in the slowest line. Single lines do not move any quicker, but they reduce the variance of the wait and thus reduce frustrations. Customers can line up behind the teller or clerk of their choice, or in one line that allows the first person in line to go to the next available server—called a single-server line. As a result, most types of businesses in which several service people handle customers have switched to the single-server line.

Firms have tried several other approaches to dealing with lines. Chemical Bank began a program where any customer who had to wait in a teller line for more than seven minutes was given $5. Hospital emergency rooms in Los Gatos, California, now offer a "No waiting" guarantee: If you wait longer than five minutes for emergency-room care, the billing department knocks 25 percent off your bill. The Manhattan Savings Bank offers live entertainment during noontime banking hours. Some hotels and office buildings have mirrors on their elevator doors in an attempt to distract people while waiting.

Sometimes just telling people how long they have to wait cheers them up. Disneyland has had to learn to comfort those in line, since a popular attraction like Star Tours can attract as many as 1,800 people in a line. Like many amusement parks, Disneyland provides entertainment for those standing in line, but it also gives people updates, in the form of signs, noting "from this point on the wait is 30 minutes." Distractions such as these help people forget how they could be spending their time if they weren't waiting in line.

—*William Boyes and Michael Melvin*

b 1. What is the main idea of the selection?

a. People are more impatient than they used to be because they have less leisure time.

b. Businesses try to attract customers by decreasing waiting time.
c. Time can be considered part of the opportunity cost of a product or service.
d. Banks, stores, and other businesses have introduced single-server lines and entertainment for customers waiting in line.

a 2. What is the main idea of the first paragraph? Choose from the choices for question 1.

3. What is the main idea of the last paragraph, using your own words?

Disneyland provides entertainment for people in line and tells them how long the wait will be.

4. Which paragraph states the main idea of the selection most directly?

the second paragraph.

5. Copy the part of the sentence from that paragraph that states the main idea of the selection most fully.

Businesses are focusing their marketing efforts on what marketers call time utility.

6. In the selection, are the following details major or minor? Write *major* or *minor* in the space following each detail.

a. Americans' leisure time has shrunk 37 percent in the last two decades.

major

b. Louis Harris conducted the survey.

minor

c. People judge a product on its full opportunity cost, including time.

major

d. Marketers call saving consumers' time *time utility*.

minor

e. Single-server lines reduce customers' frustrations.

major

f. At Chemical Bank, customers who had to wait more than seven minutes were given $5.

minor

g. Some hospital emergency rooms offer a "no-waiting guarantee."

major

h. The hospital emergency rooms are in Los Gatos, California.

minor

i. Eighteen hundred people may be standing in line for the Star Tours attraction at Disneyland.

minor

j. Disneyland informs people how long they have to wait in line and offers them entertainment while they wait.

major

Critical Thinking and Writing

We all value time but react differently to it. Do you ever refuse to do things because they take too much time? Have you ever decided not to purchase something because it would take too long for it to arrive? Have you ever left a line because it was too long? Have you ever paid more for an item to save yourself time? Write a few paragraphs describing how valuable time is to you compared to money or other valuable things. Be sure to give specific examples.

10.6 Major Details

Read this business textbook selection about advertising. Then answer the questions that follow.

Ethical Challenges
Sex in Advertising—Has It Gone Too Far?

For years, advertising flirted with sexual innuendoes but avoided being sexually explicit. Then, in a Calvin Klein jeans ad, actress Brooke Shields asked the question, "Want to know what comes between me and my Calvins?" The answer, "Nothing," raised eyebrows, sold jeans, and paved the way for a new generation of sexually provocative advertising.

Ever since a beautiful woman first posed on the hood of a new model automobile, or a handsome man first rode his horse over a mountain and lit up a cigarette, advertisers have been satisfied that sex sells products. From coffee to clothing, advertising contains sexual innuendo. A series of Bugle Boy ads currently running on MTV shows more women dressed in bikinis and tight skirts than men wearing Bugle Boy jeans. In Maidenform underwear ads, women squirm and stuff their way into constricting underwear fashions from the past. Beer marketers are notorious for relying on sexy men and women to sell their product. When the "Swedish Bikini Team," a group of shapely blondes in skimpy bathing suits, joins a group of men drinking Old Milwaukee Beer, the implication is clear—drinking this brand of beer attracts beautiful women. Although these ads range from humorous and inoffensive to obviously sexist, others cross the line into what many call crass, soft-core pornography. The epitome of advertising that provokes an uproar was Calvin Klein's explicit ad insert in *Vanity Fair* magazine. On 116 textless—and many say tasteless—pages of advertising that would make anyone's grandmother blush, readers saw naked bodies, tattoos, and motorcycles, but not many jeans.

For Calvin Klein's marketers, shocking and outraging some people is permissible if it means selling more jeans. Other advertising executives, however, ask themselves if it is ethical to offend for the sake of profit. To get expert advice and increase awareness, agencies are hiring consultants and holding seminars on sex in advertising. As a result, many sexist, exploitative, or degrading ads are disappearing. There are those, however, who argue that if the public really objected to this type of ad, the products they promote wouldn't sell. In addition, they insist, it's the role of advertisers to market products, not to serve as America's social conscience.

Issues to Consider

1. Is it ethical to use sex in advertising to attract attention when sex is not related to the product, such as in an

advertisement for industrial equipment or life insurance? Explain. What about for products related to sex, such as perfume or jeans?

2. From an ethical standpoint, what factors influence how sexually explicit an advertisement should be?

—William Pride, Robert Hughes, and Jack Kapoor

1. Write in your own words the main idea of the entire selection.

   It is a serious ethical issue whether advertising now relies too heavily on sex.

2. According to the first paragraph, what is the main change that took place?

   Flirtation with sexual innuendo turned to explicit sexual provocation.

3. What is the main event that marked the change?

   a jeans ad that was sexually explicit

4. What are some of the minor details of that event?

   The ad was for Calvin Klein. It featured Brooke Shields. She talked about what was under her jeans.

5. What is the main idea of the second paragraph?

   Ads have always used sex.

6. What are some of the major details that support that idea?

   Sex has sold automobiles, cigarettes, coffee, clothes, and beer.

7. What is the main idea in the third paragraph?

   Some advertisers think anything that sells is permissible, but others are drawing limits.

8. For each side of the controversy, what are the two major details?

Proponents say they need the sex to sell products. They also say their job is to sell. Opponents ask ethical questions and hire consultants. Many sexist, exploitative ads are disappearing.

9. Which paragraph has the most minor details?

the second

Critical Thinking and Writing

Write a few paragraphs giving your thoughts about the questions raised in the "Issues to Consider" section of the selection.

10c Noting Sequence

Writers put all of a paragraph's ideas and information in an order, or a sequence. Readers then can see how the details fit together in an overall pattern. The more you notice the pattern a writer uses, the better you can understand and remember the information.

The most widely used patterns are time order, place order, and order of importance. Once you can recognize these patterns, you can see how different paragraphs are organized.

Writers, however, do not always follow these simple patterns. Sometimes they combine patterns. In those cases, you often can notice the patterns with which you are familiar as part of the combined pattern. When writers use more complex patterns, they also often give the readers clues about the patterns.

If you pay attention to paragraph patterns, you should be able to see what the pattern is. Unless you are reading a mystery story, the writer is not trying to confuse you. Although fitting the parts of a paragraph together may be something of a puzzle, the writer wants to make that puzzle easy to solve, so you get the right picture.

10c(1) *Time Order*

Some paragraphs put the details of an event in the same order they happened. In this way, it is easy for you to see how one detail follows another. Time order is very useful for telling stories, explaining how something happens, or describing how to do or make something. Time order is sometimes called *chronology*.

Time Order Clue Words

- Time Words—*now, then, before, after soon, next, one day, in a few days, meanwhile, first, second, third, suddenly, finally*—help you know that time order is being used and how events follow one another.

Notice how the following story about the beginnings of coffee uses time order. Pay attention to the clue words.

According to Arab legend, a lone shepherd named Kaldi was roaming the hills with his herd of goats sometime around A.D. 850. One day he found his usually quiet herd behaving very strangely: old and young alike frolicked and danced, scampered up and down the rocky slopes bleating excitedly. The bewildered shepherd then hid and watched them nibbling the berries of shrubs scattered over the hillside. Soon he was overcome with curiosity and sampled the fruit. The effects were similar. He joined the dancing goats. An *imam* [holy man] passing by noticed Kaldi, and soon he too ate the berries and joined the party.

The *imam* returned to his monastery with the powerful shrub, but neither he nor the monks could identify it. They next sought advice from Mohammed. As the prayers dragged on, the *imam* dozed, and Mohammed appeared to him advising him to boil the berries of his plant in water and drink it—this, Mohammed said, would keep him awake enough to pray! The monks immediately followed this command and called the new drink *qahwah*, which means both "life-giving" and "wine." Their monastery soon became famous for its long and lively prayer meetings.

adapted from *How Did They Do That?* by Caroline Sutton

10c(2) *Place Order*

Some paragraphs describe details in the order you would see them within a room, a building, or an outdoor setting. Place order descriptions follow a regular pattern of direction in going from one place to another. The pattern may be from left to right or up to down. It may be near to far, east to west, or turning around in a circle.

When you read place order descriptions, it often helps to think of yourself as standing in one place and turning your head to see the different parts or walking from one part to the next in a regular way. Descriptions of places, settings, buildings, and groups of people usually follow place order.

Place Order Clue Words

- Location words—*near, far, in front, behind, above, below, under, over, beneath, next to, alongside, left, right, inside, outside*— help you know when place order is being used and how the description is moving through space.

The following description of sights in southern Arizona uses the order of places you see as you go along the road.

> When you travel south from Tucson to the Mexican border town of Nogales you will see many reminders of the old West. Just outside Tucson you will find Old Tucson, built by Columbia Pictures in 1939. It is now open daily as a combination Western theme park and movie/TV studio. Nearby is the Arizona–Sonora Desert Museum, displaying the plants and wildlife of Arizona and northern Mexico. Traveling south you will come across an eighteenth-century Spanish mission. Called Mission San Xavier de Bac, it is still open for daily services. Farther south are the ruins of the Tumacon Mission.

10c(3) *Order of Importance*

Some paragraphs begin with details the writer considers least important and end with the most important. The importance of the details builds up as you go through this kind of paragraph. Order of importance often is used to present reasons in support of an idea and to describe several items or events one after another.

Order of Importance Clue Words

- Words that measure importance—*first, in the first place, to start, least important, next, more important, most important, major, greatest, most* ______*er,* ______*est*—help you know if order of importance is being used.

The following discussion of cold starts with our ordinary ideas of cold weather and builds up to the very special kind of cold created by scientists. Only by going step by step can we come to see what serious cold really means. Notice how the word *coldest* three sentences from the end signals the most important part.

How cold is cold? It all depends on who's talking. To us ordinary mortals nothing in the world may be so cold as falling through the ice on a frozen lake, or huddling on a windswept mountain hoping to be rescued in dead of winter. Some may even think they are freezing to death when plunging under an ice-cold shower just out of a warm bed. Indeed, we all know what cold means. Arctic explorers would laugh at such timid ideas. Down in the Antarctic, where scientists of many nations spend pitch-dark months living on a sheet of ice two miles thick, the temperature spends most of its time at 50 or 60 degrees below zero, often with hundred-mile winds and raging blizzards. This is the cold that is cold, to them. Space people have still another standard. . . . The coldest place in which a person can live and survive is some 400 degrees *hotter* than space itself. . . . The coldest place on earth—colder even than space—is inside a machine called a cryostat. Here, scientists and engineers in thousands of laboratories and factories in many parts of the world regularly *make* cold that turns the South Pole's worst into a balmy summer day. They are inching toward such cold that there is no temperature at all—down a frozen valley that leads to Absolute Zero, 459.65 degrees below our zero of a brisk winter's day.

David O. Woodbury

EXERCISES

10.7 Sequence Clue Words

1. In the example of *time order* (page 220), circle the words that help you see that paragraph details are arranged in time order.
2. In the example of *place order* (page 221), circle the words that help you see that paragraph details are arranged in place order.
3. In the example of *order of importance* (page 222), circle the words that help you see that paragraph details are arranged in order of importance.

10.8 Sequence

Look at the following details from the example of time order (page 220). Arrange the details in their proper time order by putting 1 in front of the first thing that happened, 2 in front of the second thing that happened, and so on.

__7__ a. Mohammed advised the *imam* to drink the berries boiled in water.

__3__ b. Kaldi ate the berries and danced.

__8__ c. The drink was named *qahwah*.

__4__ d. An *imam* passed by Kaldi.

__1__ e. The goats were behaving strangely.

__6__ f. The *imam* dozed during prayers.

__2__ g. Kaldi saw the goats eating the berries.

__5__ h. The *imam* brought the shrub to his monastery.

10.9 Sequence

Reread the example of place order on page 221. Identify each place described in column A by writing the number of the correct answer from column B.

A

__4__ a. the start of the trip

__3__ b. the place farthest south on the trip

__6__ c. nearest to Tucson

__1__ d. the third stop on the trip

__2__ e. the mission more north than the other

__5__ f. the last stop before the Mexican border

B

1. Arizona–Sonora Desert Museum
2. Mission San Xavier de Bac
3. Nogales
4. Tucson
5. Tumacon Mission
6. Old Tucson

10.10 Sequence

The following examples of cold all come from the paragraph using order of importance on page 222. Using the numbers in front of each example, arrange them in order from least cold to most cold in the spaces below.

1. outer space
2. a frozen lake
3. inside a cryostat
4. the Antarctic (the south polar region)
5. a cold shower
6. Absolute Zero

least cold __5__ __2__ __4__ __1__ __3__ __6__ most cold

10.11 Sequence

Read the following paragraph from a geology textbook describing the rock formations left behind when an ice glacier melts. Then answer the questions below.

> All the rocky material dumped by a glacier after it melts is called *till*. Till is a mixed-up collection of many different sizes and shapes of pieces of rock. The rows and piles of till dumped at the edges of glaciers are called *moraines*. Till that was dumped along the sides of moving ice in a valley is called a *lateral moraine*. Lateral means on the side. A long row of till left where

the <u>front</u> of the glacier stood for a long time is called a *terminal moraine*. Terminal means at the end.

—*Joseph H. Jackson and Edward D. Evans*

1. In the paragraph, underline all the clue words that tell you what kind of order in which the details are placed.
2. Match each term in column A with its definition in column B.

	A	*B*
3	a. moraine	1. till from the front end of the glacier
4	b. till	2. till from the sides of the glacier
1	c. terminal moraine	3. till from the edge of the glacier
2	d. lateral moraine	4. rocky material left by a glacier

b 3. Which pattern most resembles the order of details followed in the paragraph?
   a. Bottom to middle to top
   b. Edge to sides to front
   c. Inside to edge to outside
   d. Past to present to future

10.12 Sequence

Read the following paragraph describing how different situations can cause stress. Then answer the questions below.

It is not just the big tragedies of life that cause stress. Happy events and small events can also increase your stress. Psychologists have, in fact, developed a scale to show how much stress can be caused by life situations. In this scale of a hundred points, Christmas rates at twelve points of stress and vacation rates at thirteen. And you thought holidays help you relax. <u>More</u> stress can be caused by achievements, such as starting or finishing school (twenty-three points), an outstanding personal victory (twenty-eight points), starting a new job (twenty-nine points), or switching careers (thirty-five points). Happy changes in personal relationships can be <u>even more</u> stressful, with gaining a new family member at thirty-nine points, pregnancy at forty, and marriage at fifty. The major tragedies, nonetheless, do cause the <u>most</u> stress, with personal injury at fifty-three, jail term at sixty-three, divorce at seventy-three, and death of a spouse at a hundred.

1. Underline the clue words in the paragraph that let you know how details are arranged. What kind of order do these clues suggest?

   order of importance

d 2. According to the paragraph, which kind of events cause the least stress?
   a. Happy changes in personal relationships
   b. Major tragedies
   c. Achievements
   d. Holidays

b 3. Which kind of events cause the most stress?
   a. Happy changes in personal relationships
   b. Major tragedies
   c. Achievements
   d. Holidays

b 4. What causes almost the same stress as pregnancy?
   a. Marriage
   b. Getting a new family member
   c. Divorce
   d. Finishing school

a 5. What causes almost the same stress as marriage?
   a. Personal injury
   b. Jail term
   c. Outstanding personal victory
   d. Changing careers

10.13 Sequence

Read the following paragraph from a travel pamphlet about Ohio. The passage describes the beauties of that state during the different seasons of the year. Then answer each question below.

> Ohio is the show that never ends. Each season, Ohio takes on a special beauty all its own. Spring is when Ohio's many gardens show off thousands of the earth's most beautiful creations. And sugar maples provide syrup just as they did for the Indians and settlers long ago. Ohio summers feature sunshine-filled skies. Build a sandcastle on any of Lake Erie's four islands or climb a sandstone cliff and picnic above it all. Ohio autumns are the time leaves flame with color. Follow the

colorful blaze of fall foliage aboard a 1910 steam engine as it chugs along the Cuyahoga River. Ohio winters often dress forests in white. Wake to a crisp, alpine morning and then cross-country ski across fresh snow. Ohio is a place for all seasons and all reasons.

1. What special activity can you enjoy in each season?

   Summer building sandcastles; climbing cliffs; picnicking

   Winter cross-country skiing

   Spring visiting gardens; tapping sugar maples

   Fall taking a train ride

2. What special feature does nature have in each season in Ohio?

   Summer sunshine-filled skies

   Winter white forests

   Spring beautiful gardens

   Fall colored foliage

3. Which season is described first? spring

   Next? summer

   Next? fall

   Finally? winter

10.14 Details

1. Of the three sample paragraphs in Exercises 10.11, 10.12, and 10.3, which paragraph places details in time order?

   the paragraph on Ohio (Exercise 10.13)

2. Which paragraph places details in place order?

   the paragraph on till (Exercise 10.11)

3. Which paragraph places details in order of importance?

   the paragraph on stress (Exercise 10.12)

10.15 Details Arranged Using Combined Methods

The sequences of details in the following three selections are arranged using a combination of methods. Read each selection and notice the sequence. Then describe the sequence in the blanks.

The first selection tells one woman's experience answering a 911 emergency line; the second reveals how Harry Houdini did his most famous trick; the last tells how naturalist John Muir decided to explore the Sierra Mountains in California.

1. It's a new day. I walk down to the basement of the public-safety building, pass through a secured entrance and walk slowly down a long, quiet corridor. My stomach tightens a bit as I approach a final locked door. It's starting all over again, and I'm a little anxious. I get some supplies from my locker. A headset, Rolodex file and "bible"—a notebook bursting with maps, charts, policy, and procedure updates that will help guide me through this day. I go down the wheelchair ramp, into the deepest, most secluded corner of the building. I'm in the Phoenix Police Communications Center, known as "911." A vitally important place, one filled with tremendous responsibility, sadness, frustration, and few rewards.

   It's a dim, noisy, and unassuming room. Four posters, one on each wall, seem out of place. They're scenic posters of beautiful places—the snow-covered mountains of Austria, an icy lake in Norway, a quaint fishing village in some faraway country. I suppose the posters are there to make us feel serene in the otherwise chaotic setting. There are four rows of small, unadorned and rather dingy cubicles, five in each row. I find one that's unoccupied and set up camp. I'm surrounded by a computer terminal, tape recorder, multiline phone console, cup of coffee, and a small photograph of my son. It's 0800 hours. I take a deep breath, say a little prayer, and hope that I don't make any mistakes that might get me on the six o'clock news. This will be my not-so-happy home for the next ten hours.

   "911, what is your emergency?" It's my first call of the day. The woman is crying but calm. She has tried to wake her elderly husband. With the push of a button I connect her to the fire department. They ask if she wants to attempt CPR, but she says, "No, he's cold and blue . . . I'm sure he's dead." I leave the sobbing widow in the hands of the fire dispatcher and disconnect from the call. I'm feeling sad, but I must move on. I have more incoming calls to take.

   It's busy this morning. The orange lights in each corner of the room are shining brightly, a constant reminder that nonemergency calls have been holding more than ninety seconds. My phone console appears to be glowing, covered with blinking red lights. It's almost hypnotic, like when you sit in the dark and stare at a lit Christmas tree, or gaze into a flickering fireplace. But then I remember that each light represents a person—person with a problem, someone in crisis.

A loud bell is ringing. It means an emergency call is trying to get through, but the lines are jammed. All operators are already on a call. I quickly put my caller on hold. He's just reporting a burglary that occurred over the weekend.

—*Tracy Lorenzano*

Time order and place order combine as she walks to her job and describes the place. As she begins to work, the events are of increasing seriousness and importance.

2. Harry Houdini's most famous escape was from a crate sunk in a river. He was handcuffed. The crate was nailed shut and tied in heavy ropes. Holes were drilled in it to make sure it sunk in the water. How did he do it? First and easiest, the handcuffs had a secret spring that opened them instantly. Next, Houdini had secretly taken a pair of nail cutters with him. As soon as his hands were free, he began cutting the nails. The moment the crate was under water, he pushed a few planks open, climbed out, and pushed the planks closed. After he and the crate were pulled out of the water, his assistants secretly removed the cut nails, and hammered in new nails. More important than the secret tricks were Houdini's skill and speed. He could work fast and control his breath for unusually long times. Most important, however, was his great courage. Even with the secret tricks and his great skill, the escape was dangerous. Many things could go wrong. Houndini had to keep a cool mind. Panic would have meant death.

In describing Houdini's method, the paragraph uses time order. It uses place order in following his "escape" from the crate. However, overall, the paragraph follows order of importance in describing his special tricks and skills.

3. In the great Central Valley of California there are only two seasons—spring and summer. The spring begins with the first rainstorm,

which usually falls in November. In a few months, the wonderful flowery vegetation is in full bloom, and, by the end of May, it is dead and dry and crisp, as if every plant has been roasted in an oven.

Then the lolling, panting flocks and herds are driven to the high, cool, green pastures of the Sierra. I was longing for the mountains about this time, but money was scarce and I couldn't see how a bread supply was to be kept up. While I was anxiously brooding on the bread problem, so troublesome to wanderers, and trying to believe that I might learn to live like the wild animals, gleaning nourishment here and there from seeds, berries, etc., sauntering and climbing in joyful independence of money or baggage, Mr. Delaney, a sheep-owner, for whom I had worked a few weeks, called on me, and offered to engage me to go with his shepherd and flock to the headwaters of the Merced and Tuolumne Rivers—the very region I had most in mind. I was in the mood to accept work of any kind that would take me into the mountains whose treasures I had tasted last summer in the Yosemite region. The flock, he explained, would be moved gradually higher through the successive forest belts as the snow melted, stopping for a few weeks at the best places we came to. These I thought would be good centers of observation from which I might be able to make many telling excursions within a radius of eight or ten miles of the camps to learn something of the plants, animals, and rocks; for he assured me that I should be left perfectly free to follow my studies. I judged, however, that I was in no way the right man for the place, and freely explained my shortcomings, confessing that I was wholly unacquainted with the topography of the upper mountains, the streams that would have to be crossed, and the wild sheep-eating animals, etc.; in short that, what with bears, coyotes, rivers, cañons, and thorny, bewildering chaparral, I feared that half or more of his flock would be lost. Fortunately, these shortcomings seemed insignificant to Mr. Delaney. The main thing, he said, was to have a man about the camp whom he could trust to see that the shepherd did his duty, and he assured me that the difficulties that seemed so formidable at a distance would vanish as we went on; encouraging me further by saying that the shepherd would do all the herding, that I could study plants and rocks and scenery as much as I liked, and that he would himself accompany us to the first main camp and make occasional visits to our higher ones to replenish our store of provisions and see how we prospered. Therefore, I concluded to go, though still fearing, when I saw the silly sheep bouncing one by one through the narrow gate of the home corral to be counted, that of the two thousand and fifty many would never return.

I was fortunate in getting a fine St. Bernard dog for a companion. His master, a hunter with whom I was slightly acquainted, came to me as soon as he heard that I was going to spend the summer in the Sierra and begged me to take his favorite dog, Carlo, with me, for he feared that if he were compelled to stay all summer on the plains the fierce heat might be the death of him. "I think I can trust you to be kind to him," he said, "and I am sure he will be good to you. He knows all about the mountain animals, will guard the camp, assist in managing the sheep, and in every way be found able and faithful." Carlo knew we were talking about him, watched our faces, and listened so attentively that I fancied he understood us. Calling him by name, I asked him if he was willing to go with me. He looked me in the face with eyes expressing wonderful intelligence, then turned to his master, and after permission was given by a wave of the hand toward me and a farewell patting caress, he quietly followed me as if he perfectly understood all that had been said and had known me always.

—*John Muir*

The opening paragraph sets an overall time order of the seasons to the selection. The second paragraph ties movement up into the hills with the changing seasons. In the second paragraph, the place order shifts between thinking about what happens in the high mountain pastures and preparations down below. The plans, told in time order, follow place order as well, as the herds start down in the valley and move higher. The time order of the preparation ends with the time order story of meeting the dog, Carlo, in the third paragraph.

CULTURAL Exchange

iron lung an airtight metal tank that encloses all of the body except the head; the tank forces the lungs to inhale and exhale through regulated changes in air pressure; used for people suffering from polio (page 208)

persnickety overparticular or extremely picky about trivial details; quality of a demanding individual who requires others to be attentive to details (page 212)

to raise eyebrows	to shock or surprise people mildly (so their eyebrows go up in surprise or disbelief) (page 217)
sexual innuendo	an indirect or subtle implication, either spoken or written, concerning anything sexual; usually derogatory (page 217)
sexist	describes an action or speech showing discrimination based on gender, especially discrimination against women; also refers to attitudes, conditions, or behaviors that promote stereotyping of women (page 217)
crass	stupid, insensitive, unfeeling (page 217)
soft-core pornography	material that depicts or describes sexual activity, often equating sex with power and violence; less explicit than hard-core material (page 217)
to doze	to sleep lightly and intermittently for short periods; to nap (page 220)
to huddle	to crowd together for protection, as from cold or fear (page 222)
Rolodex file	a circular device that holds small file cards, each one containing information about clients or friends (name, address, phone number, etc.). Cards may be added or removed at any time. (page 228)
911	an emergency phone number that directly contacts the police or medical personnel (page 228)
chaotic	confused, disordered, jumbled, or mixed up (page 228)
dingy	dirty; dark; faded; not bright (page 228)
cubicle	a very small, enclosed area of a larger room, whose walls usually do not reach the ceiling; many large companies have individual cubicles for their employees instead of walled offices (page 228)

to take a deep breath	to breathe air in deeply, especially for courage and patience when starting an unpleasant task or dealing with a difficult individual (page 228)
CPR	cardiopulmonary resuscitation, an emergency procedure in which cardiac massage, artificial respiration, and drugs are used to maintain the circulation of oxygenated blood to the brain (page 228)
the lines are jammed	the telephone lines are all busy; no one can get through (page 229)
to put someone on hold	to leave someone waiting on the telephone; to stop all activity or communication with someone; to postpone something (page 229)
plank	a piece of lumber; a wide, flat board used in building houses, boxes, etc. (page 229)
to loll	to move, stand, or recline in a lazy or relaxed manner (page 230)
to pant	to breathe rapidly in short gasps, as after exertion (page 230)
flock	a group of animals that live, travel, or feed together (page 230)
to brood	to be deep in thought; to focus one's attention on someone or something with deep concentration (page 230)
to glean	to collect or gather something bit by bit (page 230)
to saunter	to walk at a leisurely pace, in no particular hurry (page 230)
shortcoming	a deficiency; a flaw; a fault in character (page 230)
topography	the detailed, precise description of a place's land contours (e.g., the slope of hills, heights of cliffs) (page 230)

chaparral	the dense growth of mostly small-leaved evergreen shrubs and small trees, as that found in the foothills of California (page 230)
to replenish	to fill or make complete again; to add a new stock or supply (page 230)
store of provisions	a supply of food, drinking water, medicine, and the like used in camps or remote areas (page 230)
St. Bernard dog	an extremely large dog, bred in Switzerland and known for its ability to aid travelers in trouble (page 230)
GI	an ordinary soldier, usually associated with World War II; short for General Infantry (page 235)
mushroomed	grew rapidly (page 238)

Chapter 10 SELF-TEST
Reading for Information

Read the selection below about where Americans moved during the period just after World War II, from *A People and a Nation*, an American history textbook. Then answer the questions that follow. Count five points for each correct answer.

The Affluent Society, the Sunbelt, and the Suburbs

1 The Harvard economist John Kenneth Galbraith gave a name to the United States during the postwar economic boom: the "affluent society." As United States productivity increased in the postwar years, so did Americans' appetite for goods and services. During the depression and the Second World War, many Americans had dreamed of buying a home or a car. In the affluent postwar years they finally could satisfy those deferred desires. Some families bought two cars and equipped their new homes with the latest appliances and amusements. Easy credit was the economic basis of the consumer culture; when people lacked cash to buy what they wanted, they borrowed money. Consumer credit to support the nation's shopping spree grew from $5.7 billion in 1945 to $58 billion in 1961.

Growth of the Sunbelt

2 Millions of Americans began their search for affluence by migrating to the Sunbelt—roughly, the southern third of the United States, running from southern California across the Southwest and South all the way to the Atlantic coast. Among the Sunbelt's booming cities were Houston, Phoenix, Los Angeles, San Diego, Dallas, and Miami. The population of Houston, which became a center not only of the aerospace industry but also of oil and petrochemical production, jumped from 385,000 in 1940 to 1,243,000 in 1960. California absorbed no less than one-fifth of the nation's entire population increase in the 1950s—enough by 1963 to make it the most populous state in the Union (see map).

3 The mass migration to the Sunbelt had started during the war, when GIs and their families were ordered to new duty stations and war workers moved to defense plants in the West and South. The economic bases of the Sunbelt's spectacular growth were agribusiness, the aerospace industry, the oil industry, real-

estate development, recreation, and defense spending. Government policies—generous tax breaks for oil companies, siting of military bases, and awarding of defense and aerospace contracts—were crucial to the Sunbelt's development. Industry was also drawn to the southern rim by right-to-work laws; which outlawed closed shops, and by low taxes and low heating bills.

Growth of the Suburbs

4 Another mass movement in postwar America was from the cities to the suburbs. Almost as many Americans resided in the suburbs as in the cities by 1960 (see table). A combination of motives drew people to the suburbs. Some wanted to leave behind the noise and smells of the city. Some white families moved out of urban neighborhoods because African-American families were moving in. People living in row houses and apartments wanted to move into houses that had yards, family rooms, extra closets, and utility rooms. Many also were looking for a place where they could have a measure of political influence, particularly on the education their children received. Perhaps most important, for this generation of adults—who had suffered economic deprivation during the depression and separation from loved ones during the war—the home became a refuge, and family togetherness fulfilled a psychological need.

Geographic Distribution of the United States Population, 1930–1970 (in Percentages)

YEAR	CENTRAL CITIES	SUBURBS	RURAL AREAS AND SMALL TOWNS
1930	31.8	18.0	50.2
1940	31.6	19.5	48.9
1950	32.3	23.8	43.9
1960	32.6	30.7	36.7
1970	31.4	37.6	31.0

Source: Adapted from U.S. Bureau of the Census, *Decennial Censuses, 1930–1970* (Washington, D.C., U.S. Government Printing Office).

Housing Boom

5 Government funding helped new families to settle in the suburbs. Low-interest GI mortgages and Federal Housing Administration (FHA) mortgage insurance made the difference for people who otherwise would have been unable to afford a home. This easy credit, combined with postwar prosperity, produced a construction boom. From 1945 to 1946, housing starts

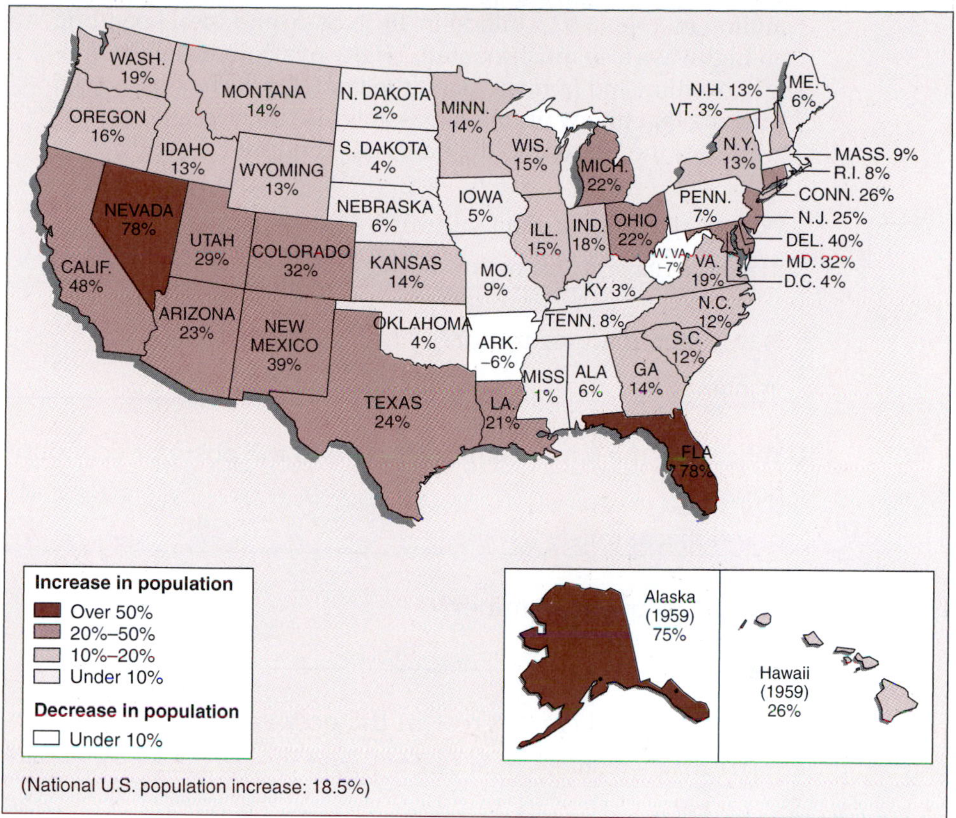

climbed from 326,000 to more than 1 million; they approached 2 million in 1950 and remained above 1.3 million in 1961. Never before had new starts exceeded 1 million.

6 To produce so much new housing so fast, contractors had to operate on a massive scale. Arthur Levitt and Sons developed a system, adopted by other companies, of using interchangeable materials and designs to build nearly identical houses on uniform, treeless lots. In 1947, the construction of Levittown, New York, began; Levittowns also arose in New Jersey and Pennsylvania. To supply the new communities, shopping malls soon dotted the countryside.

Highway Construction

7 As suburbia spread, pastures became neighborhoods with astounding rapidity. Highway construction was a central element in the transformation of rural land into suburbia. In 1947, Congress authorized construction of a 37,000-mile chain of highways, and, in 1956, President Eisenhower signed the Highway Act. Federal expenditures on highways swelled from $79

million in 1946 to $2.6 billion in 1961. State and local spending on highways also mushroomed. Highways both hastened suburbanization and homogenized the landscape. The high-speed trucking that highways made possible also accelerated the integration of the South into the national economy.

1. What is John Kenneth Galbraith's background?

   He was a Harvard economist.

2. Is this fact major or minor?

   minor

3. What was the name Galbraith gave to the postwar economic boom?

   the "affluent society"

4. Is this fact major or minor?

   major

5. How much did credit grow in the postwar period?

   more than ten times—from $5.7 billion in 1945 to $58 billion in 1961

6. Where were Americans most likely to migrate?

   to the Sunbelt

7. Name six Sunbelt cities.

   Houston, Phoenix, Los Angeles, San Diego, Dallas, and Miami

8. Which three states' population grew at the highest rate in the 1950s?

   Florida, Nevada, and Alaska

9. By what percentage did New Mexico's population grow in the 1950s?

   39 percent

10. In what year did California become the most populous state?

    1963

11. What six industries fueled the growth of the Sunbelt?

agribusiness, aerospace, oil, real-estate development, recreation, and defense

12. What three government policies supported the growth of the Sunbelt?

oil tax breaks, military base sitings, and defense and aerospace contracts

13. By what year did more people live in the suburbs than in the central cities?

1970

14. When was the last time most of the people lived in rural areas and small towns?

1930

15. What is the most important fact in paragraph 6?

House builders operated on a massive scale.

16. Which sentence in paragraph 6 contains the least important facts?

In 1947, the construction of Levittown, New York, began; Levittowns also arose in New Jersey and Pennsylvania.

17. How did Congress help the development of the suburbs?

Congress authorized construction of a national chain of highways.

18. How did highways help develop the economy of the South?

Highways made high-speed trucking possible.

19. In what order is the information in paragraph 4 presented?

time order

20. In what order is the information in paragraph 5 presented?

order of importance

Score: ______ correct × 5 points each = ______

CHAPTER ELEVEN

Using SQ3R

SQ3R is a technique or method that helps you understand what you read. It gives you a useful series of steps that can improve your comprehension. You may recognize parts of SQ3R because they were discussed under different names in earlier chapters, but SQ3R pulls together five steps into a whole system. You can use the system for your reading, especially in textbooks, newspapers, and magazines.

What is SQ3R? The letters stand for the following activities:

- *S*urvey
- *Q*uestion
- *R*ead
- *R*ecite
- *R*eview

11a Survey

When you survey, you preview. Do you remember previewing from Chapters 4 and 5? If not, look back for a quick review.

Survey means the same as *preview*. Its purpose is to give you information about what you are reading *before* you actually begin. When you survey, you do the following:

- Read the sentences that introduce the chapter.
- Read the main headings and the subheadings (look for **bold face** or *italic* print).
- Look at the illustrations and the photographs and read all the captions (sentences that explain the pictures).
- Read the checklists and the questions at the end of the selection.

- Read the introductory sentences at the beginning of the chapter.

In surveying, don't read all the material. Your purpose is *not* to read the complete piece. You want an overview. Take only a few minutes to survey.

EXERCISES

11.1 Take a Survey

Look at the English textbook selection "Giving a Talk" below. Survey it; do not read the whole piece. Then, on a separate sheet of paper, answer the following questions:

1. What do the two introductory paragraphs tell you?
2. What are the headings?
3. What questions or activities appear after the selection?

Giving a Talk

Giving a talk or a speech might bring butterflies to your stomach, make your knees knock and your palms moist, and give you a dry mouth. People who normally have no trouble talking often search for words when they are speaking in front of an audience.

How can you overcome your nervousness and be a good speaker? Remembering these five *P*'s should help—Prepare, Plan, and Practice, Practice, Practice.

Prepare

1. Choose a topic that is interesting to *you*.
2. Choose a topic that you can research if necessary.
3. If appropriate, add humorous or interesting details or personal stories that will keep your audience interested.

Plan

1. Be sure that you know exactly what you want to say. Make notes or an outline on note cards or slips of paper that you can look at during your talk. Write only key words on your

cards that will help you recall your main points and details. You do not want to read your speech.
2. If you are using illustrations or pictures, be sure they are large enough for your audience to see.
3. Ask your family or friends to set aside some time for you to practice your talk in front of them.

Practice

1. Find a quiet place to practice your talk out loud.
2. Read over your notes until you have them almost memorized. Then practice your talk by just glancing at your note cards occasionally. Find the key word, and look up again as you continue with your talk.
3. Practice in front of a mirror so you can see how you look. Your hands are busy with your note cards, but how are you standing? Are you rocking back and forth? Are you pacing like a caged lion? Try standing with your feet slightly apart so that you are comfortable. If you feel yourself getting tense, take a deep breath, and relax.
4. Listen to yourself as you practice out loud. Are you talking loudly enough without shouting? Are you stressing your main points and details? Let your voice show your feelings. Look at one or two spots while you practice. When you give your talk, replace these spots with actual people.
5. Practice in front of your family and friends. Time yourself. If you are over or under your time limit, speed up or slow down or change the length of your talk. Practice using your illustrations. Ask for comments when you finish.

If you follow the five *P*'s, you will feel confident in front of your audience. You will know that your talk is interesting and that your presentation is strong. Try to enjoy yourself.

Activity

Write notes or a short outline for a five-minute talk on one of the following topics, or choose one of your own.

a strange pet I would like to own
my favorite activity
somewhere I would like to visit

—John Stewig and Shirley Haley-James

11b Question

In the SQ3R process, the Q for *question* means that you actually produce your own questions. You identified the main headings and the subheadings when you surveyed. Now look again at the headings (usually in boldface or italic print). Turn each heading into a question and write the question on a sheet of paper.

To construct your question, you might want to use one of the following word groups:

- Why is (are)?
- How do (did)?
- When did?
- Why did?
- What is (are)?
- What does (do)?

For example, look at the headings taken from a chapter called "Six to Twelve: Relationships with Others" in a college psychology text, which appear in the left column. Then look in the right column for some sample questions prepared from the headings.

Headings	*Questions Made from the Headings*
1. Relationships with Parents	What are a child's relationships with his or her parents?
2. Reactions to Child-Rearing Styles	What are some reactions to child-rearing styles? How do children react to the different styles that parents use in bringing up their children?
3. The Impact of Divorce	What is the impact of divorce on a child?
4. The Impact of Maternal Employment	What is the impact of maternal employment? How does a mother's working affect a child?

EXERCISE

11.2 Develop Questions

Look at the selection titled "Giving a Talk" on pages 241–242. On a separate sheet of paper, write your own questions using the title and the three headings. (Do not write a question for the heading "Activity.") Student responses will vary.

11c Read

The first R, *read*, means that now you read the selection from one heading to the next heading and stop before going on. While you read, try to find the answer to the question you've made up from the heading—from the Q step in SQ3R.

Reading in this way gives you a purpose. It keeps you focused on segments (short pieces) of the text. You do not read the whole selection at once.

When you read the sentences from one heading to the next, stop before you continue. Your purpose is to read in order to answer the questions you wrote. After you answer each question, continue reading to the next heading. Repeat the process through the end of the selection.

11d Recite

The second R, *recite*, means that after you've read from one heading to the next, you stop reading and try to answer the questions you created.

When you first start using SQ3R, recite your answers out loud. As you gain more experience, say the answers to yourself. The key here is to do the following:

- Look at the questions you made up from the heading.
- Read only from one heading to the next.
- Stop before going on.
- Recite the answers to the questions.

After you answer the questions, read down to the next heading. If you can't come up with an answer, read the sentences under the heading again.

EXERCISES

11.3 Read and Recite

Look again at the selection titled "Giving a Talk" on pages 241–242. Follow the instructions below carefully.

1. Read the question you wrote from the title "Giving a Talk" (see question 1 on page 243).
2. Now read the two paragraphs beneath the title and try to find out the answer to your question. After you complete that step, *come back to read step 3 below before going on!*
3. After you read to look for an answer, recite your answer aloud. If you can't answer your question, read the section again.

11.4 Read and Recite

In the same selection, consider only the sentences from the heading "Prepare" to the heading "Plan." Follow the instructions on page 244 carefully.

1. Read the question that you wrote for the heading.
2. Now read the sentences beneath the heading to find out the answer to your question. Come back to read step 3 below before going on.
3. After you read to look for an answer, recite your answer out loud. If you can't answer your question, read the sentences again.

11.5 Read and Recite

Continue reading the selection "Giving a Talk."

1. Read from the heading "Plan" to the heading "Practice." Follow steps 1, 2, and 3 in Exercise 2 exactly.
2. Read from the heading "Practice" to the heading "Activity." Follow steps 1, 2, and 3 in Exercise 2 exactly.

11e Review

After you read the whole selection, *review* your reading. *Review* means "look again." What is the best way to look again at what you've done? Simply go back and read your questions another time. Try to answer the questions.

This time, however, do not read the material under each heading. Now you're trying to remember what you read by thinking about each question and giving an answer. If you can't answer a particular question, reread only the material under the heading that will answer your question.

EXERCISE

11.6 A Review of Your Reading

Return to the selection "Giving a Talk" on pages 241–242. Look first at all the questions that you wrote from the headings. Try to recall what you read and answer your own questions. Write the answers on a separate sheet of paper. Student responses will vary.

11.7 Review of SQ3R

Look at the selection titled "Being an Employee." Use SQ3R on your own to read the selection. Follow all the steps explained in **11a, 11b, 11c, 11d,** and **11e**.

Write down the questions you make up for the headings and the answers to those questions on a separate sheet of paper. Student responses will vary.

Being an Employee

When you get that job, you'll have cause for celebration! The looking, writing, and interviewing will be over. You'll know that all your hard work has paid off. Getting a job is a good feeling. It makes up for all the rejection you suffered each time you weren't selected. The anxiety and the tension are released, and you can relax and begin to think about the next step.

Now you can concentrate on doing your best while on your job and gaining experience you can use to boost your career. You want your employment to be successful, and you want to be ready for the next job up on your career ladder.

Survival Techniques

Performing well on a job requires some effort. Just as you developed some skills for the job search, you must develop some skills for good job performance.

Here are some things to do to make your employment a successful one:

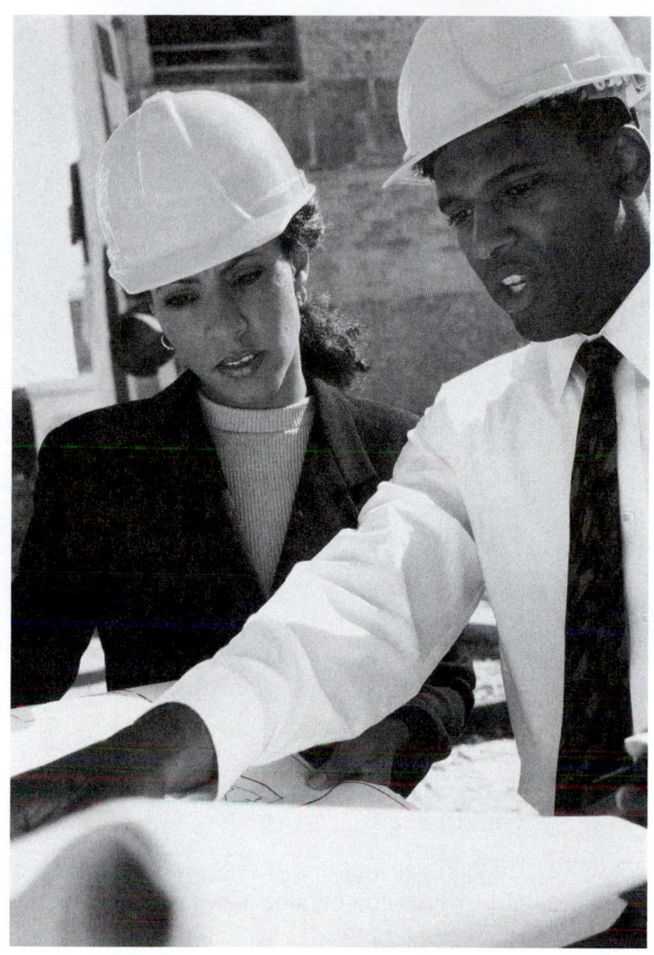

1. *Allow yourself an adjustment period.* Everyone suffers from butterflies in the stomach during the first few days. There are so many new things. It can be very difficult to enter a new environment. Things are not familiar. In addition to learning your new job, you will have to make new transportation arrangements; you will have to learn everybody's name; you will have to make new relationships; you will have to learn company policy; you will have to find out where the restroom is and where to go for lunch.

   You may also suffer from **reality shock** or the realization that what you expected and what you found are not the same. That 25-mile commute didn't seem so bad when you agreed to take this job, but a couple of weeks later the reality of just how far away you do have to travel will set in.

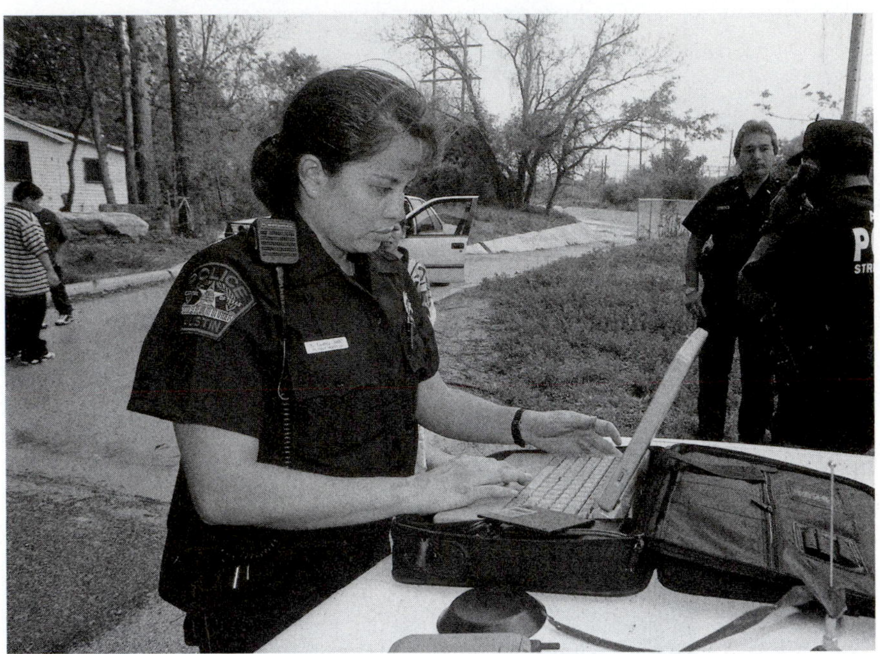

Allow yourself time to adjust to your new job.

Or maybe the work isn't as interesting as you thought it would be.

2. *Conduct yourself in a professional manner.* Nothing makes a bad impression on a boss more than an employee who acts unprofessionally.

   - Be on time.
   - Try never to be absent.
   - Dress appropriately.
   - Refrain from arguing, complaining, criticizing, and gossiping.
   - Have a pleasant attitude. Smile.
   - Put forth your best effort.
   - Be **self-motivated**. Don't rely on others to persuade you.
   - Show some **initiative**. Don't wait to be told every little thing to do.

3. *Have the right work attitude.* A good **work attitude** includes a favorable outlook, or point of view, about the job and about the working conditions. It means being willing to give an honest day's work. It means being as concerned with giving as you are with getting. The rewards for doing

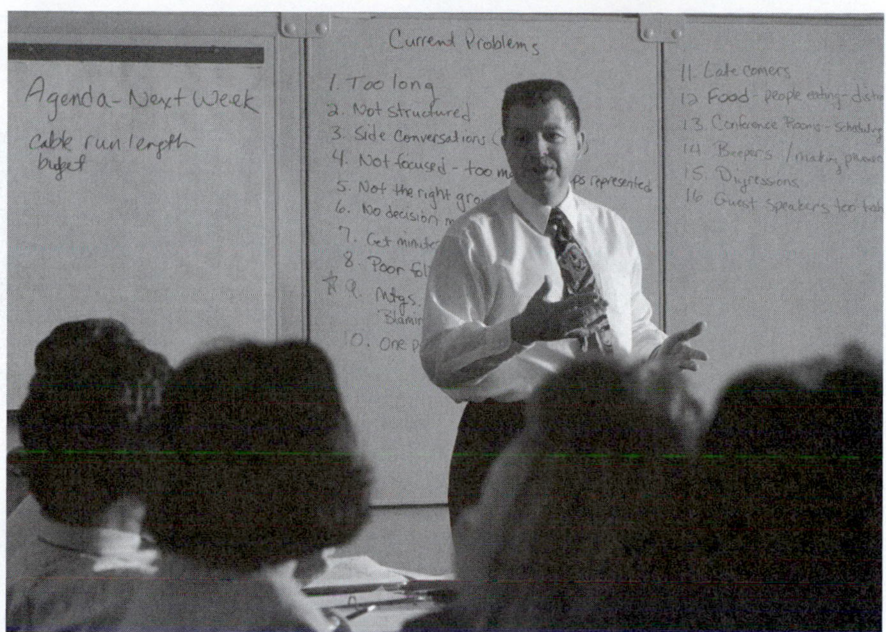

Remember to exercise competence and professionalism in the workplace.

a job well go beyond your paycheck. They come from the recognition you receive from those who have observed your ability to perform well.

4. *Show competence*. You were hired because either you already knew how to do the job or the boss thought you were capable of learning it. The boss wants someone who can carry out all the responsibilities of the job. He or she wants someone who is **competent**.

   - Always put forth your best effort.
   - Proofread any written work before turning it in.
   - Take notes of names, dates, procedures, or small details you may be apt not to remember.
   - Use good communication skills by
     —being polite on the telephone.
     —reading directions carefully.
     —using correct spelling, grammar, and punctuation.
     —pronouncing words correctly.
     —listening attentively.

5. *Practice good human relations*. Good human relations, or the ability to get along with others, are necessary in virtually every aspect of your job. You must interact with your boss,

Most jobs require interaction with other employees.

your peers, your subordinates, your customers, and visitors such as vendors of delivery people. Even the person who works alone cannot escape all human contact.

A company wants an employee who can get along with others. Employees who are difficult to get along with are uncomfortable to work with. They are poor goodwill ambassadors because they turn customers off. And these customers tell other customers of their unhappy experiences with the business.

6. *Keep yourself up to date*. It is important that you be on the lookout for ways to improve your skills and to keep them updated. Your willingness to learn emphasizes the fact that you are motivated and genuinely interested in working there. Check for training programs, conferences, workshops, seminars, and courses that are available to employees. Some of these may be paid for by the company. Read the magazines and journals of your chosen occupation. Join your professional association and attend the meetings. The professional association is an excellent source of information about what's going on in your line of work. (It's also a

good place to find out about job openings when you're ready to make your next move.)

7. *Be aware of the politicking*. Some people are not motivated by the belief that all work is honorable and that personal satisfaction comes from within. These employees act primarily on the basis of responding to who has influence and who hasn't, or who can help them and who can't. This behavior is called **politicking**. It is difficult to avoid coworkers who operate in this manner, but it is important that you are aware of their existence.

   This conversation between coworkers Joe and Marge illustrates politicking:

   Marge: You're new on the job, so I'm going to do you a favor and tell you what the politics are like around here.

   Joe: What do you mean "politics"?

   Marge: You know, office politics—whom you need to impress, who's in line for promotion, who's out to get someone else's job, who's polishing the apple, who's deadwood. . . .

   Joe: Sounds like office gossip to me.

   Marge: Well, it may sound that way to a newcomer, but to others it's a way of life on the job. They play up to the important people.

   Joe: But all I want to do is the best possible job. Isn't that enough?

   Marge: Of course, job performance is the key, but you just need to be aware of the environment you are entering—not to get involved, necessarily, but to know whom and what to avoid so that you can do your best. Remember, this company is made up of all sorts of people with all sorts of goals. How they achieve them is where the politics come in, (Pause) You puzzled?

   Joe: Yeah.

   Marge: Well, for example, Harry, who is very competent, takes criticism only a certain way. He's rather sensitive. You have to go easy. Frances is a bright, assertive young woman. She is a mover and shaker. The boss likes young self-starters like you.

So Frances is your chief competition. And Fred over there is insecure about his job. He is very afraid of young, bright talent like you. So just remember that his fear and envy could be your worst enemy. That's what I mean.

Joe: Oh, office politics!

8. *Be ready for your performance appraisal.* One way your employer can measure how well you are doing on your job is to conduct a **performance appraisal**. This is used by many employers to appraise, or judge, an employee's performance on the job. This formal review is done by your boss, usually once a year. Most employers use a form that provides a scale of rating to evaluate performance.

   Performance appraisals are generally discussed between the supervisor and the employee. This can be occasion for a frank exchange of views about the job, its responsibilities, and its potential for growth. If the employee has been honest, there should not be much difference between the employee's evaluation of him- or herself and the employer's performance appraisal. The employee may also be asked to speak freely about the job's drawbacks or problems. After both sign the form, the original copy usually becomes a part of the employee's permanent personnel record.

CULTURAL Exchange

bring butterflies to your stomach cause your stomach to feel nervous (page 241)

career ladder a series of upward job moves (page 246)

Chapter 11 SELF-TEST
Using SQ3R

Answer the following questions about SQ3R. Count five points for each answer.

1. In the term *SQ3R*, what do each of the letters stand for?
   a. S Survey
   b. Q Question
   c. R Read
   d. R Recite
   e. R Review

2. As you survey the reading, what four things do you read or look for?
   a. sentences that introduce
   b. main headings and subheadings
   c. illustrations and photographs
   d. checklist at beginning and questions at end

3. When you question, what do you ask questions about?
   You ask questions about the information that might be contained in the reading, based on the headings.

4. List five phrases you can use to construct your questions.
   a. How is (are)?
   b. How do (did)?
   c. When did?
   d. Why (or What) did?
   e. What is (are)?

5. List two things you should do when you read the selection.
   a. Look for answers to your questions.
   b. Read short segments, from one heading to the next.

6. What do you recite?
   the answers to your questions

7. How do you review?
   Try to answer each question.

8. What do you do if you can't answer a question as you review?
   Reread only the material under the heading that will answer the question.

Score: ______ correct × 5 points each = ______

UNIT 4 REVIEW TEST

Do SQ3R as you read this selection from an anthropology textbook. Write your answers to the survey and question parts of SQ3R before reading. Then answer the questions that follow the selection.

1. List the headings and subheadings of the selection.

   Nonhuman Culture

   Tools and Learning

   Is It Culture?

2. What is the title of the boxed information?

   Chimpanzee Culture

3. How many sentences or sentence groups are set off by ruled lines? What kind of information do they present?

   The three sentences or groups of sentences present important ideas in the sections.

4. What do the pictures represent?

   The two photographs show chimps and monkeys being social, using tools, and communicating.

Nonhuman Culture

Selection for increased learning capacity set the stage for the emergence of culture.

The capacity for learning has depended on the evolution of larger and more complex brains and of more intelligent species. The great evolutionary novelty of culture is that capabilities and habits are acquired through *learning*, which is socially transmitted, rather than through the more ancient process of biological heredity. (It must be stressed, though, that actual cultural responses always depend in part on genetically predetermined capacities and predispositions.)

Many animals possess learned traditions that are passed on from one generation to the next and that can be thought of as rudimentary forms of culture. As we shall see in a moment, chimpanzees and other primates possess rudimentary learned traditions. However, only among the *hominids* (members of the human family) has culture become as important a source of adaptive behavior as biological evolution based on changes in gene frequencies. Able to stand and walk erect, their hands freed entirely from locomotor and support functions, the earliest hominids probably manufactured, transported, and made effective use of tools as a primary means of subsistence. Apes, in contrast, survive nicely with only the barest inventory of tools. Hominids, ancient or modern, have probably always depended on culture for their very existence.

Tools and Learning

Experimental approaches to behavior show that most birds and mammals and especially monkeys and apes are intelligent enough to learn to make and use simple tools under laboratory conditions. Under natural free-ranging conditions, however, the capacity to make and use tools is expressed less frequently. As a result of the process of natural selection, they have become adapted to their environment through such body parts as snouts, claws, teeth, hooves, and fangs.

Although primates are intelligent enough to make and use tools, their anatomy and normal mode of existence disincline them to develop extensive tool-using traditions.

Among monkeys and apes, the use of hands for tool use is inhibited by the importance of the forelimbs in walking, running, and climbing. That is probably why the most common tool-using behavior among many species of monkeys and apes is repelling intruders with a barrage of nuts, pine cones, branches, fruits, feces, or stones. Throwing such objects entails only a momentary loss of the ability to run or climb away if danger threatens.

Among free-ranging monkeys and apes, the most accomplished tool user is the chimpanzee. Over a period of many years, Jane Goodall and her associates have studied the behavior of a single population of free-ranging common chimpanzees in the Gombe National Park in Tanzania. They have discovered that the chimpanzees "fish" for ants and termites. Fishing for termites involves first breaking off a twig or a vine, stripping it of leaves and side branches, and then locating a suitable termite nest. Such a nest is as hard as concrete and impenetrable except for certain thinly covered tunnel entrances. The chimpanzee scratches away the thin covering and inserts the twig. The termites inside bite the end of the twig, and the chimpanzee pulls it out and licks off the termites clinging to it. Especially impressive is the fact that the chimpanzees will prepare the twig first and then carry it in their mouths from nest to nest while looking for a suitable tunnel entrance (Goodall 1986).

"Anting" provides an interesting variation on this theme. The Gombe chimps "fish" for a species of aggressive nomadic driver ant that can inflict a painful bite. On finding the temporary subterranean nest of these ants, the chimps make a tool out of a green twig and insert it into the nest entrance. Hundreds of fierce ants swarm up the twig to repel the invader. "The chimpanzee watches their progress and when the ants have almost reached its hand, the tool is quickly withdrawn. In a split second the opposite hand rapidly sweeps the length of the tool catching the ants in a jumbled mass between thumb

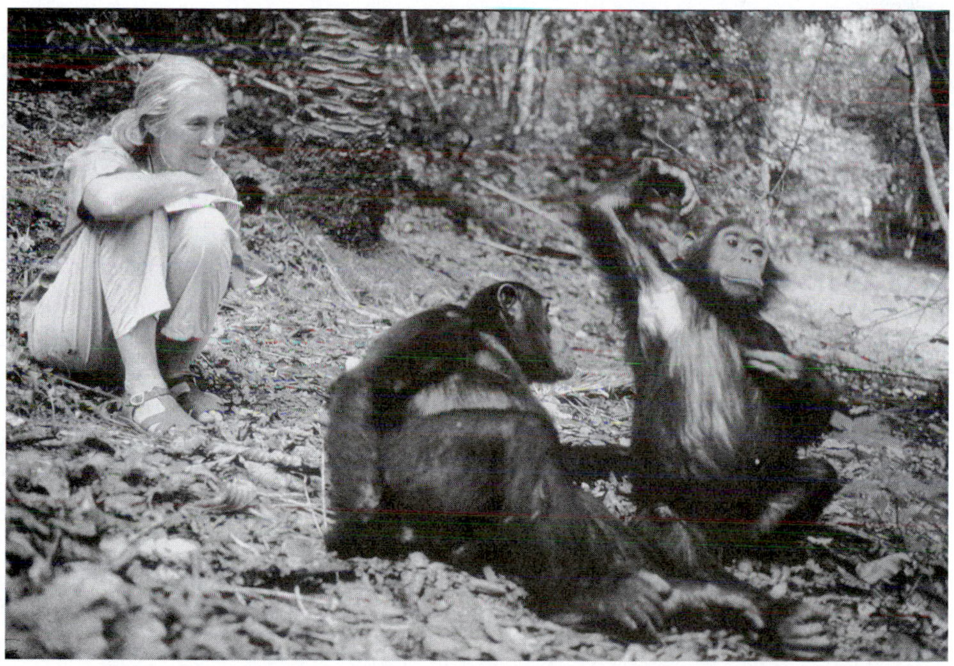

Jane Goodall
Making friends with chimps Prof and Pax in Gombe National Park, Tanzania.

and forefinger. These are then popped into the open, waiting mouth in one bite and chewed furiously" (McGrew et al. 1979:278).

In addition, chimpanzees can manufacture "sponges" for sopping up water from an inaccessible hollow in a tree. They strip a handful of leaves from a twig, put the leaves in their mouth, chew briefly, put the mass of leaves in the water, let them soak, put the leaves to their mouths, and suck the water off. A similar sponge is employed to dry their fur, to wipe off sticky substances, and to clean the bottoms of chimpanzee babies. Gombe chimpanzees also use sticks as levers and digging tools to pry ant nests off trees and to widen the entrance of subterranean beehives.

Is It Culture?

Unlike humans, chimps and other social animals do not experience continuous cultural change. Their cultures remain rudimentary and do not evolve.

There appears to be no specific genetic information that is responsible for chimpanzee termiting and anting. True, for this behavior to occur, genetically determined capacities for learning, for manipulating objects, and for omnivorous eating must be present in the young chimpanzee. But these general biological capacities and predispositions cannot explain termiting and anting. Given nothing but groups of young chimpanzees, twigs, and termite nests, termiting and anting are unlikely to occur on their own. Thus, although chimpanzees acquire complex skills such as anting and termiting, they have only a rudimentary form of culture.

Jane Goodall (1971:161) describes young chimpanzees as they learn tool use techniques to "fish for termites." They learn through trial and error; each chimp invents the technique anew as his interest is drawn to the activity. At about 18 to 22 months they begin to termite on their own. At first their behavior is clumsy and inefficient. Novices often retrieve discarded sticks and attempt to use them on their own. They become proficient at termiting when they are about 3 years old. Fishing for ants, with the risk of being bitten, takes longer to learn; the youngest chimp to achieve proficiency was about 4 years old (McGrew 1977:282).

The conclusion that anting is a learned cultural trait is strengthened by the fact that chimps at other sites do not exploit driver ants even though the species is widely distributed throughout Africa. At the same time, other groups of chimps do exploit other species of ants and in ways that differ from the Gombe tradition. For example, chimps in the Mahale mountains 170 kilometers south of Gombe insert twigs and bark into the nests of tree-dwelling ants, which Gombe chimps ignore (Nishida 1987; McGrew 1992). Similarly, there is cultural variation in tool use. Throughout the area chimpanzees sometimes peel the bark from the twigs or vines they use for termiting; in some locations they then discard the bark, whereas at Gombe, after they peel the twigs or vines, they use the bark itself as a tool for termiting (McGrew et al. 1979).

People who are skeptical about the existence of nonhuman culture claim that "Culture is what humans do." Yet if we are willing to define culture more broadly as, "group behavior that is acquired, at least in part, from social influences," then we can say that culture is present in nonhuman species (McGrew 1998). There is little evidence for teaching in nonhuman primates. But much human learning also takes place without systematic instruction (see Box 3.1).

Box 3.1 Chimpanzee Culture

If we compare the British with Americans, we find differences in dialect, cuisine, and the way people drive. Similarly, chimpanzees display different behavior patterns that vary at different locations.

- Some chimpanzees fish for ants with short sticks, eating their prey off the stick one by one, whereas others use a more efficient technique of accumulating many ants on a long wand and then sweep the ants into their mouths with a single motion.
- Some chimps mop their brows with leaves, others raise their arms while companions groom them.
- In Tanzania, chimps at Gombe routinely use sticks to probe the ground for termites, but chimps 100 miles away in the Mahale mountains do not.
- Gombe chimps don't use stones to crack nuts, even though their terrain is strewn with rocks. But Tai rain forest chimps in the Ivory Coast use stone tools even though rocks are scarce.
- At Tai, grooming chimps wipe parasites on their forearms before mashing them with their forefingers. At Gombe, groomers mash parasites on a leaf.
- Courting styles also exhibit variation, just as they do among humans. In some places, the males knock on tree trunks to attract a female's attention; in other locales, they swing vegetation around.

In a synthesis of several researchers observations (ranging over 8–38 years), primatologists report that our closet cousins display what was long thought to be a uniquely human attribute cultural variation. These findings offer the most detailed evidence yet that nonhuman animals can pick up behaviors and then convey them to others. This means that chimpanzees learn from one another, in contrast to inheriting behaviors through genetics.

All in all, researchers have found 39 different behavior patterns, including tool usage, grooming, and courtship behaviors that are customary in some communities but not in others. Primatologist Frans de Waal says the evidence is overwhelming that chimpanzees have a remarkable ability to invent new customs and technologies, and they pass these on socially. So far, there is almost no evidence of chimpanzees teaching each other and only thin evidence of chimpanzees learning by imitation. Goodall has observed wild female chimps imitating their mothers by playing with their infants the same way their mothers played with them. She has also seen young males imitating adult males in clanging empty fuel cans to make themselves seem more fierce. But in laboratory experiments chimps have failed to mimic precise procedures. For example, chimps have failed to imitate flipping a rake to make it a more efficient tool for raking bananas. It is therefore still unclear to what extent chimps learn by imitation or if they pick up behavior through ingenuity. If a young chimp sees his mother using a stick to fish out termites, he may then go find a stick and is likely to figure out how to use the tool on his own.

(Adapted from Whitten, Goodall, McGrew, Nishida, Renolds, Suguuuyama, Tutin, Wrangham and Boesch 1999, and de Waal 1999)

Marvin Harris and Orna Johnson

5. On a separate sheet of paper, write the answers to each of your SQ3R questions. Student responses will vary.

6. What is the relation between culture and the ability to learn?

   Learning allows capabilities and habits to be passed on from one generation to another. These socially transmitted capabilities and habits are what we call culture.

7. To what degree do animals use tools? What limits their tool use?

   Although most birds and mammals can learn to use simple tools, they do not do so much in nature.

   They become adapted to nature by evolution of body parts and so have less need for tools.

8. What is the most common use of tools for apes and monkeys? Also list two other main tool uses observed in nature.

   The main use is throwing objects at invaders.

   Chimps have been observed fishing for ants and termites.

   They also have been observed sponging up water, as well as using "sponges" to clean themselves.

9. What are the genetic aspects of termiting? What are the cultural aspects? Why is this only a basic form of culture?

   Genetic aspects are the capacity for learning and for manipulating objects, as well as a wide taste in eating.

   The cultural aspect is learning to use twigs on the termite nests.

   The culture is limited because the learning has a high degree of individual trial and error, so there is little teaching and not much advancement of culture.

10. What are six examples of cultural variation among groups of chimps? Why is cultural variation significant?

    1. short sticks versus long wands for anting
    2. mopping own brows versus companion grooming
    3. sticks for termiting versus no sticks
    4. stone tools versus none
    5. mashing parasites between forefingers versus on a leaf
    6. courting by knocking tree trunks versus swinging vegetation

    Cultural variation shows learning from others in the group.

11. What is more important for chimp learning, imitation or teaching?

    Imitation. Teaching is rarely observed.

12. Write *major* or *minor* in the blanks to indicate the importance of each of the following facts in the context of this selection.

major a. Apes have only a few tools.

minor b. Hooves and fangs are adapted to the environment

major c. Monkeys and apes throw objects to chase intruders.

minor d. Objects thrown include nuts and feces.

minor e. Termite nests are as hard as concrete.

minor f. Making a termite stick involves stripping off leaves.

major g. Chimpanzees carry their prepared sticks while they look for tunnel entrances.

major h. Researchers have found 39 different behavior patterns showing cultural variation.

major i. Teaching has not been observed among chimps.

minor j. Chimps use their opposite hands to sweep ants off sticks.

Critical Thinking and Writing

In what ways are the chimpanzee's use of the culture they pass along like human culture? In what ways are they different? Write a few paragraphs evaluating how close chimpanzee culture is to human culture.

UNIT FIVE

Interpreting What You Read

CHAPTER 12

Interpreting Fact and Opinion

CHAPTER 13

Using Inference

CHAPTER TWELVE

Interpreting Fact and Opinion

Understanding the ideas and details that a writer presents is an important part of reading, but it is not everything. You must also be able to interpret what you read.

You need to be able to interpret your reading so you can know not only what the writer says but also what meanings you can take away from the reading. Interpretation involves deciding what you believe about your reading and what you need to think more about. Interpretation also involves finding the ideas and the conclusions that are suggested by the reading but that are not stated directly.

Not everything a writer writes is necessarily true. The writer gives both facts and opinions. The writer claims only that the facts are true. The opinions are merely what the writer thinks, not what everyone necessarily would agree with. For example, consider this statement by someone deciding which notebook computer to buy.

> The 3.4 GigaHerz processor, 512 MB graphicfast SDRAM with full connectivity options, all in a 4-pound ultra-thin package make the Maximind SuperXJ Notebook the best computer buy around today.

Several facts appear in this sentence. The speed of the processor (3.4 GigaHerz), the size of the graphics processor (512 MB), the connectivity options, and the weight are all facts. However, whether this is the best system and the best buy is a matter of opinion. Some people may prefer other computers that fit their needs better or that they consider a better value for their money.

Of course, it is not always easy to keep facts and opinions apart. Sometimes the writer presents as fact something that others would not agree with. Just try to get two people who were fighting to agree who threw the first punch! In this kind of situation, what one person believes is a fact to the other is just an opinion.

Sometimes the writer gets facts wrong. For years, people wrongly said that Columbus discovered the Americas. They never stopped to think that, coming from Asia, Native Americans had made the discovery long before. Even when correct facts are available, some writers do not always check their facts.

At other times, the writer may mix facts and opinions together so closely it is impossible to tell where facts end and where opinions begin. Philosophers argue about what a fact is and what an opinion is. Most people have opinions they believe represent facts.

For most practical purposes, however, we can tell fact from opinion in our reading.

- *Facts are statements that tell what really happened or what really is the case.* A fact is based on direct evidence. It is known by actual experience or observation.
- *Opinions are statements of belief, judgment, or feeling.* Opinions show what someone thinks about a subject. Some opinions, of course, are based more on facts than others are. Such well-supported opinions are more reliable than others. Still, all opinions are just somebody's views; they are not facts.

Read the following statements about the world population:

1. In 1950, the total world population was 2.5 billion; in 1980, the world population was 4.5 billion. The world population is now 6.5 billion.
2. The United Nations believes the world population is likely to double (to 13 billion) by the year 2100.
3. It seems we must stop this terrifying problem of the growth of the world population before it is too large for the planet's resources.

Sentence 1 is a statement of fact. National and international agencies keep population records, which are available in many reference books. Notice that the sentence presents no opinion about the size of growth or whether the decrease in the growth rate is good or bad.

Sentence 2, even though it gives numbers and a reliable source, is just an opinion. The sentence simply predicts what might be rather than what definitely will be. A prediction is an opinion about what might happen in the future. The words *believes, will, likely,* and *by* tell us that the statement is only an opinion about the future. This opinion is not necessarily the opinion of the author, who never expresses agreement or disagreement with it. The opinion is that of the United Nations. (It is fact that representatives of the United Nations did state this opinion.)

Sentence 3 is an example of the author's opinions. The opening phrase—*It seems . . .* —lets us know an opinion follows. People may disagree on whether we *must* do something, what constitutes *terrifying* or *too large*, or what population the *planet's resources* can maintain. Some people argue that the earth can support many more people than it currently does; others say that it is not up to humans to determine who and how many can be born; still others see this as a problem that can be handled and is therefore not terrifying; and some say we can do something if we want to, but we have a choice. Words such as *must, terrifying, problem,* and *too large* all present individual judgments.

Opinion Clue Words

- Some words give an opinion by evaluating or making a judgment. Words such as *ugly, pretty, safe, dangerous, clever, stupid, well-dressed, sloppy, desirable,* and *hateful* always express someone's judgment.
- Some words clearly state that an opinion follows. You know that an opinion is going to be expressed when the writer says *I believe, I think, in my opinion, I feel,* and *I suggest.*
- Some words show that doubt may exist about a statement. These words indicate that a statement is not always true or that other opinion are possible: *usually, often, sometimes, on occasion, probably, perhaps, likely, plausible, possible,* and *maybe.*

EXERCISES

12.1 Opinion Clue Words

In each statement of opinion, underline the clue words that let you know that you are reading an opinion, not a fact.

1. Finding a good job seems to get harder every year.
2. Even for simple jobs, employers usually expect you to have completed college.
3. Desirable jobs seem to require both advanced training and experience.
4. Only clever or lucky people wind up with work they like.
5. I believe I am going to have to work very hard to find a job I will be happy with.

12.2 Fact and Opinion

Write *F* before each statement of fact; write *O* before each statement of opinion. Then circle any words that help you recognize what is fact and what is opinion.

__O__ 1. In many families today, television seems to be an electronic babysitter.

__O__ 2. Some critics of television claim that violence on television leads to violence in real life.

__F__ 3. Children watch an average of three-and-a-half hours of television a day, as reported by a National Education Association survey.

__F__ 4. Cable television provides its subscribers with many alternatives to the major networks, as you can see by looking at television schedules.

__O__ 5. The quality of television programming has declined dramatically over the last five years.

__O__ 6. *The West Wing* is one of the finest shows on television today.

__O__ 7. Children probably learn more about gender roles from watching television than from watching their parents.

__F__ 8. According to scholarly studies, women reporters now cover major stories on all news shows on all networks.

12.3 Fact and Opinion in a Textbook Selection

Read this selection from an American history textbook. Then answer the questions that follow.

Nat Turner's Revolt Inspires Fear

In 1831 an insurrection in Virginia startled and terrified slave owners everywhere. This uprising was led by Nat Turner. Turner, a slave, had been taught to read by one of his owner's sons. When the white boys were sent to school and Turner was sent to work in the fields, however, he became deeply embittered. Encouraged by his mother, Turner grew up to be a preacher of considerable ability. He came to believe that he had a divine mission to deliver black people from bondage.

Turner was able to gather together a band of slaves and organize a revolt. The uprising, first planned for the Fourth of July, was postponed when Turner fell ill. Turner and his band finally attacked a number of white homes on August 21, 1831. Before the end of the rebellion, about 160 people of both races had been killed. Turner and nineteen others were caught and hanged.

—*Henry F. Graff*

1. List at least three facts in this selection.

   Nat Turner led a slave uprising in Virginia in 1831. Turner, a slave, was able to read. Turner grew up to be a preacher. The uprising was originally planned for July 4, but took place on August 21. About 160 people were killed in the uprising. Turner was caught and hanged. Turner believed he had a divine mission.

2. List at least two opinions in the selection.

   The revolt startled and terrified slave owners. When sent to work in the fields, Turner became deeply embittered. Turner was a preacher of considerable ability.

12.4 Fact and Opinion in Product Information

In presenting their products, corporations often mix facts with strongly stated opinions. Read the description of the 2005 Jaguar XK from the corporation website. Then answer these questions.

The 2005 XK

Style, exhilaration and performance

Jaguar designers have evolved the 2005 XK's shape into something so lean and taut it seems but a muscle reflex away from pouncing on its prey. Its 4.2-liter V8 engine isn't just inspired by Jaguar' s rich legacy of racing success. It became the basis for the XK race car after it recently secured America's oldest sports car championship by winning the 2003 Trans Am Title. Drive the newly redesigned XK and you will feel not only its race-bred power, but also its profound refinement. The 2005 XK. Born with the heart of a champion. Lives to satisfy the soul.

XK8: Engage its 6-speed automatic transmission and the growl of the 4.2-liter engine quickly turns into a perfectly pitched roar. More than 86 percent of the V8 engine's torque is available from as low as 2,000 rpm, creating effortless acceleration that has been a Jaguar trait since the first XK sports car startled the world a half century ago. New for 2005 are a lower front bumper, side sills, and rear bumper, as well as larger dual exhaust tailpipe finishers.

XKR: At the heart of the XKR is a 4.2-liter V8 that beats to the rhythm of an Eaton Roots-type supercharger with twin air-liquid intercoolers. The output figures are powerful: 390 horsepower at 6000 rpm and 399 lb-ft of maximum torque at 3500 rpm. For 2005, the XKR receives the same enhanced body along with a restyled mesh grille, a larger trunk spoiler, and new quad exhaust tailpipe finishers.

1. List all the facts in paragraph 1.

   none

2. List the opinions in paragraph 1.

   The car is destined to reward its driver. The road has pleasures, which the driver will experience.

3. Are the opinions in paragraph 1 expressed directly or indirectly? Why?

   Indirectly through a question, to get the reader to agree at the same time as giving the reader a sense of making his or her own judgment.

4. List the facts in the second paragraph.

   The XK has a 4.2-liter V-8 engine.

   The race version won the 2003 Trans Am race.

   The Trans Am is America's oldest sports car championship.

5. List some of the opinions in the second paragraph

   The shape is lean and taut.

   The shape seems ready to pounce on its prey.

   The car is inspired.

   Jaguar's racing history is a rich legacy.

   You will feel power and refinement.

   The car has the heart of a champion.

   The car will satisfy your soul.

6. List the facts about the XK8 in the third paragraph

   It has a 6-speed transmission.

   It has a 4.2-liter engine.

   86% of the torque is available at 2000 rpm.

   This year's model has lower bumpers and sills and larger tailpipe finishers.

7. List some of the opinions in the third paragraph

   The engine growls and then gives a perfectly pitched roar.

   Acceleration is effortless.

   Effortless acceleration is a Jaguar trait.

   The first XK startled the world.

8. List the facts about the XKR in the fourth paragraph.

   It has a a 4.2-liter V-8 engine.

   The engine has an Eaton Roots-type supercharger with twin air-liquid intercoolers.

   The engine produces 390 horsepower at 6000 rpm and 399 lb-ft of torque at 3500 rpm.

   The 2005 model has a restyled grille, a larger spoiler, and new tailpipe finishers.

9. List some of the opinions in the third paragraph.

   The engine beats to a rhythm.

   The output figures are powerful.

10. Which fact is repeated most? Why?

    The engine is a 4.2-liter V-8. This fact suggests power.

11. How can you describe the other facts selected and presented?

    They all emphasize the power of the engine.

12. How would you describe the opinions expressed?

    The opinions express power and impressiveness that satisfy the driver.

13. Which paragraphs have more fact or more opinion? Why?

    The opening paragraphs have fewer facts and more opinions while the last paragraph has more facts and fewer opinions. This is because the XKR model described in the last paragraph has the most powerful engine, which provides the most impressive facts. The earlier paragraphs build up an emotional impression that attracts the reader and leads them to desire the most expensive model. Or at least they associate the car with the facts concerning the most expensive model.

CULTURAL Exchange

West Wing	a popular TV program about a fictional U.S. president (page 270)
insurrection	the act of open revolt against civil authority or a constituted government (page 271)
embittered	bitter; resentful (page 271)
preacher	an individual who publicly talks about religion or morals for an occupation (page 271)
divine mission	a particular job or duty that someone believes God has chosen for him or her to do or accomplish in life; implies urgency and necessity to complete the job (page 271)
gratuitous	unnecessary, unwarranted, or unjustified (page 277)
flippant	expressing disrespectful humor or casualness (page 277)
insidious	working or spreading harmfully in a subtle or alluring manner intended to entrap (page 277)
Valium	a tranquilizer used in the treatment of anxiety and tension, as a sedative, and as a muscle relaxant (page 277)
Congressional hearing	a meeting of senators, members of Congress, or both, to investigate the workings of government policies and bureaucracy (page 277)
"drug favorable" film	a film that portrays drugs, their use, and their sale in a good and positive way (page 277)

to endow an academic chair	to provide a great sum of money for the purpose of establishing an academic specialty (e.g., English, European History, or Women's Studies) in a particular field at a university (page 278)
"I don't buy that."	I don't believe that; I don't accept that as true (page 278)

Chapter 12 SELF-TEST
Interpreting Fact and Opinion

Read the following magazine story about how one movie star feels about the way radio, television, and movies encourage drug abuse. Then answer each of the questions that follow. Count five points for each correct answer.

Paul Newman: "It's an Epidemic"

"Take a moment to think what our children's environment would be like if radio stations decided not to play records with pro-drug messages, if movie studios refused to distribute pictures with gratuitous drug scenes, and if television networks declined to air programs with casual and flippant remarks about drugs."

The speaker is Paul Newman. When he talks about drug abuse, it's from the perspective of a parent who has lost a child to what he calls "the insidious killer of our best and brightest."

Scott Newman, the actor's son by his first wife, Jacqueline Witte, died November 20, 1978, at age 28, after mixing alcohol and Valium. . . .

To demonstrate his concern on the drug issue, Newman appeared at a Congressional hearing on March 20, when his daughter Susan testified during an inquiry into television's role in glamorizing substance abuse.

Newman, however, is uneasy about the government's shadow looming over Hollywood. "It's dangerous," he said. "It's something government should not be involved with. The fact they are getting involved is an admission that we can't police ourselves. It will be an evolving process, but I think we will because we have to. I think you can bring some pressure to bear on the major studios to avoid it when they can."

Asked if he supported an addition to the ratings system to warn of "drug favorable" films, he said: "I can live with that."

The Scott Newman Center was founded by the family four years ago. Among its goals are reshaping media's treatment of drugs and reaching youngsters before they become involved. It produces educational films, advises moviemakers and backs an awards program for TV writers, producers and directors who accurately depict substance abuse.

The center recently was affiliated with the University of Southern California, and Paul Newman donated $1.2 million for operating expenses and to endow an academic chair in the School of Pharmacy. "I think people look at drug abuse and think problems of this size are unmanageable," Newman said. "I don't buy that. This effort is worth it."

—*Parade*

1. Put a check mark before each statement that accurately reflects Newman's opinions.

✓ a. Radio, movies, and television often carry pro-drug messages.

✓ b. Drugs hurt young people.

___ c. The government should crack down on filmmakers.

✓ d. Young people are influenced by pro-drug messages.

✓ e. The entertainment industry is not policing itself.

✓ f. The entertainment industry should police itself.

___ g. The drug problem is too big to manage.

___ h. Newman donated $1.2 million to fight drug abuse.

___ i. A drug rating system will solve the problem.

2. Which of the following statements represent a fact and which represent an opinion? Write *F* or *O* on the blank before each statement.

F a. Newman's child died from substance abuse.

O b. Newman has the viewpoint of someone who lost a child.

O c. The government's involvement shows that the entertainment industry has not been able to control its presentation of drugs.

F d. Newman's family founded the Scott Newman Center.

O e. The center will be able to influence how the media portray drugs.

O f. A rating system that warns of "drug favorable films" is an acceptable action.

3. Read the following sentences. Put a *T* in front of every fact that is true, according to this article, and a *W* before every statement that Paul Newman wishes were a fact.

W a. Movie studios refuse to distribute pictures with gratuitous drug scenes.

T b. Scott Newman's sister testified before Congress.

T c. Television airs programs with casual remarks about drugs.

W d. Hollywood has a drug rating system.

T e. Awards are given for TV writers who accurately depict substance abuse.

Score: ______ correct × 5 points each = ______

Critical Thinking and Writing

In what ways can the media improve their treatment of drug and alcohol abuse? Write a few paragraphs to express your views.

CHAPTER **THIRTEEN**

Using Inference

Writers often tell you more than they say directly. They give you hints or clues that help you read between the lines. Using these clues to gain a deeper understanding of your reading is called *inferring*. When you *infer*, you go beyond the surface details to see other meanings the details suggest or imply.

Inference in some ways is like a guessing game, but not a wild guessing game. You must look carefully at the facts and the details in the reading. You must add your own knowledge and experience to those details. Then you can judge what other things are likely to be true, even though they are not said directly. You cannot always be certain the inferences you make are absolutely right. However, if you follow hunches based on evidence and reasonable judgments, you can be fairly sure about some things, even if they are only hinted at.

For example, a story begins in the following way:

> Suzanne looked down at the speedometer. Eighty-five. She tightened her grip on the steering wheel. Suddenly she heard a siren behind her.

You already know many things that haven't been said: Suzanne is in an automobile. She is driving it. She is going 85 miles an hour. She is breaking the law by going too fast. The siren is likely to be that of a police car pulling her over to give her a ticket.

How do you know these things? Because your experience gives the stated facts meaning. You know that speedometers are in cars; the driver is the one who usually looks at the speedometer and grips the steering wheel; the speed is usually given in miles per hour on cars in the United States; speed limits in this country do not exceed 70 miles per hour; and when people drive cars faster than the speed limit, the police often stop them by following them and turning on sirens.

Writers rely on readers' being able to make inferences. It would be unnecessary and no doubt boring for the writer of Suzanne's story to spell out all the details that most readers can easily infer. The writer can tell the story more quickly and forcefully by depending on the reader to fill in parts of the picture. The more a writer can rely on a reader's inference skills, the more the writer can focus on the really important elements of the story. These elements make the story interesting or important.

Actually, you use inference not only when you read but also when you participate in almost every aspect of life. You constantly use it, for example, to understand how other people are behaving. In this sense, we are all like the great detective Sherlock Holmes, looking for clues to make inferences about people.

Let's say you are sitting around the lunchroom with some friends, making your usual jokes and small talk. You make a perfectly ordinary comment about an incident in class involving someone who is not there. Suddenly Sam, who is sitting at the table, gets angry. "Why don't you get off her case. I don't have time for this," he shouts. Then he grabs his books and storms away.

Everyone at the table immediately infers that something is bothering Sam. How do your friends know that? They used their own background knowledge. When somebody gets angry, we usually infer that there is a cause. However, the mood at the table was pleasant, and there seemed no obvious cause for Sam's anger. Everybody at the table also infers that what is bothering Sam has something to do with your comment. It might be either the person who you were talking about or what you said, even though your remark at first seemed harmless enough. The people at the table can infer this because Sam got upset right after your remark. Further, he referred to your remark and to the person. You know from experience that often people seem to get angry over harmless remarks when those remarks reflect something on their minds.

You have to be careful, however, that your inferences do not go too far beyond the available evidence. If you make a guess on too little information, you are likely to be wrong. In this example, there isn't enough evidence to know exactly what is bothering Sam. People might start making guesses. Maybe Sam just started a relationship with the girl you were talking about. Maybe he is on edge about an exam coming up. Maybe he is still angry about a similar remark you made about *him* two weeks ago. Each explanation is possible, but without more evidence there is no sure way of knowing. If one member of your group reports that Sam has been having a hard time asking the girl you were discussing for a date, then you might infer that that was what was really bothering him. Without that extra evidence, it is wiser to ask Sam, "What's bothering you?" Otherwise, you might guess incorrectly and do something inappropriate. Inferences must be based on valid information, not just on vague suspicions and wild guesses.

You regularly use inference in looking at scenes, whether in photographs, movies, television programs, or real life. Inferences help you know what the scene is all about.

Look at the picture on this page. On the blank lines, write a sentence explaining the point of the picture — that is, what you think the picture is all about.

Student responses will vary.

____

____

You probably wrote something like "A schoolboy is counting on his fingers." That description makes sense. Now think about how you came to your statement. How did you know the picture showed a boy rather than a girl? How did you know that the child is in school? How did you know that he is using his fingers for counting? These things are not shown directly. You came to all these conclusions by inferring from the details in the picture.

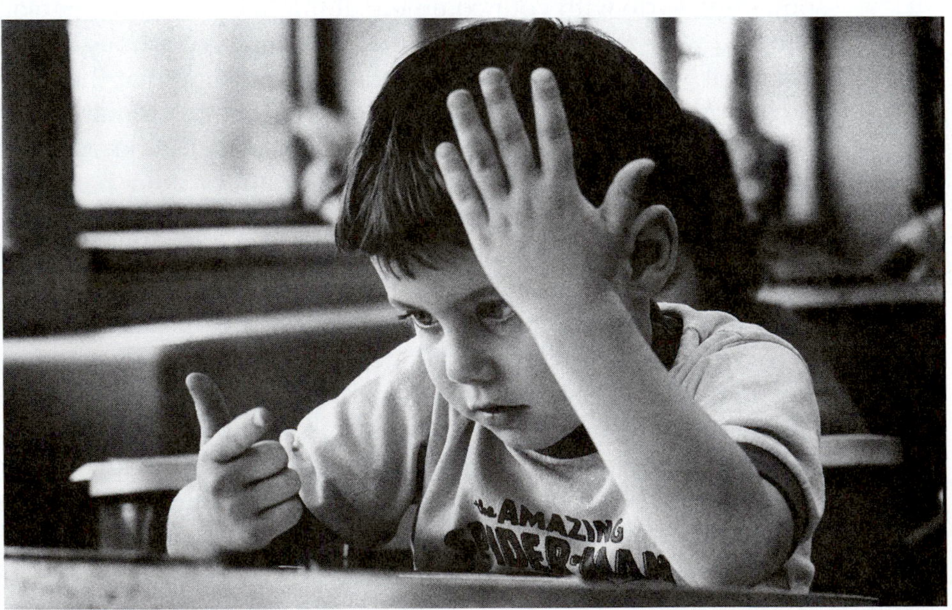

Write down some of the clues that helped you infer that the child is a boy.

____

____

Most likely the haircut and the Spiderman t-shirt together gave you the impression that the child is a boy. We often use clothing and hairstyle to judge people's gender.

What clues made you believe that the child is in school?

____

____

Was it that the child is sitting behind a desk? Was it the hint of other desks and children in a straight row behind the child? Was it the big windows?

What made you believe that the child is counting? Why did you not infer that the child is pointing with his right hand and waving with his left?

____

____

Most likely, a combination of factors led to your inference. Other inferences about the age of the child, that the child is in a classroom, that the child is staring at his fingers and concentrating very hard all fit together in the inference that he is doing finger arithmetic.

The clues we get from the picture help us figure out what is going on. We infer meanings from things we actually see. Inferences help us complete the picture, fill in important information.

Look at this cartoon and apply your inference skills to answer the questions that follow.

b 1. The woman wearing a hat is Mr. Dithers's
   a. teacher.
   b. wife.
   c. secretary.
   d. mother.

a 2. The cake had
   a. many candles.
   b. very large candles.
   c. few candles.
   d. no candles.

d 3. The cake baked itself because
   a. it was a no-bake cake.
   b. the day was very hot.
   c. the oven didn't work.
   d. the candles made a lot of heat.

c 4. Mr. Dithers is
   a. a young man.
   b. about twenty years old.
   c. an old man.
   d. dead.

To answer the questions, you had to use inference skills. None of the information required to answer the questions is stated directly in the cartoon, but you were able to draw on your own knowledge.

For question 1, how did you know to choose *b*, Mr. Dithers's wife? First, you probably inferred that two women having lunch might be talking about their husbands. You also inferred that a wife might make a birthday cake for her husband. The other answers don't seem to be correct. Nothing in the cartoon suggests that the woman is either Mr. Dithers's teacher or his secretary. It's *possible* that either of these choices is correct, of course. But *b* seems much more likely than *a* or *c*. Choice *d* does not seem right. Mr. Dithers's mother would look much older than the woman in the hat.

For question 2, we must infer that the cake had many candles. Only *a* is correct. Few or no candles would not give off the necessary heat. We know nothing about the size of the candles. Choices *b, c,* and *d* are incorrect.

For question 3, we can infer that the cake baked itself because of all the candles. Choice *d* is correct here. Nothing in the cartoon suggests choice *a, b,* or *c.* (We never learn just why the candles were lit *before* the cake was baked. Usually we light candles on a cake that already is baked. Still, the absence of reality does not keep us from enjoying the cartoon.)

For question 4, we must infer that Mr. Dithers is an old man. We know from experience that the older we get, the more candles are placed on our birthday cakes. The custom, as you know, is that each year is represented by its own candle. A young man's cake would not have enough candles for it to bake itself. Twenty candles *might* bake a cake, but an old man's cake would have more candles and, as a result, would give off more heat. Mr. Dithers might be old enough for you to think him dead, but we don't bake birthday cakes for people in their graves. Only choice *c* is the correct inference; choices *a, b,* and *d* are incorrect.

Now read the following description. Inferences turn the plain facts into an amusing and surprising story.

The Last Wild West Stagecoach Robbery

It was pulled off by a woman in 1898. Pearl Hart and Joe Boot, her accomplice, robbed the Globe, Arizona, stage. Pearl Hart was 27 and working in an Arizona mining camp as a cook. She convinced Joe Boot that there was more money to be made robbing stages. As the Globe stage turned a bend, the two robbers were waiting, armed with rifles. The three passengers, a drummer, a dude, and a Chinese gentleman, were thrown to the floor and ordered to "shell out." The drummer gave $390, the dude $36, and the Chinese $5. The coach was then ordered on its way. The last stage holdup had netted $431. During their escape, Pearl and Joe became hopelessly lost and then were drenched in a tremendous storm. Three days later they were found (rather than caught) by the local sheriff. When the prisoners arrived in Florence, Pearl was asked, "Would you do it again?" She replied, "Damn right, pardner." Boot got 35 years, Pearl got only 5. She was the sole female prisoner in the Yuma Territorial Prison, and the governor was relieved when he released her after 2½ years. She was next heard of in 1903, when she was arrested at Deming, New Mexico, for conspiring to pull a train robbery, but she was released for lack of evidence. She was last seen in 1924, a small, innocent-looking 53-year-old woman, busy reminiscing — at the Pima County Jail.

David Wallechinsky and Irving Wallace

c 1. What can you infer about women and stagecoach robberies from this story?
   a. Women often robbed stagecoaches.
   b. Women never robbed stagecoaches.
   c. A woman robbing a stagecoach was surprising.

b 2. These two robbers were
   a. experienced and skillful.
   b. inexperienced and unlucky.
   c. lucky and successful.

b 3. Pearl Hart
   a. was ashamed of her criminal activity.
   b. liked the idea of being a robber.
   c. was talked into crime by evil friends.

You can infer that women stagecoach robbers were surprisingly rare. Several details in the paragraph and your own background knowledge of the Old West help you. Even though she was the brains of the operation, Pearl got the shorter sentence, which implies that the judge was not used to sentencing women criminals. She was the only female prisoner, and the governor was relieved to release her — as though he was not used to having female prisoners. The correct answer to question 1 is *c*.

You can infer that the two robbers were inexperienced because they got lost and did not hide very well. Being caught in the rain and being found by the sheriff also imply that their luck was bad. The correct answer to question 2 is *b*.

Finally, you can infer Pearl Hart's attitude toward being a criminal from her talking Joe Boot into the crime, her tough words during the robbery and after it, her later criminal career, and her reminiscing. The correct answer to 3 is *b*.

Building Inference Skills

- Try to read beyond the words. Fill in details, information, and ideas based on the writer's suggestions and your own background knowledge.
- Ask yourself questions about your reading. In the selection about the stagecoach robbery, you might have asked yourself what was special or surprising about the story or whether

these stagecoach robbers were amateurs or experts. Questions help you put together the details of the piece to make inferences.

- If the writer describes a person, try to understand the person from how the person moves, what the person says, and what the person looks like. You can infer things about someone's character from what the person does. Build a picture in your mind of what the person is like.
- If you have a hard time seeing how information fits together in a selection or what the selection's meaning is, try using inference skills. Sometimes a single inference can make sense of a whole picture. Imagine how pointless the picture of the schoolchild on page 282 would appear if you could not infer that he is doing finger arithmetic.
- If you cannot easily answer a question about what you have read, remember to use inference skills. Return to the reading looking for clues that will help you figure out the answer.
- Try to predict what might happen next. From a series of events, you often can infer the outcome. Being able to predict outcomes is an important part of inference.
- Try to generalize about what you have read. When you *generalize,* you infer extended meanings. These meanings go beyond the particular information in the reading. You form principles, or rules, based on what you've read. For example, from the picture on page 282, you might infer this general idea: *Schoolchildren sometimes count on their fingers.* Based on the picture, the inference is valid.

EXERCISES

13.1 Inference from an Advertisement

Look carefully at the advertisement on the following page and answer the questions below. You must use inference skills to answer each question.

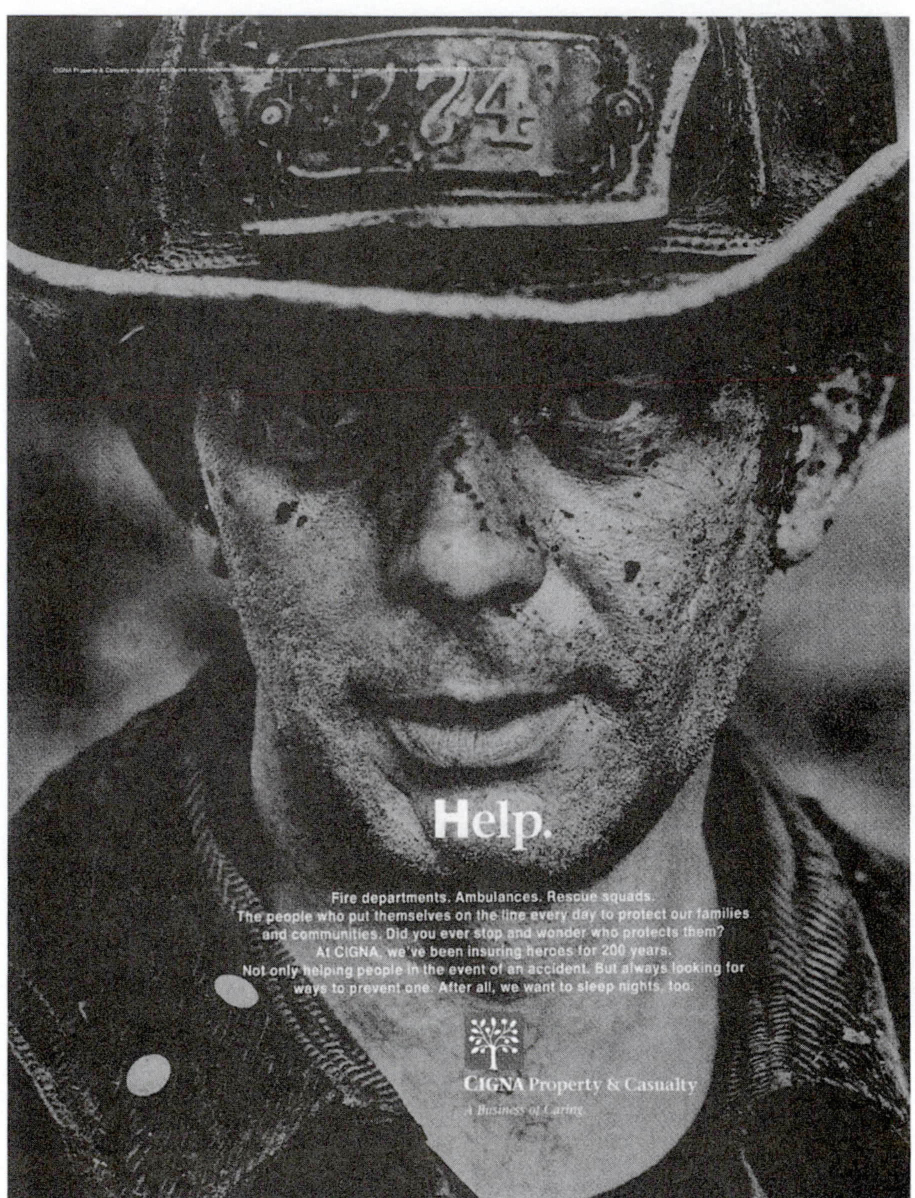

c 1. You can infer that the person in the picture is
   a. an ambulance driver.
   b. an insurance agent.
   c. a firefighter.
   d. a family member.

b 2. You can infer that the person in the picture has just
a. met with an insurance agent.
b. fought a fire.
c. suffered an accident.
d. gotten ready for work.

a 3. You can infer that the person is
a. brave.
b. selfish.
c. cautious.
d. accident-prone.

4. List some clues that helped you answer questions 1, 2, and 3.

the helmet and badge

the dirt on the face

d 5. You can infer that the headline "Help" refers to
a. what the person in the picture provides.
b. what we all need for security.
c. what the Cigna company provides.
d. all of the above.

e 6. From the text, you can infer that the Cigna company
a. protects the community protectors.
b. is part of the community.
c. helps people.
d. is quietly heroic like members of the fire, ambulance, and rescue squads.
e. is all of the above.

7. List some clues that helped you answer question 6.

"insuring heroes"

"who protects them? At Cigna"

"protect *our* families" "want to sleep nights, too"

"looking for ways to prevent one"

13.2 Inference from a Paragraph

Read the following paragraph about how businesses show off how great they are to attract customers. As you read, think of the inferences you can make about the businesses and their claims. Then use your inference skills to answer the questions that follow.

There is an old story about a downtown city block that had five restaurants on it. The first restaurant boasted in a big sign in the window, "THE BEST RESTAURANT IN THE CITY." The next restaurant on the block had a bigger sign with bigger letters, "THE BEST IN THE STATE." The sign in the window of the third restaurant topped them both, "THE BEST RESTAURANT IN AMERICA." A fourth restaurant would not be beat, "THE WORLD'S BEST." Just at the end of the block a small, ordinary-looking lunch counter had a little sign with small letters, "the best restaurant on this block."

__c__ 1. The signs were put up by
   a. food critics from local newspapers.
   b. gourmets who had eaten at the restaurants.
   c. the restaurant owners.
   d. the same person in all five cases.

__d__ 2. The owners of the five restaurants
   a. were all telling the truth.
   b. had visited many other restaurants to compare food.
   c. all own very good restaurants.
   d. are willing to say anything to attract customers.

__d__ 3. The restaurant owner least likely to be thought of as exaggerating the truth is the
   a. first.
   b. second.
   c. fourth.
   d. last.

__b__ 4. The owner of the last restaurant
   a. has no confidence in the food served there.
   b. is poking fun at the other restaurant.
   c. believes his or her restaurant is not as good as the other restaurants.
   d. believes the other restaurant owners are telling the truth.

13.3 Inference from a Cartoon

Look at the cartoon on the facing page and answer the following questions using your inference skills.

__b__ 1. You can infer that the elephant in the front is
   a. a professional ballet dancer.
   b. practicing to be a ballet dancer.

"Don't trample on a young girl's hopes and dreams, Roy."

c. a truly graceful ballet dancer.
d. making fun of ballet dancers.

__a__ 2. You can infer that the two elephants in the back are
a. parents of the elephant in the front.
b. ballet trainers.
c. schoolmates of the elephant in front.
d. strangers to the elephant in front.

__d__ 3. You can infer that Roy has
a. always wanted to be a ballet dancer.
b. encouraged the young elephant to be a ballet dancer.
c. little respect for the art of ballet dancing.
d. just made negative comments about the young elephant's dancing.

__c__ 4. You can infer that the elephant speaking
a. believes the young elephant is really a fine dancer.
b. has no sense of what it takes to make a good dancer.
c. is concerned about her daughter's feelings.
d. believes in telling the truth.

d 5. The word *trample* is especially appropriate here because
   a. you can crush someone's hopes merely by saying something negative.
   b. elephants trample things underfoot merely by walking.
   c. the young elephant ballerina is surely trampling objects on the ground as she dances.
   d. all of the above.

13.4 Inference from an Advertisement

Look at the advertisement on page 293. On the following lines, describe what inferences you draw from the ad and what clues led you to those inferences. Student responses will vary.

The drug problem is very serious. The picture is of a young child. The paragraphs below the picture describe drug problems of the young and what parents can do.

CULTURAL Exchange

stage	a shortened form of *stagecoach,* a four-wheeled horse-drawn vehicle formerly used to transport mail, parcels, and passengers over a regular route in the Old West (page 285)
dude	a stylishly dressed man from the city (page 285)
to shell out	to pay money for something (page 285)
brains of the operation	the person who does the planning (page 286).

America's Drug Problem Is Not As Big As You Think.

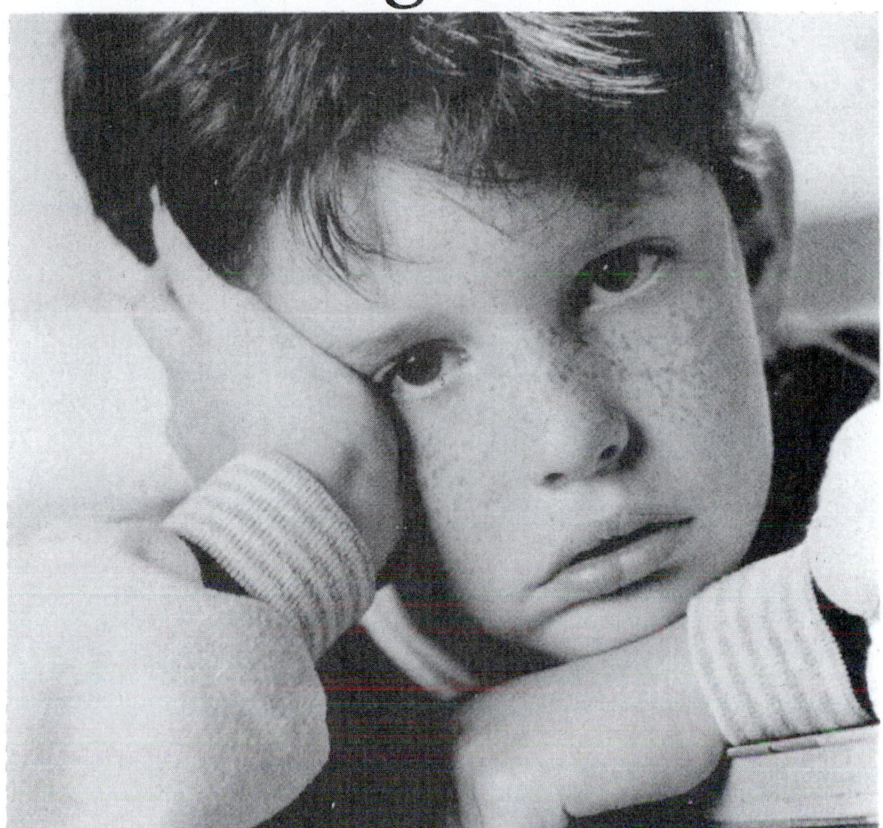

It can start as a dare. Or youthful curiosity. Or it may be a way to escape problems at home. Whatever the reasons, studies show that an alarming number of young children are trying drugs. Unfortunately, too many parents still do not believe that *their* kids are at risk.

The truth is, it's never too early to start teaching your kids about the dangers of drugs. If you're not sure how to talk to them, call 1-800-624-0100 and ask for a free booklet called *Growing Up Drug-Free – A Parent's Guide To Prevention*. Call today, because if you don't take care of little problems, they can easily grow into big ones.

Partnership for a Drug-Free America®

Chapter 13 SELF-TEST
Using Inference

Read the following selections from magazines and textbooks. Then answer the questions after each. Count four points for each correct answer.

1. Five days a week, Al Jury wears the tan uniform of the California Highway Patrol, pushing paper on felony cases involving drugs, drunks and manslaughter. On the seventh day, the 6-foot-1, 192-pounder slips on a striped shirt, tucks a yellow flag into the back pocket of his white pants, steps into the National Football League—and lays down the law.

   The football season opens Sunday. It's Jury's ninth year as an NFL official, his 17th as a highway patrolman. If the big guys start throwing punches, he's both. "It's the same as being a police officer. You break it up," says Jury.

   You won't find a butcher, a baker or a candlestick maker, but the NFL's 107 officials (15 crews of seven each, plus two swingmen) include a foot doctor, golf course director, motivational speaker, lawyer, longshoreman and bank boss, to name just a few occupations. They can tackle real-world jobs because, unlike other pro sports, these officials don't work four or five games a week—just one—and they had better get that one right.

   —Gary Mihoces

___d___ 1. From this passage, you can infer that
   a. being a football referee is a full-time job.
   b. being a referee of professional football pays a lot of money.
   c. football referees find their regular work boring.
   d. football referees hold other jobs during the week.

___b___ 2. Refereeing a football game
   a. reminds all referees of their weekday work.
   b. reminds some referees of their weekday work.
   c. is the most important thing in the referee's life.
   d. is not important to the referees.

___b___ 3. Referees for the National Football League
   a. all have athletic weekday jobs.
   b. include professional men.
   c. are made up of all kinds of people.
   d. all have college degrees.

2. Sam John Passarella has plenty of time. As a prison inmate in Tennessee, convicted of charges involving assault and kidnapping, he has served 11 years of a term extending into the next century, but he gardens now and says he doesn't give much thought to his "red date," or scheduled release, in 2013.

"I don't even care that much about getting out as long as I can continue to work with flowers, especially roses," he said. In his mid-40s, Passarella still has the face of an acolyte, but he weighs more than 400 pounds, and when he moves, it is like the docking of a ship.

We walked in single file through narrow aisles of a greenhouse at the Middle Tennessee Reception Center in Nashville, a holding facility for prisoners awaiting transfer to other institutions. Passarella recited the names of the plants as we passed through, and when he came to a bench where there were rose cuttings taking root in containers, he said almost in awe, "Look at that; we're bringing life into the world."

—*William Ellis*

__a__ 4. From Passarella's crimes and sentence, we can infer that he
   a. at one point was a dangerous man.
   b. believes he was unjustly accused and convicted.
   c. will return to a life of crime.
   d. is incapable of gentler feelings.

__b__ 5. From his lack of concern about when he will be released, we can infer that Passarella
   a. likes prison more than the outside world.
   b. finds gardening the most important thing in his life.
   c. knows he will return to crime if he leaves prison.
   d. earns a good living from gardening inside the prison.

__d__ 6. An *acolyte* is someone who assists a priest. From the description "Passarella still has the face of an acolyte," we can infer that he looks
   a. guilty.
   b. angry.
   c. sick.
   d. innocent.

__c__ 7. Overall, we can infer that
   a. Passarella has a split personality.
   b. the prison has a good rehabilitation program.
   c. gardening has changed Passarella.
   d. Passarella will never commit another crime.

3. Sound is made when the particles that make up a gas (such as air), a liquid (such as water), or a solid (such as iron or wood) move rapidly back and forth. This back-and-forth motion is called *vibration*. When an object vibrates in air, the object pushes air outward from itself in a series of airwaves. When these waves strike our ears, we hear a sound. For example, when a gong is struck, the gong vibrates. The metal shell of the gong moves first in one direction, then in the opposite direction. When any portion of the shell moves in one direction, it squeezes together air particles in its path as it shoves them outward. As the same portion of the shell moves in the opposite direction, the air particles behind it are spaced out. (Of course, when the air on one side of the vibration portion is being squeezed together, the air on the other side is being spaced out.) The alternate squeezing and thinning out of air particles produces sound waves.

—*Martin C. Keen*

__d__ 8. We can infer that if we stop a gong from vibrating,
- a. air will be squeezed together.
- b. the gong will continue to move back and forth for a few minutes.
- c. the sound will get softer.
- d. the sound will stop.

__c__ 9. If you shake a wood stick back and forth in the air rapidly enough, we can infer that
- a. the stick will break from air pressure.
- b. air will be squeezed on both sides of the stick at the same time.
- c. a sound will be produced.
- d. the stick will move to where the air is thinner

__a__ 10. We can infer that on a planet with no air a gong that is struck will
- a. make no sound.
- b. make a louder sound.
- c. send its sound out over a greater distance.
- d. not vibrate.

4. The Bedouin people think most highly of people who show loyalty. To them, loyalty does not mean that one is devoted to a country, a place, or a leader. Loyalty means being faithful to one's family and tribe.

The Bedouin take pride in their ancestors. They do not admire a hero from an ordinary or poor family as much as one who comes from an honored family. They particularly respect those who have inherited a good name and then have passed it on to their children.

A man's position among the black-tent people depends upon his ancestors, relatives, and fellow tribesmen. If they are honored, he is also honored. If they are disgraced, he too is disgraced. Therefore, one carefully guards the honor of his family, his lineage, and his tribe.

A man can protect his family's honor by being brave and generous and by giving protection to those who ask for it. He also guards it by carefully watching the women of his family.

A Bedouin woman cannot bring honor to her family, but she can bring disgrace. Even if a woman only looks as if she has done wrong, she may be killed. The honor of her family depends upon her virtue.

—*Merwyn S. Garbarino and Rachel R. Sady*

__c__ 11. Based on this passage, you can infer that a Bedouin man will feel disgraced if he
   a. does not succeed at business.
   b. needs to ask for help from his brothers.
   c. does nothing when a member of his family is insulted.
   d. does not help a stranger who asks for assistance.

__a__ 12. From this passage, you can predict that if a Bedouin woman betrays her husband with another man, the
   a. woman will be punished.
   b. other man will be punished.
   c. husband will ask for a divorce.
   d. woman will be forgiven.

__b__ 13. From this passage, you can infer that the Bedouin people
   a. respect people who leave their families to seek success on their own.
   b. respect people who value their families above all else.
   c. blame government officials who use their power to get special favors for their families.
   d. are self-centered.

__d__ 14. You can infer from this passage that Bedouin women are
   a. treated as the equals of men.
   b. always listened to carefully when they tell their side of a story.

c. respected for the many things they do.
d. not respected as much as men.

b 15. You can infer from this passage that the Bedouins
a. are a peaceful people.
b. center their lives around their families.
c. are not concerned with status and honor.
d. are quick to recognize individual excellence.

5. Heard about the couple who divorced after 70 years of marriage? "We didn't want to hurt the kids, so we waited until they died," they explain. Such black humor captures the anguish of many couples. Should we split up, or stay together for the sake of the children?

Stay, experts once advised; protect your kids from the fallout of a broken home. Then in the '60s, they began backing divorce: The trauma is temporary, and more fulfilled parents rear happier, better-adjusted children. We listened. Forty-five percent of kids born in the 1980s will see their parents divorce before they're 18, as opposed to 11 percent in the 1950s. The new advice was based on changing values and psychological theory, not empirical data. Now, long-term national studies, which monitored large numbers of families and schoolchildren, reveal that the effects of splitting are not so rosy. While unhappy parents can cause problems for children, it seems divorce may provoke greater problems. Kids suffer in ways we didn't anticipate.

Children reared by only one birth parent are twice as likely to drop out of school or become teenage parents, and are one-and-a-half times more likely to be unemployed after leaving school. This occurs regardless of a parent's race and educational background, say sociology professors Sara McLanahan of Princeton University and Gary Sandefur of the University of Wisconsin in *Growing Up with a Single Parent: What Hurts, What Helps* (Harvard University Press, 1994).

—*Roberta Pollack*

c 16. We can infer that the divorced couple in the joke
a. really enjoyed raising children.
b. stayed very close to their children, even after the children were grown.
c. did not feel even adult children could cope with their divorce.
d. did not keep secrets from their children.

___b___ 17. We can infer from the joke that people
   a. take divorce lightly.
   b. worry about the effect of divorce on children.
   c. can work together in raising children even if they feel like divorcing.
   d. think divorces work better for old people.

___a___ 18. We can infer that divorces in families with children
   a. have increased since the 1950s.
   b. have decreased since the 1950s.
   c. have stayed the same since the 1950s.
   d. are at the same level as divorces in families without children.

___d___ 19. We can infer that experts before the 1960s advised parents to
   a. divorce if they find it necessary.
   b. send children to counseling to protect them from the effects of divorce.
   c. remarry as soon as possible after getting a divorce.
   d. avoid divorce to protect children.

___c___ 20. We can infer that experts in the 1960s
   a. were more sensitive to the needs of children.
   b. had access to new facts that suggested divorce did no permanent harm to children.
   c. thought divorce was better for children than a bad marriage.
   d. tended to be divorced themselves.

___b___ 21. We can infer that experts now advise parents
   a. never to get a divorce.
   b. that children can be hurt by divorce.
   c. to follow their feelings about divorce.
   d. that staying married causes no problems for children.

___c___ 22. We can infer that the new advice is based on
   a. more and better values than in the past.
   b. more and better theories than in the past.
   c. more and better facts than in the past.
   d. more open-minded thinking than in the past.

___a___ 23. We can infer that family experts
   a. have switched their opinions back and forth.
   b. have been consistent in their opinions.
   c. are affected only by facts.
   d. have no reason or logic to their advice.

d 24. From the facts presented in the final paragraph, we can infer that children of divorce
   a. are always raised by only one parent.
   b. seek an independent path in life.
   c. never emerge from their problems.
   d. are more likely to have difficulties at school and work.

d 25. From the study reported in the final paragraph, we can also infer that
   a. children of well-educated families have the same amount of problems as children of less-educated families.
   b. race has no influence in the kinds or amount of problems families and children have.
   c. well-educated parents are more likely than less-educated parents to know how to protect their children from the harmful effects of a divorce.
   d. children of divorce have more problems than children from the same race and education group raised by both birth parents.

Score: ______ correct × 4 points each = ______

UNIT 5 Review Test

Read this selection from a marketing textbook, which describes the crime problem in shopping malls. Then answer the questions that follow.

Coping with Shopping Mall Crime

To escape the crowding, dirt, and crime of the cities, thousands of Americans flocked to the suburbs in the 1950s and 1960s. With the growth of the suburbs came the shopping mall, a refuge of piped-in music, bright lighting, and clean surroundings, where parents could safely drop off their children for a few hours on Saturday. Their biggest fear would have been that the youngsters might spend too much money. These days, however, malls are becoming less like havens and more like city streets, where crime is on the rise.

Not long ago, a woman was murdered at an upscale Los Angeles shopping center. After the murder, business dropped dramatically, and rent for retail space plummeted from $6.00 a square foot to $2.50. Increasingly, crime affects mall site selection. Real estate consultants report that retailers are avoiding malls with a reputation for crime whether the reputation is substantiated or not. Prudential Realty Group's institutional investment management unit affirms that the agency always examines an area's crime potential. If a mall doesn't provide excellent security, says the unit's managing director, his organization probably won't invest in a store there.

To combat car theft, vandalism, and violent attacks on customers, mall developers, managers, and retailers must spend more on security. At a meeting of shopping center security directors, those attending agreed that security spending has risen from 5 percent of a center's budget to about 20 percent. The biggest chunk of security budgets goes toward hiring and training staff, and then paying the well-trained, highly visible personnel. But maintaining such a security staff is only one step that malls are taking to restore peace of mind to investors, employees, and customers. They also utilize elaborate video camera systems, some with lenses that can zoom in on license plates. Security officers carry beepers, walkie-talkies, and even special night-vision binoculars. Lighting plays an important security role. One Long Island shopping center installed a system that illuminates its ten-thousand-car parking lot as brightly as a baseball field. Other security measures include escorting customers to their cars, distributing written safety information, offering optional valet parking, and employing plainclothes police to patrol malls, as well as mounted police to patrol parking lots.

Many law enforcement officials insist that mall crime is not soaring; the public simply has a heightened awareness of it. Because neither federal, state, and local law enforcement agencies nor retail organizations keep records of crimes occurring specifically in shopping malls, it is difficult to separate real events from fear-driven rumors. At a joint meeting of the U.S. Senate Law and Public Safety Committee and the Assembly of Senior Citizens, however, state police officials, crime victims rights groups, and representatives from various states' Attorney General's offices took the problem quite seriously. Although those attending acknowledge that developers and managers cannot guarantee absolute protection to thousands of people every day, malls must bear the costs of dealing with this increasing problem.

—William Pride and O. C. Ferrell

Put an *F* in front of each statement that represents a fact and an *O* in front of each statement that represents an opinion. If the statement represents an opinion, write the name of the person or group who holds that opinion on the blank line following the statement.

__F__ 1. Thousands of Americans flocked to the suburbs in the 1950s and 1960s.

____

__O__ 2. Youngsters might spend too much money.

parents

__O__ 3. Shopping malls are becoming less like havens and more like city streets.

the writer of the selection

F 4. After a murder, business dropped in a Los Angeles mall.

F 5. Retailers avoid malls with a reputation for crime.

O 6. A mall with less than excellent security is a bad investment.
Prudential Realty Group

F 7. Security spending has risen from 5 percent to 20 percent of a shopping center's budget.

F 8. Security officers use electronic equipment.

O 9. Mall crime is not soaring.
law enforcement officials

O 10. Malls have much crime.
public

F 11. No government or business organization keeps statistics on mall crime.

O 12. Mall crime is a serious problem. many groups at the U.S. Senate Committee and Assembly of Senior Citizens hearings

O 13. Malls must pay the cost of security. many groups at the U.S. Senate Committee and Assembly of Senior Citizens hearings

14. Put a check mark beside each statement you can correctly infer from the selection.

✓ a. People did not like the dirt and crime of cities.

___ b. People in the 1950s did not enjoy the cities as much as we do now.

_______ c. Before the 1950s, there was not much crime in the cities.

___✓___ d. Shopping malls are likely to be built in suburbs.

_______ e. People really enjoy listening to piped-in music.

___✓___ f. Piped-in music increases a sense of safety.

___✓___ g. Parents now worry more about their children spending time at a mall than they did in the 1960s.

_______ h. Young people hanging out at food courts upsets shoppers.

___✓___ i. Electronic devices help identify crimes and criminals.

___✓___ j. Night brings special security problems.

___✓___ k. Plainclothes police catch people engaged in crime.

___✓___ l. People are deterred from crime when they see security agents.

___✓___ m. People feel safer when they see security agents.

___✓___ n. Dark parking lots are dangerous.

_______ o. Mall security aims entirely at catching criminals.

_______ p. Mall security is aimed entirely at stopping crime.

_______ q. Mall security is aimed entirely at making customers feel safe.

___✓___ r. Mall security aims at catching criminals, stopping crime, and making customers feel safe.

___✓___ s. If customers don't feel safe, they are less likely to shop at a mall.

___✓___ t. Mall owners want to make customers happy.

_______ u. Law enforcement agencies are concerned with malls making a profit.

_______ v. Shoppers have no say in the discussion over mall security.

_______ w. Local governments will help maintain mall security because of the importance of malls to the local economy.

_______ x. The problem of shopping mall crime is likely to be solved.

UNIT SIX

Writing to Read

CHAPTER FOURTEEN

Critical Reading

Not everything that appears in print or on the Internet is true, right, or to be accepted without question. Just because somebody wrote something doesn't mean you need to believe it, just as you may not go along fully with every person you talk with.

When you talk with people, you are constantly evaluating and making judgments about what they say. You sense some people know more on the topic and have better judgment. You sometimes suspect some people are trying to get you to do something because it serves their interests. You are aware that some people are more honest or candid than others. You know when people spend more time on being pleasant than on getting the work done, and you know when they push their activities so hard and fast they do not consider your perspective and concerns.

In the same way, you need to evaluate what you read. You need to consider how knowledgeable and trustworthy the writer is and what viewpoints or perspectives the writer offers. You should examine how factually accurate the writing is and how trustworthy and based on evidence its opinions are as well as how the authors try to persuade you. Reading well is reading critically.

The previous two chapters presented some of the basic skills of critical reading. Spotting what is fact and what is opinion is the first step to seeing how well supported ideas are with evidence. Noticing what writers don't tell you directly but want you to infer helps you see where their argument is headed. It also helps you judge whether you really want to go where they suggest. Below are three groups of questions to ask yourself as you read. The questions concern the credibility of the author or publication, the facts or information presented, and the reasoning used.

14a Who Writes, and Where Is It Published

1. AUTHOR: *Can you identify who has written or gathered the material?*

On the Internet and elsewhere, some material appears that cannot be traced back to any source. You should be suspicious about material that has no identifiable source for two reasons. First, you have no way to evaluate the trustworthiness, expertise, or credibility of the source. Second, no one stands behind the material to be held responsible if it is false or misleading.

2. EXPERTISE: *Does the writer have knowledge, expertise, or credibility on the topic?*

If the writer is a known expert or holds a position that requires knowledge and credibility in a particular area, then his or her words on that subject carry more weight than those of just any person who ventures an opinion. Information about a disease from a licensed medical doctor has some believability, but that from a doctor who is head of a major research hospital has even more. Sometimes the believability comes from the organization the person speaks for or through. For example, statistics from the U.S. Census Bureau have a powerful believability due to the procedures and trustworthiness of the organization. Information from websites prepared by major nonpartisan organizations has greater reliability than that from an unknown or fly-by-night source.

3. QUALITY: *Does the publication have some reputable quality control?*

While anyone with a computer and an Internet connection can now put up his or her own website, the work of only a small number of writers is chosen to appear in certain journals or on websites that have careful selection and review procedures. Thus, a story from a major newspaper or news website such as CNN or the *Los Angeles Times* has greater authority than a rumor posted on a private blog. Articles in a respected academic journal usually have gone through an especially rigorous review process. Similarly, books from reputable presses or articles in major reference books, such as the *Encyclopedia Britannica*, have the credibility that comes from the trustworthiness of the publisher.

14b What Facts are Presented

4. EVIDENCE: *Does the author provide enough appropriate evidence to back up the view presented?*

If a writer seems to be presenting his or her own views with no facts to back them up, or with facts that may back another point, but not this, then you should suspect the accuracy of what they write.

5. ACCURACY: *Is the author's information accurate?*

One of the best ways to check accuracy is to compare the information with that presented by other reliable sources. Another way is to ask how the information was collected and checked.

6. COMPREHENSIVENESS: *Does the author take into account information and ideas from other knowledgeable people in the area, or does the writer seem to be asserting his or her own views only?*

This is not to say that you should distrust every new and different perspective. Rather, someone who presents a new point of view must be especially full in providing evidence and answering objections from established points of view.

14c How the Authors Think

7. REASONING: *Are the ideas presented logically and consistently?*

One point needs to follow another in a logical way. Important parts of the topic need to be covered and not left out. If the writer asks you to make a big leap of thinking for no good reason or leaves you wondering how you got from the statements at the beginning to those at the end, you are right to have doubts and ask questions.

8. BIAS: *Does the author push a point of view without giving proper respect to the other side?*

An author who dismisses opposition out of hand and without careful argument is not likely to present a full, careful, and fair picture of the subject. While an author need not agree with other views, he or she at least needs to take them seriously. If the author does not, you ought to suspect bias.

9. WORLDVIEW: *Does the author seem to take for granted a view of the world that you or other readers are likely to find controversial?*

People who write from extreme worldviews may write with great certainty and confidence about ideas that may look more doubtful from other perspectives. While you certainly should consider ideas from people with different perspectives, you need to evaluate each fact and idea carefully on its own merits.

These questions will help you decide what you should take from each piece of reading, what you should suspect, and what you may want to find out more about before coming to conclusions.

EXERCISES

14.1 Critical Reading of an Essay

Read Paul Newman's comments on drugs in our society on pages 277–278 in chapter 12. On a separate piece of paper, evaluate it in relation to each of these concerns:

1. author
2. expertise
3. quality
4. evidence
5. accuracy
6. comprehensiveness
7. reasoning
8. bias
9. worldview

14.2 Critical Reading of a Textbook

Using the nine questions above, critically evaluate the reading selection on MTV in exercise 10.2 on page 205–206. Use a separate sheet of paper.

14.3 Critical Reading of an Internet Site

Locate an Internet site that discusses MTV. On a separate sheet of paper, critically evaluate the site using the nine questions above.

Then compare your evaluation of the website with your evaluation of the textbook selection on MTV that you evaluated in exercise 14.2.

Critical Reading on the Internet

Find three Internet sites on one of the following topics:

global warming

school testing

choosing a career

back pain

acupuncture

a recent president of the United States

Evaluate and compare the three websites in terms of each of the nine questions listed above.

Chapter 14 SELF-TEST
Critical Reading

In your own words, explain the meaning and importance of each of the following criteria for critically evaluating reading means. Score five points for each correct definition and five points for each correct identification of importance.

1. Author

   meaning: Is the writer of the piece identified?

   importance: If no one takes responsibility for the information, it cannot be trusted.

2. Expertise

   meaning: Does the author know much about the topic?

   importance: Someone who knows and has experienced more on the topic, as well as being more respected, is more to be believed and trusted.

3. Quality

   meaning: Does the publication have standards for the quality of material it publishes?

   importance: Information and ideas from publications with high standards are more likely to be credible.

4. Evidence

   meaning: Does the author present facts to back up his or her ideas and claims?

importance: If a claim is backed by strong evidence, it is more believable.

5. Accuracy

meaning: Is the author careful to get the facts right?

importance: If the facts are not precisely right, the author is either careless or trying to shade the truth. In either case, such an author is to be trusted less.

6. Comprehensiveness

meaning: Is the author aware of the full range of facts and ideas on the subject?

importance: An author who shows knowledge of more of the facts and ideas is likely to take more into account and is also likely to have thought through alternative views.

7. Reasoning

meaning: Is the argument and reasoning logically presented?

importance: You need to be able to follow and accept an author's reasoning in order to accept his or her conclusions. Lack of logic should make you suspect the ideas.

8. Bias

meaning: Does the author seem to favor one perspective over all others?

importance: If the author has a one-sided view, he or she may not be representing fairly views and facts that do not support the favored view.

9. Worldview

meaning: Does the author have a view of life that predetermines his or her view on the subject?

importance: If the author has a predetermined view on the subject, he or she may not be considering all relevant facts and ideas fairly and equally.

Score: ______ correct answers × 5 points each + 10 free = ______

CHAPTER FIFTEEN

Underlining, Listing, and Summarizing

Most of reading goes on inside your head. Your eyes see dark spots on paper, and your brain makes meaning out of those spots and remembers that meaning. This is a lot of activity to keep straight inside your head. You often can get and remember more meaning from reading if you do some of the work outside your head.

Marking the most important parts of your reading in one way or another allows you to see more easily how these parts fit together into a total meaning. Writing down the main points of a reading selection also can refresh your memory about what you have read. Finally, the simple act of marking something down impresses that idea on your mind.

There are many ways to mark down directly the ideas from your reading. Most involve writing. Through your writing, the ideas you get from reading turn into words with which you yourself have worked.

This chapter discusses three ways of writing to read. The first, underlining, requires you to mark the main points of meaning in a selection. The second, listing, requires you to put down these points in your own writing. The last, summarizing, requires you to put the ideas together by writing your own statement about the selection. Underlining is a bit active. Listing is more active. Summarizing is most active and thus is the best method for helping you understand and remember meaning. The skills you learn when you do underlining and listing help you summarize.

15a Underlining

By underlining main ideas and major details when you read, you actively mark what you think is most important in a passage. Later, if you ever need to reread or look over the passage, the underlining will draw your eye to the most important parts.

Underlining

- Underline only in books that belong to you. Do not underline in library books, borrowed books, or books that belong to your school. Underlining is a personal process. Your underlining may interfere with other people's use of a book.
- Mark the main ideas and the major details differently. Underline the main ideas with a double line and the major details with a single line, or use two different colors of high lighter pens.
- Find main idea sentences by following the suggestions on page 153. Underline the sentences (or parts of sentences) that state the main idea of a paragraph. If the main ideas are only implied, write your own main idea sentence in the margin.
- Find major details by following the suggestions on page 211. Underline the major details.
- Use circles, brackets, asterisks, numbers, or any other symbol to mark parts that are especially interesting or important to you. If you note ideas in a sequence, number them 1, 2, 3, 4, and so on.
- Write notes or comments to yourself in the margins. The margins are good places to put down your own thoughts as you read. Notes in the margin can help you connect ideas from different parts of the reading. Notes also can help you connect your reading to other things that you have read, that your teacher said, or that you have experienced.

Look at the following example of how a student underlined a selection from a book about how to drive a car. This selection describes everything you have to do before you turn the car key. Notice how the student's underlining and notes help organize the many details so the overall meaning can be seen easily.

Predriving Checks

Before entering — Before getting into the car, make sure that nothing is in its path. Clear the windows, if necessary. Enter your car from the curb side. If you must enter the car from the street side, approach the door from the front of the car. From this position, you can see and *Entering* — avoid approaching traffic. When it is safe to do so, open the door and get into the car. Close and lock the door quickly.

Clearing — Once inside the car, you can put the key in the ignition while you make remaining predriving checks. Clear all objects from the front and rear window ledges. These items can block your view and also become hazards if they slide off during a sudden stop. Be sure all windows are clean.

Seating — Seat yourself comfortably with your back against the seat and your arms and legs slightly bent. Rest your left foot on the floor beside the clutch or brake pedal. Rest the heel of your right foot on the floor and the ball of your foot on the gas pedal. Grasp the steering wheel with both hands. To position your hands properly, think of the steering wheel as a clock. Place your left hand between the 9 and 10 o'clock positions. Place your right hand *Adjust* — between the 2 and 3 o'clock positions. Move the seat forward or backward until you are comfortable and can reach all the controls. Make sure you can see over the steering wheel. If necessary, use a cushion. Adjust the head restraint so that it is directly behind the middle of the back of your head.

Don't Forget — Once you are properly seated, fasten your safety belt and make sure that all passengers have fastened theirs. Next, check the mirrors. Adjust the inside mirror so that you can see out of the entire rear window. Adjust the outside mirror so that you can see the area to the left of your car and only a small part of the side of your car.

Duane R. Johnson and Donn W. Maryott

EXERCISES

15.1 Underlining

1. Read the selection about Mathematical Skills in Infancy on pages 195–197. Underline the important information in the passage.
2. Review Chapter 12 of this textbook (pages 267–279) by underlining.

15.2 Underlining

1. Underline a chapter in a textbook assigned in another course. Use underlining and other marks to highlight important information.
2. Underline the following selection from a criminal justice textbook. The selection deals with how our ideas about punishment have changed since ancient times.

Punishment in Historical Perspective

Ancient societies did not have prisons; instead, they used other forms of punishment. Some favored public humiliation and ridicule, especially for minor offenses, to teach offenders a lesson and to deter other individuals from violating social norms. In some societies, punishment often took the form of restitution; offenders would be expected to compensate their victims for the wrongs they had committed. In other societies, punishment was more retributive and involved fines, banishment from the society, corporal punishment, or execution (Farrington, 1996).

Ancient societies and their medieval counterparts developed many types of corporal punishment, including beating, whipping or flogging, branding, mutilation, and the use of devices such as the rack and pillory. Torture in medieval Europe was common, both as a punishment and as a means of making individuals confess to alleged offenses. Corporal punishment in the Western world lasted well into the nineteenth century when, thanks to efforts begun a century earlier by criminal justice reformers in Britain, Italy, and elsewhere, it finally fell out of favor. It did not disappear altogether, however; flogging remained a possible form of legal punishment in Great Britain for at least some offenses until 1967. In the United States, floggings occurred in Delaware as late as 1952, and Delaware did not ban them until 1972 (Walker, 1998). Flogging and other corporal punishment are prohibited by various international human rights treaties but continue to be practiced in many nations in the Middle East and elsewhere.

incarceration confinement in prison or jail following conviction of a crime

As a form of punishment, confinement (or **incarceration**) did not really exist anywhere in the world before the eighteenth century. Some offenders *were* confined even in ancient times, but not as a form of punishment. Instead, they were confined until they could be tried or until they could be given some other form of punishment, such as flogging or banishment. In one exception to this general rule, debtors in medieval Europe were confined until they could pay the money they owed.

Several institutions resembling prisons were established during the sixteenth century in Britain and other parts of Europe. The first was the *workhouse*, in which poor people lived and had to work hard under the supervision of guards. Workhouses were developed to help the poor by providing them with food and lodging and helping them to learn good work habits, but, in effect, they were a way of confining them and controlling their behavior. A second quasi-prison that developed during this time was the *house of correction*, in which people charged with minor offenses lived and, like their workhouse counterparts, had to work hard under the supervision of guards. Finally, the *gaol* (jail) also developed and was used to detain suspects until they could be tried. But until well into the eighteenth century, incarceration in prison or jail as a form of punishment was not used (Foucault, 1977).

That changed by the end of the eighteenth century, in large part due to the efforts of the European criminal justice reformers noted earlier. These reformers were appalled by the massive use of torture and executions in Europe and argued that punishment should be proportional to the offense. They were also appalled by the conditions in the European prisons that were used to hold people for the reasons just cited. Their efforts helped improve prison and jail conditions but also gave rise to the idea that imprisonment should replace corporal punishment as the dominant mode of punishment. Thus, as the 1700s passed, more and more people were punished by being put behind bars. Although that was a reform over corporal punishment, the prisons in which they were put continued to suffer from terrible conditions. They were filthy and overcrowded; men, women, and children were confined together, as were violent and minor offenders. Rape and other abuses were common. The crowded and dirty conditions made communicable diseases rampant, and these diseases routinely killed inmates, guards, and even, sometimes, lawyers and judges. At the same time, many British prisoners who were awaiting *transportation*, or banishment, to Australia lived in the hulls of ships docked in England and often never left for Australia. The conditions in the hulls were often even worse than those in the prisons.

Criminal justice reformers continued to call attention to all these decrepit conditions. One British reformer, John Howard, wrote a 1777 book in which he said that prisons should become places in which offenders could learn the error of their ways and repent the offenses they had committed. His work helped motivate Britain to build prisons, which came to be called **penitentiaries**, designed to accomplish this goal. The age of the modern prison had finally begun (Foucault, 1977).

penitentiaries early prisons that were built to hold inmates so they could repent for their offenses

Critical Thinking and Writing

Some people argue that we need to be tougher on criminals, locking up more of them for longer periods. Other people find that too many of our youth are being locked up for nonviolent offenses. And others feel there is discrimination in who winds up in prison. Write your views on our current practices of sending people to prison. Use evidence and arguments to back up your views.

15b Listing

When you read, you can list the ideas and the major details. By writing the ideas and the details on a sheet of paper, you are an even more active reader than you are when you simply underline. You pay special attention to ideas and details and check out whether you understand the meaning fully. Also, when you organize the list later on, you can organize the reading in your own mind.

The wording for the list can come from the original material or can be your own rephrasing. You can copy whole sentences and phrases, or you can shorten them, as long as you keep the main point. Choosing your own phrasing makes you think even more actively about the meaning.

Making a list is like taking notes or writing an informal outline. When you are done, you have your own statement of what is important in the reading.

Read the information about listing ideas and information in the box on this page. Then look at one student's list of ideas and information made from the selection on predriving checks (page 317).

Predriving Checks

outside, check road and windows are clear

get in car safely, from curb if possible

clear ledges and windows

sit comfortably, place hands and feet

adjust seat, head restraint, safety belt, mirrors

In this list, the student includes all the main things that must be done but leaves out all the specific details, such as exactly where the hands should be placed on the wheel.

Listing Ideas and Information

- Find the main ideas by following the suggestions in Chapter 8. Write these main ideas on notebook paper, starting at the left margin of the paper. You can copy the entire main idea sentence as it appears in the reading, shorten it, or put the idea in your own words. Or you can jot down a few key phrases, as long as they capture the main idea.
- Find the major details by following the suggestions on page 211. List these details beneath the main ideas they support. List each detail separately. Indent the details a bit so you can tell the details from the main ideas. Again, you need not copy whole sentences; phrases will do. Use either your own wording or the wording of the original, as long as you capture the meaning.

EXERCISES

15.3 Ideas and Information

1. List the major ideas and details from the selection about Jean Paul Getty on pages 202–203.

   Jean Paul Getty made most of his money on his own.

   He made his money on oil dealings.

   He started in business in Oklahoma, but he went on to deal around the world.

   He was the richest man in the world, worth between $2 billion and $4 billion.

2. Review Chapter 13 on inference, pages 280–293, by listing the important information.

   Inference helps us read between the lines by using hints and clues.

   Inferences cannot be certain, but if we are careful we can be fairly sure of what they suggest.

   Writers rely on inference.

   We use inference in all aspects of life—for example, in figuring out what people are feeling.

15.4 Ideas and Information from Textbooks

1. Study a chapter from a textbook assigned in another course by listing the important ideas and information. Use a separate sheet of paper.
2. List the important ideas and information from the textbook selection on the history of punishment on pages 318–320. Use a separate sheet of paper.
3. Read the following selection from a study skills textbook. This selection discusses how to improve study habits outside the classroom. On a separate sheet of paper, list the important ideas and information that you find in the selection. Student responses will vary.

Improving Your Academic Performance

Having wisely chosen an academic major and related courses, how do you then maximize your performance within your course of study? To improve your academic performance, you will first need to assess the following factors: how much time you have available to study, how much of that time you actually devote to study, and the circumstances under which you typically study. This analysis should point to out-of-class factors (e.g., when you are studying, with whom you are studying) that will need to be altered to improve your in-class performance.

Analyzing Your Study Habits

Preparing a weekly schedule is one way to clarify how much time could be devoted to study. For example, if you have allocated 56 hours per week for sleep, 20 hours for a part-time job, 10 hours for eating, 5 hours for exercising, 5 hours for personal grooming, 17 hours for attending class, and 5 hours for commuting to school, you would still have an additional 50 hours left for study and other activities. Assuming that you allocated about 3 hours per weekday to study, you would have some time each day for other pursuits, and your weekends would be essentially free for whatever you choose.

After you have determined how much time you could reasonably devote to study, you will need to determine exactly how much time you are actually studying and the circumstances surrounding your studying. Keeping a study log for at least a week, including the weekend, could greatly illuminate your study habits. Simply have a notepad available to record when you study, where you study, what you study, what you accomplish when you study, and how alert you are when you study. Your log may indicate that you are devoting less time to study than you thought, frequently shifting activities in your study time, often studying when your energy is low, studying in settings where you are easily distracted, studying at the last minute, and accomplishing little in your study sessions. Recording your study habits will help you pinpoint what needs to be changed to improve your academic performance.

One way to pinpoint deficiencies in your study habits is to use the information recorded in your log to answer the following questions. Answering yes to several items indicates that your study habits are far less effective than they could be.

- I seldom set definite goals for how much studying I should do.

- I have never tried to keep a time schedule for regulating my study.
- I frequently put off studying until it is too late to get my assignments completed on time.
- When I do try to study on a regular basis, something usually interferes.
- I probably devote less than 10 hours per week to study.
- Ten or 15 minutes is about as long as I can concentrate without getting restless.
- My place of study sometimes gets cluttered with magazines and other material that could distract me from studying.
- Bull sessions frequently occur where I study.
- Daydreams keep interfering with my studies.
- I have never consciously tried to reinforce any of my study behaviors.

Critical Thinking and Writing

Using the methods and concepts described in this selection, write a few paragraphs in which you analyze your own study habits and describe how you might improve them.

Changing Out-of-Class Behaviors

Probably any course you take will involve some out-of-class commitments (e.g., reading course materials, writing papers, studying for exams). Without certain requisite out-of-class activities, your time in class can be wasted. You will need to evaluate the recommendations in this section in terms of the information obtained from analyzing your study habits.

Allocating Your Time If your time assessment revealed insufficient time for study, your overall schedule will need to be altered. The amount of study time needed varies somewhat from major to major. One survey (Schuman et al., 1985) of study time for weekdays and weekends showed that pre-professional natural science students (e.g., premedical) reported studying an average of 3.9 hours daily, natural science students 3.6 hours, social science students 3.2 hours, and humanities students 3 hours. Consequently, if a typical humanities student were taking 15 credit hours and studying an average of 3 hours per day (or 21 hours weekly), that student would be studying about 1.4 hours per week for every credit hour taken.

The estimates of study time reported in the preceding research are generally consistent with what many professors expect from students (i.e., at least an hour of out-of-class study for every hour that a student is scheduled to be in class). You may want to use this criterion as an initial guideline for reallocating your study time. Once you make time available for study, you must then address the more important issue of how you use that time.

Using Time Effectively Don Dickinson and Debra O'Connell's work (1990) with education majors provides a good example of what is meant by effective use of study time. The students recorded the time they spent reading, reviewing, and organizing. *Reading* included both initial reading and rereading of course material. *Reviewing* included going back through the material to underline important content, rereading underlined material, reading class notes, reading headings (surveying), and trying to recall material. *Organizing* referred to integrating material into some meaningful pattern, such as finding primary and secondary concepts in the material, combining lecture and reading notes, and writing answers to course objectives in one's own words. When the amounts of time that students reported for reading, reviewing, and organizing were compared with their exam scores, organizing proved to be the factor that best discriminated between the high and the low scorers. High-scoring students spent 76 percent more time organizing than did low-scoring students.

Effective use of study time is also reflected in how well you match your tasks with available time slots. For example, a half hour between classes would not be enough time to complete a major reading assignment, but could be a good time to review class notes and develop questions that you want to ask in class. A brief time slot might also be a good time to survey a chapter, paying particular attention to the major issues addressed in that chapter. Similarly, you might use the time to identify the major concepts in the notes just taken in class or make plans for the remainder of the day.

Choosing an Optimal Setting If you frequently find yourself sitting down to study only to be tempted to do something else, perhaps you need to make changes in the place(s) where you study. A number of researchers (Beneke & Harris, 1972; Briggs et al., 1971; Fox, 1962) have demonstrated that you can increase the likelihood of studying in a given setting by devoting that area exclusively to study. To ensure that an area is associated only with study, you should leave your place of study whenever you begin to think of anything inconsistent with study. However, before you leave, work one more problem, read one more page, or complete a small portion of your assignment. The next time you sit down to study, you might work two problems, read two more pages, or complete a larger portion of your assignment after getting the impulse to stop studying. This strategy helps you maintain a relationship between that setting and studying, as well as work through your impulse to stop studying.

Keep your study area free of distracting materials (e.g., photographs of your girlfriend or boyfriend). Such stimuli frequently lead to behaviors that are incompatible with studying, such as fantasizing. (Save those thoughts for your study breaks.) Similarly, if you want to study with others, study only with those who stay focused on the subject matter. The library is often a good place for study, because studying is the primary activity associated with the library. Many libraries also have rooms for small-group study.

Improving Your Reading Comprehension Possibly no factor is more fundamental to your academic success than your ability to comprehend reading material. One of the most widely used models for promoting reading comprehension is the **SQ3R method** developed by Francis Robinson (1970). Survey, question, read, recite, and review are abbreviated in the SQ3R title to make it easier to remember. Although you may not choose to use all these strategies with every reading assignment, the SQ3R method does combine these strategies into one integrated model.

Survey, the first step in the SQ3R method, involves examining a chapter's headings and subheadings to get a general outline of the material to be studied. Surveying can also include reading topic sentences and summary statements at the end of the chapter. Once you have surveyed the material, the second step is to create *questions* from section headings. You can begin the questioning process by turning the first heading into a question. Your next step is to *read* the section with the idea of finding the answer to that question. After reading the first section, pause and *recite* the answer to your question. One useful means of reciting is to write down your answer from memory in the margin of the text. If you dislike making notes, then underline your answers. You first must think of your response to the question, and then look for key passages that reflect your answer. Don't worry about underlining until after you have read the entire section and have actually identified the important answers to your question. After completing your recitation for the first section, repeat the same procedure (i.e., question, read, and recite) for every section in the chapter. When you complete the assignment, you are then ready for the final step—a brief *review* of all the major concepts in the chapter.

Completing Major Projects You may have little difficulty with short-term assignments, but find it difficult to complete major projects on time. The following strategies should contribute to both the quality and timely completion of your long-term projects.

1. Break your project down into smaller tasks that can typically be done on a daily basis. Delaying work on a project often results from thinking of it as a single task rather than as a collection of smaller tasks.
2. Formulate a time schedule for completing these various tasks, leaving buffer time at the end. In other words, don't schedule your project to be completed the day it's to be submitted.
3. Generate ideas for a topic by keeping an idea sheet of possible topics in your notebook. Then select two or three ideas that have the greatest appeal to you.
4. Identify information related to possible topics by using standard indexes, such as *Psychological Abstracts* or *The Current Index to Journals in Education*. Many libraries now have computer systems linked to the standard indexes, making the process of finding relevant resources much easier.
5. Ultimately set the topic for which a manageable amount of information has been identified. Some topics can have too much information (i.e., hundreds of citations) and others too little (i.e., one or two citations). Of course, the manageability of information can be altered by narrowing or broadening an initial topic.
6. Once you have a list of potential references for the topic chosen, peruse the abstracts for these references to see which articles are truly relevant to your topic. Most computer searches supply abstracts with the references.
7. Begin making notes from the articles that you believe will be most useful in developing your topic. Take your notes on cards (e.g., 5-by-8-inch index cards) and give each card a topic label. Be sure to write the complete reference on each card so you will not have to relocate the reference later to get specific citation information (e.g., volume number of publication, page numbers for article).
8. Write an outline from your cards. This task will be much easier if you first categorize your cards by topics, then arrange these topics in a logical sequence, and finally logically order the cards within each topic area.

9. Write a rough draft from the outline. The information on your cards can be used to expand on the points in your outline. The major points to be addressed in your paper should be identified in the introduction.
10. Revise and edit your paper several times. Be sure that the points identified in your introduction are clearly and coherently addressed in the paper. The process of revision will be simplified if you use a word-processor rather than a typewriter. If you use a word-processing program, be sure to use a programmed spell check to correct any spelling errors. Do not allow grammatical mistakes and typographical errors to detract from the readability of the paper.

Reinforcing Effective Study Because many of the most potent academic reinforcers (such as a high mark on a term paper and an A in a course) do not immediately follow your daily study activities, you may need to arrange for intermediate payoffs. Actually, one of the best ways to reinforce studying is to follow study time with a fun activity. Even such a modest reward as reading the newspaper or looking through a magazine can serve as a short-term reinforcer for completing a specified amount of work. Beyond these natural reinforcers, you may wish to establish a credit system in which each segment of work is worth a certain amount of credit toward tangible items or weekend privileges.

If you are questioning the merits of rewarding your own study efforts, consider the findings of a research study conducted by Heffernan and Richards (1981). On the basis of interviews with students who had tried to improve their study behavior, the researchers classified half of the participants as successful and half as unsuccessful. The successful students were those who had increased their study time by at least 50 percent and maintained that change for one semester or longer. All the students had previously reported studying less than ten hours per week and were concerned about their study habits. Whereas 75 percent of the successful students reported using some type of self-reward, only 8 percent of the unsuccessful students used self-rewards.

—*Robert Williams and James Long*

15c Summarizing

In summarizing, you combine all the main ideas and the major details of a reading passage into a new, shorter statement. This statement fits together all the important parts into a connected whole.

When preparing a summary, you think about meaning even more actively than you did with listing. As with listing, you must think about what is important and how to phrase each idea briefly. In addition, you must think about how the parts fit together, and you must show that connection in the way you write the summary.

The summary should be about a quarter or a third as long as the original. To make a short summary, you have to think carefully about what is really important in the passage and what is not. Underlining or listing main ideas and major information can help you decide what to include in your summary. Crossing out minor information in the original also can help you decide what not to include.

Once you decide what information to include, you must put together the main ideas and the major details in readable sentences. You must show the connection between ideas and facts. The words for the summary can be either your own words or words from the original reading. Usually, in fact, the wording of a summary is a mixture of the two. More important, the wording must be brief. State the main points and leave everything else out. The summary, however, must be written in complete sentences that fit together smoothly. Unlike a list, which can include phrases, a summary must be a readable piece of writing.

Writing a Summary

- Read and make sure you understand the passage you want to summarize. Use a dictionary to check the meaning of all words about which you feel uncertain.
- Identify the main ideas and the major details of the reading selection by either underlining or listing.
- Make the main idea of the selection the most important sentence of the summary. This usually is the first sentence of the summary.
- Rewrite the information you underlined into sentences that show the connections among facts and ideas. You may combine several facts or facts and ideas into a single sentence, as long as the ideas do not get confused.

- Omit extra words in your summary and emphasize the important words.
- Make sure that you present the ideas and the information in an organized way that follows the meaning of the original. Don't jump suddenly from one point to the next. Use connecting words—*first, second, on the other hand, because*, and *although*—to show how the statements fit together. Use sentences that bring together related ideas, facts, or examples.

The following sample summary is based on the selection on predriving checks that you read as an example of underlining on page 317, and listing, on page 321. Notice how the summary uses the ideas, information, and even words picked out by underlining and listing. The summary then combines them into readable sentences that fit together as a single unit.

Before getting into a car, make sure the car's path and windows are clear. Then enter the car safely, from the curb side if possible. On the inside, make sure no objects on the ledges can slide around or block your vision. Then sit comfortably, with feet on the pedals and hands on the steering wheel. You can then adjust the seat, the head restraint, the seat belt, and the mirrors to fit your position.

To understand more fully how to write a summary, examine the process by which one student summarized a passage from a geology textbook. First, the student read the passage through for overall understanding. She had a pencil in hand to circle any words she needed to look up and to underline parts she thought were important. As you read the passage, notice the parts she marked.

What Causes Earthquakes?

People have tried to explain the cause of earthquakes since earliest times. Some people thought that quakes were sent from heaven to punish the wicked. Others believed that the earth rested on the backs of animals. When these creatures moved the earth would tremble, causing earthquakes.

We now have more scientific explanations of the causes of these destructive earth tremors. <u>Earthquakes are evidence that some process is at work below the surface of the earth.</u> Large

> bodies of magma may be in motion. These and other internal movements can result in a sudden release of energy by breaking the overlying, brittle rocks.
>
> During earthquakes, rocks beneath the surface are clearly bent and broken. In other cases deformation takes place slowly and without recognizable earthquake shocks. For example, in a drill hole in the Great Valley of California, earth movements have been measured for years. The rocks here are moving at a rate of about one meter per century.
>
> Another example of slow earth movements is at a winery in Hollister, California. By chance it was built on a fault associated with the San Andreas Fault Zone. Over the years there have been slow, steady movements without accompanying earthquakes. The winery building, originally a rectangle, has been pulled into a diamond shape. The land at this particular location moves about one centimeter a year.
>
> In some places pressure slowly builds up until the rocks break and quickly snap back into position. The faulting releases energy that may have built up in the rocks for hundreds or thousands of years. This sudden burst of energy causes vibrations that travel through the rocks. These vibrations are an earthquake. Most earthquakes are so small that they can be detected only by sensitive instruments. But when violent earthquakes occur in inhabited areas, they can cause great destruction and human misery.
>
> In large earthquakes most of the stored energy is released in the first movement along the fault surface. However, energy may continue to trickle off in *aftershocks*. These shocks are much less severe than the main shock and may continue for months after the initial earthquake.
>
> *American Geological Institute*

The student looked up the words *magma* and *fault* in the glossary at the back of the textbook. (If there had been no glossary, she would have used a dictionary.) She then looked over all the parts she underlined and made sure she understood what the whole passage was about.

She noticed the entire passage answered the question in the title: What causes earthquakes? She then realized the main idea of the passage would be the part that most directly answered the question. She found two related main idea sentences: "Earthquakes are evidence that some process is at work below the surface of the earth.... These and other internal movements can result in a sudden release of energy by breaking the overlying, brittle rocks." She combined the opening question and these two sentences into a single main idea sentence. She used that sentence to start her summary: "Earthquakes occur when internal movements of the earth suddenly release energy by breaking the overlying brittle rocks on the earth's surface."

The passage was mostly about the way scientists explain earthquakes today. The student felt that all the old explanations in the first paragraph were minor and should be left out. From the rest of the passage, she kept the major details of the explanation and eliminated most details of the examples.

Throughout, she combined sentences and eliminated extra words to bring out the main ideas in as few words as possible. Here is her final summary:

> Earthquakes occur when internal movements of the earth suddenly release energy by breaking the overlying brittle rocks on the earth's surface. During earthquakes, rocks are clearly bent and broken. Elsewhere, rocks may be slowly deformed over many years. Then the pressure may build up until the rocks break and snap back into position. This break releases the built-up energy in the rocks and causes vibrations to travel through the rocks. Most earthquakes are so small that they can be barely detected, but large violent earthquakes can destroy inhabited areas. In large earthquakes, smaller aftershocks may follow after the first large movement of the rocks.

EXERCISES

15.5 Summarizing Paragraphs

Summarize in one or two sentences each of the following paragraphs from an article about children who go to school at home.

> While other 15-year-olds are struggling through geometry, the periodic table and the agony of high-school social life, Gabriel Willow is blissfully pondering the body angles of fish, the mysteries of evolution, origami and anything else that intrigues him. "I've got a pile of about 12 fish books," says the teenager, who lives in rural Maine. "I'm looking for fish with the most exaggerated shapes that I can do in origami, things like puffer fish and angler fish, barracudas." What educational institution allows such freedom? None. Gabriel has spent virtually all of his school years at home. For an exceptionally bright, self-motivated kid, home-schooling is a salvation, he says. "Everything isn't divided up into half-hour learning

periods," he says. "I can pursue my own interests as far as I want to take them."

Home-schooling allows Gabriel Willow to explore his own interests.

Although it sounds radical, home-schooling is legal in all 50 states. The Department of Education estimates that more than 350,000 children are home-schooled (out of 49 million kids in grades K through 12). A majority come from fundamentalist families who want to teach morality along with the three R's. Other parents just want to get their kids out of deteriorating public schools, says Patrick Farenga of Holt Associates in Cambridge, Massachusetts, which publishes a newsletter for home-schoolers. Home-schooling isn't popular with many educators, who worry—legitimately—that the average parent doesn't know enough to teach at home. To help make sure that home-schooled kids get what they need, each state has its own rules. This is a daunting challenge for even committed parents. For guidance, they can turn to groups like Farenga's, specialists in local school districts and community-college faculties.

Parents provide home-schooling for over 350,000 children for a variety of reasons. Groups provide help in meeting state rules.

It's not easy being a teenager under any circumstances, but some home-schoolers say being away from regular school actually is a relief. Barbara Alexander took her sons Elye and Ben out of their local public school in rural Vermont a decade ago when Elye was in sixth grade and Ben was in third grade because both boys were academically frustrated. As they got older, the community became their classroom and they worked with a retired college professor, a veterinarian, farmers and woodsmen. "If you're just used to being with kids your own age, you lose touch with everyone else," says Elye. He thinks his home-schooling experience made him more self-reliant when he entered Harvard four years ago. The adjustment wasn't difficult: "No one else had come to college before either." But his mother has had a hard time adjusting since Ben went off to Cornell this fall. For home-teachers, she says, "this empty-nest thing isn't easy."

—*Barbara Kantrowitz*

Home-schooling provides a better emotional and social environment for some children.

15.6 Summarizing Newspaper Articles

Summarize each of the following short newspaper articles. Use the blanks provided after each selection.

WASHINGTON—At least two new moons—and perhaps two others—have been discovered in the orbit of Saturn, the ringed planet already was known to have 18 natural satellites large enough to be called moons.

Astronomers Amanda S. Bosh of the Lowell Observatory near Flagstaff, Arizona, and Andrew S. Rivkin of the University of Arizona announced Thursday that they spotted the new moons in Saturn photos taken by the Hubble Space Telescope.

Bosh said the photos were snapped May 22 during a rare time that Saturn's dust rings were seen edge-on, a celestial event known as the Earth ring crossing. During this time, the bright reflected light from the rings is dimmed and independent moons can more easily be sighted.

Two of the moons in the photos may be previously discovered bodies known as Atlas and Prometheus. Those moons were discovered by the Voyager spacecraft in 1980, but the latest sighting was in a slightly different location than where the moons were thought to be, based on the Voyager findings.

—Associated Press

Scientists have discovered at least two new moons orbiting Saturn.

LONDON—Jack the Ripper, the notorious 19th century murderer of London prostitutes, was an American surgeon, the authors of a new book, "The Lodger," said Monday.

British police officer Stewart Evans and Paul Gainey, a police press officer, claimed to have solved one of the world's greatest mysteries, naming Dr. Francis Tumblety as the killer.

Their claim is based on an unpublished letter written in 1913 by Chief Inspector John Littlechild, head of the special branch of London's Scotland Yard.

The letter, found in an antiquarian bookseller's collection, named Tumblety as the prime suspect. But he fled to the U.S. and police failed to track him down. There were no more Ripper-style murders in London after Tumblety left. But similar murders took place in Nicaragua and Jamaica which Tumblety may have committed.

—Reuters

Jack the Ripper may have been an American, based on an unpublished letter.

Godzilla to Bite the Dust

TOKYO, July 15—This time Godzilla is really going down for the count.

After 21 films in which the Japanese science-fiction monster has died only to rise again, the makers of his next film say it will definitely and positively and absolutely be the creature's last rampage across the screen.

Shogo Tomiyama, chief producer of the Toho Company, maker of the Godzilla films, told reporters today that after 21 adventures there were just no more new ideas left.

Godzilla first appeared on the screen in 1954, a giant dinosaur awakened from a long sleep at the bottom of the Pacific Ocean by hydrogen bomb tests who sets out to destroy Tokyo.

Mr. Tomiyama said in the dinosaur's last appearance, "Godzilla vs. Destroyer," set for release in December, the monster attacks Hong Kong.

—Reuters

Godzilla will die for the last time in a new movie.

NEW YORK—Remember the one about alligators in the sewer?

Well, here's another story for the annals for urban legends, only this one's for real: A 3-foot long alligator with a fat tail was captured in a small lake in the borough of Queens.

After several fishermen reported seeing the creature, it emerged, hissing, from Kissena Park Lake and was captured bare-handed by a day-camp worker with experience at handling reptiles.

"The guy just swooped down and grabbed the alligator," marveled park ranger Deborah Schreyer. "And I wrapped a big rubber band around its mouth."

The alligator, a male about 3 to 5 years old, was named Kissena.

"We believe that this is a released pet," Parks Commissioner Henry Stern said yesterday. "We know that because it's well-fed with a very fat tail, and it's calcium-deficient from lack of sunlight, probably because it was indoors."

The reptile's former owner "probably thought it was very cute until it got big," Stern said, adding, "It reminds me of the Ogden Nash poem: 'The trouble with a kitten is that, eventually it becomes a cat.' "

It is illegal to keep alligators as pets in New York City. The New York Herpetological Society agreed to pick the creature up and find it a suitable home.

Stern said the discovery of the alligator Wednesday was definitely an isolated occurrence.

"We found no other alligators in the lake," he said. "We're lucky this one wasn't thrown in the sewer."

A three-foot alligator was caught in a lake in Queens.

___

___

15.7 Summarizing a Textbook Selection

Summarize the following excerpt from a chapter in a history textbook. The selection deals with an ancient tribe of people in the Southwest. Use a separate sheet of paper. Student responses will vary.

Many Cultures Arise North of Mexico

Hundreds of different cultures and languages developed among the Indians who settled the North American continent north of Mexico. These different peoples are often grouped by geographical regions where people had similar ways of life. As in Mesoamerica, archeologists have found evidence that several distinctive cultures emerged as early as 1000 B.C. Some were influenced by the Mesoamerican civilization to the south. Trade, agriculture, and arts flourished, and different forms of political organization developed.

The Anasazi Build Cities in Cliffs and Canyons

By the first century A.D., a people known as the Anasazi had created a farming culture in the dry lands of the Southwest—present-day Arizona, New Mexico, Colorado, and Utah. The name Anasazi was given them by the Navajo Indians, who much later discovered the ruins of their huge, many storied homes. In the Navajo language *Anasazi* means "strange ancient ones."

The early Anasazi probably learned farming techniques about 1500 B.C. from the peoples of Mesoamerica. Corn, beans, and squash became their staple foods.

The Anasazi at first lived in dugout houses roofed with logs. About A.D. 700, as the population increased, they began to build houses of stone or sun-baked clay called adobe. Communities grew more crowded, and society became more complex. Houses were built close together and on top of each other. Hundreds of people in the community worked together to build huge "apartment houses," which were several stories high and had many rooms. People hauled logs long distances to make the framework and roof; they cut blocks of sandstone for the walls. The Spaniards who arrived several hundred years later called these huge buildings *pueblos*, which means "towns" in Spanish.[1]

Many pueblos were built in canyons or high on steep cliffs. One of the largest, Pueblo Bonito (in present-day New Mexico), took more than a hundred years to build and was completed about A.D. 1085. It had 650 rooms and could house well over a thousand people. Nearby pueblos in the same canyon were almost as large. Every great pueblo had a central room or *kiva* used for community ceremonies and religious rituals. Colorful murals decorated the walls of the kiva.

As farmers in a dry land, the Anasazi were dependent on natural forces, and these were the center of their religion. The Anasazi devised a kind of "sun clock" to track the seasons and the cycles of the sun. Men oversaw the rituals that people hoped would bring good hunting, enough rain, and successful crops. Women in Anasazi society owned all the houses and property and headed family clans.

The Anasazi culture stretched over a huge area in the Southwest. Networks of wide roads linked central pueblos with outlying villages and other centers. The people traded with Mexican Indians for copper and feathers and with Indians of the Great Plains for buffalo meat. Their only farm animals were turkeys, but they kept dogs as pets.

---

[1]This term is now used both for the buildings and for the present-day Indians, such as the Zuni and Hopi, who are the Anasazi's descendants.

About 1150, a very long drought struck the central area of Anasazi culture. Gradually all the great pueblos were abandoned. The Anasazi moved away to join neighboring groups, and the first great culture of the Southwest vanished.

The Hopewell People Carry on Widespread Tradition

About the fifth or fourth century B.C., a highly organized farming society developed in the Ohio River valley. Living in villages along the river, these people became known as "Mound Builders" because of the large earthen mounds they constructed. Some of these structures were burial mounds, and others were ceremonial mounds in the shape of animals such as snakes, turtles, or birds. The Mound Builders traded widely along the rivers and lakes, acquiring copper from the northern Great Lakes region, seashells from the Gulf of Mexico, and mica (a shiny mineral) from people to the east. Their artists worked with wood, stone, and copper to make ornaments and household objects. The Mound Builders' way of life, called the "Hopewell culture,"[2] spread over the central part of the continent from what is now Wisconsin to the Gulf Coast and as far west as present-day Kansas. The Hopewell way of life lasted for about a thousand years, until A.D. 400 or 500.

The Mississippian Culture Borrows from Mesoamerica

Both ideas and goods were exchanged in the trade among the Indian peoples of the Americas. By about A.D. 1200, people along the lower Mississippi River had built the most advanced culture north of Mexico. Their culture, which archeologists call the Mississippian, was influenced by ideas from Mesoamerica. Mississippian society was divided into strict classes under a ruler known as the Great Sun. In the center of the walled villages stood steep-sided earth pyramids with wooden temples on the flat summits. High-ranking nobles built their homes on smaller mounds, and other mounds were used for burials. Religion included the Mesoamerican idea of a feathered serpent god.

—*Marvin Perry et al.*

[2]The culture was named for a farmer in southern Ohio, on whose land archeologists discovered mounds and objects from this culture.

15.8 Summarizing More Textbook Selections

1. Summarize the passage about World War II inventions on page 190. Use a separate sheet of paper.

2. Study Chapter 11 of this textbook by summarizing it. Use a separate sheet of paper.
3. Summarize the passage from an economics textbook (pages 213–214). Use a separate sheet of paper. Student responses will vary.

CULTURAL Exchange

9 and 10 o'clock positions	just above halfway up the left-hand side of the steering wheel, as though the wheel were a clock (page 317)
2 and 3 o'clock positions	just above halfway up the right-hand side of the steering wheel, as though the wheel were a clock (page 317)
radical	politically extreme (page 333)
fundamentalist	holding religious beliefs about the literal truth of the Bible or other sacred text. Fundamentalists can be believers in any religion, but in the context of this selection the reference is to fundamentalist Christians (page 333)
alligators in the sewer	a legendary story about alligators living in the subways and underground tunnels of New York City (page 335)
urban legends	tall tales about modern life that circulate among people who live in cities (page 335)

Chapter 15 SELF-TEST Underlining, Listing, and Summarizing

Read the following magazine selection about the teasing children receive and how parents can help their children understand and cope with the teasing. Then, on a separate sheet of paper, list important ideas and information from the article. On another sheet of paper, summarize the same article. Count five points for each important statement you include in the list (up to ten statements) and the summary (up to ten statements). Student responses will vary.

Teaching about Teasing

Nine-year-old Laura looks like a younger version of any magazine cover girl—tall, long limbed, slender. But don't try telling her that. For the last two years, Laura has been teased about being too thin. Other children call her a "stick" and tell her she looks "weird."

"She comes home upset, telling us the kids at school are calling her names because she's skinny," says her mother, Patricia Graves, of Fayston, Vermont. The teasing has turned Laura from a self-assured child into one who's worried about how she fits in. "It's made her cry and feel bad about herself," Graves says.

Laura's experience isn't unique: Seven- to 10-year olds tease each other all the time. While some teasing is good-natured and can be shrugged off or responded to with a similar wisecrack, mean-spirited taunts can really hit home. "Kids are needling each other, so they go for whatever's available," explains Leon A. Rosenberg, Ph.D., director of the Johns Hopkins Children's Mental Health Center, in Baltimore. "But when children spot a kid who seems to be a little more vulnerable or who embarrasses easily, then the teasing will focus on him and whatever seems to upset him most, usually his physical appearance," Rosenberg says.

Theodore R. Warm, M.D., a child psychiatrist in the pediatrics department at Rainbow Babies and Children's Hospital, in Cleveland, defines teasing as a deliberate attempt to create tension in someone else. When a peer calls him stupid, the insult cuts deep because a child this age doesn't have the intellectual maturity or self-confidence to defend himself. The insult hurts because it seems real.

Interestingly, most kids first learn a form of teasing at home: Games like peekaboo and "I've got your nose!" are good-natured forms of teasing that help children through various stages of development, Warm says.

Such benign teasing is a positive way for parents to interact with kids. In fact, most child-development experts say that children who aren't exposed to teasing at home may have more difficulty handling it when it occurs at school. "Teasing is part of what's known as incidental learning," says Edward Christophersen, Ph.D., professor of pediatrics at Children's Mercy Hospital, in Kansas City, and author of *Beyond Discipline* (Overland Press). "No one actually tries to teach a child to do it but they often learn it through our interactions with them.

Teasing Is Part of Growing Up

Trading barbs is completely normal in children ages 7 to 10, for several reasons. At this age, kids begin to select friends based on more than just a shared love of coloring or singing songs. Now they want to fit in and be with kids who look or act like them. And, as isolating as it is for the victim, teasing is very unifying for the teasers, who often band together to make up jokes or pranks. Children also tease as a way of expressing competitiveness. In school, kids are constantly being tested and ranked, both in academics and in sports, and teasing is a simple form of one-upmanship.

Growing communication skills contribute to the increase in teasing as well. Between ages 7 and 10, a child's vocabulary and understanding of language are sharpening; he's learning to express more sophisticated thoughts and to attach value to his observations. While a younger child may innocently remark that another child is overweight, a 7- or 8-year-old has learned to add a value—in this case, a negative one—to the idea that someone is heavy. Thus an overweight child now gets labeled "Fatso."

Teasing also gives kids a pleasurable feeling of control, over others or over a situation. Teasers quickly learn that a clever taunt will produce two things: laughter from other children and a reaction from the victim. In his research, Warm found that the vast majority of the children he studied said that they tease their peers because it's fun.

Parents Can Help Kids Cope with Teasing

It may help to view this painful rite of passage as an opportunity for your child to learn that she can handle adversity. Try these tips to help her through the rough spots.

- *Listen—and sympathize.* Let your child tell you, in her own words and at her own pace, what happened. Then tell her that you appreciate how she feels. Say, "That must have hurt your feelings" or "I know it feels bad to be called names." Resist the urge to talk about how mean the other kids are or to downplay the importance of her feelings. When she's calm, ask your child how she handled the teasing. Ask simply, "What did you do then?" This takes the emphasis off the teaser's behavior and encourages your child to see that she has a role—that she's not merely a victim.
- *Offer encouragement, not lectures.* This is where many well-meaning parents slip up—by telling the child what he should have done. Instead, bite your tongue and keep the conversation going by asking him, "What happened then?"
- *Fix what you can.* In many cases, kids are teased about superficial things—a lunch box, a haircut—that parents dismiss as silly. But that's a mistake, says Dorothea M. Ross, Ph.D., a professor at the University of California at San Francisco and author of *Childhood Bullying and Teasing* (American Counseling Association). "Parents shouldn't buy a child all new clothes," she says, "but often they can modify something to help eliminate the teasing." Sometimes, she says, spending money on more fashionable blue jeans or a new backpack is the simplest solution.
- *Develop a strategy together.* Talk with your child about what she can do the next time she's teased. Simply ignoring a teaser may seem like the simplest advice, but it's very hard to do—and the teaser will usually up the ante until he gets a reaction. Instead, Ross advises parents to encourage their child to take action without being confrontational. For instance, your child can adopt a carefree altitude, as if he's not bothered by the taunts, and maintain a confident but not threatening posture: standing up straight, arms relaxed, looking the teaser in the eye. He might come up with a nonaggressive response like agreeing with the teaser ("You're right. I am a slow runner. So what?"). Try role-playing at home to help your child practice these new strategies, Ross says. "The fact that the child is standing up to them is usually enough to throw the teasers off. And it

gives a child a great boost when he actually gets the teasers to back down."

- *Set the right example.* If you want your child to take another kid's words less seriously, you'll have to act nonchalant yourself. Acknowledge that it is important, but don't make an issue of teasing. Then it's more likely that your child won't either. "In the end," says Warm, "a parent's attitude will have a big impact on how a child views teasing."

—Martha Schindler

Score: ______ important statements × 5 points each = ______

CHAPTER SIXTEEN

Keeping a Reading Journal

It is one thing to understand the words a writer has written. It is another to feel that the words are important to you. Skillful reading is not just understanding the words. It also is connecting the words with your life, so the words become part of you. Skillful reading is discovering personal meanings for yourself—by making the words part of your thinking, your experience, and your life. Simply stop for a minute to think about how what you are reading relates to what you have already experienced, what you know, and what you feel.

A good way to take that extra moment is to write about your reading. Keep a notebook, or a journal, just for your personal thoughts about your reading. Every time you read something, take an extra five minutes to write down a few ideas about your reading.

What kinds of things can you write about in this journal? It's best to keep a number of questions in mind (see the box on page 345). When you write a journal entry, you should try to follow up on your thoughts. Don't worry about grammar or spelling. For every statement that you make, ask yourself why you believe that or what experiences or feelings lie behind the statement. If one idea leads to another, continue writing about the new idea. The more you put your thoughts on paper, the more you will see how the reading connects with things that are important to you.

Before you read what one student wrote in her journal in response to the selection about opportunity costs (pages 213–214), read "Questions to Answer in Your Reading Journal" on page 345.

Whenever I buy anything, I usually think about how much money I have to pay directly and whether I have enough to cover it in my wallet or checking account. That's often a real mistake because I sometimes leave myself without the money to buy other things I might like even more. I may see a real neat leather jacket in one store and spend my whole week's salary on it, except what I know I need for food and rent. And then I think it might be really great to go to a comedy show with some friends, but I don't have any money left. So I don't have anywhere to show off my neat new leather jacket. So the cost of the jacket was not just the money, but it was the lost opportunity to hang out with my friends. I really need to think through my purchases better.

Questions to Answer in Your Reading Journal

- How do you feel about the subject of the reading? Are your feelings similar to the writer's?
- Which parts of the reading seemed exciting? dull? funny? depressing? outrageous? Why did you feel that way?
- Do you feel sympathy with any of the people described in the reading?
- What experiences have you had that are similar to the events described in the reading?
- What people do you know who are similar to the people described in the reading?
- What places or situations or problems in the reading resemble those that you know?
- How do your opinions about the subject compare with the writer's? With which statement do you particularly agree or disagree?
- What is the writer trying to say?
- How important to you are your beliefs on this subject?
- Has the writer changed your mind or made you start thinking about a new point of view? How?
- How convincing are the ideas and the arguments that the writer presents?
- How might some people disagree with the writer?
- As you were reading, what ideas went through your mind?
- Did the reading remind you of other thoughts you have been having? Which thoughts?
- How does the reading connect with any subject you have been thinking about?
- Did you have any new thoughts after finishing the reading? What were those thoughts?

After reading the selection about John Muir's trip into the Sierra Mountains (pages 229–231), another student wrote this journal entry:

I know just how John Muir must have felt. I love to hike and camp. When the spring rains end and the hills start to dry out, I just have to get my hiking boots and backpack out of the closet. I must have hiked all the trails in the state and half of them in the surrounding states. I can hike from morning to evening with sixty pounds on my back. But all the time I am looking at the mountain flowers, breathing clean air, and feeling the warm sun on me. And then I look out to spectacular views. Because I have to go to school and work, I can only go for a few days at a time. If I had my way, though, I would spend months at a time up in the mountains. My dream job is to be a park ranger at one of the national parks. I'm going to try to do that this summer.

In both cases, the students gained a better understanding of their original reading by looking at the feelings and thoughts that were set in motion by the reading.

EXERCISES

16.1 A Reading Journal

Begin a reading journal. Every time you have a reading assignment (or whenever your teacher suggests), write fifty to one hundred words describing your feelings and thoughts about the reading. This will be particularly useful as you read the selections in the second half of this textbook.

16.2 Personal Thoughts

Reread the selection about Paul Newman's opinions on drugs and the entertainment industry (pages 277–278). Do you agree or disagree with him? Write a paragraph describing your own thoughts on the subject.

16.3 Personal Experiences

Read the following comic piece about how children eat. Does this passage remind you of anything you used to do as a young child or that you have seen young children do? On a separate sheet of paper, write a paragraph describing your experiences with how kids eat. You may want to discuss whether these experiences fit the ways of eating described in the selection.

How to Eat Like a Child

Peas Mash and flatten into thin sheet on plate. Press the back of the fork into the peas. Hold fork vertically, prongs up, and lick off the peas.

Animal Crackers Eat each in this order—legs, head, body.

Sandwich Leave the crusts. If your mother says you have to eat them because that's the best part, stuff the crusts into your pants pocket or between the cushions of the couch.

Spaghetti Wind too many strands on the fork and make sure at least two strands dangle down. Open your mouth wide and stuff in spaghetti; suck noisily to inhale the dangling strands. Clean plate, ask for seconds, and eat only half. When carrying your plate to the kitchen, hold it tilted so that the remaining spaghetti slides off and onto the floor.

Ice-Cream Cone Ask for a double scoop. Knock the top scoop off while walking out the door of the ice-cream parlor. Cry. Lick the remaining scoop slowly so that ice cream melts down the outside of the cone and over your hand. Stop licking when the ice cream is even with the top of the cone. Be sure it is absolutely even. Eat a hole in the bottom of the cone and suck the rest of the ice cream out the bottom. When only the cone remains with ice cream coating the inside, leave on car dashboard.

Spinach Divide into little piles. Rearrange into new piles. After five or six maneuvers, sit back and say you are full.

—Judith Viorst

CULTURAL Exchange

John Muir	late nineteenth-century American naturalist who wrote about the beauties of the mountains of California (page 346)
Victorian	referring to the late nineteenth century (page 348)
Meet Me in St. Louis	A 1944 movie about the St. Louis World's Fair of 1904 (page 348)

Chapter 16 SELF-TEST
Keeping a Reading Journal

Read the following magazine essay about how a grown woman now looks back on her happy childhood. Then, on a separate sheet of paper, write a journal entry exploring your reactions to the essay. Because your journal will be personal to you and different than anyone else's, there are no right answers. However, to evaluate how much you were able to develop your thoughts, count ten points for each sentence that expresses a new thought of yours and develops your reaction to the essay.

The Burden of a Happy Childhood

Every time I described the house to friends—the two porches, the bay windows, the balcony over the front door, the stone tubs on either side of the front steps that, before they crumbled, always held geraniums—they said, "It sounds wonderful."

"No, it's not wonderful," I'd protest. "It's too narrow, even if it runs deep, and why in a town of beautiful houses my grandfather had to buy that one...." Then I'd stop, partly because no amount of words could disabuse my listeners of the notion that all big Victorian houses resembled the charmer in *Meet Me in St. Louis*, and partly out of guilt. How could I say such things about three tall stories of white clapboard that had housed my grandparents, a widowed great-aunt, an aunt, the husband she acquired at 56, my parents, my sister, myself and, on occasion, whatever distant relatives were passing through.

Oh, yes, I forgot. Until I was 19, there was a cocker spaniel named Judy and in my earliest childhood a series of canaries, all of which were named Dickie and all of which flew away because my aunt trusted them to stay on their perches when she cleaned their cages out of doors.

My grandfather bought the house in 1920. My mother's wedding reception was in the backyard; my aunt's, when she finally married, on the first floor; my sister's, on the second. I remember coffins in the first-floor bay window (there is nothing like an old-fashioned New England upbringing to acquaint you with life's realities) and, in the same place, the narrow bed in which my father died. It was there so he could have a view of the main street. My grandmother and I loved that view. When

I was little we would sit in the window, she in her rocker, I in a hard cut-velvet-upholstered chair, and monitor the passersby.

The house was across the street from a little beach, and after our morning dip our grandfather sluiced my sister and me with the garden hose. Years later my aunt's husband sluiced my daughters and, eventually, my niece after their dips. In my grandfather's day the garden was beautiful. After his death my grandmother, who was not one for gardening, said there was nothing nicer than a nice green lawn. Perhaps there isn't, but I have always missed his rosebushes and peonies and his patches of sweet william and pansies.

Recently, after 77 years as one family's residence, the house was sold. "How dreadful for you!" friends said. Not at all. What in my childhood had been not only my home but also my fortress, because outside of it lurked every grade-school classmate who didn't like me, had become my prison. As long as it was the place to which I fled whenever my life as an adult became too hard to bear, I was immured in childhood. I was also incapable of calling the apartments in which I lived with my husband and, later, my children "home." Home was where members of my family, some of whom were long gone, were forever baking apple pies, smoking pipes while patting the dog, reading *The Providence Evening Bulletin* and crocheting elaborate bedspreads.

An unhappy childhood can cripple, but so can one as blessed as mine. You go through life with the sense that something has been mislaid, something you think that, with luck, you can find again. Only you can't, because what you're looking for is unconditional love. My family was too strict to spoil a child, but I knew, even before I knew the words, that they would betray me only by dying. As long as they lived, my cradle would never fall.

If you're smart you give up the search early on, but that is hard when the house in which you lived your joy is still yours for the wandering. Furthermore, the ghost I met in every room was not that of a grandparent or the father who died when I was 20 but of my past self. In most particulars she was pretty much the person I am today. But I have lost forever, and mourn, the innocence that had her greeting every morning as if it were the world's first.

Today, though, the house is gone and with it a sadness I wore as a turtle wears its shell. The old radiators are in the side yard and a big hose is hanging out the third-floor window. Its buyers are updating the heating system, gutting the attic. The door on which I had painted "Artist's Den, Keep Out" has disappeared, and once the painters move in, my family's fingerprints will disappear too. But when its new occupants first toured the house, the real-estate agent reported that they said it had "good vibes." So the family that once owned it is still there, not only in my memory but in its laths and beams and solid—oh, so solid—foundation.

—Mary Cantwell

Score: ______ sentences with new thoughts
× 10 points each = ______

UNIT 6 REVIEW TEST

Answer the following questions about writing to read.

1. Put a check mark before each of the things you might underline or otherwise mark in your reading.

_______ a. important information in library books

✓ b. main idea sentences

✓ c. major details

_______ d. weird, but minor, facts

_______ e. the writer's opinion

✓ f. your own thoughts

_______ g. unintentionally funny sentences

✓ h. what is especially interesting or important to you

_______ i. ideas you want your friend to notice when you return the book

✓ j. main ideas

_______ k. all facts

d 2. When you list main ideas and major details from your reading, you

a. should always use the exact words from the book.
b. should always rephrase the material in your own words.
c. can add your own thoughts.
d. can combine your phrasing with the reading's phrasing.

3. Put a check mark before some of the ways you can organize the meaning of the reading in your own mind as you list important ideas and information.

✓ a. Turn the list into a word map.

✓ b. Identify main ideas.

✓ c. Afterward, reorganize the information.

✓ d. Mark important sentences in the book.

✓ e. Indent the major details underneath main ideas.

✓ f. Connect main ideas with your own experiences.

✓ g. Write notes to yourself between items in the list.

✓ h. Rephrase the information in your own words.

4. List six steps in writing a good summary.

   a. Read and understand the selection to be summarized.

   b. Identify the main ideas and major details.

   c. Make the main idea of the selection the first sentence of the summary.

   d. Rewrite the material into sentences that connect important pieces of information.

   e. Leave out extra words.

   f. Keep your writing organized.

c 5. In writing a reading journal, you should
   a. try to make complicated sentences.
   b. practice writing correctly.
   c. follow and develop your thoughts.
   d. not wander from the information and ideas of your reading.

6. On a separate sheet of paper, list five questions you may ask about your reading in your reading journal. Student responses may vary, but they can be selected from the list on page 345.

Reading Selections

These selections will help you practice the reading skills you've learned so far. The questions for each selection check your understanding of what you read. In some cases, you will be able to answer the questions without returning to the selection; in other cases, you will want to return quickly to specific passages before you choose an answer. Returning to the selection to check *every* answer will slow you down and make your reading a chore. Try to remember as much as you can when you read each piece. However, when you are not certain about something, it's best to check back before writing an answer.

You'll notice that numbers and letters in parentheses appear in boldface type at the end of each question. They refer to the chapter and section in the first part of this book where the skill you need for answering the question is explained. If you are still stumped after you've checked the selection again, turn to the appropriate section of the handbook and review your skills.

Three approaches help you learn new words in each selection. Before the selection, key words are listed with their definitions in a section called "Word Highlights." When a difficult word appears in the selection, you can look it up easily. Following the selection, the "Cultural Exchange" explains terms with particular cultural meanings. In addition, a vocabulary exercise appears at the end of the questions on each piece. The vocabulary exercises ask questions about the uses and meanings of new words. You will want to add the new words to your reading, writing, and speaking vocabularies as soon as possible. This means writing the words down, using them in sentences, and following the other guidelines given in Chapter 1. You also should keep a list of other words you don't know in each selection. Check their meanings and learn them, too.

The writing assignments provided for each selection will help you think critically about what you have read. In responding to the selection, first, you will write informally in your reading journal. Use separate sheets of paper for other writing assignments. You may have to summarize important points in the reading, compare experiences presented in the reading with your own experiences, or express your opinion about a point raised in the reading.

The works chosen for this section will teach you, amuse you, and make you think. You'll find articles, essays, and sections of books, newspapers, and magazines. This anthology provides a varied program of reading similar to that required of today's college student.

1 Climates in the United States and Canada

Thomas Baerwald and Celeste Fraser

An area's location—North, South, near water or mountains—determines its weather pattern. These patterns of weather are called climates. An understanding of climate can help someone plan a vacation, decide on a region to live in, or consider what kind of business or farming to work with. As you look over the maps, charts, and other information in this selection, consider what the climate is like where you live, what causes that climate, and how that climate influences what grows there and how people live.

Getting Started

Use SQ3R as you read this selection. **(11)** Write your questions on a separate piece of paper.

Word Highlights

hallmark (¶2)	a distinctive feature that identifies something
annual (Table 1)	yearly

ON THE WEB

A good introductory site on world climate can be found at **<http://www.blueplanetbiomes.org/climate.htm>.**

Data on climate from cities and regions around the world can be found at **<http://www.worldclimate.com/>**.

Many world maps are available at **<http://www.geographic.org/maps/maps.html>**.

The United States and Canada
Climates

Latitude, elevation, and distance from oceans affect the climates of the United States and Canada. Canada lies farther north than most of the United States except for Alaska, and generally has a colder climate. Both nations have climate differences between east and west, partly because the Rocky Mountains block moisture-laden winds from the Pacific Ocean. The eastern slopes of the Rockies and the plains lie in a **rain shadow**, an area of reduced rainfall on the leeward side of high mountains.

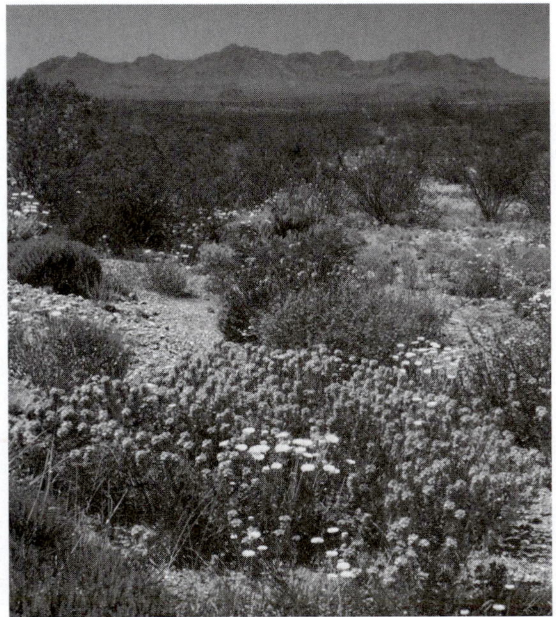

Arid Climate

Big Bend National Park, which marks part of Texas's border with Mexico, has little rainfall for most of the year. Winter rains, however, can lead to spectacular wildflower displays in the spring. **PHYSICAL PROCESSES** *Do you think this landscape looks the same all year? Explain.*

Humid Continental Climate

Warm summers and cold winters are a hallmark of humid continental climate regions. The colorful trees on this Vermont farm indicate the arrival of cool autumn temperatures.
CLIMATES *What regions of the United States and Canada have the same climate as Vermont?*

Climatic Differences

The data for these five cities show the variety of climate zones throughout the United States. Temperature, rainfall, and snowfall are all indicators of climate.
CLIMATES *Which city in the table has the highest average July temperature?*

Table 1 Climate Conditions of Selected U.S. Cities

CITY	AVERAGE MONTHLY TEMPERATURE (°F)		AVERAGE ANNUAL PRECIPITATION (IN.)	AVERAGE ANNUAL PRECIPITATION (DAYS)	AVERAGE ANNUAL SNOWFALL (IN.)
	January	July			
Chicago, IL	21	73	33.3	127	40.3
Dallas–Ft. Worth, TX	44	86	29.5	78	3.1
Miami, FL	67	83	57.6	129	0.0
New York, NY	32	76	42.8	119	26.1
Seattle, WA	39	65	38.6	158	12.8

Source: National Oceanic and Atmospheric Administration

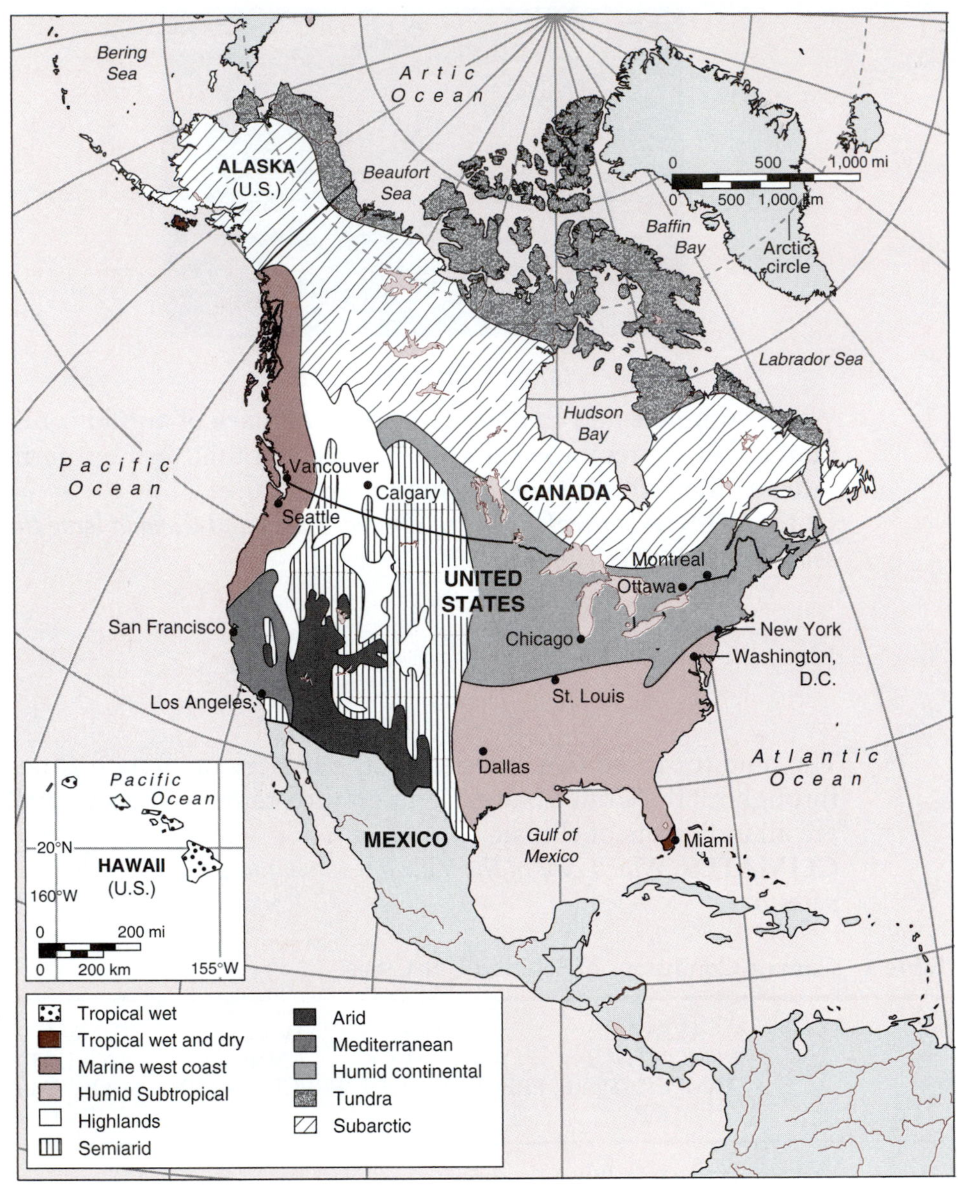

Assessment

1. **Key Term** Define rain shadow.
2. **Map Skills; Regions** Which cities on the map are located in the humid subtropical climate zone?

3. **Critical Thinking; Analyzing Causes and Effects (a)** Why is Canada's climate generally colder than that of the United States? **(b)** How can a colder climate have economic effects for both individuals and businesses?

EXERCISES

Understanding Main Ideas

___b___ 1. The main idea of the selection is to explain **(9)**
   a. seasonal weather patterns in the United States and Canada.
   b. the different climates in the United States and Canada.
   c. locations of warm and cool areas in the United States and Canada.
   d. why temperatures tend to be coolest in northern climates.

___b___ 2. The main point of the "Climate Conditions" chart is to show **(8c)**
   a. the average monthly temperatures of five cities in the United States.
   b. the temperature and precipitation differences among climate zones.
   c. the amount of rainfall in most areas of the United States.
   d. where the five climate zones are located.

___d___ 3. The main idea of the paragraph under the heading "Climates" is that **(8c)**
   a. Canada is colder than the United States.
   b. Plains regions are dry.
   c. Mountains can block rain.
   d. The climates of the United States and Canada have similarities and differences.

Finding Information

___c___ 1. One reason for the different climates in the east and the west is the **(10)**
   a. location of the Pacific and Atlantic oceans.
   b. large arid climate area separating the two coasts.
   c. mountains that stop moist winds from the Pacific.
   d. low elevation of many states in the Midwest.

d 2. The "Climate Regions" map shows that Alaska is near **(7)**
a. Hudson Bay and the Arctic Ocean.
b. the Bering Sea and Baffin Bay.
c. the Gulf of Mexico and Atlantic Ocean.
d. the Arctic Ocean and Bering Sea.

b 3. According to the "Climate Regions" map, Miami is closest to **(7)**
a. the equator.
b. the Tropic of Cancer.
c. the Pacific Ocean.
d. latitude 40 North.

4. Using the "Climate Regions map," write the name of the climate zone for these cities: **(7)**

Dallas Humid subtropical

Montreal Humid continental

Miami Tropical wet and dry

Seattle Marine west coast

Los Angeles Mediterranean

New York Humid continental

Chicago Humid continental

c 5. The chart entitled "Climate Conditions of Selected U.S. Cities" shows precipitation measured in **(7)**
a. inches and feet.
b. feet and temperature.
c. days and inches.
d. degrees and miles.

c 6. Which of the cities on the chart entitled "Climate Conditions" has the greatest average total amount of rainfall? **(7)**
a. Chicago
b. Dallas
c. Miami
d. New York
e. Seattle

e 7. Which of the cities on the chart entitled "Climate Conditions" has the greatest average days of rainfall? **(7)**
a. Chicago
b. Dallas

c. Miami
d. New York
e. Seattle

___a___ 8. Which of the cities on the chart entitled "Climate Conditions" has the greatest average total amount of snowfall? **(7)**
a. Chicago
b. Dallas
c. Miami
d. New York
e. Seattle

Interpreting

___d___ 1. From the answers to questions 6, 7, and 8 just above and other data on the chart, we may reasonable infer that **(13)**
a. If a city gets a lot of rain, it will also get a lot of snow.
b. A city that has more total days of precipitation will necessarily have more total precitation,
c. If a city does not have average temperatures below freezing, it will never get snow.
d. Rains in Seattle on average deliver less rain than those in Miami.

___b___ 2. We can infer that San Francisco has an average temperature that is **(13)**
a. warmer than that of Los Angeles.
b. cooler than that of Miami.
c. warmer than that of Vancouver.
d. cooler than that of Ottawa.

___c___ 3. We can infer that Chicago's climate is most similar to the climate of **(13)**
a. New York
b. St. Louis
c. Ottawa
d. Seattle

___a___ 4. We can infer from the inset of Hawaii that the islands **(13)**
a. have rain throughout the year.
b. are dry throughout the year.
c. have a dry season and a rainy season.
d. have four seasons with different weather in each.

a 5. Juneau, the capital of Alaska, is halfway down the narrow strip that extends the south part of the state. From the map, we may infer that the climate of Juneau is **(13)**
   a. Marine West Coast
   b. Tundra
   c. Subarctic
   d. Humid Continental

b 6. Nome is in the north of Alaska, on the Bering Sea near the Arctic Circle. From the map, we may infer that the climate of Nome is **(13)**
   a. Marine West Coast
   b. Tundra
   c. Subarctic
   d. Humid Continental

b 7. Fairbanks is as far north in Alaska as Nome, near the Arctic Circle, but it is far inland, near the border with Canada. From the map, we may infer that the climate of Fairbanks is **(13)**
   a. Marine West Coast
   b. Tundra
   c. Subarctic
   d. Humid Continental

Vocabulary

Many of the terms in this selection refer to either geography or to weather and climate. In the space before each of the words in column A, write a *G* if the word refers to an aspect of geography and *W* if it refers to climate or weather. Some of the words refer both to geographical regions and to climate types; before these terms place a C. Then, in the space after each, write the number of the appropriate definition from Column B.

Column A

W a. arid 6
C b. continental 12
G c. elevation 1
W d. humid 7
G e. latitude 2
C f. leeward 9

Column B

Geographic terms
1. Height above sea level
2. Measure of how near a place is to the equator or north or south poles
3. Large level areas
4. Mountainsides
5. areas

C g. marine 13

C h. Mediterranean 16

W i. moisture-laden 8

G j. plains 3

W k. precipitation 10

G l. regions 5

G m. slopes 4

C n. subarctic 15

C o. subtropical 14

C p. tropical 11

Weather terms

6. Dry
7. Wet
8. Heavy with water
9. The side protected from the wind, the opposite of windward
10. rain and snow

Climate area terms

11. areas near the equator
12. areas in the middle of large land masses
13. areas over or near oceans
14. areas near the tropics but with a less extreme climate
15. areas near the north or south poles but with a less extreme climate
16. areas having climates like that in the south of Europe.

WRITING PRACTICE

Writing in Your Journal

1. Write a few paragraphs describing the climate in your area and what that means in terms of daily weather.
2. Write about how the climate affects the choices you make about activities, work, vacations, and other aspects of life. How might your life change if the climate in your region were to change?

More Writing Practice

1. Write answers to the SQ3R questions you wrote for this selection. **(11)**
2. Many scientists and other concerned with the environment believe we are currently in a period of climate change due to human activities which affect the atmosphere. Using the search times "climate change" or "global warming" find out

what scientists are saying about the future of the planet. Summarize what you find in a few paragraphs. **(15)**

Internet Activities

1. After identifying the climate in your own location, examine a map of world climates (such as at http://www.blueplanetbiomes.org/climate.htm). By comparing that map to a geographic map, make a list of other countries and cities that would have similar climates to yours elsewhere on the planet.
2. For several cites across the U.S. and Canada, check the weather at <http://www.nws.noaa.gov> or <http://www.weather.com>. Is that weather consistent with what you would predict from the climate? Why? If not, explain how it varies from what you might expect.
3. Examine the lists of weather warnings or advisories at <http://www.nws.noaa.gov/> and compare those warnings to the kind of climates in each region where there is a warning. What can you infer about the relationships between climate and the kinds of extreme weather and weather dangers that might occur there. **(13)**

2 Teachings of Confucius

By Iftikhar Ahmad, Herbert Brodsky, Marylee Susan Crofts, and Elizabeth Gaynor Ellis

Confucius is a Chinese philosopher known for his strong belief in harmony and order. His teachings were so influential, the values they express are still taught and followed today. As you read this passage, think about the values that you try to follow in your life and how they match to the teachings of Confucius.

Getting Started

1. When you think of a teacher of values, who comes into your mind? Do you think of Dr. Martin Luther King Jr. or Gandhi? Do you think of a family member, teacher or community figure? Do you think of a philosopher or a religious leader? What values did these people teach? Make a list of the teachers who have taught you values, and under each list the values you associate with them. **(5a)**
2. Confucius emphasized that leaders should set models for the people who they are responsible for. Freewrite for several paragraphs about how those with authority do or do not set a model for you. **(5d)**

Word Highlights

philosopher (¶1)	a lover of wisdom, someone who searches for general truths
analects (¶2)	selected short writings
mandate (¶4)	a command from authority
filial (¶6)	relating to a son or daughter
piety (¶6)	showing respect and obedience

ON THE WEB

There are many web tributes to the teaching of Confucius, of varying quality. A good set of links is to be found at **<http://chineseculture.about.com/msubconfucius.htm>** A scholarly introduction to Confucius's thought is available at the online *Stanford Encyclopedia of Philosophy* to be found at **<http://plato.stanford.edu/entries/confucius/>** A full downloadable English translation of the Analects of Confucius is available at **<http://classics.mit.edu/Confucius/analects.html>**

Confucius (kuhn FYOO shuhs),* China's best-known philosopher, was born in about 551 B.C. The disorder and suffering caused by constant warfare disturbed Confucius. He developed ideas about how to restore peace and ensure harmony.

2 Confucius visited the courts of various princes, hoping to convince them to put his ideas into practice. Disappointed, he returned home, where he taught a small but loyal group of followers. After his death, his followers collected his teachings in the *Analects*.

3 **Five relationships.** To restore order, Confucius taught that five relationships must govern human society. They are the relationships between ruler and ruled, father and son, older brother and younger brother, husband and wife, and friend and friend. In all but the last relationship, one person has authority over another. In each, said Confucius, the superior person should set an example for the inferior one.

> If a ruler himself is upright, all will go well without orders. But if he himself is not upright, even though he gives orders, they will not be obeyed.

4 According to Confucius, the superior person is also responsible for the well-being of the inferior person. A supporter of the Mandate of Heaven, he said that the ruler must provide good government for his subjects. The ruler's subjects, in turn, owed the ruler loyalty and obedience.

---

*When Europeans reached China, they heard about the thinker Kong Zi (kuhng dzuh), or Master Kong. They pronounced the name Confucius.

5 To Confucius, relationships involving the family are the key to an orderly society. One of those relationships—the relationship between father and son—is very much like that between the ruler and the ruled.

6 Like a ruler, the father must set an example for his son and look after his family. The father takes the credit—or blame—for his children's actions. The son, in turn, is expected to honor and obey his father. Confucius stressed this idea of filial piety, the duty and respect that children owe their parents.

7 **Influence.** Confucius created a guide to proper behavior based on ethical, or moral, principles. In his teachings, he placed the family and the good of society above the interests of the individual. He also stressed loyalty, courtesy, hard work, and service.

8 Confucius placed great emphasis on education. "By nature, men are pretty much alike," he said. "It is learning and practice that set them apart." The importance of education as well as other Confucian ideas would shape Chinese government, as you will read.

9 In time, Confucian ideas came to dominate Chinese society. As China expanded across Asia, Confucianism influenced the cultures of Korea, Japan, and Vietnam as well.

Cultural Exchange

The Analects	A book of Confucius's wise sayings (¶2)
Mandate of Heaven	the belief that China's rulers were granted authority from the gods. When they lost the Mandate of Heaven, it was proper to remove them from office. (¶4)
Filial piety	showing respect and obedience to one's parents **(¶6)**

EXERCISES

Understanding Main Ideas

b 1. Which of the following sentences best sums up the main point of the selection? **(9c)**

a. "Confucius, China's best-known philosopher, was born in about 551 B.C."

b. "He developed ideas about how to restore peace and ensure harmony."
c. "Confucius placed great emphasis on education."
d. "In time, Confucian ideas came to dominate Chinese society."

c 2. The topic of paragraph 3 is **(8c)**
a. the core path all relationships must follow for success.
b. how older and younger brothers should get along.
c. Confucius's belief about the five human relationships.
d. the struggle of Confucius to gain acceptance in China.

d 3. The main idea of paragraph 3 is that **(8c)**
a. All relationships involve authority.
b. Being a good example is the most important part of a relationship.
c. The relationship between friend and friend is different from all others.
d. The five relationships are important to keeping order in society.

a 4. The main idea of paragraph 7 is stated in **(8c)**
a. the first sentence.
b. the middle sentence.
c. the last sentence.
d. the title of the paragraph.

d 5. The main idea of the sentence "As China expanded across Asia, Confucianism influenced the cultures of Korea, Japan, and Vietnam as well" is that **(8a)**
a. Chinese culture became more important than other Asian cultures.
b. Korea, Japan, and Vietnam grew just as quickly as China.
c. Confucius traveled across all parts of Asia.
d. Confucian ideas spread as China grew.

Finding Information

1. List the five relationships Confucious said were important for society. **(10a)**

a. between ruler and ruled
b. between father and son
c. between older brother and younger brother
d. between husband and wife
e. between friend and friend

d 2. In what relationship did Confucius say one person did not have authority over another? **(10a)**
   a. between husband and wife
   b. between father and son
   c. between older brother and younger brother
   d. between friend and friend

b 3. According to Confucius, which relationship is key to an orderly society? **(10a)**
   a. between ruler and ruled
   b. between father and son
   c. between business and family
   d. between friend and friend

c 4. In his teachings, what did Confucius place above the interests of the individual? **(10a)**
   a. honor and admirable behavior
   b. family and faith
   c. the good of society and family
   d. the advancement of culture

Interpreting

a 1. It is opinion that **(12)**
   a. the interests of families are more important than of individuals.
   b. Korea, Japan, and Vietnam are parts of Asia.
   c. Confucius was in born in about 551 B.C.
   d. Confucius visited various princes to put his ideas into practice, but was rejected.

a 2. It is fact that **(12)**
   a. Confucius was a philosopher in China.
   b. Confucius was Asia's only philosopher.
   c. Most of the world's philosophers were in Asia.
   d. Asia developed philosophy for the world.

b 3. We can infer from this selection that Confucius's philosophies **(13)**
   a. were very popular during his lifetime.
   b. became more popular after his death.
   c. have suddenly become very popular.
   d. were never considered important.

a 4. Based on the long quote given in paragraph 3, we can infer that (**13**)
   a. only a moral leader is sure to be followed.
   b. the actions of a leader do not affect actions of followers.
   c. Confucius valued followers who were loyal even to corrupt leaders.
   d. leadership comes from giving strong orders.

d 5. Based on the last paragraph in this selection, we can infer that (**13**)
   a. Confucian philosophies have spread all over the world.
   b. Confucian ideas are based on strong leadership.
   c. Confucian followers are all Chinese.
   d. Confucianism had a major impact on Asia.

b 6. We can infer that Confucius thought (**13**)
   a. men and women were equally responsible for social harmony and order.
   b. men should take more responsibility and authority than women.
   c. women are capable of taking on major social responsibilities.
   d. mothers have little importance in children's lives.

Vocabulary

Each of the following words is made of two or more word parts. In column A, break the word in two or more parts to show the word parts. In column B, write the meaning of the word.

	Column A	*Column B*
disorder	dis/order	confusion
ensure	en/sure	make certain
warfare	war/fare	military conflict
relationship	relation/ship	being connected
authority	author/ity	power to command or decide
superior	super/ior	higher in rank
inferior	in/ferior	lower in rank
upright	up/right	honest, virtuous
well-being	well/being	happiness, healthiness, and prosperity

government	govern/ment	system of ruling
obedience	obe/dience	the following of commands
Confucian	Confuc/ian	following the beliefs of Confucius
Confucianism	Confuc/ianism	the belief system associated with Confucius

WRITING PRACTICE

Writing in Your Journal

1. Do you agree with Confucius's views on obedience to authority, whether ruler over ruled, parent over child, elder child over younger, husband over wife? To what extent and in what situations do you think the inferior should listen to and respect the superior? To what extent do you accept the concepts of superior (or more powerful) and inferior (less powerful) in any of these relationships? Write in your journal your thoughts about Confucian ideas of authority and obedience.

2. In what roles does Confucius consider women? In what roles does he consider only men? What do you infer from this selection not mentioning daughters or mothers? How would you describe Confucius's ideas about gender and gender roles? How might these views have affected societies that have adopted Confucian values? Write in your journal what you infer to be Confucian views of women and your thoughts about those views. (**16**)

More Writing Practice

1. Write a description of a person you consider a leader and to whom you listen. What makes you want to follow what he or she says? What kinds of ways do you follow the person? What characteristics make you want to follow him or her?

2. Make a list of the values you consider important. For each of those values, write a paragraph describing and explaining the value, perhaps giving an example.

Internet Activities

1. Go to <**http://chineseculture.about.com/msubconfucius.htm**> and find links to pages that present Chinese characters representing words important to Confucian thought. Try copying those character in your own drawing, and write in your own words the meaning of those characters.
2. Also at <**http://chineseculture.about.com/msubconfucius.htm**>, find a website that provides quotations from Confucius's *Analects*. Copy down quotations that make sense or are of interest to you. Compare your choices with the choices of your classmates and explain what you liked about each quotation.

3 Gunfire at Night

Paul Gordon

The sudden horror of gunshots before midnight, right below the writer's window and . . . ? Read this true story, which shows the effects of a frightening, violent act on a city neighborhood.

Getting Started

On a separate sheet of paper, make a word map on the topic *gunfire at night*. (**6b**)

Word Highlights

silhouetted (¶2)	outlined
welled (¶4)	rose to the surface, ready to flow
calamity (¶10)	a disaster; terrible distress
votive (¶13)	expressing a wish, desire, or vow
homeboy (¶16)	neighborhood gang member

ON THE WEB

Many websites, both governmental and public, are devoted to information on gangs. The National Alliance of Gang Investigators Associations (NAGIA) **<http://www.nagia.org/>** provides links to most local and national law enforcement agencies concerned with gang violence.

An example of a comprehensive public page is Gangs or Us **<http://www.gangsorus.com/>**.

The National Gang Crime Research Center **<http://www.ngcrc.com/index.html>** provides access to research on the topic.

Above the battered desks at Hollywood's Homicide Division hangs a wooden sign: "Our day begins when your day ends."

2 This time, the detectives' day began just before midnight when the sound of a gunshot rattled my bedroom window. I looked out. Silhouetted in the fire of a second shot, I saw the figure of a man crouched over the sidewalk across the street. A third muzzle flash — an orange disk with a white-hot core — burned into the ground.

3 The man rose. Purposeful but unhurried, he moved off into the shadows down the darkened street. Behind him on the sidewalk lay the dim, slack shape of a body.

4 I ran down the staircase two steps at a time, around the tall hedge and out past the security fence. In the lighted bedroom window, I could see my wife crying into the telephone; the street was empty. Ahead in the moonlight, I could make out the slumped form. Blood welled over the curbstone into a darkening pool.

5 In less than a minute, a police car rounded the corner and drew up at an angle, blocking the street. Two more police cruisers, lights flashing, closed off the block. An officer fed out a roll of yellow tape between utility poles and directed me to a strip of grass beneath a burned-out street lamp.

6 The detectives arrived. Neighbors in their nightclothes began to gather. Paramedics worked on the victim — a young man, we saw now. All useless.

7 An officer filled out a white field report and told me to get my things. I was an eyewitness.

8 At the Hollywood station, beneath the "Our day begins" sign, eight or nine of us were seated, most street people from an abandoned parking lot across from where the shots were fired. It was after 1 A.M. Someone made a pot of coffee, and we waited in silence for the detectives to arrive.

9 About 3 A.M., I gave my statement. I was, it turned out, a poor eyewitness. The shooter, was he large or small? Young or old? Black or white? With shock, I found that I didn't have the faintest idea. The nature of the killing — its cool, deliberate, almost ritual brutality — was what I had retained. The facts, like the gunman himself, had faded without a trace.

10 The next day was warm and sunny. The street was quiet. People with shopping bags walked down toward the traffic on Santa Monica Boulevard. Across the street, a narrow dark stain remained

on the sidewalk. A few scraps of yellow police ribbon hung from a lamp post. Otherwise, all trace of the night's calamity seemed to evaporate in the sunlight.

11 But as I watched, a woman passing by leaned down and lightly touched the dark spot on the sidewalk. A few minutes later another crossed herself, her lips moving with a silent prayer, and went on. A group of children, running toward their school, paused and fell silent. A teenage girl shook her fists at the ground and pinched away angry tears.

12 All day long, people — some I recognized from the neighborhood and some I didn't — passed the spot where the boy had fallen. It had the quality of ceremony.

13 That evening, someone laid out an offering — two votive candles and a glass of water — in the narrow strip of grass beside the street. Through the night the tiny pools of light flickered on a silent train of mourners.

14 The visitation continued the next day, and then the next. I noticed unfamiliar trucks parked on the block, and singing and guitar music from behind the fences. More candles appeared on the grass. Then there were flowers and a painted wooden crucifix. Families came by, and one day at noon a church group stood with Bibles in their hands and held a meeting by the sidewalk.

15 Toward the evening on the third day, I saw my downstairs neighbor walk across the street with his daughter. She had just turned 9. At the spot in the grass, they stood together. He talked quietly while she looked solemnly up at him. For some minutes they stood together, hand in hand, before they walked back across the street.

16 A neighbor who knew the slain boy told me that he was only 17. It was said he had decided to take a walk down the street for pizza that night. He was not a gang member, people said, but his brother was. And he was wearing homeboy colors, they said, so that was how and why it all had happened the way it did. We didn't know. The case remained unsolved.

17 Other visitors came. Curious onlookers cruised the street, and once a brightly painted pickup with three young men in the cab and the stereo booming crept past. At the end of the block the men yelled, shook their fists in the air and sped away.

18 One day, I came home in the middle of the afternoon to find a crowd of young men with headbands and tattoos, drunk and singing, kicking at the grass by the candles. I heard someone shout, "*¡Es todo!*" ("That's all!").

19 Then the street was full of police cars, and two men in handcuffs were spread-eagle on the ground. The candles and crucifix were scattered in the gutter. The next morning a street-cleaning truck swept them away.

20 *The death of José Guadalupe Medina is believed to be gang-related and is still unsolved because of lack of positive identification from witnesses, police say.*

CULTURAL Exchange

roll of yellow tape	special tape used by the police to mark off an area where a crime has been committed; it keeps unauthorized people out of the taped-off area. (¶5)
paramedic	a person who is trained to give emergency medical care, but who is not a doctor or nurse; most emergency vehicles are staffed with a paramedic. (¶6)
to cross oneself	to move one's hand in the shape of a cross on the body; to begin to pray; to ask God for help (¶11)
headband	a piece of cloth worn around the head; gang members may wear special headbands to distinguish themselves from one another. (¶18)
spread-eagle	lying face-down on the floor or ground, with arms and legs stretched out; this is the usual position in which police search criminal suspects for weapons. (¶19)

EXERCISES

Understanding Main Ideas

__d__ 1. Which of the following phrases best expresses the topic of this selection? **(8b)**

a. Police cars at night
b. Events at a Hollywood police station
c. Violence in the city
d. Murder in a city neighborhood

2. State the main idea of the selection in your own words. **(8)** Student responses will vary.

An anonymous murder on a city street has powerful effects on a neighborhood.

3. In your own words, state the main idea of paragraph 9. **(8c)**

I was a poor witness because the brutal killing wiped out memories of the shooter.

Finding Information

c 1. When he hears the shots, the writer **(10a)**
a. calls the police.
b. goes to the police station.
c. rushes down the steps.
d. fills out an eyewitness form.

b 2. When asked by the police to give his statement, the writer **(10a)**
a. describes the killer as a young black man.
b. realizes that he cannot remember anything about the gunman.
c. refuses to cooperate because of the brutal killing.
d. is standing on a strip of grass beneath a burned-out street lamp.

c 3. On the day after the shooting, **(10a)**
a. all memories of the event have vanished.
b. the murdered boy's gang returns to avenge his death.
c. people go past the spot of blood on the street as if in a ceremony.
d. the police close off the street with yellow tape.

4. Arrange the following details in the proper sequence. Put a 1 before the first detail, a 2 before the second detail, and so on. **(10c)**

2 a. The writer's wife is crying in the lighted bedroom window.

6 b. A teenage girl shakes her fist at the ground.

10 c. Two men in handcuffs are spread-eagle on the ground.

3 d. The police close off the block.

9 e. A downstairs neighbor talks with his daughter on the strip of grass.

7 f. Someone lays out two votive candles and a glass of water.

1 g. A man crouches over the sidewalk, outlined in the fire of a gunshot.

8 h. A church group holds a meeting on the sidewalk.

4 i. The detectives arrive.

5 j. The writer gives his statement.

Interpreting

1. Write an *F* before each statement of fact from the selection; write an *O* before each statement of opinion. **(12)**

F a. I ran down the staircase two steps at a time.

F b. The detectives arrived.

O c. All useless.

F d. A group of children, running toward their school, paused and fell silent.

O e. It had the quality of ceremony.

F f. More candles appeared on the grass.

a 2. We can infer from the wooden sign at Hollywood's Homicide Division that **(13)**
   a. much of police work takes place when regular citizens are asleep.
   b. the police do jobs other than police work at night.
   c. an alarm or phone call wakens police officers in the middle of the night.
   d. for the police, the beginning of the day is just like the end.

d 3. The police arrived in less than a minute because **(13)**
   a. they heard the gunshots.
   b. they regularly patrol the neighborhood where the killing took place.

c. an officer saw the killer move down the dark street.
d. the writer's wife called them on the phone.

___c___ 4. We can infer that people brought flowers and candles **(13)**
a. as gifts for the dead boy's family.
b. to cheer up the neighborhood after the violence.
c. to honor the dead boy's memory.
d. in appreciation of the police department's help.

___c___ 5. The neighbor standing with his nine-year-old daughter is probably telling her **(13)**
a. to help clean up the street.
b. never to talk to strangers.
c. about the senselessness of violence and murder.
d. always to obey her parents.

___b___ 6. The boy probably was killed because **(13)**
a. someone wanted to steal his money.
b. a rival gang member saw him in the kind of clothing worn by the neighborhood gang.
c. the killer was jealous that the boy was going out with the killer's girlfriend.
d. a seventeen-year-old should not be in the streets at midnight.

___d___ 7. From the last paragraph, we can infer that **(13)**
a. the police now take better care of the people in the neighborhood.
b. more candles and crucifixes will arrive to honor the slain boy.
c. teenagers with headbands and tattoos have moved into the neighborhood.
d. new violence scatters the memories of the dead boy.

Vocabulary

Complete each sentence by filling in the blank with one of the following words from the selection. **(1c)**

battered	ritual
purposeful	brutality
slack	flickered
abandoned	solemnly
deliberate	onlookers

1. That was no accident; with a ___deliberate___ push, she knocked her brother off the bicycle.
2. The puppy was chained to a tree for days, apparently ___abandoned___ by its owner.
3. Just before the power died, our lights ___flickered___ and then went out completely.
4. His actions were ___purposeful___ —that is, intentional— and we could assume only that he had planned things carefully for a long time.
5. Damaged by heavy use, the old ___battered___ wheelbarrow lay overturned in the dirt.
6. Each step followed in order with the seriousness of a religious ceremony, so that for Esteban, studying for a test was like a ___ritual___.
7. Not gently, but with unnecessary ___brutality___, the father scolded the child for playing with the telephone.
8. With great seriousness of purpose, the union members marched ___solemnly___ past the coffin of their slain leader.
9. No one turned away from the scene; the ___onlookers___ stared in horror as the murderer dashed between the houses and vanished in the darkness.
10. The rope was ___slack___, limp and loose, and the boat bobbed up and down in the breeze.

WRITING PRACTICE

Writing in Your Journal

Write a description of a frightening or sad event you witnessed or were part of.

More Writing Practice

1. Write about the events you think led up to the killing described in the selection. Use your imagination; draw on sensory details—colors, actions, sounds, smells. Show the scene

clearly to someone who did not see it. Describe the characters and events.

2. What steps can we take to reduce the violence in U.S. cities? Write a page to express your views on the issue.

Internet Activities

1. Just as spontaneous memorials were created where the murder occurred as described in this selection, the Internet has become a place for memorials for the deaths of many kinds of people. Do a Web search on the term "memorials" and describe a few sites you find. You may also wish to narrow your search to a specific category, such as "firemen memorials" or "drive-by shooting memorials."
2. Do a Web search on "gang violence" along with the name of your city or state to find out about the gang activity in your region.

4 Angry Fathers

Mel Lazarus

This childhood memory was written by the well-known cartoonist of the "Momma" and "Miss Peach" comic strips. He tells how his father reacted to one of his misdeeds. In this selection, the author reveals both his and his father's ideas about teaching children the right way to behave.

Getting Started

Do you think that corporal—that is, physical—punishment is a good way for parents to teach their children the difference between right and wrong? Make a list of what you consider to be the pros and cons of this kind of punishment. **(6a)**

Word Highlights

listless (¶2)	idle; sluggish
casino (¶3)	a public room for entertainment especially for gambling
sheetrock (¶4)	wallboard used in construction
anonymous (¶4)	nameless; unsigned
battering ram (¶5)	heavy beam used to knock down walls and gates
inconspicuous (¶10)	not easily noticeable
blighted (¶11)	ruined; demolished
approbation (¶11)	approval; support
abstractions (¶14)	ideas separate from experience
reproach (¶23)	blame; criticism; rebuke
spectacle (¶25)	public performance or display

ON THE WEB

Many resources are available on the Internet giving advice to parents on forms of disciplining children and adolescents. Two examples are **<http:// www.keepkidshealthy.com/adolescent/adolescentdiscipline.html>** and **<http://www.disciplinehelp.com/>**. Frequently asked questions about discipline are answered by The National Committee to Prevent Child Abuse at **<http://www.kidsource.com/kidsource/content/discipline.3.19.html>**. A Web search on "adolescent discipline" or "child discipline" will turn up many more, expressing various points of views.

Daddy's going to be very angry about this," my mother said.

2 It was August 1938, at a Catskill Mountains boarding house. One hot Friday afternoon three of us—9-year-old city boys—got to feeling listless. We'd done all the summer-country stuff, caught all the frogs, picked the blueberries and shivered in enough icy river water. What we needed, on this unbearably boring afternoon, was some action.

3 To consider the options, Artie, Eli and I holed up in the cool of the "casino," the little building in which the guests enjoyed their nightly bingo games and the occasional traveling magic act.

4 Gradually, inspiration came: the casino was too new, the wood frame and white Sheetrock walls too perfect. We would do it some quiet damage. Leave our anonymous mark on the place, for all time. With, of course, no thought as to consequences.

5 We began picking up a long, wooden bench, running with it like a battering ram, and bashing it into a wall. It left a wonderful hole. But small. So we did it again. And again. . . .

6 Afterward the three of us, breathing hard, sweating the sweat of heroes, surveyed our first really big-time damage. The process had been so satisfying we'd gotten carried away; there was hardly a good square foot of Sheetrock left.

7 Suddenly, before even a tweak of remorse set in, the owner, Mr. Biolos, appeared in the doorway of the building. Furious. And craving justice: When they arrived from the city that night, he-would-tell-our-fathers!

8 Meantime, he told our mothers. My mother felt that what I had done was so monstrous she would leave my punishment to my father. "And," she said, "Daddy's going to be very angry about this."

9 By 6 o'clock Mr. Biolos was stationed out at the driveway, grimly waiting for the fathers to start showing up. Behind him, the front porch was jammed, like a sold-out bleacher section, with indignant guests. They'd seen the damage to their bingo palace, knew they'd have to endure it in that condition for the rest of the summer. They, too, craved justice.

10 As to Artie, Eli and me, we each found an inconspicuous spot on the porch, a careful distance from the other two but not too far from our respective mothers. And waited.

11 Artie's father arrived first. When Mr. Biolos told him the news and showed him the blighted casino, he carefully took off his belt and—with practiced style—viciously whipped his screaming son. With the approbation, by the way, of an ugly crowd of once-gentle people.

12 Eli's father showed up next. He was told and shown and went raving mad, knocking his son off his feet with a slam to the head. As Eli lay crying on the grass, he kicked him on the legs, buttocks and back. When Eli tried to get up he kicked him again.

13 The crowd muttered: Listen, they should have thought of this before they did the damage. They'll live, don't worry, and I bet they never do that again.

14 I wondered: What will my father do? He'd never laid a hand on me in my life. I knew about other kids, had seen bruises on certain schoolmates and even heard screams in the evenings from certain houses on my street, but they were those kids, their families, and the why and how of their bruises were, to me, dark abstractions. Until now.

15 I looked over at my mother. She was upset. Earlier she'd made it clear to me that I had done some special kind of crime. Did it mean that beatings were now, suddenly, the new order of the day?

16 My own father suddenly pulled up in our Chevy, just in time to see Eli's father dragging Eli up the porch steps and into the building. He got out of the car believing, I was sure, that

whatever it was all about, Eli must have deserved it. I went dizzy with fear.

17 Mr. Biolos, on a roll, started talking. My father listened, his shirt soaked with perspiration, a damp handkerchief draped around his neck; he never did well in humid weather. I watched him follow Mr. Biolos into the casino. My dad — strong and principled, hot and bothered — what was he thinking about all this?

18 When they emerged, my father looked over at my mother. He mouthed a small "Hello." Then his eyes found me and stared for a long moment, without expression. I tried to read his eyes, but they left me and went to the crowd, from face to expectant face.

19 Then, amazingly, he got into his car and drove away! Nobody, not even my mother, could imagine where he was going.

20 An hour later he came back. Tied onto the top of his car was a stack of huge Sheetrock boards. He got out holding a paper sack with a hammer sticking out of it. Without a word he untied the Sheetrock and one by one carried the boards into the casino.

21 And didn't come out again that night.

22 All through my mother's and my silent dinner and for the rest of that Friday evening and long after we had gone to bed, I could hear — everyone could hear — the steady bang bang bang bang of my dad's hammer. I pictured him sweating, missing his dinner, missing my mother, getting madder and madder at me. Would tomorrow be the last day of my life? It was 3 A.M. before I finally fell asleep.

23 The next morning, my father didn't say a single word about the night before. Nor did he show any trace of anger or reproach of any kind. We had a regular day, he, my mother and I, and, in fact, our usual sweet family weekend.

24 Was he mad at me? You bet he was. But in a time when many of his generation saw corporal punishment of their children as a God-given right, he knew "spanking" as beating, and beating as criminal. And that when kids were beaten, they always remembered the pain but forgot the reason.

25 And I also realized years later that, to him, humiliating me was just as unthinkable. Unlike the fathers of my buddies, he couldn't play into a conspiracy of revenge and spectacle.

26 But my father had made his point. I never forgot that my vandalism on that August afternoon was outrageous.

27 And I'll never forget that it was also the day I first understood how deeply I could trust him.

CULTURAL Exchange

Catskill Mountains	area located in southeastern New York, immediately west of the Hudson River, with rounded, forested summits and deep valleys. Dams on the numerous streams have created artificial lakes. The Catskills are a year-round recreation area, and tourism is important to the region's economy. (¶2)
boarding house	a house that provides guests with a room and meals, on either a temporary or long-term basis. (¶2)
bingo	a popular game played with cards on which numbered squares are covered as numbers are called out (¶3)
traveling magic act	an entertainment in which a magician travels from place to place performing magic acts for groups of spectators (¶3)
"You bet."	sure; certainly; without a doubt (¶24)
God-given right (n.)	unquestionable permission to do something (¶24)
to play into something	to go along with; to agree with (¶25)

EXERCISES

Understanding Main Ideas

b
_______ 1. Overall, the main idea of the selection is that **(9)**

a. the writer was much luckier than his two friends.

b. the father's reaction showed the writer that trust taught more responsibility than humiliation and revenge.

c. idle children often get into mischief that gets people angry at them.

d. adults sometimes let their anger and frustration lead them to punish their children in ways that are not always effective.

d 2. What is the main idea of the sentence "I knew about other kids, had seen bruises on certain schoolmates and even heard screams in the evenings from certain houses on my street, but they were those kids, their families, and the why and how of their bruises were, to me, dark abstractions"? **(7a)**
   a. The writer knew that some children had bruises.
   b. The writer heard some children scream at night.
   c. The writer does not believe that the bruises he sees or the screams he hears are real.
   d. The writer doesn't understand how or why parents hit their children.

c 3. What is the main idea of the sentence "And I also realized years later that, to him, humiliating me was just as unthinkable"? **(8a)**
   a. The writer's father did not think about humiliating his son.
   b. Years pass before the writer understands his father.
   c. The writer's father did not believe that humiliating his son was acceptable either.
   d. The writer's father thought that humiliating his son was cruel, but necessary.

d 4. Which paragraphs describe the reaction of the boarding-house guests? **(8b)**
   a. paragraphs 7 and 8
   b. paragraphs 9 and 11
   c. paragraphs 9, 10, and 11
   d. paragraphs 9, 11, and 13

a 5. Which paragraphs describe the damage to the casino? **(8b)**
   a. paragraphs 5 and 6
   b. paragraphs 6 and 7
   c. paragraphs 7 and 8
   d. paragraphs 21 and 22

Finding Information

b 1. How old was the writer when the events he describes in this selection took place? **(10a)**
   a. 6 years old
   b. 9 years old
   c. 11 years old
   d. 13 years old

c 2. Who is Mr. Biolos? **(10a)**
a. Artie's father
b. Eli's father
c. The boarding house's owner
d. The writer's father

b 3. Which of the following descriptions does not fit the crowd waiting for the arrival of the boys' fathers? **(10a)**
a. indignant
b. inconspicuous
c. once-gentle
d. craving justice

a 4. What did Artie's father do when he arrived? **(10a)**
a. He took off his belt and gave his son a whipping.
b. He took his son aside and talked to him.
c. He knocked his son down and kicked him.
d. He stared at his son and then got in his car and drove away.

c 5. What did Eli's father do when he arrived? **(10a)**
a. He took off his belt and gave his son a whipping.
b. He took his son aside and talked to him.
c. He knocked his son down and kicked him.
d. He stared at his son and then got in his car and drove away.

d 6. What did the writer's father do when he arrived? **(10a)**
a. He took off his belt and gave his son a whipping.
b. He took his son aside and talked to him.
c. He knocked his son down and kicked him.
d. He stared at his son and then got in his car and drove away.

d 7. The reactions of the three fathers are told in order of **(10a)**
a. time.
b. increasing drama.
c. increasing seriousness.
d. all of the above.

c 8. The writer's father views corporal punishment as **(10a)**
a. a necessary evil.
b. a God-given right.
c. a crime.
d. an effective way to discipline children.

a 9. Overall, this selection is arranged according to **(10c)**
a. time order.
b. place order.
c. order of importance.
d. a combination of methods.

Interpreting

1. Put an *F* in the blank before each statement that is a fact and an *O* in the blank before each statement that is an opinion. After each opinion, write who holds that opinion. **(12)**

F a. The casino walls were made of wood and Sheetrock.

O b. The casino walls were too perfect.
Artie, Eli, and the writer

F c. Mr. Biolos told the boys' mothers what they did.

O d. Artie and Eli got the punishment they deserved.
the crowd

F e. The writer's father repaired the casino.

O f. Humiliating a son was unthinkable.
the writer's father

O g. His father can be trusted.
the writer

c 2. From the statement, "My mother felt that what I had done was so monstrous she would leave my punishment to my father," we can infer that **(13)**
a. when the writer was a boy, mothers did not discipline their children.

b. she thinks the writer fears being punished by his father more.
c. the writer's mother sometimes punishes him.
d. the writer's mother does not know how to punish him for such a serious offense.

___a___ 3. From the sentence, "I knew about other kids, had seen bruises on certain schoolmates and even heard screams in the evenings from certain houses on my street, but they were those kids, their families, and the why and how of their bruises were, to me, dark abstractions," we can infer that **(13)**
a. The writer's parents have never hit him.
b. The writer only imagined he saw bruises and heard screams.
c. Some of the writer's friends have been beaten by their parents.
d. The writer does not believe that parents beat their children.

___d___ 4. From the phrase, "with practiced style" in paragraph 11, we can infer that **(13)**
a. Artie's father practices whipping.
b. Artie's father is a criminal.
c. Artie's father has whipped Artie once or twice before.
d. Artie's father has whipped Artie several times before.

___b___ 5. From paragraph 13, we can infer that the boarding-house guests believe that corporal punishment is **(13)**
a. cruel, but necessary.
b. harmless, effective, and justified.
c. cruel, ineffective, and unjustified.
d. ineffective, but justified.

___c___ 6. From paragraph 24, we can infer that the writer's father believes that corporal punishment is **(13)**
a. cruel, but necessary.
b. harmless, effective, and justified.
c. cruel, ineffective, and unjustified.
d. ineffective, but justified.

Vocabulary

1. The following words from the selection name degrees of anger. Look up each word in a dictionary. Then write the definition in the space after the word. Finally, number the words

in order of least to most angry in the spaces provided before each word. **(3)** Numbering may vary.

5 a. furious uncontrollably angry

6 b. craving justice having an overwhelming desire to correct a wrong

3 c. angry strongly displeased

4 d. indignant angry at a moral wrong

7 e. raving mad insane with anger

1 f. upset agitated

2 g. mad resentful

2. The writer uses informal, colorful, conversational language throughout this selection. Use context to figure out the meaning of each of the following phrases. Then write each definition in the blank provided. **(1c)**

a. some action (¶2) excitement

b. the summer-country stuff (¶2) rural activities

c. our anonymous mark (¶4) a sign of our presence that others would not attribute to us

d. the sweat of heroes (¶6) the sign of great labor

e. tweak of remorse (¶7) the smallest feeling of guilt

f. like a sold-out bleacher section (¶9) crowded with many people

g. with practiced style (¶11) knowing what he was doing

h. an ugly crowd (¶11) a violent, angry gathering

i. order of the day (¶15) rule

j. dizzy with fear (¶16) anxious

k. on a roll (¶17) having momentum from earlier success

l. hot and bothered (¶17) upset

m. a conspiracy of revenge and spectacle (¶25) people making a big show of getting even

WRITING PRACTICE

Writing in Your Journal

Write a few paragraphs in your journal describing a time a parent or another adult punished you or otherwise made you aware of a wrongful deed.

More Writing Practice

1. Write a one-paragraph summary of the lesson the writer learned from the events described in this selection.
2. Imagine that you run an advice column. Write a 200-word letter in which you respond to the writer's father's request for advice about what to do in this situation.

Internet Activities

1. The topic of spanking or corporal punishment is still a controversial one, with some people and groups believing it is wrong in all cases and others viewing it as appropriate under certain conditions and when used in a careful, thoughtful, moderate way. Do a Web search on "spanking" or "corporal punishment." Select several sites with different points of views. Describe the position and point of view of each. If you can, see if a religious, moral, or philosophical perspective lies behind the point of view expressed in each.
2. Fathers, when angered, may do many unusual things. Do a Web search on the term "angry father" and collect some of the more interesting stories that turn up.

5 Please Straighten Out My Life

Stephanie Winston

Has life ever seemed so confusing that you didn't know what to do or where to begin? Stephanie Winston is an expert in getting people organized. Here she gives a few basic rules for starting to put your life in order. As you read, think about whether her ideas can help you.

Getting Started

Do SQ3R as you read this selection. **(11)** Write your questions here. Student responses will vary.

How can someone else help you straighten out your life?

Why is a single notebook necessary?

How do you divide up a problem into segments?

What does aggravating mean here? How do you rank projects?

What are the items in the problem-solving checklist?

ON THE WEB

Checklist.com **<http://www.checklists.com/>** provides free checklists for almost every aspect of life. Organizedliving.com **<http://www.organized-living.com/>** also offers articles, checklists, links, personal tests, and many other resources for organizing your life. Get Organized Now **<http://www.getorganizednow.com/>** offers tips and products. The National Association of Personal Organizers **<http://www.napo.net/>** includes in its activities a National Get Organized Week and an annual convention of organizing professionals.

Word Highlights

clients (¶1)	customers for a service
principles (¶3)	rules
staples (¶5)	basic supplies
isolate (¶6)	separate out
inventory (¶7)	supplies
fundamental (¶9)	basic
significant (¶10)	important
adjacent (¶11)	next to
articulating (¶14)	clearly stating
impetus (¶14)	push force energy
temperament (¶15)	personality feelings

It is not uncommon for clients to approach me with the cry, "Please straighten out my life." Their daily life seems overwhelming, and organizing it seems hopeless. Such people cannot see that specific, smaller difficulties must be resolved before the whole becomes manageable. Some clients, on the other hand, feel confronted by so many tiny problems that they are defeated by their very quantity.

2 The first step toward taking things in hand is to define just what a "problem" is. Never yet, in my experience, has a situation been so complex that it couldn't be unraveled.

3 To begin, provide yourself with a notebook — either loose-leaf or spiral-bound — small enough to carry around with you. This notebook will become your "master list" — a single continuous list that replaces all the small slips of paper you're probably used to. Use the notebook to keep track of all errands, things to do or buy, and general notes to yourself about anything that will require action. This basic organizing technique is the first in a series of principles that will appear throughout the book highlighting the prime rules of organization.

Principle #1 Use a Single Notebook for Notes to Yourself

4 Choose a time with no distractions and sit down with your notebook and pencil. List six elements in your life that need to be put in order. Forget about straightening out your life as a whole. Instead, focus on things like these:

5 I spend so much time looking for kitchen utensils that cooking a meal takes hours. How can I make my kitchen "work" properly?

I want to start woodworking again, but my books and tools are all over the house. What do I do to get them together?

The living room is always a mess because I don't know what to do with all those magazines and newspapers I haven't read.

I'm always running out of soap, toilet paper, and other household staples. How can I plan more effectively?

It takes me forever to get ready in the morning and I'm always late for work. How can I streamline the "up and out" process?

How can I plan enough time for special projects that I like to work on and still leave a comfortable margin for household, family, and other activities?

6 Substitute your own examples for mine, and you've completed the first step. If your mind tends to blur when you try to isolate problems, the "movie" technique may help. Take a deep breath and relax. Then close your eyes and mentally run through a typical day, letting it unroll like a movie. "I get up, brush my teeth . . ." and so on. When you come to a scene or situation that creates a problem, write it down. While you are screening your day's movie, remember that you may not be consciously aware of some problems but your mind and body are. If your stomach lurches or your muscles tighten or your head aches when you come to a particular scene, then you can be sure you have locked onto a problem.

7 If, for example, a twinge of tension occurs at the idea of brushing your teeth, perhaps you're always running out of toothpaste — a problem in maintaining an inventory control system for household supplies. Or, the toothpaste might be there, but the medicine chest is so jammed that a dozen other things fall into the sink every time you reach into the cabinet.

8 Write down each problem as you come to it, then shut your eyes again, relax, and continue. List no more than six problems, otherwise the list itself may overwhelm you!

9 This procedure of problem definition illustrates a fundamental rule of organizing — every life situation, no matter what it may be, can be divided into its significant parts. Stated as a principle:

Principle #2 Divide Up a Complex Problem into Manageable Segments

10 Some of the problems on your list will be fairly straightforward. A messy clothes closet, for example, is a small area with one function, and organizing it is a fairly simple procedure. But changing your morning ritual so that you're on time for work is a considerably more complex matter. It may involve changing your habits, revising your time schedule, reorganizing your bathroom or laundry system — or all of these things. Keeping Principle #2 in mind, the next step is to divide the *complex* problems on your list into more manageable units. These more complex situations usually fall into one of two categories:

11 1. *Physical areas: Rooms*. If an entire room needs reorganizing, you must first isolate its various problem areas. Stand in the doorway of the room and, choosing any corner at random, mentally block out an area about five feet square. Cast a sharp eye over every inch of that area to inspect it for "knots." In the living room, a knot might be a sloppy desk and work area, a disorganized wall unit with books piled in disarray, or an inconvenient and unappealing furniture arrangement. Whatever jars your nerves or sensibilities is a fit subject for reworking. List these specific "knot" areas on your master problem list under the general problem of which they are a part. Block out another five foot square area immediately adjacent to the first and repeat the process. Follow this procedure until you have checked the entire room and have a complete list of individual elements to work on.

12 2. *Processes or systems*. To break down a process or a system into its manageable parts, use the same movie technique, mentally running through the particular process that's giving you trouble. Each time you feel tension about an action or function, write it down. For instance, the stumbling blocks in the "up-and-out-in-the-morning" process might include some of the following: alarm clock rings too softly; cannot move quickly in the morning; don't have time to decide what clothes or accessories to wear; kitchen always messy so cooking breakfast is a chore.

13 There is one very significant step that provides the bridge between defining the problem and finding the solution. On a scale of one to ten, rank each of the six major items on your list according to how much it irritates you. Stated as a principle:

Principle #3 After Articulating a Small Group of Projects, Rank Them by Number According to How Aggravating They Are

14 A problem that creates serious tension is a #1; one that could wait until next year is #10. Write the number next to each item on your list. This is a very important impetus to action. You may end up with two problems which are #1, two #2, one #5 and one #7. Do *not* try to arrange the problems 1, 2, 3, 4, 5, 6 in numerical order of importance. People tend to get so involved in figuring out which problem is fifth and which is sixth or whatever, that they lose sight of what they're trying to accomplish. If any of your six major problems can be subdivided . . ., rank those subdivisions in the same way. . . .

15 With this step of ranking, the process of establishing order is well and truly begun. The issues have been outlined, priorities have been set, and a foundation for action has been laid. All that remains before actually tackling the problems is to set a specific and regular time for organizing work. If you can't choose a good time, play a little game with yourself. Imagine that for the next several weeks you have a fixed appointment with yourself that you note in your appointment calendar as if it were a regular medical or dental appointment. Your "appointments" could be every day for an hour, or every day for fifteen minutes, or twice a week for two hours each, or an hour a week; whatever is practical in terms of other responsibilities and your own temperament. If you know you'll start getting jittery after half an hour, don't set a two-hour appointment because it will be "good for

you" or you "ought" to. Instead, be kind to yourself and give yourself appointments that you know you can keep and handle.

16 But remember, these are firm appointments and must be kept, except in case of emergency. Making this commitment to yourself will be one of the smartest things you ever did.

Problem-Solving Checklist

17 Before you begin, review this checklist, which summarizes your first steps.

18
1. Select and list in your notebook no more than six problems at one time.
2. Break the complex problems on the list into manageable units.
3. Rank the problems and their units according to aggravation level.
4. Turn to the appropriate section or sections of this book and solve the first #1 problem on the list; do not omit any units.
5. Go to the next #1 item, then the #2s, and so on until all the problems have been solved.
6. Choose another set of problems and follow the same steps.

CULTURAL Exchange

to take things in hand — to take control of things, especially when circumstances have allowed things to get out of control (¶2)

loose-leaf or spiral-bound — two types of notebooks: a loose-leaf notebook has three large metal rings that open and close; it holds sheets of paper with three holes. A spiral-bound notebook has a long piece of wire that is wrapped around in the shape of a spring to hold the sheets of paper together. (¶3)

to streamline — to make more efficient; to simplify by getting rid of unnecessary items or actions (¶5)

to blur — to become unclear or indistinct in appearance (¶6)

to mentally run through	to go over or review something in one's mind; to think about and to plan activities in one's mind before actually doing them (¶6)
to lurch	to stagger; to move quickly, in a single uncontrolled motion (¶6)
ritual	a regularly followed procedure; for example, a morning ritual might include getting up, reading the paper, having a cup of coffee, and taking a shower; the same thing every day without change (¶10)
to jar one's nerves	to upset someone's calm disposition; to shock someone's senses (¶11)
"up-and-out-in-the-morning" process	one's morning ritual; the things one must do every morning to get up (out of bed) and out of the house in time for school or work (¶12)
chore	an everyday duty or job that is often perceived as unpleasant or time-consuming (¶12)
jittery	very nervous (¶15).

EXERCISES

Understanding Main Ideas

__d__ 1. The main idea of this selection is that **(9)**
- a. the author knows how to straighten out her clients' lives.
- b. you should rank your problems.
- c. complex problems are more difficult to solve than simple ones.
- d. to begin to organize your life, you must define and rank specific problems.

__c__ 2. The main idea of paragraph 6 is **(8c)**
- a. to substitute your own examples.
- b. to relax when your mind blurs with a problem.

c. that the "movie" technique will help you remember problems.
d. that your muscles tightening is a sign you have locked onto a problem.

__d__ 3. The main idea of paragraph 10 is **(8c)**
a. simple problems are easy to solve.
b. changing the morning ritual is a complex problem.
c. some problems are more complex than others.
d. complex problems can be divided.

__c__ 4. The main idea of paragraph 10 is stated in the **(8c)**
a. first sentence.
b. second sentence.
c. fourth sentence.
d. last sentence.

Finding Information

__b__ 1. To define your problems, you should write down **(10a)**
a. all your problems on slips of paper.
b. six problem areas in a single notebook.
c. your biggest problem on a large sign.
d. all your problems in a single notebook.

__b__ 2. The "movie" technique is to **(10a)**
a. go to the movies to forget your problems.
b. relax and mentally go over your activities, as though they are part of a movie.
c. take a movie of your activities so you can watch yourself.
d. watch a movie on problem solving.

__d__ 3. A complex problem should be **(10a)**
a. put aside if it is too hard to handle.
b. attacked directly as a single unit.
c. put off for a few days while you think about it.
d. broken down into smaller parts that you can handle.

__c__ 4. You should rank your problems according to **(10a)**
a. the order in which you thought of them.
b. how important they are.
c. how upsetting they are.
d. how hard they are to solve.

__a__ 5. Principles 1, 2, and 3 are arranged according to **(10c)**
a. time order.
b. space order.

c. order of importance.
d. order of difficulty.

6. Write *major* before each important detail and *minor* before each less important detail. **(10b)**

minor a. You should keep short appointments with yourself.

major b. Making appointments with yourself can help you plan your time.

major c. Complex situations usually involve either physical areas or processes.

minor d. You may have problems deciding what to wear.

major e. Feeling tense about a situation is a sign of a problem area.

minor f. Feeling tense about brushing your teeth may be a sign that your medicine cabinet is a mess.

Interpreting

c 1. It is a fact that **(12)**
a. complex problems always can be broken down into simple ones.
b. ranking problems by how much they upset you is better than putting them in numerical order by importance.
c. rooms sometimes have disorganized areas.
d. problems should be written down in a single notebook.

a 2. This selection is mostly based on **(12)**
a. the opinion of someone with a lot of experience.
b. the opinion of someone with no experience.
c. fact.
d. scientific theories.

c 3. We can infer from this selection that **(13)**
a. people need to solve all their problems to feel more organized.
b. you should have no problem remembering your problems.
c. solving just a few problems gives people some sense of relief and control.
d. getting out of the house in the morning is easier than straightening out a messy closet.

4. Put a check mark next to each statement that is a correct inference you can draw from the selection. **(13)**

✓ a. After acting on the three principles here, a disorganized person should not feel hopeless about getting organized.

____ b. Rules help solve all life's problems.

✓ c. Not knowing what to do in complex situations makes people feel overwhelmed.

✓ d. Becoming organized requires planning and clear thinking.

____ e. Being organized or disorganized is just a state of mind.

✓ f. It is possible to straighten out your life, no matter what the mess.

✓ g. If you work on a few clearly defined problems, you probably will have more success than if you work on many problems all at once.

____ h. Your closet will never get organized.

Vocabulary

This selection includes several positive words related to being organized and several negative words related to being disorganized. These positive and negative words are mixed together in column A. On the first blank after each word, write the number of the correct definition from column B. On the second blank, write *P* if the word is positive or *N* if the word is negative. (**1c, 2**)

A		
overwhelming	6	N
manageable	3	P
technique	7	P
tension	4	N
twinge	8	N
disarray	1	N
inconvenient	9	N
unappealing	10	N
appointment	5	P
commitment	2	P

B

1. confusion
2. promise to do something
3. possible to be controlled
4. state of feeling nervous
5. agreement to do something at a certain time and place
6. too much to handle
7. a method of doing something
8. a small nervous feeling
9. not very easily done
10. not attractive

WRITING PRACTICE

Writing in Your Journal

Write a paragraph discussing whether you are organized or disorganized and why you think so.

More Writing Practice

1. Go back to the SQ3R exercise at the beginning of this selection and write the answers to your questions. **(11)**
2. Following the techniques described in this selection, write down six problems that bother you. Then break down the more complex problems into smaller parts. Rank the problems and their parts according to how much they irritate you.

Internet Activities

1. Mindtools offers useful advice on how to construct a list of things to do. After reading the advice on this website, construct a list for yourself. **<www.mindtools.com/stress/WorkOverload/ToDoLists.htm>**
2. Many companies sell products to help you organize your life, time, work, or house. Using "personal organization products" as a search term, examine a number of websites that sell such products. Then share with your classmates the most useful or most bizarre products you find.

6 Changing Roles Alter Buying Behavior

William M. Pride and O. C. Ferrell

How much influence do children have in spending money? What effect does children's spending power have on America's economy? Read this selection from a college textbook in marketing for some interesting (and surprising) answers to these questions.

Getting Started

Before you read, freewrite on the topic *children spending money.* **(6d)** As you read, underline what you think is most important in the selection. **(14a)**

Word Highlights

marketer (¶1)	someone concerned with buying and selling
discretionary (¶1)	for use without any restrictions
peer (¶1)	an equal; someone of the same age or with the same rank, status, or class
apparel (¶3)	clothing
clout (¶4)	power
astute (¶5)	sharp; clever
per se (¶5)	exactly

ON THE WEB

The U.S. Center for Media Literacy **<http://www.medialit.org/>** and the Canadian organization Media Awareness Network **<http://www.media-awareness.ca/>** have much information for parents and teachers to help educate children about all aspects of the media, including advertising and marketing.

Commercial practices targeting children on the Internet are discussed at **<http://www.net-consumers.org/erica/policy/practices.htm>**.

In some ways they are a marketers' dream. They have billions of dollars in discretionary income—and spend most of it. Although their individual purchases are small, they buy regularly, often in response to peer pressure. They are heavily influenced by the hours of television advertising they see each week. And, as a result of today's smaller families and the increase in the number of two-income households, they have more to say about family purchase decisions than ever before.

2 "They" are children, of course, a group whose spending habits are attracting the attention of more and more marketers. One recent study estimates that the thirty million U.S. children 4 to 12 years old receive about $4.7 billion annually from allowances, gifts, and odd jobs. Of that amount, they spend a total of $4.2 billion each year on snacks ($1.4 billion), toys and games ($1.1 billion), movies and sports ($771 million), video games ($766 million), and gifts ($164 million), engaging in some 280 independent purchase transactions annually. Children thirteen to nineteen account for even greater yearly expenditures: $30.5 billion of their own money.

3 But children's financial muscle does not end there. Researchers estimate that children directly influence more than $40 billion in adult purchases each year. A Nickelodeon/*USA Today*/Yankelovich Youth Monitor study found that children are extremely aware of brands and have considerable input into their

parents' selections of apparel, cereal, snacks, cars, videocassette recorders, televisions, and personal computers. Many children are involved in actual household purchasing, especially food; in a recent Teenage Research study, half the teen girls surveyed reported shopping for groceries at least once a week. Recognizing this indirect purchasing power that children have, a growing number of marketers are approaching the youths directly. The National Dairy Board, for example, now airs milk commercials with youth appeal, and Procter & Gamble has developed a Crest for Kids toothpaste.

4 How did children acquire such buying clout? Researchers point to several factors. As the number of working couples and single-parent households increased, many parents shifted certain household responsibilities onto children's shoulders. Thrust into adult roles, children have ended up with more influence over the family's purchases, and they also tend to spend increased amounts of money themselves. In addition, many older, professional couples have fewer children. These parents can afford to lavish more on their children, including extra spending money for such items as Fisher-Price Toys' $225 children's camcorder and the My First Sony line of electronics gear for children. The bandwagon effect is yet another factor: when one marketer begins to focus on children, competitors follow suit, encouraging even more children's purchases. McDonald's Corp., for example, has aimed advertisements for its hamburgers, meal kits, and parties at children for years; now Hardee's Food Systems, Inc., and Wendy's International Inc. are doing the same.

5 Astute marketers realize that children actually represent three markets: current consumers, influential consumers, and future buyers. Because children are steadily developing brand awareness and product preferences that someday will translate into purchasing decisions, even companies not selling youth products per se are beginning to pay attention to children. Marketers are overcoming their traditional reluctance to sell directly to children, realizing that, out there somewhere, tomorrow's bigticket customer is playing video games today.

Sources: "Children Come of Age as Consumers," *Marketing News*, Dec. 4, 1987, p. 6; Kim Foltz, "Kids as Consumers: Teaching Our Children Well," *Adweek*, Nov. 30, 1987, p. 40; Ellen Graham, "Children's Hour," *The Wall Street Journal*," Jan. 19, 1988, p. 1; James U. McNeal, *Children as Consumers* (Lexington, Mass.: Lexington Books, 1987); Noreen O'Leary, "Study Portrays Children as Complex, Savvy Media Mavens," *Adweek*, Nov. 30, 1987, p. 42.

CULTURAL Exchange

two-income household	a family in which both parents work (¶1)
allowance	money given to a child weekly to do with as he or she wants (¶2)
odd job	any one of a variety of tasks, especially physical ones, needing to be done as it occurs, but not providing a steady, continuous pattern of work (¶2)
big-ticket customer	a customer who usually spends a lot of money; someone who buys very expensive items (¶5).

EXERCISES

Understanding Main Ideas

__b__ 1. The topic of this selection is **(8b)**
  a. marketing products.
  b. children's spending patterns.
  c. doing surveys of children.
  d. the bandwagon effect.

__c__ 2. Which of the following is the main idea of this selection? **(9)**
  a. Children have more to say about family purchase decisions than ever before.
  b. Children are important members of society.
  c. Children have a good deal of power as buyers and consumers.
  d. Marketers are overcoming their lack of interest in selling to children.

__a__ 3. Which of the following is the main point of paragraph 2? **(8c)**
  a. Children from four to nineteen have lots of money to spend.
  b. Thirty million U.S. kids under age twelve spend over $4 billion each year.

c. Children engage in about 300 independent purchase transactions annually.
d. Marketers are paying more and more attention to children's spending habits.

4. On the blank lines, in your own words, write the key idea of each of the following sentences. **(8a)**
   a. "Researchers estimate that children directly influence more than $40 billion in adult purchases each year."

   Children influence what adults buy.

   b. "As the number of working couples and single-parent households increased, many parents shifted certain household responsibilities onto children's shoulders."

   Children have more responsibilities than before.

   c. "Because children are steadily developing brand awareness and product preferences that someday will translate into purchasing decisions, even companies not selling youth products per se are beginning to pay attention to children."

   Companies are paying attention to children because children are future buyers, too.

Finding Information

d 1. As a group, children ages four to twelve spend most on **(10a)**
   a. video games.
   b. toys and games.
   c. movies and sports.
   d. snacks.

2. Write an *F* next to each statement that is a fact and an *O* next to each statement that is an opinion. **(12)**

O a. Children are a marketer's dream.

F b. Children between thirteen and nineteen spend over $30 billion of their own money.

F c. Procter & Gamble has developed a Crest for Kids toothpaste.

O d. Children have major input into parents' selection of certain products.

F e. Wendy's is aiming advertising at children.

Interpreting

d 1. From the statement that children "have billions of dollars in discretionary income — and spend most of it," we can infer that children **(12)**
   a. have no sense of value regarding money.
   b. should not be given so much money by their parents.
   c. misuse the financial power placed in their hands.
   d. do not save much of their own money.

b 2. About their buying behaviors, we can infer that children are **(12)**
   a. not influenced by advertising.
   b. very much influenced by their friends.
   c. not influenced by milk commercials with youth appeal.
   d. careful about spending on hamburgers and other fast foods.

b 3. As families continue to shrink in size and as more and more parents work, we can safely infer that children will have **(13)**
   a. less influence on family purchase decisions.
   b. more influence on family purchase decisions.
   c. less time to make purchases.
   d. help in making decisions from caregivers other than parents.

c 4. We can infer that marketers believe children who develop "brand awareness" when they are young will **(13)**
   a. reject those brands when they become adults.
   b. purchase video games for their children.
   c. remain loyal to those brands into adulthood.
   d. spend their money wisely and thoughtfully as adults.

5. Put a check mark next to each of the general statements below that you believe you can safely infer from the selection. **(13)**

✓ a. Some adults value their children's suggestions in making purchasing decisions.

✓ b. Patterns established when we are children influence our behaviors as adults.

___ c. Children's independence should be encouraged but controlled.

✓ d. Children are a very strong force in the U.S. economy.

___ e. Adults are models for children in many areas of life.

Vocabulary

On the blank lines, write your own definition for each word in italics. Whenever possible, use word part clues from the phrase in which the word appears. **(1c, 2)** Do not use a dictionary.

1. "One recent study *estimates*"

   makes guesses based on other information

2. "Children thirteen to nineteen account for even greater yearly *expenditures*: $30.5 billion of their own money."

   spending

3. "Researchers estimate that children directly *influence* more than $40 billion in adult purchases each year."

   affect

4. "Children . . . have considerable *input* into their parents' selections."

   influence; suggestions

5. "Half the teen girls *surveyed* reported shopping for groceries."

   questioned

6. "The National Dairy Board, for example, now *airs* milk commercials with youth appeal."

   broadcasts on television and/or radio

7. "How did children *acquire* such buying clout?"

   get

8. "These parents can afford to *lavish* more on their children, including extra spending money."

   spend generously

9. "The *bandwagon effect* is yet another factor: when one marketer begins to focus on children, competitors follow suit, encouraging even more children's purchases."

   follow-the-leader pattern

10. "Marketers are overcoming their traditional *reluctance* to sell directly to children."

    unwillingness; lack of enthusiasm

WRITING PRACTICE

Writing in Your Journal

Write a few paragraphs describing how much money you had available for spending when you were in grade school. What did you spend the money on? What forces affected your decisions to buy?

More Writing Practice

1. Write a paragraph to summarize this selection. **(15c)**
2. Should children be given money by parents and relatives, and should they have the right to spend it freely? Write a paragraph to explain and support your opinion.

Internet Activities

1. Many products for children are available for sale on the Internet. By using search terms like "shopping children" or "children's products," you can see the range of products for children. Share some of the more interesting ones you find with your classmates.
2. Examine the website of a restaurant chain, candy, or food product popular with children. See how the site is designed to appeal to children. Then write up what you notice in a few paragraphs.

7 Rock 'n' Roll

Jean Folkerts and Stephen Lacy

Have you ever wondered how rock 'n' roll music was born? Did you know that rock 'n' roll, country, and gospel music have a connection? In this article, the history of rock 'n' roll as a foundation for today's popular music is explored. As you read, think about the types of music you enjoy and the connections it may have to good ol 'rock 'n' roll.

Getting Started

1. In this selection, the roots and beginnings of rock 'n' roll in country, blues, and gospel music are explained. Think about everything you know about the early history of rock 'n' roll music and draw a word map. **(6b)** Use a separate piece of paper.
2. Think about current types of popular music. Did they suddenly pop up, or did they develop from earlier styles? Choose one kind of current music and freewrite about what styles went into making up the style. Using specific examples of groups and songs may help you think about how music styles are related. **(6d)** Use a separate piece of paper.

Word Highlights

rhythm (¶1)	the pattern of beats over time in music
vitalized (¶1)	gave life to
executives (¶4)	people who run corporations

ON THE WEB

Numerous online resources are devoted to the history of rock 'n' roll and to individual artists, groups, styles, and regions. This site **<http://www.history-of-rock.com/>** provides a good overview of rock history.

The Rock and Roll Zone offers a range of resources, including many links. **<http://www.rocknrollzone.com/>**

The Rock and Roll Hall of Fame has information on all its inductees plus a listing of events that happened this day in rock history. **<http://www.rockhall.com/home/default.asp>**

By using a search engine such as Google, you can find many more resources on rock 'n' roll and other forms of music such as blues, gospel, and country that went into making rock 'n' roll.

CULTURAL Exchange

rhythm and blues	a kind of blues music that has a strong beat (¶1)
hillbilly	a person from the mountainous regions of the south and mid-Atlantic states. The term is usually considered a derogatory ethnic slur. Here, however, it is used positively to identify the music of the region. (¶2)
cover	to record a song originally performed by another artist (¶2)
disc jockey	a radio announcer who plays recorded music (¶3)
trash	worthless (¶4)

Elvis Presley incorporated rhythm and blues with rockabilly roots to establish himself as a rock 'n' roll star.

Blending Music to Make Rock 'n' Roll

People disagree about who invented rock 'n' roll, but everyone agrees that it vitalized the recording industry. Many say that Louis Jordan's rhythm and blues music of the 1940s was rock 'n' roll. Others argue that Bob Wills and his Texas Playboys' western swing of the 1930s was the root of rock 'n' roll. Other influences include urban blues singers such as T-Bone Walker, who adopted Les Paul's solid-body electric guitar during the late 1940s. Elements of gospel music can also be heard in early rock 'n' roll.

2 Without question, however, rock 'n' roll was born in the deep South, and it emerged from rhythm and blues. By living in the South, young musicians were able to hear the black R&B and white hillbilly music that formed the core of rock 'n' roll. Two streams emerged. One involved identifiable rock 'n' roll music from rhythm and blues, by musicians such as Little Richard, Bo Diddley, and Chuck Berry. The other stream was the rockabilly music, which dated to Bob Wills but incorporated more rhythm and blues. Early rockabilly musicians, such as Johnny Cash, Carl

Perkins, Buddy Holly, and Elvis Presley, folded gospel and rhythm and blues into their music. Often they covered R&B artists' music, as Elvis did with Big Mama Thornton's "Hound Dog." At the same time, some African American artists, such as Chuck Berry, found influence in the country music they heard growing up in the South.

swing: Big band music played with a jazz rhythm that was popular during the 1930s and early 1940s. Swing enjoyed a revival during the 1990s.

bop: Jazz that developed during the 1940s as a reaction to big band swing music. Usually performed by small groups with fast tempos and conflicting rhythms. Also called be-bop.

jump music: Small band music that merged swing and electric blues during the late 1940s: Jump developed into rhythm and blues music.

3 Alan Freed, a Cleveland disc jockey, helped to popularize the music in the North. His show boomed in popularity after June 1951, when he began playing the R&B records he had heard on African American radio stations. Freed called the music "rock 'n' roll."

4 Though early rock 'n' roll made African American rhythms more acceptable to white audiences, the major recording companies resisted. Company executives saw no future in music that adults considered too loud, and the sexual energy demonstrated in rock 'n' roll dancing alarmed adults. This was "trash" music to most white people older than age eighteen. Early production and distribution of rock 'n' roll were left to small record companies such as Sun Records of Memphis and Chess Records of Chicago. Figure 11.1 illustrates the evolution of rock 'n' roll and other strains of music in the United States.

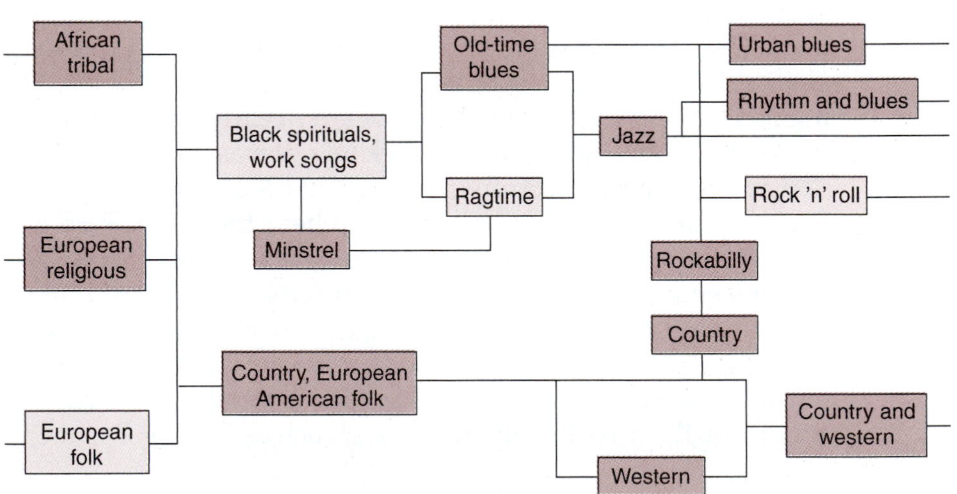

Figure 11.1

EXERCISES

Understanding Main Ideas

c 1. The main idea of the selection is **(9)**
   a. Rock 'n' roll was born in the deep South.
   b. No one knows who invented rock 'n' roll.
   c. Rock 'n' roll combined music of whites and blacks.
   d. White adults did not like rock 'n' roll music at first.

d 2. The main idea of the sentence in paragraph 3 that begins "Alan Freed, a Cleveland disc jockey," is that Freed **(8a)**
   a. listened to African American radio stations.
   b. had a popular radio show in Cleveland.
   c. renamed rhythm and blues music "rock 'n' roll."
   d. helped popularize African American music in the North.

b 3. The main idea of Paragraph 2 is that **(8c)**
   a. rockabilly music incorporated rhythm and blues.
   b. black R&B musicians and white rockabilly musicians influenced each other
   c. Little Richard, Bo Diddley, and Chuck Berry were early rock 'n' roll musicians.
   d. Elvis covered Big Momma Thornton's recording of "Hound Dog."

a 4. The main idea of paragraph 4 is that **(8c)**
   a. early rock 'n' roll faced a lot of resistance.
   b. only small record companies gave rock 'n' roll a chance.
   c. older adults immediately disliked this new form of music.
   d. the start of rock 'n' roll was an easy one.

Finding Information

d 1. T-Bone Walker adopted **(10a)**
   a. a country music playing style.
   b. the songs of Johnny Cash.
   c. a new form of gospel music.
   d. the solid-body electric guitar.

c 2. Early rockabilly musicians included **(10a)**
   a. Elvis Presley and Chuck Berry
   b. Johnny Cash and Carl Perkins
   c. Carl Perkins and Big Momma Thornton
   d. Chuck Berry and Alan Freed

3. From the diagram of the evolution of rock 'n' roll, identify where these kinds of music fit historically. In the space before each type of music write *O* if it is one of the oldest origins of rock 'n' roll, *M* if is one of the middle forms that were part of the transition from older to contemporary music, *C* if it is a current form of popular music, and *N* if has no relation to the origin of rock 'n' roll. **(10b)**

M a. minstrel

O b. European religious

M or C c. jazz

M d. rockabilly

N e. opera

C f. country and western

O g. African tribal

M h. work songs

C i. urban blues

N j. disco

M k. American folk

M l. ragtime

O m. European folk

4. Write *major* next to all the major details listed below and *minor* next to all the minor details. **(10b)**

major a. Rock 'n' roll music was born in the deep South.

minor b. Rockabilly dated to Bob Wills.

major c. Major recording companies resisted rock music.

major d. Swing music played a part in the development of rock 'n' roll.

minor e. Chess Records is located in Chicago.

Interpreting

1. Write an *F* before each fact that appears in the selection, an *O* before each opinion that appears in the selection, and *N* for an opinion that does not appear in the selection. **(12)**

N a. Bob Wills and the Texas Playboys is a silly name for a band.

O b. Louis Jordan played the first rock 'n' roll music.

F c. Rock 'n' roll emerged from rhythm and blues.

O d. There was too much sexual energy in rock 'n' roll dancing.

O e. Rock 'n' roll is too loud.

F f. Sun Records of Memphis produced early rock recordings.

d 2. We can infer that Chuck Berry **(13)**
 a. enjoyed country music as he grew up.
 b. traveled North when he was young.
 c. played more country music than rock 'n' roll.
 d. listened to rhythm and blues

b 3. We can infer that Les Paul played what kind of music? **(13)**
 a. gospel
 b. western
 c. rhythm and blues
 d. rock 'n' roll

c 4. We can infer that big recording companies **(13)**
 a. never produced rock 'n' roll recordings.
 b. were quick to see that rock 'n' roll would be profitable and identified early stars.
 c. produced rock 'n' roll only after the small companies were successful with it.
 d. were not concerned about the racial issues raised by early rock 'n' roll.

5. Referring to the diagram of the evolution of rock 'n' roll, check all the statements we can appropriately infer **(13)**

✓ a. Ragtime and western music did not influence each other.

___ b. Black spirituals were not influenced by European music.

✓ c. Jazz has roots in both African and European music.

___ d. Rock 'n' roll eliminated all other forms of music.

✓ e. Jazz influenced rhythm and blues more than it influence country.

___ f. Old-time blues and urban blues were almost exactly the same.

✓ g. Black music was more influenced by European religious music than it was by European folk music.

Vocabulary

Use a word from the following list to fill in each blank in the numbered sentences. **(1c)**

a. adopted
b. blues
c. boomed
d. influence
e. resisted
f. strains
g. urban

1. Fashion choices of popular movie stars will often __d__ clothing trends.
2. The saxophone is a typical instrument heard in __b__ music.
3. I grew up in an __g__ neighborhood with busy streets and lots of office buildings.
4. When our aunt visited from Georgia, my little sister __a__ our aunt's southern accent.
5. Many __f__ of the common flu virus can make you sick.
6. The housing market __c__ after interest rates went down.
7. I __e__ the extra slice of pizza to save room for dessert.

WRITING PRACTICE

Writing in Your Journal

1. In your journal, write about current kinds of music that are related to rock 'n' roll. What groups or artists would you associate with these types of music? In what way do they show the influence of rock 'n' roll? In what way do they carry on or change rock 'n' roll traditions? **(16)**
2. In your journal, write about the ways the history of rock 'n' roll involved issues of race. Are there racial differences in how music developed? To what extent did the kinds of music developed by different races influence each other, and to what extent did they stay separate? Do you think there were racial differences in who listened to which kind of music? How did rock 'n' roll challenge racial patterns? How might this piece of musical history also be a lesson about cultural or racial acceptance? How might music have changed people's thoughts about people different from themselves? **(16)**

More Writing Practice

1. Write several paragraphs about your experiences of and feelings about rock 'n' roll. Did you or do you listen to it a lot? Do you consider it old-fashioned, and do you now prefer more current types of music? Who were your favorite artists? Do you still like them?
2. This selection gives an example of how older people may have different tastes in music than younger people and may even attempt to discourage younger people's music. Is that still the case? What kinds of music would you consider the favorites of young people today? In your experience, do older people appreciate current music? Do they try to interfere with or support the music? What do your parents think about the music you like? Write several paragraphs on what older people today think about youth music.

Internet Activities

1. Search the Web for your favorite rock 'n' roll musicians from the 1950s or 1960s to see what you can find out about them, their music, and their popularity. Collect the information in your own file. Be sure to give the source of each piece of information or file you copy.
2. Search the Web to find out about the history of rock 'n' roll in your city or state. Collect the information in your own file. Be sure to give the source of each piece of information or file you copy.

8 Toughlove

Dann Denny

What should parents do when their teenage children get out of control? Should they be understanding and forgiving? Or should they be strict and demanding? This article from a Bloomington, Indiana, newspaper describes some parents' solution to problem teenagers. This group of parents follows the philosophy of Toughlove. As you read this selection, think about what Toughlove means and how well the Toughlove method might work with people you know.

Getting Started

Freewrite on the subject of problem teenagers and their parents. **(6d)** Use a separate sheet of paper.

Word Highlights

adolescents (¶4)	teenagers
licensed (¶4)	officially approved
therapist (¶4)	a person who helps with social and psychological problems
propagating (¶6)	making known spreading
invariably (¶6)	always
modify (¶9)	change
misconceptions (¶9)	wrong ideas
tenets (¶11)	strong beliefs
ostracized (¶15)	shut out of a group; shunned

ON THE WEB

The website of the Toughlove International organization at <http://www.toughlove.org/> describes the organization, provides links to local chapters, and offers other resources. An online magazine devoted to helping families live well with their teenagers is at **<http://www.parent-teen.com/>**.

Advocates for Youth is an international organization devoted to the needs and rights of young people. **<http://www.advocatesforyouth.org/>**

Finally, the American Bar Association Center on the Children and the Law provides resources to understand the rights of youth. **<http://www.abanet.org/child/home2.html>**

John, a 14-year-old boy, is a gifted artist. But he also has a violent temper, having kicked a hole through his bedroom wall, physically assailed his parents and threatened his school teacher with bodily harm. His No. 1 goal? To get expelled from school.

2 "He's on a course toward self-destruction," says his mother, kneading her brow with the tips of her fingers. "And he doesn't seem to care."

3 Angie, a 15-year-old girl, has been expelled from a private school for lying and truancy. Her mother, a single parent, is desperately searching for a school that will take her.

4 John and Angie are just two of the many adolescents who have caused their parents enough grief to drive them to Bloomington's Parents in Crisis, one of the more than 800 support groups across the United States and Canada patterned after the Toughlove philosophy of David and Phyllis York. The Yorks (each a licensed family therapist) founded Toughlove in Doylestown, Pennsylvania, in 1978, formulating their principles while dealing with their own wayward daughter.

5 "Toughlove is a loving solution for families that are being torn apart by unacceptable adolescent behavior," writes York in the *Toughlove* manual. "It's the same kind of loving approach we used when our little children had to take their medicine. We knew they did not like it but we insisted on their taking it anyway."

6 York feels many of today's parents have been duped by books, movies and magazines propagating the notion that

understanding, active listening and tender loving care will invariably produce well-behaved children.

7 "With some children these approaches seem to work," admits York. "Toughlove is for those many parents whose teenagers will not accept tender loving care—not from their parents, teachers, guidance counselors or other concerned adults."

8 "Some of these kids are as big and as strong as their parents," says Dick Sanders, whose wife (Carole) co-founded Parents in Crisis in 1982. "They can be abusive, both physically and verbally. And with many of them, no amount of persuasion will get them to change their behavior."

9 "The Yorks say what these out-of-control kids need is Toughlove—a firm-but-loving attempt to modify the behavior of an insubordinate child. Unfortunately, the word often conjures up a bushel of misconceptions.

10 "When some people think of Toughlove they think, 'Oh, yah, those are the parents who throw their kids out of the house,' " says Carole. "That's not it at all. We love our kids enough to be tough on them rather than bail them out of jail or make excuses for their irresponsible behavior."

11 One of the Toughlove tenets is to "take a stand," or, as York puts it, "make real demands with real consequences." This often takes the form of a contract drawn up by parents (and signed by the adolescent) in which unacceptable behavior is clearly defined and its consequences outlined.

12 If the child violates one of the contract's stipulations, he may lose a privilege (such as talking to his friends on the telephone), or forfeit the use of something (such as his stereo or the family car).

13 "My husband recently cleaned everything out of my son's room," says one mother. "All that was left was his mattress. By improving his behavior, he can get his things back."

14 If an adolescent's contract violation involves vandalism, he may have to get a job and earn enough money to pay for the damage.

15 "We are trying to show them that they can do anything they want to, but that there are consequences for socially repulsive behavior," says Dick. "That's a fact of life. If an adult behaves irresponsibly, he may be ostracized, arrested, or fired. Our ultimate goal is to help our children become responsible citizens."

16 "And we try to never surprise a kid with a consequence," says Carole. "By explaining ahead of time what the consequences will be, it's really up to the child whether he suffers them or not."

17 In every case, banishing one's child from the house is the last resort, done only after every other option has been exhausted.

18 "It's hard," admits Carole. "But sometimes when a child comes home he finds a note on the front door with a quarter and list of phone numbers of Toughlove parents he can call. Each of the parents has agreed to put him up for the night."

CULTURAL Exchange

to knead one's brow	to massage one's forehead with one's fingers, especially for relief from a bad headache or stress (¶2)
support group	a group of individuals sharing a similar problem or difficulty; the purpose of the group is to offer its members advice, support, and sympathy without judging them. (¶4)
to take one's medicine	to accept or endure without complaining an unpleasant consequence one has deserved; to accept a punishment for having done something wrong or bad (¶5)
bushel	a large quantity; a lot (¶19)
to bail someone out of jail	to pay a fixed sum of money to have someone released from jail until his or her trial (¶10)

EXERCISES

Understanding Main Ideas

c 1. The main idea of this selection is that **(9)**

a. John and Angie are out of control.
b. some parents are too soft with their children.
c. a group of parents is trying to help their problem teenagers through the Toughlove philosophy.
d. the Toughlove philosophy was developed by David and Phyllis York.

d 2. The topic of paragraph 4 is **(8b)**
a. adolescents.
b. the Toughlove philosophy.
c. the experience of David and Phyllis York.
d. John, Angie, and the Yorks' daughter.

d 3. The main idea of paragraph 4 is that **(8c)**
a. parents go to Toughlove support groups.
b. children drive their parents to take action.
c. David and Phyllis York developed the Toughlove philosophy.
d. Toughlove is a way to deal with wayward adolescents.

d 4. The main idea of paragraph 6 is that **(8c)**
a. understanding will produce well-behaved children.
b. books, movies, and magazines propagate ideas of understanding.
c. York feels that parents love their children.
d. York feels that parents don't always need to be understanding.

Finding Information

b 1. How many parent-support groups based on the Toughlove philosophy are there across the United States and Canada? **(10a)**
a. 600
b. 800
c. 50
d. 100

d 2. The Bloomington support group is called **(10a)**
a. Toughlove Parents.
b. Parents' Support Group.
c. Toughlove.
d. Parents in Crisis.

c 3. The Toughlove philosophy says that insubordinate children most need **(10a)**
a. tenderness and understanding.
b. rules and punishment.
c. firmness and love.
d. being thrown out of the house.

a 4. Parents and adolescents following the Toughlove method **(10a)**

a. sign a contract.
b. talk over their disagreements.
c. forgive one another.
d. rely on outsiders to enforce discipline.

d 5. According to the Toughlove philosophy, children should **(10a)**

a. be surprised by the consequences of their actions.
b. be punished whenever the parents decide.
c. always be well behaved.
d. be aware of the consequences of bad behavior ahead of time.

a 6. Punishments mentioned in the article include all of the following *except* **(10a)**

a. not allowing the child out of the house.
b. taking away the child's belongings.
c. making the child pay for damages.
d. banishing the child from the house.

Interpreting

1. Write an *F* if the statement is a fact or an *O* if the statement is an opinion. **(12)**

F a. Angie has been expelled from a private school.
F b. Angie's mother is searching for a school.
O c. Angie's mother is desperate.
F d. John is fourteen years old and Angie is fifteen.
O e. John is a gifted artist.
F f. John kicked a hole through his bedroom wall.
O g. John's goal is to get expelled from school.
O h. John is on a course toward self-destruction.

d 2. "Tender loving care will invariably produce well-behaved children" is **(12)**

a. a fact.
b. the opinion of the Yorks.
c. the opinion of many parents.
d. the opinion the Yorks believe that many parents hold.

___c___ 3. You can infer that John and Angie **(13)**
   a. cannot be helped.
   b. will be in trouble with the police.
   c. may be helped by the Toughlove method.
   d. will definitely become better behaved through Toughlove.

___b___ 4. You can infer that the parents described here **(13)**
   a. are disgusted with their children.
   b. are worried about their children.
   c. enjoy punishing their children.
   d. are mean and cruel.

___d___ 5. You can infer that the parents described here believe that **(13)**
   a. you can force children to obey.
   b. love solves all problems.
   c. teenagers get into trouble no matter what you do.
   d. teenagers sometimes behave better if they know the rules ahead of time.

___c___ 6. If a teenager damages school property, you can predict that a Toughlove parent probably would **(13)**
   a. get angry with the teenager.
   b. pay for the damage.
   c. make the teenager pay for the damage.
   d. banish the child from the house.

___a___ 7. You can infer that the Toughlove method **(13)**
   a. has helped some families cope with problem children.
   b. is the best method for dealing with problem children.
   c. cannot work because the teenagers become even angrier.
   d. is approved by all family therapists.

___c___ 8. From this article, you can infer that **(13)**
   a. all children need strict rules.
   b. parents should not try to understand and listen to their children.
   c. parents should not be afraid to be strict with their children.
   d. children should do what their parents tell them to do.

Vocabulary

1. The words in column *A* describe teenagers or their problems mentioned in the article. On each blank, write the number of the correct definition from column *B*. **(1)**

	A	B
5	a. truancy	1. not obeying parents or teachers
7	b. wayward	2. the willful destruction of property
2	c. vandalism	3. not to be relied upon
6	d. abusive	4. disgusting
4	e. repulsive	5. skipping school
1	f. insubordinate	6. insulting
3	g. irresponsible	7. wild; uncontrollable

2. The words in column *A* have to do with agreements about rewards and punishments used to help change teenagers' behavior. On each blank, write the number of the correct definition from column *B*. **(1)**

	A	B
3	a. consequences	1. give up
2	b. stipulations	2. specific terms of an agreement
5	c. privilege	3. results
1	d. forfeit	4. the breaking of a rule
6	e. contract	5. a special thing one is allowed to do
4	f. violation	6. a legal agreement

WRITING PRACTICE

Writing in Your Journal

Describe in a paragraph what your parents did when you misbehaved as a teenager and whether or not that method worked. **(16)**

More Writing Practice

1. In a paragraph, summarize the Toughlove philosophy and method. **(15c)**
2. In a paragraph, answer the following question: When you are a parent of teenagers, will you treat them the same way your parents treated you? Explain why or why not.

Internet Activities

1. The term *toughlove* has become so popular it is used in many contexts that have little to do with providing help for teenagers and young adults. Do a Web search on "toughlove" and collect some of the more unusual situations it is used in. Then explain to your classmates how the word is being used and whether or not you think the use is appropriate.
2. Sometimes toughlove is associated with situations or institutions that are considered abusive. Look at **<http://www.teen-liberty.org/>** and other sites you can find through a Web search that consider toughlove a form of child abuse. After reading their materials, discuss what the appropriate limits should be to a toughlove approach. You may wish to examine again the main website of toughlove.org to see what limits that organization itself suggests.

9 My World Now

Anna Mae Halgrim Seaver

As more and more people survive to older ages, the issue of life quality for senior citizens draws more and more attention. Here, an elderly woman describes her life in a nursing home.

Getting Started

Draw a word map that presents the interests and activities of someone you consider "old." **(6b)**

Word Highlights

rehabilitation (¶2)	recovery healing
Alzheimer's (¶3)	a disease that leads to loss of memory and logic
turnover (¶4)	change of workers
utensils (¶11)	knives, forks, and spoons
demise (¶13)	death
pureed (¶15)	strained
Chablis (¶16)	a white wine

ON THE WEB

SeniorNet **<http://www.seniornet.org/>**, in its many resources for older people, includes information about nursing homes and assisted living facilities. It also has a bulletin board where people share their experiences in nursing homes and family members discuss their concerns about placing a loved one in a nursing home.

A resource site to help people consider what kind of care their parents or other elderly loved ones might need is at **<http://www.aging-parents-and-elder-care.com/>**.

This is my world now. It's all I have left. You see, I'm old. And, I'm not as healthy as I used to be. I'm not necessarily happy with it but I accept it. Occasionally, a member of my family will stop in to see me. He or she will bring me some flowers or a little present, maybe a set of slippers — I've got 8 pair. We'll visit for awhile and then they will return to the outside world and I'll be alone again.

2 Oh, there are other people here in the nursing home. Residents, we're called. The majority are about my age. I'm 84. Many are in wheelchairs. The lucky ones are passing through — a broken hip, a diseased heart, something has brought them here for rehabilitation. When they're well they'll be going home.

3 Most of us are aware of our plight — some are not. Varying stages of Alzheimer's have robbed several of their mental capacities. We listen to endlessly repeated stories and questions. We meet them anew daily, hourly, or more often. We smile and nod gracefully each time we hear a retelling. They seldom listen to my stories, so I've stopped trying.

4 The help here is basically pretty good, although there's a large turnover. Just when I get comfortable with someone he or she moves on to another job. I understand that. This is not the best job to have.

5 I don't much like some of the physical things that happen to us. I don't care much for a diaper. I seem to have lost the control acquired so diligently as a child. The difference is that I'm aware and embarrassed, but I can't do anything about it. I've had 3 children and I know it isn't pleasant to clean another's diaper. My husband used to wear a gas mask when he changed the kids. I wish I had one now.

6 Why do you think the staff insists on talking baby talk when speaking to me? I understand English. I have a degree in music and am a certified teacher. Now I hear a lot of words that end in "y." Is this how my kids felt? My hearing aid works fine. There is little need for anyone to position their face directly in front of

mine and raise their voice with those "y" words. Sometimes it takes longer for a meaning to sink in; sometimes my mind wanders when I am bored. But there's no need to shout.

7 I tried once or twice to make my feelings known. I even shouted once. That gained me a reputation of being "crotchety." Imagine me, crotchety. My children never heard me raise my voice. I surprised myself. After I've asked for help more than a dozen times and received nothing more than a dozen condescending smiles and a "Yes, deary, I'm working on it," something begins to break. That time I wanted to be taken to a bathroom.

8 I'd love to go out for a meal, to travel again. I'd love to go to my own church, sing with my own choir. I'd love to visit my friends. Most of them are gone now or else they are in different "homes" of their children's choosing. I'd love to play a good game of bridge, but no one here seems to concentrate very well.

9 My children put me here for my own good. They said they would be able to visit me frequently. But they have their own lives to lead. That sounds normal. I don't want to be a burden. They know that. But I would like to see them more. One of them is here in town. He visits as much as he can.

10 Something else I've learned to accept is loss of privacy. Quite often I'll close my door when my roommate — imagine having a roommate at my age — is in the TV room. I do appreciate some time to myself and believe that I have earned at least that courtesy. As I sit thinking or writing, one of the aides invariably opens the door unannounced and walks in as if I'm not there. Sometimes she even opens my drawers and begins rummaging around. Am I invisible? Have I lost my right to respect and dignity? What would happen if the roles were reversed? I am still a human being. I would like to be treated as one.

11 The meals are not what I would choose for myself. We get variety, but we don't get a choice. I am one of the fortunate ones who can still handle utensils. I remember eating off such cheap utensils in the Great Depression. I worked hard so I would not have to ever use them again. But here I am.

12 Did you ever sit in a wheelchair over an extended period of time? It's not comfortable. The seat squeezes you into the middle and applies constant pressure on your hips. The armrests are too narrow and my arms slip off. I am luckier than some. Others are strapped into their chairs and abandoned in front of the TV. Captive prisoners of daytime television; soap operas, talk shows and commercials.

13 One of the residents died today. He was a loner who, at one time, started a business and developed a multimillion-dollar company. His children moved him here when he could no longer control his bowels. He didn't talk to most of us. He often snapped at the aides as though they were his employees. But he just gave up; willed his own demise. The staff has made up his room and another man has moved in.

14 A typical day. Awakened by the woman in the next bed wheezing — a former chain smoker with asthma. Call an aide to wash me and place me in my wheelchair to wait for breakfast. Only 67 minutes until breakfast. I'll wait. Breakfast in the dining area. Most of the residents are in wheelchairs. Others use canes or walkers. Some sit and wonder what they are waiting for. First meal of the day. Only 3 hours and 26 minutes until lunch. Maybe I'll sit around and wait for it. What is today? One day blends into the next until day and date mean nothing.

15 Let's watch a little TV. Oprah and Phil and Geraldo and who cares if some transvestite is having trouble picking a color-coordinated wardrobe from his husband's girlfriend's mother's collection. Lunch. Can't wait. Dried something with puréed peas and coconut pudding. No wonder I'm losing weight.

16 Back to my semiprivate room for a little semiprivacy or a nap. I do need my beauty rest, company may come today. What is today, again? The afternoon drags into early evening. This used to be my favorite time of the day. Things would wind down. I would kick off my shoes. Put my feet up on the coffee table. Pop open a bottle of Chablis and enjoy the fruits of my day's labor with my husband. He's gone. So is my health. *This* is my world.

CULTURAL Exchange

nursing home a private establishment that takes care of the very sick and the elderly because their families are unable or unwilling to take care of them; often such an establishment takes on an air of abandonment, uselessness, and finality. (¶2)

diaper	a piece of soft cloth, folded around the legs and the waist, serving as underpants for babies, the elderly, or individuals who cannot control their bowels (¶5)
gas mask	a device worn around the face to protect a person from breathing poisonous gases or very bad odors (¶5)
. . . words that end in "y"	refers to baby-talk, such as *doggy, horsey, beddy-bye*, etc. To an elderly adult confined to a nursing home, such talk could seem disrespectful, mocking, or belittling. (¶6)
Great Depression	the financially devastating economic depression that took place in the 1930s. At the height of the Depression in 1933, one American out of every four was jobless. The situation continued throughout the 1930s, shaking the foundations of Western capitalism. (¶11)
to control one's bowels	to have the ability to wait as long as it takes to reach a bathroom before defecating. It is often difficult for the elderly and sick or injured people to control their bowels; babies cannot control their bowels, and young children are slowly taught how to control theirs. (¶13)
chain smoker	a person who smokes almost continuously, often lighting one cigarette from the end of the previous one (¶14)
Oprah and Phil and Geraldo	the names of three popular talk-show hosts in the 1980s and 1990s (¶15)
transvestite	a person who likes to wear the clothing of the opposite sex (¶15)
the fruit of one's labor	the rewards or benefits of one's hard work (at the end of the day, at retirement, etc.) (¶16)

EXERCISES

Understanding Main Ideas

c 1. What is the key idea of the sentence "He or she will bring me some flowers or a little present, maybe a set of slippers—I've got 8 pair"? **(8a)**
   a. The writer needs slippers.
   b. The writer prefers flowers to slippers.
   c. People bring the writer small gifts.
   d. The writer has 8 pairs of slippers.

a 2. What is the key idea of the sentence "There is little need for anyone to position their face directly in front of mine and raise their voice with those 'y' words"? **(8a)**
   a. The writer can understand normal speech.
   b. The writer does not understand baby talk.
   c. The writer understands English.
   d. People who use baby talk to communicate with the writer are wasting their time.

b 3. What is the key idea of the sentence "After I've asked for help more than a dozen times and received nothing more than a dozen condescending smiles and a 'Yes, deary, I'm working on it,' something begins to break"? **(8a)**
   a. When the staff ignores the writer, she breaks things.
   b. The writer is frustrated by her requests being ignored.
   c. The writer has asked for help, and has been ignored, dozens of times.
   d. The nursing-home staff ignores the writer's requests for help.

c 4. What is the key idea of the sentence "Quite often I'll close my door when my roommate—imagine having a roommate at my age—is in the TV room"? **(8a)**
   a. The writer's roommate often watches TV.
   b. The writer does not like her roommate.
   c. The writer closes her door when her roommate is not there.
   d. The writer is too old to have a roommate.

c 5. What is the main idea of paragraph 7? **(8c)**
   a. The writer has a reputation for being disagreeable.
   b. The staff often ignores the writer's requests for help.

c. Making her feelings known gave the writer a reputation for being disagreeable.
d. The writer has tried to make her feelings known.

b 6. What is the main idea of paragraph 14? **(8c)**
a. The writer's roommate has asthma.
b. To the writer, each day is like any other.
c. The writer has to wait over an hour for breakfast.
d. Most residents of the nursing home use wheelchairs.

d 7. Which sentence from the selection best presents the main idea of the entire selection? **(9)**
a. "One day blends into the next until day and date mean nothing."
b. "I am still a human being. I would like to be treated as one.
c. "I don't want to be a burden."
d. "I'm not necessarily happy with it, but I accept it."

Finding Information

b 1. Which paragraphs describe the writer's condition? **(10a)**
a. paragraphs 2–3
b. paragraphs 5–6
c. paragraphs 11–12
d. paragraphs 14–16

d 2. Which paragraphs describe a typical day in the nursing home? **(10a)**
a. paragraphs 3–4
b. paragraphs 11–12
c. paragraphs 12–13
d. paragraphs 14–16

c 3. The author's children **(10a)**
a. live out of town and can't visit often.
b. can't afford the nursing home.
c. visit as frequently as they can.
d. don't like visiting the nursing home.

Interpreting

1. Write an *F* before each statement about the selection that is a fact and an *O* before each statement that is an opinion. **(12)**

__O__ a. The staff at the nursing home is basically pretty good.

__O__ b. The writer does not want to be a burden to her children.

__O__ c. The writer's son visits as much as he can.

__O__ d. The writer is "crotchety."

__O__ e. Every day at the nursing home seems much the same.

__F__ f. When one of the residents died, another man moved into his room.

__b__ 2. We can infer that what the writer feels toward the residents who are "passing through" is **(13)**
   a. pity.
   b. envy.
   c. frustration.
   d. admiration.

__d__ 3. From the way that staff members talk to the writer, we can infer that they view residents of the nursing home as **(13)**
   a. animals.
   b. adults.
   c. objects.
   d. children.

__c__ 4. We can infer that the writer's children **(13)**
   a. view their mother as a burden.
   b. are selfish.
   c. are well-intentioned but busy.
   d. are selfless.

__d__ 5. We can infer that the residents of the nursing home watch TV because **(13)**
   a. they like it.
   b. they find it educational.
   c. they do not care to talk to each other.
   d. there is nothing else to do.

__b__ 6. We can infer from the details in paragraph 8 that the writer **(13)**
   a. is incapable of doing what she used to do.
   b. is prevented by circumstance from doing what she used to do.
   c. is prevented by her children from doing what she used to do.
   d. no longer wants to do what she used to do.

b 7. We can infer from the details in paragraph 11 that the writer has lost her right to **(13)**
   a. privacy.
   b. personal choice.
   c. dignity.
   d. respect.

a 8. From the writer's description of a typical day in the nursing home, we can infer that she feels **(13)**
   a. bored.
   b. angry.
   c. tired.
   d. depressed.

b 9. We can infer from this selection as a whole that the writer believes that old people **(13)**
   a. are superior to young people.
   b. have a right to be treated with dignity and respect.
   c. should never be put in nursing homes.
   d. should try to be happy where they are.

Vocabulary

The phrases in column *A* refer to the behavior or attitude of either the residents or the staff at the nursing home. In the first space before each phrase, place the number of the definition from column *B* that best defines each italicized word. Then, in the second space before each phrase, identify to whose behavior or attitude each phrase refers by writing the letter *R* (for "Resident") or the letter *S* (for "Staff"). Use context and word part clues to figure out the meaning of the words. **(1)**

		A
9	R	a. aware of our *plight*
3	R	b. robbed several of their mental *capacities*
7	S	c. *invariably* opens the door
10	R	d. lost the control acquired so *diligently*
4	S	e. begins *rummaging* around
6	R	f. my mind *wanders*
1	R	g. being "*crotchety*"

8 S h. a dozen *condescending* smiles
5 R i. smile and nod *gracefully*
2 S j. insists on talking *baby talk*

B

1. grouchy; disagreeable
2. speech used with an infant or very small child
3. abilities
4. searching through in a disorganized way
5. politely; with courtesy
6. strays; fails to stay focused
7. always; inevitably
8. disdainful; superior
9. difficult situation or condition; predicament
10. with great care and effort

WRITING PRACTICE

Writing in Your Journal

Write a few paragraphs comparing the writer's life with the life of an elderly person you know. **(16)**

More Writing Practice

1. In a paragraph, contrast the life the writer lives in the nursing home with the life she lived before.
2. The writer makes a point of telling us that the people in the nursing home are called "residents." Why? Write a one-page essay arguing for the use of this or another term.

Internet Activities

1. While nursing homes or other assisted living arrangements sometimes await elderly people as they become ill or frail, more older people are living vigorous active lives than ever before. Numerous programs and organizations have developed to provide active opportunities for senior citizens. Elderhostel **<http://www.elderhostel.org/>** organizes learning and

travel opportunities for older people. Examine the opportunities at this site or find other opportunities for older people through a Web search.

2. One of the most threatening illnesses that now affects the elderly and often requires placement in a nursing home is Alzheimer's disease. But new methods of care are being developed every day. By searching the Web, find out what you can about Alzheimer's disease and the latest discoveries about it.

10 In Praise of the F Word

Mary Sherry

In high school and college, do you know anybody who got an F in a course or was afraid of getting an F? What do you think about teachers who give Fs? Do you think teachers should give Fs at all? In this selection, Mary Sherry, a high school teacher, explains why she believes in letting students fail.

Getting Started

Freewrite for a page or so on F grades. What do you think about them? Have you ever gotten an F? What effect has an F or the fear of an F had on you? **(6d)**

Word Highlights

impediments (¶4)	obstacles
trump card (¶4)	winning card
composure (¶6)	state of being calm and collected
environments (¶8)	surroundings
testimony (¶9)	stated evidence

ON THE WEB

The question whether grades have gotten too easy goes under the name *grade inflation*. An introduction to the controversy over whether there has been grade inflation appears in an issue of the *Harvard Education Newsletter* **<http://www.edletter.org/past/issues/2000-if/grades.shtml>**

Also, an overview of the controversy is at **<http://complit.rutgers.edu/palinurus/>**.

Data on grade inflation appears at **<http://www.gradeinflation.com/>**.

Tens of thousands of 18-year-olds will graduate this year and be handed meaningless diplomas. These diplomas won't look any different from those awarded their luckier classmates. Their validity will be questioned only when their employers discover that these graduates are semiliterate.

2 Eventually a fortunate few will find their way into educational-repair shops — adult-literacy programs, such as the one where I teach basic grammar and writing. There, high school graduates and high school dropouts pursuing graduate-equivalency certificates will learn the skills they should have learned in school. They will also discover they have been cheated by our educational system.

3 As I teach, I learn a lot about our schools. Early in each session I ask my students to write about an unpleasant experience they had in school. No writers' block here! "I wish someone would have had made me stop doing drugs and made me study." "I liked to party and no one seemed to care." "I was a good kid and didn't cause any trouble, so they just passed me along even though I didn't read well and couldn't write." And so on.

4 I am your basic do-gooder, and prior to teaching this class I blamed the poor academic skills our kids have today on drugs, divorce, and other impediments to concentration necessary for doing well in school. But, as I rediscover each time I walk into the classroom, before a teacher can expect students to concentrate, he has to get their attention, no matter what distractions may be at hand. There are many ways to do this, and they have much to do with teaching style. However, if style alone won't do it, there is another way to show who holds the winning hand in the classroom. That is to reveal the trump card of failure.

5 I will never forget a teacher who played that card to get the attention of one of my children. Our youngest, a world-class charmer, did little to develop his intellectual talents but always got by. Until Mrs. Stifter.

6 Our son was a high school senior when he had her for English. "He sits in the back of the room talking to his friends," she told me. "Why don't you move him to the front row?" I urged, believing the embarrassment would get him to settle down. Mrs. Stifter looked at me steely-eyed over her glasses. "I don't move seniors," she said. "I flunk them." I was flustered. Our son's academic life flashed before my eyes. No teacher had ever threatened him with that before. I regained my composure and managed to say that I thought she was right. By the time I got home I was feeling pretty good about this. It was a radical approach for these times, but, well, why not? "She's going to flunk you," I told my son. I did not discuss it any further. Suddenly English became a priority in his life. He finished out the semester with an A.

7 I know one example doesn't make a case, but at night I see a parade of students who are angry and resentful for having been passed along until they could no longer even pretend to keep up. Of average intelligence or better, they eventually quit school, concluding they were too dumb to finish. "I should have been held back," is a comment I hear frequently. Even sadder are those students who are high school graduates who say to me after a few weeks of class, "I don't know how I ever got a high school diploma."

8 Passing students who have not mastered the work cheats them and the employers who expect graduates to have basic skills. We excuse this dishonest behavior by saying kids can't learn if they come from terrible environments. No one seems to stop to think that—no matter what environments they come from—most kids don't put school first on their list unless they perceive something is at stake. They'd rather be sailing.

9 Many students I see at night could give expert testimony on unemployment, chemical dependency, abusive relationships. In spite of these difficulties, they have decided to make education a priority. They are motivated by the desire for a better job or the need to hang on to the one they've got. They have a healthy fear of failure.

10 People of all ages can rise above their problems, but they need to have a reason to do so. Young people generally don't have the maturity to value education in the same way my adult students value it. But fear of failure, whether economic or academic, can motivate both.

11 Flunking as a regular policy has just as much merit today as it did two generations ago. We must review the threat of flunking and see it as it really is—a positive teaching tool. It is an expression of confidence by both teachers and parents that the students

have the ability to learn the material presented to them. However, making it work again would take a dedicated, caring conspiracy between teachers and parents. It would mean facing the tough reality that passing kids who haven't learned the material—while it might save them grief for the short term—dooms them to long-term illiteracy. It would mean that teachers would have to follow through on their threats, and parents would have to stand behind them, knowing their children's best interests are indeed at stake. This means no more doing Scott's assignments for him because he might fail. No more passing Jodi because she's such a nice kid.

12 This is a policy that worked in the past and can work today. A wise teacher, with the support of his parents, gave our son the opportunity to succeed—or fail. It's time we return this choice to all students.

CULTURAL Exchange

F	a letter grade in the American school system; it is a failing grade. The letter grades are A = excellent, B = very good, C = average, D = below average, F = unsatisfactory. Often a plus (+) or a minus (–) follows the grade. (title)
adult-literacy program	an educational program for adults who have never completed their formal education, or for those who do not know how to read, write, or do basic math (¶2)
high-school dropout	a person who leaves (drops out of) high school before graduating (¶2)
writer's block	the total inability to write anything because absolutely no ideas come to the writer; the writer's mind is blocked. (¶13)
to get by	to barely escape failure; to minimally succeed (¶5)
to be held back	to fail the academic year, which means that a student has to repeat the same grade the following year (¶7)
to be at stake	to be in danger or at risk (¶11)

EXERCISES

Understanding Main Ideas

__c__ 1. The main idea of paragraph 4 is that **(8c)**
   a. students do poorly because of drugs and other problems.
   b. teachers want students to concentrate.
   c. teachers have to get students' attention.
   d. the threat of failure is one way to get students' attention.

__d__ 2. The main idea of the incident involving the writer's son and Mrs. Stifter is that **(9)**
   a. charming students cannot talk themselves out of every situation.
   b. Mrs. Stifter was one tough teacher.
   c. high-school seniors are too old to be treated like children.
   d. Mrs. Stifter got the writer's son to work by threatening to fail him.

__a__ 3. The main idea of paragraph 8 is **(8c)**
   a. stated in the opening sentence.
   b. stated in the second sentence.
   c. stated in the last sentence.
   d. implied.

__a__ 4. The main idea of paragraph 9 is that night students **(8c)**
   a. are motivated by a fear of failure.
   b. have experienced problems.
   c. have made education a priority.
   d. want to improve their jobs.

__d__ 5. The overall idea of the selection is most directly stated in **(8)**
   a. paragraph 1.
   b. paragraph 2.
   c. paragraph 5.
   d. paragraph 11.

Finding Information

__c__ 1. The ideas in paragraph 4 are arranged in **(10c)**
   a. time order.
   b. space order.
   c. order of importance.
   d. no particular order.

a 2. The incident involving the writer's son and Mrs. Stifter is told in **(10c)**
   a. time order.
   b. space order.
   c. order of importance.
   d. no particular order.

c 3. The ideas and details in paragraph 11 are presented in **(10c)**
   a. time order.
   b. space order.
   c. order of importance.
   d. no particular order.

Interpreting

b 1. We can infer that students who are in adult-literacy programs **(13)**
   a. dropped out of school earlier to earn money.
   b. were never threatened with failure in regular school.
   c. had too many problems to succeed earlier.
   d. will never learn the skills they missed earlier.

b 2. We can infer that the writer's son did not work hard because **(13)**
   a. of family problems.
   b. no one had demanded that he work.
   c. his mother protected him.
   d. he didn't like English.

b 3. We can infer that students who say "I should have been held back" **(13)**
   a. do not understand what good students they are.
   b. feel they would have learned more if more had been demanded of them.
   c. are trying to get on the teacher's good side.
   d. are happy that they got away with less work than they might have.

c 4. We can infer that the author's students do not have writer's block in writing about unpleasant experiences in school because they **(13)**
   a. usually don't have writer's block.
   b. like writing for her.
   c. have plenty of unpleasant experiences to discuss.
   d. know how to complain and enjoy doing it.

d 5. It is the writer's opinion that **(12)**
   a. good students always work hard.
   b. students never work hard unless they are threatened.
   c. school is not relevant to students' lives.
   d. many students need to be pushed to work hard at school.

a 6. It is also the writer's opinion that teachers **(12)**
   a. sometimes do not push students enough.
   b. enjoy failing their students.
   c. think it is always wrong to fail students.
   d. know how to be kind in a way that works.

b 7. When the writer says that "teachers would have to follow through on their threats," we can infer that if they don't, students **(13)**
   a. will threaten them back.
   b. won't believe the threat of failure enough to start working.
   c. will find their own way of succeeding at school.
   d. will complain in later years that their teachers let them off too easily.

Vocabulary

Determine the meaning of the following words using word part clues. In each word, circle those word parts that provide clues. Then write the meaning of the word on the line beside it. **(1d)**

1. validity truth; correctness
2. semiliterate only partly able to read
3. do-gooder somebody who tries to help others
4. equivalency being the same as
5. chemical dependency reliance on drugs
6. abusive treating poorly

WRITING PRACTICE

Writing in Your Journal

Write a few paragraphs about a time you concentrated and worked hard in school because a teacher was serious about failing students.

More Writing Practice

1. Write a paragraph to explain what the writer of this selection believes happens to students when teachers use the threat of failure.
2. Should teachers fail students, or should they assure through any possible strategies that all students pass? Write your views in a page or so.

Internet Activities

1. The grade distributions for many colleges and many courses are posted on the Internet. Using the search term "grade distribution" along with the name of your school, see if you can find out about grade distribution where you are.
2. If students fail too many courses, of course, they flunk out of school, which means fewer students are retained or stay on. Good retention rates are important for both high schools and colleges. See what you can find out about programs to prevent school dropouts by searching on "preventing dropouts." Share with your classmates in a discussion what you have found and the conclusions you came to.

11 How to Spell

By John Irving

Because English borrows from so many languages, spelling of English words is full of surprises. Even skilled writers can have spelling difficulties. Here famous novelist John Irving tells of his struggles in learning to spell and presents some useful tips and rules. As you read the article think about which of these tips might help you.

Getting Started

1. Are you a good speller? Even if you are, many people have trouble spelling words that others find easy. Think back to when you were first learning to spell. What words were especially difficult for you to spell? How did you eventually learn those words? Did you develop any kinds of tricks to help you remember those spellings, like " 'i' before 'e' except after 'c'?" Write about those first experiences with spelling.
2. Think of all those words you find hard to spell or you feel uncertain about whenever you write them. Spell them as best you can on your own. After reading this selection and following its tips, go over the list to see if you would change any of the spellings.

Word Highlights

ubiquitous (¶8)	to be found everywhere
antidote (¶10)	a substance that counteracts a poison
antechamber (¶10)	a small room in front of a bigger one, a waiting room
antecedent (¶10)	an earlier term which affects a later one, such as the noun before a pronoun
medieval (¶15)	the historical period in Europe between about 500 and 1400 A.D.
tangible (¶18)	able to be touched.

ON THE WEB

Standard rules for English spelling can be found at the English Club **<http://writing.englishclub.com/spelling.htm>** and at the appropriately named website Absolutely Ridiculous English Spelling! **<http://www.say-it-in-english.com/SpellHome.html>** The history of English spelling, which accounts for its strangeness, can be found at the free on-line encyclopedia, Wikipedia. **<http://en.wikipedia.org/wiki/Spelling>**

International Paper asked John Irving, author of *The World According to Garp*, *The Hotel New Hampshire*, and *Setting Free the Bears*, among other novels—and once a hopelessly bad speller himself—to teach you how to improve your spelling.

2 Let's begin with the bad news.

3 If you're a bad speller, you probably think you always will be. There are exceptions to every spelling rule, and the rules themselves are easy to forget. George Bernard Shaw demonstrated how ridiculous some spelling rules are. By following the rules, he said, we could spell fish this way: ghoti. The "f" as it sounds in enough, the "i" as is sounds in women, and the "sh" as it sounds in fiction.

4 With such rules to follow, no one should feel stupid for being a bad speller. But there are ways to improve. Start by acknowledging the mess that English spelling is in—but have sympathy: English spelling changed with foreign influences. Chaucer wrote "gesse," but "guess," imported earlier by the Norman invaders, finally replaced it. Most early printers in England came from Holland; they brought "ghost" and "gherkin" with them.

5 If you'd like to intimidate yourself—and remain a bad speller forever—just try to remember the 13 different ways the sound "sh" can be written:

shoe
sugar
ocean
issue
nation
schist
pshaw
suspicion
nauseous
conscious
chaperone
mansion
fuchsia

Now the good news

6 The good news is that 90 percent of all writing consists of 1,000 basic words. There is, also, a method to most English spelling and a great number of how-to-spell books. Remarkable, all these books propose learning the same rules! Not surprisingly, most of these books are humorless.

7 Just keep this in mind: If you're familiar with the words you use, you'll probably spell them correctly—and you shouldn't be writing words you're unfamiliar with anyway. USE a word—out loud, and more than once—before you try writing it, and make sure (with a new word) that you know what it means before you use it. This means you'll have to look it up in a dictionary, where you'll not only learn what it means, but you'll see how it's spelled. Choose a dictionary you enjoy browsing in, and guard it as you would a diary. You wouldn't lend a diary, would you?

A tip on looking it up

8 Beside every word I look up in my dictionary, I make a mark. Beside every word I look up more than once, I write a note to myself—about WHY I looked it up. I have looked up "strictly" 14 times since 1964. I prefer to spell it with a k—as in "stricktly." I have looked up "ubiquitous" a dozen times. I can't remember what it means.

9 Another good way to use your dictionary: When you have to look up a word, for any reason, learn—and learn how to *spell*—a new word at the same time. It can be any useful word on the same page as the word you looked up. Put the date beside this new word and see how quickly, or in what way, you forget it. Eventually, you'll learn it.

10 Almost as important as knowing what a word means (in order to spell it) is knowing how it's pronounced. It's government, not goverment. It's February, not Febuary. And if you know that anti- means against, you should know how to spell antidote and antibiotic and antifreeze. If you know that ante- means before, you shouldn't have trouble spelling antechamber or antecedent.

Some rules, exceptions, and two tricks

11 I don't have a room to touch on all the rules here. It would take a book to do that. But I can share a few that help me most: What about –ary or –ery? When a word has a primary accent on the first

syllable and a secondary accent on the next-to-last syllable (sec′ re′ tar′ y), it usually ends in –ary. Only six important words like this end –ery:

cemetery	monastery
millinery	confectionery
distillery	stationery (as in paper)

12 Here's another easy rule. Only four words end in -efy. Most people misspell them—with –ify, which is usually correct. Just memorize these, too, and use –ify for all the rest.

stupefy	putrefy
liquefy	rarefy

13 As a former bad speller, I have learned a few valuable tricks. Any good how-to-spell book will you teach you more than these two, but these two are my favorites. Of the 800,000 words in the English language, the most frequently misspelled is alright; just remember that alright is all wrong. You wouldn't write alwrong, would you? That's how you know you should write all right.

14 The other trick is for the truly *worst* spellers. I mean those of you who spell so badly that you can't get close enough to right way to spell a word in order to even FIND it in the dictionary. The word you're looking for is there, of course, but you won't find it the way you're trying to spell it. What to do is look up a synonym—another word that means the same thing. Chances are good that you'll find the word you're looking for under the definition of the synonym.

Demon words and bugbears

15 Everyone has a few demon words—they never look right, even when they're spelled correctly. Three of my demons are medieval, ecstasy, and rhythm. I have learned to hate these words, but I have not learned to spell them; I have to look them up every time.

16 And everyone has a spelling rule that's a bugbear—it's either too difficult to learn or it's impossible to remember. My personal bugbear among the rules is the one governing whether you add –able or –ible. I can teach it to you, but I can't remember it myself.

17 You add –able to a full word; adapt, adaptable; work, workable. You add –able to words that end in e—just remember to drop the final e: love, lovable. But if the word ends in two e's, like agree, you keep them both: agreeable.

18 You add –ible if the base is not a full word that can stand on its own: credible, tangible, horrible, terrible. You add –ible if the root word ends in –ns: responsible. You add –ible if the root word ends in –miss: permissible. You add –ible if the root word ends in a soft c (but remember to drop the final e!): force, forcible.

19 Got that? I don't have it, and I was introduced to that rule in prep school; with that rule, I still learn one word at a time.

Poor President Jackson

20 You must remember that it is permissible for spelling to drive you crazy. Spelling had this effect on Andrew Jackson, who once blew his stack while trying to write a Presidential paper. "It's a damn poor mind that can think of only one way to spell a word!" the president cried.

21 When you have trouble, think of poor Andrew Jackson and know that you are not alone.

What's really important

22 And remember what's really important about good writing is not good spelling. If you spell badly but write well, you should hold your head up. As the poet T. S. Eliot recommended, "Write for as large and miscellaneous an audience as possible"—and don't be overly concerned if you can't spell "miscellaneous." Also remember that you can spell correctly and write well and will be misunderstood. Hold your head up about that, too. As good old G. C. Lichtenberg said, "A book is a mirror; if an ass peers into it, you can't expect an apostle to look out"—whether you spell "apostle" correctly or not.

CULTURAL Exchange

Norman	the French conquerors of England in 1066 A.D. (¶4)
gherkin	a small cucumber used for pickles (¶4)
bugbear	an irritating problem (¶16)
prep school	a private high school (¶19)

EXERCISES

Understanding Main Ideas

__a__ 1. What is the main idea of this section? **(9)**
   a. Spelling is tough, but a few tricks can make it easier.
   b. Spelling is a necessary skill that adults must learn.
   c. Spelling is hard for everyone—even famous authors.
   d. Spelling is only important for people in careers that use writing.

__c__ 2. The main idea of paragraph two is that **(8c)**
   a. "fish" and similar words can be spelled in more than one way.
   b. following each and every spelling rule is not always a good idea.
   c. English is full of conflicting spelling rules and weird exceptions.
   d. famous authors can get away with not using correct spelling.

__b__ 3. Paragraph six suggests that to improve your spelling, you should **(8c)**
   a. buy an expensive dictionary and read through it regularly.
   b. build vocabulary by using new words and learn to spell them.
   c. only use words in your writing that you know how to spell.
   d. focus on terms you know and learn how to spell those first.

__a__ 4. The purpose of paragraph fourteen is to give a tip on how to **(8b)**
   a. find words in the dictionary you aren't sure how to spell.
   b. look up the synonym for a word you want to replace.
   c. use the dictionary for purposes other than spelling.
   d. shame people who are truly the worst spellers.

__d__ 5. The main idea of paragraph fourteen is in **(8c)**
   a. the first sentence
   b. the last sentence
   c. the third sentence
   d. the fourth sentence

__b__ 6. The main idea of the sentence in paragraph thirteen which begins "Of the 800,000 words in the English language . . . is **(8a)**
   a. English has more words than any other language.
   b. *Alright* is a misspelling.

c. *All wrong* is correctly spelled.
d. Most English words are misspelled.

Finding Information

__c__ 1. How many times has John Irving had to look up the word "strictly?"
a. A dozen times.
b. Six dozen times in the last 10 years.
c. 14 times since 1964.
d. More times than he can remember.

__a__ 2. The term "anti-" used in "antibiotic" and "antifreeze" means
a. against.
b. before.
c. secondary.
d. primary.

__c__ 3. In the entire English language, how many words end in "-efy?"
a. fourteen
b. six
c. four
d. none

__d__ 4. Which is most frequently misspelled?
a. stupefy
b. incomprehensibilities
c. medieval
d. all right

5. Put a check mark before the different ways the article suggests using a dictionary. **(3)**

____ a. find the history of a word
__✓__ b. learn the meaning of a word
__✓__ c. see the correct way a word is spelled
__✓__ d. find synonyms for a word
____ e. check if a word should be capitalized
__✓__ f. discover a word's pronunciation
____ g. lend it
__✓__ h. write notes in it to help your memory
____ i. find tricks for being a better writer
__✓__ j. browse through it

6. Write *major* before each important detail and *minor* before each less important detail.

major a. Foreign influences changed the spellings of some English words.

minor b. There are 13 different ways the sound "sh" can be written.

major c. It's important to know not only what a word means, but how to pronounce it.

minor d. John Irving has trouble spelling the word "ecstasy."

minor e. T. S. Eliot wrote, "Write for as large and miscellaneous an audience as possible."

Interpreting

1. Place F before facts present in this selection and O before opinions. (12)

O a. "No one should feel stupid for being a bad speller."

F b. "90 percent of all writing consists of 1000 words."

O c. "You shouldn't be writing words you're unfamiliar with."

F d. There are "800,000 words in the English language."

O e. "It is permissible for spelling to drive you crazy."

c 2. This selection is mostly based on the **(9)**
   a. history of the dictionary from past to present.
   b. top reasons people have trouble with spelling.
   c. advice and spelling experiences of John Irving.
   d. recent book published by a popular fiction writer.

d 3. Based on the statement that printers brought the words *ghost* and *gherkin* from Holland we can infer that **(13)**
   a. people from Holland were the best printers in Europe.
   b. the Dutch like pickles and terror stories.
   c. all printers came from foreign lands.
   d. the letter combination *gh* is used in writing Dutch.

a 4. We can infer from the presentation in paragraphs sixteen through nineteen of the rule for words ending in –able and –ible that **(13)**
   a. some rules are too complex to remember.
   b. anyone can learn spelling rules.
   c. that this rule is important to remember.
   d. John Irving has a poor memory

c 5. We can infer from the story about Andrew Jackson in paragraph twenty that **(13)**
   a. President Jackson was a good speller.
   b. President Jackson was a creative thinker.
   c. President Jackson became frustrated over spelling.
   d. President Jackson wondered whether he had a "damn poor mind."

b 6. Based on the statement "if you spell badly but write well, you should hold your head up," we can infer that (13)
   a. correct spelling is just as important as strong writing skills.
   b. being a strong writer is more important than good spelling.
   c. grammar and spelling are key to great writing.
   d. only professional writers are good at spelling.

Vocabulary

Write each of the words below in the blank space of the sentence in which it best fits.

exceptions	propose
ridiculous	browse
intimidate	distillery
chaperone	synonym
schist	miscellaneous
fuchsia	apostle
acknowledging	

1. Although he tried to __intimidate__ me by standing to his full six foot six inch height, I did not budge.
2. The __fuchsia__ planted in front of the classroom building is in full blossom.
3. Ten responses did not fit any category, so we classified them as __miscellaneous__.
4. While __acknowledging__ criticisms, the candidate still held to her conclusions.

5. The rule did not allow any ___exceptions___, so Joe had to pay the fine.
6. Karen used the time in the waiting room to ___browse___ through magazines.
7. Because the cliff was made of ___schist___, the rock broke off easily and small fragments piled up at the bottom.
8. The philosopher did not find a single ___apostle___ to carry his message.
9. While in Scotland, the McLaren family visited more than one ___distillery___.
10. Is it possible not to look ___ridiculous___ when wearing a Star Trek costume?
11. Some students distracted the ___chaperone___ as others snuck out behind the gym.
12. So now that you have graduated, what do you ___propose___ to do?

WRITING PRACTICE

Writing in Your Journal

1. Write in your journal about a time that spelling errors caused you some embarrassment or trouble or when good spelling served you well. **(16)**
2. Spelling bees are competitions to see who is the best speller. Based on your feelings about spelling and the views presented in this selection, do you think spelling bees are good ideas? Do they help improve students' spelling or do they just increase bad feelings? Write in your journal your feelings about spelling bees.

More Writing Practice

1. Write a letter of advice to a younger brother or sister in junior high school who is struggling with learning to spell.
2. After looking at the various proposals for reforming English spelling (at the Websites listed under Internet fun), write an

essay presenting your views on whether English spelling should be simplified.

Internet Activities

1. There have been many attempts to reform English spelling to be more consistent. The Simplified Spelling Society says it is "Werking for pland chanje in english spelling for the bennefit of lerners and uzers evrywair." They can be found at **<http://www.spellingsociety.org/>**.

   A fuller history of reform proposals can be found at **<http://www.barnsdle.demon.co.uk/spell/>**.

2. As confusing as English language spelling is, it gets more confusing with the differences between British and American versions. Two webpages that discuss those differences can be found at **<http://writing.englishclub.com/spelling_ukus.htm>**.

   < http://www.gsu.edu/~wwwesl/egw/jones/differences.htm>.

3. The webpage of the National Spelling Bee can be found at **<http://www.spellingbee.com/>** in addition to news of the most recent contest it includes the words used in each round. It also includes spelling activities.

4. Computer spell checkers can make many funny errors because English words that sound the same but have different meanings may be spelled in different ways. There are many versions of a humorous poem that highlights this problem. To find the poem use the search words "spell check poem humor" in Google or other web search engine. After looking at these try writing your own funny poem or story using spelling confusions.

12 Dealing with Interpersonal Conflict

Roy M. Berko, Andrew D. Wolvin, and Darlyn R. Wolvin

Try as we might, we cannot avoid at some time getting into a conflict. The writers of this communications textbook selection help us understand how we make conflict a positive experience that helps us achieve our goals. As you read this selection, see how the ideas presented here help you understand the last conflict you were in.

Getting Started

Use SQ3R as you read this selection. **(11)** Write your questions on a separate sheet of paper.

Word Highlights

precipitate (¶1)	bring about; cause
perceive (¶3)	to recognize or understand
interdependent (¶3)	depending on each other
intrapersonal (¶3)	within a person
dysfunctional (¶5)	not accomplishing a useful end; not helpful
negotiations (¶6)	discussion to work out an agreement
latent (¶8)	potential or hidden; not open
intractability (¶13)	how stubborn or hard to solve a problem is
psychosomatic (Fig. 7.2)	a physical condition influenced by emotions

ON THE WEB

A good list of Internet resources on interpersonal conflict is gathered at **<http://www.mapnp.org/library/intrpsnl/conflict.htm>**.

The Internet and email have brought new opportunities and forms of conflict. An article about how to handle Internet conflict is at **<http://www.enotalone.com/article/2440.html>**.

Particularly unpleasant email conflict is known as *flaming*. A guide to flaming is at **<http://www.advicemeant.com/flame/>**.

When you hear the word *conflict* what do you think? If you are fairly typical, your list includes such terms as a *fight, dissension, friction, strife, confrontation, struggle,* and *clash*. These terms tend to be negative, and many of us have been taught to think of conflict as a totally negative experience, something to be avoided at all costs. In truth, conflict in and of itself is a natural process that can be negative or positive, depending on how it is used. The Chinese word for *crisis* is made up of two components (Figure 7.1). The top one stands for "danger" and the bottom part stands

Figure 7.1 In Chinese, the words *danger* and *opportunity* are components of the word *crisis*.

for "opportunity." Most people recognize the danger part in conflict, but few recognize the opportunity. Conflict can promote relational changes, bring people together, precipitate personal growth, and aid in gaining personal and relational insights.

Conflict Defined

2 "**Conflict** is natural, the inevitable result of individual differences, limited resources, and differences in role definitions." The most common sources of conflicts are individual differences in age, sex, attitudes, beliefs, values, experience, and training; limited human, financial, technical, time, and space resources; and differences in the definitions of various relationships. Conflict is part of everyone's life.

3 The process of conflict begins when one person perceives that another person has caused him or her to experience some type of frustration; thus they experience interference from each other in accomplishing their goals. This frustration, if put into words, would sound like this: "I want (your personal concern, need, want) ________, but (the person perceived as frustrating you) ________ wants (his or her concern, need, want) ________." From these feelings or statements comes a conflict situation in which incompatible activities occur. These activities prevent, block, or interfere with each other or in some way irritate the participants. "Any situation in which one person perceives that another person, with whom he or she is interdependent, is interfering with his or her goal achievement may be defined as a **conflict situation**. . . . If it is not expressed in some way, but kept bottled up inside, it is an **intrapersonal conflict**."

4 Some people may try to avoid conflict at any cost. In fact, one study indicated that "students try to avoid about 56 percent of their conflicts. They become skilled at turning away from conflict." This sort of behavior is generally not desirable. Conflict can be healthy because it allows for the communication of differing points of view, which can lead to important changes.

5 Just as conflict can serve a useful function, so too can it be dysfunctional. Conflict is detrimental when it stops you from doing your work, threatens the integrity of a relationship, is personally destructive, endangers the continuation of a relationship or your ability to function within it, is so upsetting that it causes physical or mental damage, or leads you simply to give up and become inactive in a relationship or life in general.

Levels of Conflict

6 As with all heightening of emotions, conflict develops sequentially and can be understood by examining the levels it travels through. These steps seem present in every type of conflict ranging from neighborly spats to family disagreements, marital problems, labor negotiations, and international incidents. The levels are:

7 *Level 1: No conflict*. At this stage, the individuals face no key differences in goals.

8 *Level 2: Latent conflict*. One person senses a problem and believes that goal differences exist. Yet the other gives no sign of noticing such differences, or tries to deny that differences exist.

9 *Level 3: Problems to solve*. The people express concerns that focus on interests. They choose to confront the problem and take the courage to face the risks associated with that confrontation. The goals do not include personal attacks that move the conflict toward a destructive orientation.

10 *Level 4: Dispute*. There is a problem to solve that carries with it a needs-centered conflict. The individuals fight about an issue but insert frequent personal attacks that move the conflict toward a destructive orientation.

11 *Level 5: Help*. When the people can no longer manage their dispute because they've gotten out of control, they often seek help. The help can be from friends, relatives, or a professional such as a psychologist, counselor, social worker, conciliator, mediator, arbitrator, or adjudicator. It is best if the third party is neutral and invited to participate rather than intrudes. The assistance can be directive or nondirective, but unless required to do so by law the third party should manage, not solve, the conflict. Individuals forced into a solution, such as in labor-management conflicts, almost always hold resentment.

12 *Level 6: Fight or flight*. If the help fails, or the parties become so angry that they don't think of asking for help, they either move against and try to defeat or destroy one another, such as in declaring war, or they try to escape from the situation, such as when a teenager runs away from home. It is at the fight stage that physical and verbal aggression, battering, or murder may take place. At the flight level, getting divorced or quitting a job may be the chosen action.

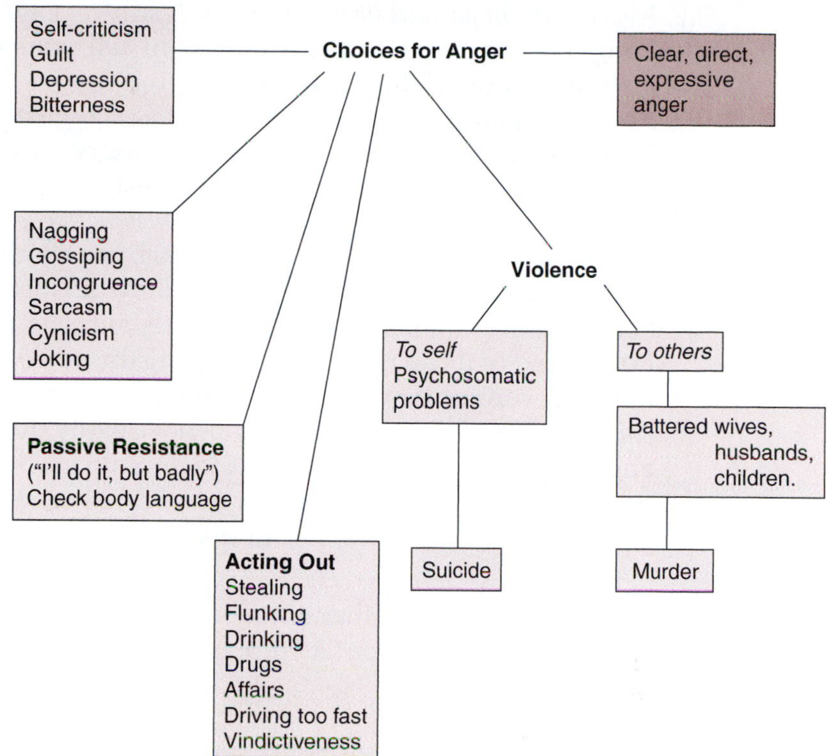

Figure 7.2 Choices for Anger

13 *Level 7: Intractability*. When people remain at the fight-or-flight level for a long period of time, sustaining the conflict becomes more important than resolving it, that is, the conflict gains a life of its own. People abandon hope for a constructive solution. The conflict may continue until the parties destroy one another or lose the will to continue to fight.

The Role of Personal Anger in Conflict

Explaining their reactions to conflict, many people say something like "He made me mad" or "I was so angry I couldn't control myself." These are statements expressing the emotion of anger.

There are some techniques that can affect your interpersonal expression of the anger so that it can be a constructive rather than a destructive action. Consider, for example, these suggestions:

16 1. *Do not react immediately when you are angered*. Although old, the count-to-ten technique is often effective.

2. *Never make important decisions in the heat of an angry moment.* That is not the time to fire anybody or tell your spouse or lover that your relationship is over.
3. *Recognize your diminished capacity for clear thinking.* You are likely to make mistakes when you are angry; at these times your memory is not functioning at its best.
4. *Use the extra energy generated by anger constructively.* When you experience anger (or its first cousin, fear), your body activates its fight-or-flight mechanism. This results in an increased flow of adrenalin that makes you temporarily stronger than usual. But instead of throwing china or beating the office machinery, mow the yard or move a filing cabinet.
5. *Apologize if necessary.* If you really behave badly during a fit of anger, you may decide it is best to apologize to those who have been affected. A simple "I'm sorry; I was angry," will probably do. You will have to decide what is needed and appropriate.

17 Above all, remember that emotions touch every facet of our lives and that anger and conflict represent a stimulus to action for each of us.

Dealing with Another Person's Anger in Conflict

18 To deal with someone's anger, one expert advises, "Don't let them dump on you; it only encourages their craziness." Instead, you must determine what is the best behavior for you and then carry it out. If you give in to another's emotional blackmail (e.g., threats that she or he will leave you or stop being your friend), you have set a pattern by which that person can control you in the future. And the more you give in, the more the person will use the same ploy again.

19 Remember that in a conflict situation the other person is often attacking you when you are not really the cause of the problem, cannot solve the problem, or are not directly related to the problem. It may simply be that you are the first person who wandered on the scene after an incident happened. Or it may be that you are the only person available. Or by the position you occupy in relation to the other person, you are a likely scapegoat. The best approach to follow in any of these situations is to allow the person to vent his or her frustrations, while you remember that the attack is not really against you and try not to react personally.

CULTURAL Exchange

Chinese word	Chinese writing builds words out of pictures that show ideas. Often, two or more idea pictures are put together to make a more complex idea. (¶1)
scapegoat	a person who is blamed even though he or she is clearly not at fault (¶19)

EXERCISES

Understanding Main Ideas

b 1. The main idea of this selection is that **(9)**
   a. there are a number of steps involved in a conflict.
   b. although conflicts may be negative, they can also present you with many opportunities.
   c. if you are involved in a conflict, don't give in to the other person's emotional blackmail.
   d. many people try to avoid a conflict at any cost.

a 2. The main idea of the selection is most clearly expressed in **(9)**
   a. paragraph 1.
   b. paragraph 2.
   c. paragraph 5.
   d. paragraph 6.

d 3. The main idea of paragraph 4 is that **(8c)**
   a. students try to avoid 56 percent of their conflicts.
   b. students are generally highly skilled at turning away from conflict.
   c. people shouldn't avoid all conflict; sometimes it can be healthy.
   d. some people try to avoid conflict at any cost.

b 4. The main idea of paragraph 18 is that **(8c)**
   a. angry people are crazy.
   b. if you give in to angry threats, you are setting a dangerous pattern.

c. emotional blackmail occurs when someone threatens to leave you or stop being your friend.
d. there are many ploys that an angry person may use to get the best of an argument.

___c___ 5. The main idea of paragraph 19 is that **(8c)**
a. you are a scapegoat if a person is attacking you unreasonably.
b. you shouldn't take conflicts so personally, because the situation is rarely your fault.
c. often in a conflict situation, you are attacked even though you are not the real cause of the problem.
d. conflict situations can be very stressful emotionally, but you must remember to remain calm.

Finding Information

___b___ 1. A conflict situation may be defined as one in which **(10a)**
a. people are angry at one another and argue as a result of that anger.
b. one person feels that another person stands in the way of achieving his or her goals.
c. feelings are not expressed but are kept bottled up inside.
d. one person tries to avoid confronting another, even though it might be healthier to do otherwise.

___c___ 2. A conflict becomes dysfunctional when **(10a)**
a. you begin attacking the other person.
b. your family problems are the focus of the conflict, and you need the help of a counselor.
c. the conflict leads you to become inactive, in a relationship or in life in general.
d. you do not confront the person who is attacking you, missing an opportunity for greater understanding.

___a___ 3. A conflict may be described as latent if **(10a)**
a. one person feels that goal differences exist, but the other either does not notice or denies such differences.
b. the conflict arises because one person involved has psychological problems.
c. the problem that surfaces has to do with a needs-centered conflict, which results in a number of personal attacks.
d. one person gives in to the other's threat to discontinue the friendship or relationship.

d ______ 4. To make the expression of your anger constructive, you should **(10a)**
   a. find out who is to blame for the situation.
   b. react immediately when you are angered.
   c. listen carefully to the other person's point of view.
   d. not react too suddenly or impulsively.

d ______ 5. The levels of conflict are arranged according to **(10c)**
   a. time order.
   b. order of seriousness.
   c. space order.
   d. both a and b.

6. Write *major* in the blank before each important detail and *minor* before each less important detail. **(10b)**

major ______ a. Many people recognize the danger part in conflict, but few recognize the opportunity.

minor ______ b. The Chinese word for *crisis* is made up of two components.

major ______ c. Conflict can be healthy because it allows for the communication of differing points of view.

minor ______ d. One study showed that students avoid 56 percent of their conflicts.

major ______ e. If the parties in conflict need help, it is best if the third party is neutral and invited to participate rather than intrudes.

minor ______ f. When you are angry, instead of throwing china, you should try mowing the lawn.

c ______ 7. The word map labeled Figure 7.2 shows **(6b, 7)**
   a. different emotions.
   b. kinds of conflict people might have.
   c. ways people can act when angry.
   d. trouble that comes from unsolved conflicts.

Interpreting

b ______ 1. It is a fact that **(12)**
   a. conflict is a totally negative experience, one to be avoided at all costs.
   b. when one person feels that another is interfering with his or her goal achievement, a conflict situation occurs.
   c. if you let people dump on you, they will become crazy.

d. those who use emotional blackmail to manipulate family and friends are in need of professional help.

__b__ 2. This selection is mostly based on **(12)**
a. opinion and conjecture.
b. social science research.
c. the opinion of someone with no experience.
d. fact.

__a__ 3. We can infer from this selection that **(12)**
a. many people miss important opportunities for greater understanding because of their fear of conflict.
b. most people understand that conflicts may be healthy, but they do not know how to explain this to those who are attacking them.
c. a conflict will typically progress through each of the levels of conflict described in paragraphs 7–13.
d. students are particularly cowardly when it comes to conflicts.

4. Put a check mark next to each statement that can be reasonably inferred from the selection. **(13)**

__✓__ a. Conflicts become increasingly destructive as the individuals involved feel less able to solve them.

__✓__ b. The rewards of confronting a given conflict can be considerable.

_____ c. In dealing with a conflict, it is probably best to seek professional help.

__✓__ d. If you don't express your anger in constructive ways, you will likely make a conflict worse.

_____ e. You should avoid apologizing for a fit of anger; to do so would be to encourage another's craziness.

_____ f. If people are using you as a scapegoat, you have probably given them the impression that you are an easy target for their anger.

__b__ 5. We can infer from Figure 7.2 that **(13)**
a. all ways of expressing anger are equally destructive.
b. some ways of expressing anger are less destructive than others.
c. anger hurts only the person who is angry.
d. anger is a simple emotion.

Vocabulary

Words listed in a sentence tend to be in some ways similar and in some ways different. Each of the following sentences from the selection has a list of words (shown here in italics). Those words appear in a list following the sentence. On the blank line after each word, define the word to show how the meaning of each word differs from every other. On the last blank line, write how all the words are similar. **(1)**

1. "If you are fairly typical, your list includes such terms as *fight, dissension, friction, strife, confrontation, struggle,* and *clash.*"

   a. fight an open conflict or a battle

   b. dissension a disagreement, a difference of opinion

   c. friction things not going smoothly

   d. strife discord, unhappy argument against each other

   e. confrontation facing each other with opposite views

   f. struggle continuing effortful actions against each other

   g. clash a head-on meeting of opposites

   All imply a disagreement between opposing people.

2. "The help can be from friends, relatives, or a professional such as a *psychologist, counselor, social worker, conciliator, mediator, arbitrator,* or *adjudicator.*"

   a. psychologist a person specializing in how people think

   b. counselor a person offering advice

   c. social worker a person specializing in how people get along

   d. conciliator someone who brings together disputing people

   e. mediator a person who comes between disputing people

   f. arbitrator a person who offers a solution to a dispute

   g. adjudicator someone who decides a resolution to a dispute

   All are professionals who help people with social problems.

Select the best meaning for each of the italicized words, based on context and word part clues. **(1c,1d)**

c 3. ". . . a conflict situation in which *incompatible* activities occur. These activities prevent, block, or interfere with each other."

a. unhappy
b. sudden
c. not fitting together
d. likely to make one upset

b 4. "Conflict is *detrimental* when it stops you from doing your work, threatens the integrity of a relationship . . ."
a. very great
b. harmful
c. in your mind
d. between two people

a 5. ". . . frequent personal attacks that move the conflict toward a destructive *orientation*."
a. direction
b. meeting
c. introduction
d. meaning

b 6. "The assistance can be directive or *nondirective*, but unless required to do so by law the third party should manage, not solve, the conflict."
a. telling you what to do
b. letting people find their own path
c. uncertain
d. confused

d 7. "Recognize your *diminished* capacity for clear thinking. You are likely to make mistakes when you are angry."
a. indirect
b. improved
c. emotional
d. lessened

b 8. "Above all, remember that emotions touch every *facet* of our lives . . ."
a. day
b. part
c. feeling
d. person

a 9. ". . . anger and conflict represent a *stimulus* to action for each of us."
a. prod
b. obstacle
c. question
d. type

WRITING PRACTICE

Writing in Your Journal

Write in your journal about a conflict you experienced recently. Did you resolve the conflict? How? If not, what happened? Looking back, would you now act differently? Do the ideas and information in this selection help you understand what went on and how you might have acted differently?

More Writing Practice

1. Write the answers to the SQ3R questions you wrote for this selection. **(11)**
2. List and summarize the seven levels of conflict. **(15b, c)**
3. Remember the last time a friend of yours got into a conflict with a boss, a teacher, or a girl- or boyfriend. Use the information in this selection to write a letter helping the friend understand what happened and offering advice about how the situation might be resolved most constructively.

Internet Activities

1. Interpersonal conflict is far from the only kind of conflict. Do a Web search on the term "conflict" and see how many different kinds of conflict you can find. Share your results with your classmates.
2. For every kind of conflict there is some kind of specialist who will attempt to resolve it. Search on the term "conflict resolution" and see how many kinds of conflict resolution specialists you can find.

Casebook

Romance, Love, and Marriage

Casebook

The next few pages present different perspectives on romance, love, and marriage. They are here for you to read, enjoy, and discuss in whatever way you, your classmates, and teacher decide is best. Reading should be informative, but also fun and thought-provoking. We hope you find these selections to be all three.

Romance and love are such forces in people's lives that there is no end to discussions of them—what they mean, how to find them, how to keep them alive. And there is no end to how people will try to use the power of romance and love to sell products. This casebook starts off with a series of advertisements, and you can easily spot many more examples on TV and in magazines.

Several selections then present some of the many ways people are now using to find their mates. The first two pieces deal with dating and the hustle of our busy lives. A short article describes a new method for meeting lots of potential partners really fast: speed dating. A cartoon links love to the fast-paced technology of the modern world. An article from *Time* magazine describes the revival of the old profession of matchmaking.

But what people look for in relationships is not necessarily the truth about what they get. "Search for a Soul Mate, or Love the One You're With?" describes research on the effect of holding either of two common beliefs about relationships. Then a pair of articles from a gender studies textbook compares media stories of the power of love to transform bad men to the realities of relationships.

Many people see marriage as the culmination of a relationship, even people with same-sex partners. A *Glamour* magazine article highlights the desire for marriage in "Here Come the Brides!" A political cartoonist humorously calls attention to the complex issue of gay marriage, as well there are many benefits of marriage as explained in "The Importance of Marriage Is Being Overlooked."

While current controversies surrounding marriage present it as a traditional, unchangeable institution, historians and anthropologists are aware of the many changes that have occurred over time and the many variations that occur across cultures. The newspaper story "Marriage: The State of the Union" raises the question of how marriage will change in our time.

Love in the Marketplace: Four Advertisements

"Mum" is the word!
The Alluring Charm of a Dainty Woman
ALL the attractiveness of beauty, social grace, and winning personality can be so easily set at naught by the neglect of one important attribute of feminine loveliness—personal daintiness.
It is so easy not to realize that one is subject to the unpleasant odor of perspiration. Almost never are you conscious of this unpleasantness yourself. And the subject is so delicate that your closest friend would not speak about it.
A simple precaution
But really careful women, women to whom complete personal attractiveness means so much, take a simple precaution that protects them absolutely from even the thought of an unpleasant body odor—for all day and evening.
"Mum" is the original and truly effective deodorant cream—pure white in color and easy and pleasant to use. "Mum" is applied as you dress, to the underarm and wherever perspiration is closely confined. The instant perspiration occurs, "Mum" immediately robs it of its disagreeable odor.
"Mum" is the tried, approved and safe deodorant. It has been used for years by millions of women who would not think of entrusting their personal daintiness to mere soap-and-water cleanliness nor to makeshift substitutes which give only temporary relief.
An important use
Dainty women are also grateful to "Mum" for its effectiveness when used on the sanitary napkin. In this important use "Mum" is essential to women's poise and peace of mind.
You will find "Mum" at every drug store, 25c. and 50c. (Special introductory size of "Mum" will be sent to you postpaid for 10c.)
Be sure to read our special offer, introducing to you "Amoray," the exquisitely perfumed Talc.
"Mum" prevents all body odors
Special Offer: We want you to know of "Amoray"—a new idea for the toilette of the fastidious woman. Although a talc of the finest Italian grind, astonishingly soft and smooth, "Amoray" is something more. It is perfumed by a costly process with the fragrance of many flowers from the fields of France. It is really a perfume in powder form.
In order to introduce "Amoray" to you, we shall be glad to send you a 25c jar of "Mum" and a 25c container of "Amoray"—both for 40c postpaid. The coupon is for your convenience.
"Mum" used on the foot neutralizes the acids of perspiration and makes silk hosiery last longer.
MUM
A Delicate Deodorant
SPECIAL OFFER COUPON
March, 1927
Mum Mfg. Co., 1100 Chestnut St., Philadelphia
Enclosed is ______ for offer checked ☐ Special Offer—25c "Mum" for personal daintiness and 25c "Amoray" Talc, cool and comforting, perfumed with a rare and exotic fragrance—50c worth for 40c postpaid. ☐ Introductory size of "Mum", 10c postpaid.
Name
Address
City

THE FOREVERMARK IS USED UNDER LICENSE.

didn't know she had a tattoo

didn't know she'd hog both sides of the bed

didn't know she'd become CEO

didn't know she'd have twins

somehow, always knew she was the one

The Three Stone Earrings
for your past, present and future.
Visit the Design Gallery at
adiamondisforever.com

A DIAMOND IS FOREVER
DIAMOND TRADING COMPANY

Drink
Coca-Cola
Delicious and Refreshin
NNE GIBSON and
PH SCOTT on location
SARI MARITZA
PARK LANE
ESHED for the

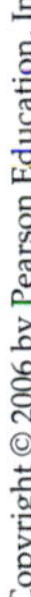

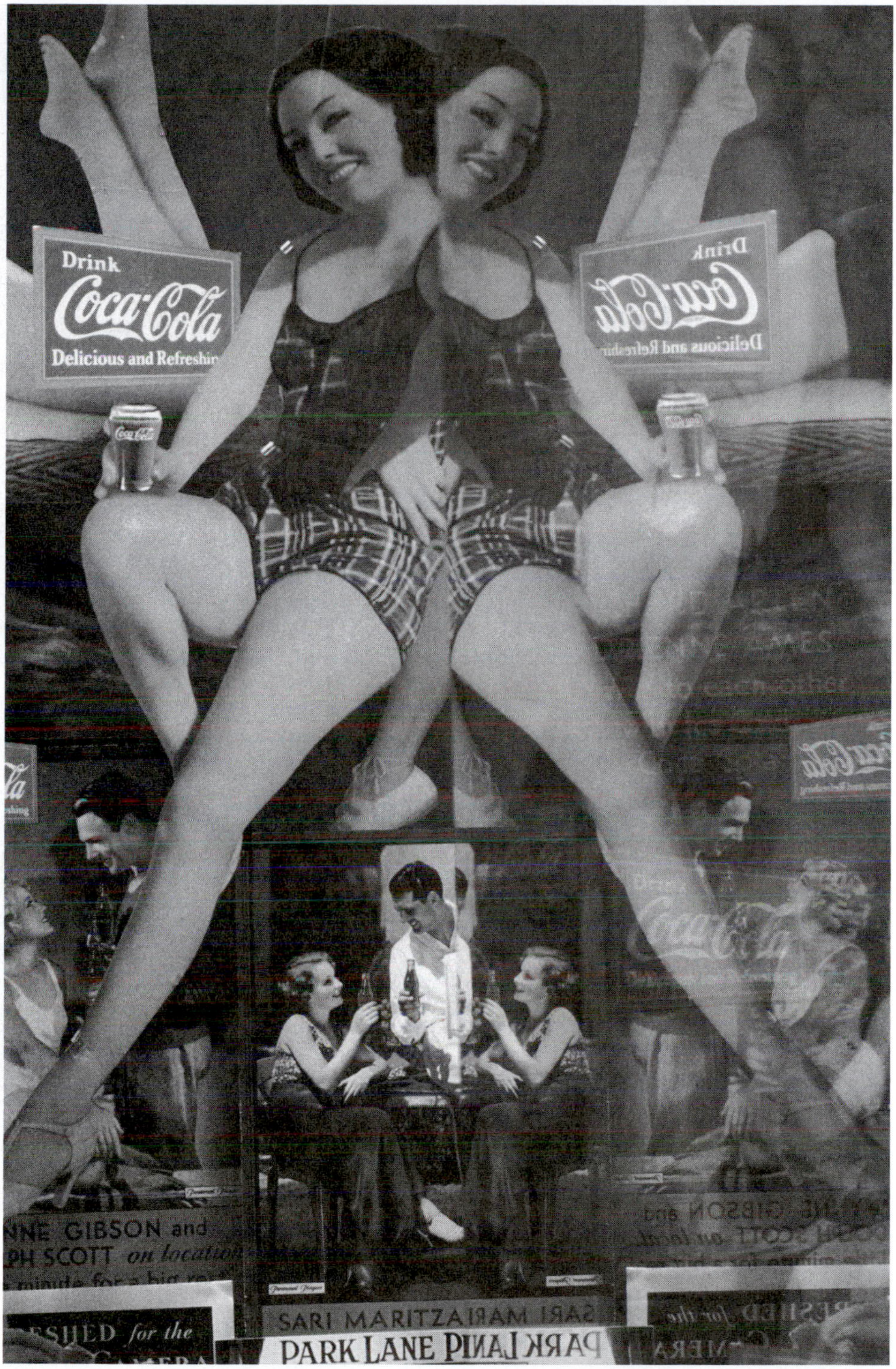

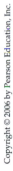

EXERCISES

1. How do these advertisements use romance to sell their products? What is the link between the products and romance? In what way and to what extent are the products likely to provide the satisfactions they promise?

2. Find and describe two advertisements on television that use romance and love. Discuss how they represent romance and love and how they use those emotions to sell products.

3. Using specific examples discuss whether you think those advertisements that use love and romance glorify those feelings, debase them, present an unrealistic view, or are helpful to people in satisfying their desires.

Zero to Romance in Three Minutes Flat

Sora Song

Since 1999, when a Los Angeles rabbi, Yaacov Deyo, co-author of *Speed Dating: The Smarter, Faster Way to Lasting Love*, divined a way to get Jewish singles to mingle, scores of speed-dating services have popped up, offering time-pressed lonely hearts a chance to meet dozens of prospective partners in a single evening. One such service, HurryDate, launched in New York City two years ago, now runs dating events in 50 cities in the U.S., Canada and Britain—and points with pride to its first engaged couple (set to wed this June). TIME went to a session in New York City to survey the scene.

2 Nearly 100 buoyant singles arrived at a low-lit downtown lounge and were outfitted with name tags, numbers and scorecards. The women stayed seated while the men hustled among them, meeting for three minutes apiece in a highly structured, musical chairs–style round robin. The sessions are designed for equal numbers of both sexes, but women outnumbered men at

"You say you love me, but I'm not on your speed dial."

this event, so each woman ended up with unexpected (but welcome) rest periods.

3 Conversations revolved mostly around careers. Few were memorable. One speechwriter had so little to say about himself that it was hard to imagine him putting words in other people's mouths. Of the 20 guys I talked with, none left more than a nebulous memory.

4 At the end of the evening, we turned in our scorecards, with each potential mate marked yes or no. Albert, No. 52, was thrilled. "I felt like a kid in a candy store," he said. "And I walked out of there with a buzz." I left with more of a headache—but also with the phone numbers of two lawyers, Sandy and Margarita. They're girls. And we're going to a bar next week to dish about guys.

Cupid Academy

Lisa Takeuchi Cullen

ELIZABETH BIONDI WANTS TO BE A matchmaker. After a devastating breakup with a boyfriend last summer, the Detroit social worker decided to channel her romantic energy into something constructive. She had always enjoyed setting friends up on dates—why not strangers? So late last month Biondi, 25, hopped on a plane to New York City and enrolled in matchmaking school.

2 Biondi is in good company. Dating services have blossomed over the past few years to become a billion-dollar industry. Though the Internet fueled that explosion, real-life matchmakers with names like Great Expectations and It's Just Lunch are popping up around the country like valentines in J. Lo's mailbox. The Matchmaking Institute, which offers the nation's first certification course for would-be Cupids, opened in October and is attracting students from as far away as Singapore. It helps that the modern-day yenta looks less like Sylvia Miles in *Crossing Delancey* and more like Alicia Silverstone in NBC's *Miss Match:* young, attractive and a long way from loserdom—just like her clients. Hey, even Paula Abdul is rumored to have met her boyfriend through a matchmaker.

3 The Internet is playing a double role in matchmaking's revival. On the one hand, the ubiquity of online dating—1 in 10 Web surfers uses those sites, which get 40 million hits a month—

has eased Americans' hang-ups about paying a third party to set up dates. On the other, Web-dating singles have grown increasingly weary of the attending aggravations—the overly flattering photos, the fibbing bios, the less-than-honorable intentions, the inevitable letdown of that first date.

4 Online-dating sites are responding by trying to be more like real-life matchmakers. The fastest growing site, eHarmony.com, draws 10,000 new users a day with a 436-question screen. Match.com, the largest of the services, recently added its own test as well as an advice site manned by live therapists. "We can get into the nuances of chemistry and attraction too, but on a mass scale," says Trish McDermott, vice president of romance for Match.com.

5 But many singles seem to crave the human touch. "People like to think matchmakers are in it not just for money but because they have a sixth sense," says Darren Star, creator of *Miss Match*. "A matchmaker is part psychologist, part psychic."

6 Those who come to the Matchmaking Institute believe they have the magic; they just need to learn the spells. Over a frozen weekend in late January, half a dozen students gathered at the institute's downtown Manhattan headquarters, a loft dominated by a lipstick red wall, a well-stocked bar and two sleepy Chihuahuas. The students were greeted by the school's co-founders, Lisa Clampitt, 39, a veteran matchmaker in a miniskirt and knee-high suede boots, and Jerome Chasques, 34, an amiable Frenchman with an international singles-events business. Nestling into black leather lounge chairs amid animal-print cushions, the students list their qualifications. Alayna Tagariello, 29, works in public relations and plays host to singles parties. Nelson Hitchcock, 35, an events coordinator, recounts the time he helped arrange a friend's elaborate proposal. Lia Woertendyke, 18, a high school senior, uses paste-on tattoos as conversation starters at parties. All the students this weekend are 35 or younger. All but one are single.

7 The institute describes itself as a "school of matchmaking and relationship sciences," but it soon becomes clear that its teachings are far from exact. Of the 22 hours of intensive training, a good many are spent on the decidedly unscientific business of assessing and handling clients, many of whom need help far beyond the introduction. Some require sober advice about wardrobe or hygiene. Others need schooling on how not to sabotage a date with obnoxious behavior. Some matchmakers, including

Clampitt, have degrees in social work or psychology. Still, she warns, "matchmaking is not therapy. You've got to be real careful about boundaries." She advises clients with serious issues to get professional counseling. . . .

8 So far, no marriages have resulted from the efforts of Matchmaking Institute graduates. One date, however, did come out of the January course: Clampitt sent Biondi, the pretty, blond social worker from Detroit, for a sushi dinner with a New York lawyer. "He was a perfect gentleman," according to Biondi, who says they keep in touch. Who knows? Cupid may have found a mark.

Search for a Soul Mate, or Love the One You're With?

Karen S. Peterson, USA TODAY

Some people believe there is one special soul mate somewhere in the universe meant just for them. But others say that's romantic mumbo jumbo. A deep bond develops only after years of working to make a relationship last.

2 The soul mate theory is the stuff of movies and fairy tales, as well as fodder for researchers who study love for a living. But many marital therapists tend to believe the opposite, pitching their tents in the "work it out" camp.

3 Now, research to be presented Friday in Atlanta to the American Psychological Society says neither belief is "right" or "wrong"—either can lead to a successful relationship. The work-it-out partners "do manage to work hard on their relationships, but not necessarily harder than those who are satisfied soul mates," says Renae Franiuk, a researcher at the University of Wisconsin–Stevens Point.

QUICK QUESTION

Which theory of love do you think holds the most water?

Soul mate: Believe that success is based on whether people are "right" for each other, that bonds exist before two people meet, that partner must be the most amazing person one has ever met, that a person can't marry unless passionately in love.

Work-it-out partners: Believe that effort is more important than compatibility, that love grows and is not "found," that most marriages fail because people won't work at them, that one can be happy with most reasonable partners.

4 The two theories are part of a new field that investigates how attitudes and beliefs about relationships formed before couples even begin dating may influence how the romance plays out.

5 The idea of a soul mate is often credited to the philosopher Plato, who said a perfect human was tragically split apart and we are destined to spend our lives trying to find our missing other. The concept has been gaining steam for the past couple of years, ever since a Gallup Poll found that most young adults believe in soul mates.

6 The idea is catching the public's imagination. Increasing numbers of self-help books and Web sites trumpet how to find the mate destiny has reserved for you.

7 But the idea of soul mates draws stinging reviews from many who monitor the future of marriage. Atlanta psychiatrist Frank Pittman, author of *Grow Up!*, says it sounds like "magic. It is an irresponsible effort at bypassing the hard work, the negotiation, battles and experiences of being together. The idea is like cotton candy. It is something that goes down easily without having to chew it."

8 Franiuk, however, says those who believe in soul mates will fight to make the relationship work.

9 Those who think they have found the right one "will work very hard to stay with him or her," she adds. "They will go out of their way to exaggerate their partner's strengths or downplay their flaws. They will frame a negative as a positive, such as calling a selfish partner 'somebody who will stand up for himself.' "

10 There is a hitch, however. If a partner decides his or her love is not a soul mate after all, the disillusioned one may bail out early. The fear is "well, if this one is a dud, I'd better move on quickly." These lost souls "will exaggerate a (current) partner's flaws and downplay strengths," Franiuk says. "They are very dissatisfied."

11 Franiuk's research team was formed at the University of Illinois–Urbana-Champaign. She has spent six years formally studying 1,500 college students, most of them single, and interviewing hundreds more. The majority filled out questionnaires; about 100 were tracked for eight months. Both men and women tend to the romantic view, she finds. Overall, about 50% strongly buy into the soul mate theory, while only about 15% strongly endorse the work-it-out concept. The rest are neutral.

12 The practical partners, those who believe in working it out, are smack in the middle on the satisfaction charts, Franiuk says. They are less satisfied than soul mates who believe they have

found their one and only, but happier than romantics who think they have linked up with the wrong partner and must move on.

13 Not all experts concerned about the chances of happily-ever-aftering pooh-pooh the idea of looking for one's soul mate. Diane Sollee, founder of the Coalition for Marriage, Family and Couples Education, refuses to pour cold water on those who believe in a destined love.

14 But she cautions that looking for a soul mate "is OK if partners realize that finding this mate who feels so right is just the first step in a long process. And that (process) will focus on how to make love last and to grow together as life mates," not just soul mates.

According to the Media . . . Bad Men Can Be Transformed by Women's Love

Linda Brannon

Movies are filled with images of selfish, roguish scoundrels transformed into heroes by women's love (Aronson & Kimmel, 1997). Self-absorbed scoundrel Rick Blaine (played by Humphrey Bogart) becomes a hero in the film *Casablanca* out of love for Elsa (Ingrid Bergman). Indeed, his love was so great that he gave up that love for the Allied cause—a true hero. Charlie Allnut (again, Humphrey Bogart) is transformed from a drunk into a hero by the love of Rose (Katharine Hepburn) in *The African Queen*. Humphrey Bogart was not the only actor who played this transformation repeatedly. Clark Gable also experienced a change for the better through the love of a woman in many movies.

2 Women have been affected by these portrayals, coming to believe that their love has the power to transform a bad man into a good one. *New York Times* columnist Anna Quindlen (reported in Aronson & Kimmel, 1997) asked female readers to choose a mate—either a kind, faithful, careful man or a roguish, self-interested scoundrel, and the vote was overwhelmingly for the nice guy. When she identified one as Ashley Wilkes and the other as Rhett Butler, however, some women felt differently. One woman said, "Well, that's different. . . . Rhett Butler's never been loved by me.

When I love him, he'll change" (Aronson & Kimmel, 1997, p. 32). This quotation demonstrates the extent to which some women believe in the transformational power of their love, a romantic fantasy perpetrated by the media.

According to the Research . . . Bad Men Are Dangerous to the Women Who Love Them

Linda Brannon

When women hope to change bad men through love, they put themselves in danger of being victimized by these men. Perhaps some scoundrels change through love, but many remain scoundrels who harm the women who love them. Violence directed toward women shows a different pattern than violence directed toward men (Heise, Ellsberg, & Gottemoeller, 1999). Women are more likely than men to be victimized by family members or intimate partners, putting women in danger of physical, psychological, and sexual abuse. Indeed, these types of abuse tend to co-occur, and women who experience one will likely be targets of the others as well. In addition, abuse typically occurs over a period of time, including repeated incidents. Women are abused in a variety of ways and at a high rate—over 25% of women reported some type of abuse by an intimate partner (Tjaden & Thoennes, 2000).

2 Women may be reluctant to leave an abusive partner, partly for the reasons that attracted them to the partner. In addition, the notion that "he will change," and "this time will be the last time he will hit/be unfaithful to/humiliate me," allows women to believe that their abusive partners will become the men they fantasized. Another factor that keeps women with abusive partners is the women's emotional commitment to these men combined with the men's lower commitment to their partners. The partner whose emotional commitment is higher has lower power in the relationship (Sprecher & Felmlee, 1997), putting women who love scoundrels at risk. Their love binds them to men who care less than their female partners do.

3 Women who do leave an abusive partner do not necessarily escape the danger they have experienced. Indeed, women who leave abusive partners are at increased risk for harm (Tjaden & Thoennes, 2000). Angry, resentful, or jealous former partners may stalk and do violence to the women who have left them. Indeed, women are more likely to be killed by an intimate partner during a separation than when living with these violent men. Staying with them is also dangerous—women experience over 1.3 million physical assaults from male partners each year. Therefore, the romantic notion that the love of a woman can transform a bad man into a good one appears more often in movies than in daily life.

EXERCISES

1. The articles on Speed-dating and the school for matchmakers, as well as the advertisement for Perfectmatch.com present different services to help people find partners. Based on what you have experienced and heard, do you think any of these three approaches is likely to work? Would you use any of these three services. Why or why not?

2. The cartoon "You say you love me. . . " links love with technology. What is the humor in the cartoon? What serious point is the cartoonist making? In that other ways has technology influenced our sense of love, marriage, and dating?

3. Do you believe in looking for a soul mate as a partner or are you more inclined to work out relationships with people you may think are less than perfect matches for you? Explain your answer in light of Karen S. Peterson's article on pages 484–486.

4. Describe your ideal partner and how you are likely to meet him or her.

5. Do you think your relationship will change the person you love? Do you think it will change you? How and in what way? Would you put up with aspects you don't like of your loved one? Which characteristics? Do you think these will change over time in the relationship? Are there aspects you will not put up with? Explain your answer.

6. How can relationships hurt people? Do you know of a case where someone has been in a relationship that has been harmful? What resulted? Did he or she eventually break the relationship off? Did this person then find a more positive relationship?

Here Come the Brides!

Jon Barrett

Sarah Landreman, 26 . . . Growing up as the youngest of 12 children in a conservative Catholic family, I watched most of my brothers and sisters get married, so I can't remember a time when I didn't want a big, fancy wedding of my own. When I realized I was gay in high school, I figured it would never happen.

2 **Kristin Broomfield, 30 . . .** I dated guys all through college, though I never had a real boyfriend. Friends of mine were in serious relationships, but that felt alien to me. After I met Sarah at a club on September 19, 2002, that changed in a hurry. When I kissed her that night—my first kiss with a woman—I finally understood what people meant when they talked about fireworks. Within a month, we had moved into a condo, and by Christmas, we were engaged. I was pretty nervous about how my family would react. Like Sarah's family, we're a big Catholic clan.

3 **Sarah**: I think that our families initially were uneasy. But we felt strongly that, whether it was legally binding or not, we wanted to declare our love in front of everybody—and that we shouldn't miss out on what should be the best day of our lives simply because we were two *women* in love.

4 **Marie Broomfield (Kristin's mom)**: When Kristin told me that she and Sarah were engaged, I was a little surprised. Their relationship seemed to get serious really fast. She was so happy, though, that I couldn't help feeling that way, too.

5 **Helen Landreman (Sarah's mom)**: When Sarah told us, my husband and I didn't know what to think. Then, as we talked, I realized that my other kids had fallen in love and gotten married. Why not Sarah? My husband saw things differently. He was so afraid that the ceremony would be against the church that he said he wouldn't be able to attend.

6 **Jennifer Meyer (one of Sarah's sisters and a matron of honor)**: I asked Sarah if she and Kristin were going to kiss during the ceremony, because my kids, who are eight, six and two, were going to be there; I don't want them to be exposed to too much. Sarah just joked, "I guess we can go in the bathroom to make out." But I wanted her to think about it—for me, and for the rest of the family.

7 **Sarah**: My family's reactions hurt, especially my father saying he wouldn't be at the wedding; I had always been Daddy's little girl. I respected his decision but was determined not to let it ruin our plans for the wedding we'd dreamed of—a traditional, formal affair. We didn't want to wear suits or go barefoot on the beach, like some gay couples. We wanted a *wedding* wedding.

8 **Kristin**: Getting married in a Catholic church was totally out of the question. So we chose an elegant art gallery near the city where we live, Sun Prairie, Wisconsin.

9 **Sarah**: I know some women who've had to beg their grooms to get involved in the wedding; when you have two brides, that's no problem. We divided up the ceremony chores: I did the music and Kristin did the flowers. We went for traditional rings—platinum bands inset with princess-cut diamonds. I remember thinking the jewelry store was getting a good deal. How often do they get to sell *two* engagement rings to the same couple? When I went shopping for my dress, some of the employees at the stores looked startled when I said I was marrying a woman. Fortunately, everyone was helpful and kind.

10 **Kristin**: We registered at Bed Bath & Beyond and Target. But friends said they couldn't find my list at Target, so I went online to see: Sarah had listed me as the groom! I later told her, "Well, I guess we know who wears the pants in this family."

11 **Sarah**: About a month before the wedding, I was at my parents' house and my father pulled me aside. I had come to peace with the fact that he wouldn't be at the ceremony, although it still stung. But he surprised me. "At confession today, I asked the priest if I could come to your wedding," he told me. "He said yes. So I'll be there." I gave him a huge hug. It wasn't until I got in the car that I screamed "My dad's coming!" and burst out crying.

12 **Kristin**: Both sets of parents and most of our brothers and sisters attended the wedding. All told, we had about 120 guests. It was a beautiful Friday evening in June, with just a little bit of rain for good luck. Our bridesmaids and matrons of honor were the first to go down the aisle, and then Sarah and I each walked

on our own to the music of Pachelbel's Canon. I went before her, and I was already teary. Then when Sarah came in, I just lost it. She was so beautiful.

13 **Sarah**: When I walked down the aisle, I didn't see anyone but Kristin. And I was so proud to declare my love. Except for a small section written by the Unitarian minister, Kristin and I wrote the ceremony ourselves. We wanted to explain that we *are* a couple, and now, a family, "It is an amazing blessing to find someone with whom to share your life," we wrote. "In fact, it's amazing to have experienced the million of happy circumstances that have shaped us so that we could be here, now together."

14 **Kristin:** We ended the ceremony with a kiss, after all. How ridiculous it would have been if, at the culmination of this wonderful event, we had patted each other on the back and said. "Right on."

15 **Jennifer:** In the end, I felt silly for being so concerned about the kiss. It didn't make me uncomfortable, and my kids sat right up in front! The ceremony was so honest and beautiful to everyone who saw it—gay or straight. It was just about finding someone to love.

16 **Sarah:** Our reception was the best party ever. There was an open bar, a DJ and a cupcake cake with two brides on top. We had our first dance to Kelly Clarkson's song "A Moment Like This," and later we each took a turn with our dads. My mom, sisters and nieces all sang "We Are Family," and I couldn't stop smiling. Then my dad—who I never expected to do anything—got up and welcomed Kristin to our family. He had never made a toast at any of his kids' weddings. He was telling me what he had never said to my face: "Sarah, this is OK with me."

17 **Kristin:** After it was all over we swept ourselves away for a weeklong honeymoon in Puerto Rico. We had relaxing massages, hiked and went swimming in waterfalls. It was completely perfect.

18 **Sarah:** When I was a little girl, as many times as I dreamed about weddings, I never pictured one like ours. And I'm not talking about the fact that I married a woman. I mean, I never pictured finding someone this perfect for me. I got the wedding of my dreams, sure, but more important, I got my soulmate.

ALL WE WANT IS A MARRIAGE, A MORTGAGE AND MANY YEARS TOGETHER
HELP! IT'S AN ASSAULT ON FAMILY VALUES!!
GAYS
POLS
WASSERMAN
© '00 BOSTON GLOBE
DIST. BY L.A. TIMES SYNDICATE

The Importance of Marriage Is Being Overlooked—Decreasing Popularity of Marriage

Linda J. Waite

Married people drink, smoke, and abuse substances less; live longer; earn more; are wealthier; and have children who do better. Yet, many public policies undermine marriage.

2 Marriage seems to be less popular with Americans now than in the past. Men and women are marrying for the first time at much older ages than their parents did. They are divorcing

more and living together more often and for longer periods. Perhaps most troubling, they are becoming unmarried parents at record rates.

3 What are the implications, for individuals, of these increases in nonmarriage? If marriage is thought of as an insurance policy—which the institution is, in some respects—does it matter if more people are uninsured or are insured with a term rather than a whole-life policy?

4 It does matter, because marriage typically provides important and substantial benefits, to individuals as well as society. Marriage improves the health and longevity of men and women; gives them access to a more active and satisfying sex life; increases wealth and assets; boosts children's chances for success; and enhances men's performance at work and their earnings.

5 Perhaps the most disturbing change in marriage appears in its relationship to parenthood. Today, a third of all births occur to women who are not married, with huge, but shrinking, differences between blacks and whites in this behavior. One-fifth of births to white mothers and two-thirds of births to blacks currently take place outside marriage. Although about a quarter of the white unmarried mothers are living with someone when they give birth, so that their children are born into two-parent—if unmarried—families, very few black children born to unwed mothers live with their fathers, too.

6 These changes in marriage behavior are a cause for concern because, on a number of important dimensions, married men and women do better than those who are unmarried. The evidence suggests that is because they are married.

7 **Healthy behaviors.** Married people tend to lead healthier lives than otherwise similar men and women who are not. For example, a 1997 national survey about problem drinking during the past year compared the prevalence of this unhealthy behavior among divorced, widowed, and married men and women. Problem drinking was defined as drinking more than subjects planned to, failing to do things they should have done because of drinking, and/or drinking to the point of hurting their health. Responses showed much lower rates of problem drinking for married than for unmarried men and extremely low reports of this condition for married or unmarried women. Excessive drinking seems to be a particularly male pattern of social pathology, one that females generally manage to avoid.

8 However, unmarried women report higher levels of other unhealthy acts than married women, in particular "risk-taking behavior." Risk taking reflects accidents around the house, while in the car, or on the job caused by carelessness; taking chances by driving too fast or doing things that might endanger others; and/or having serious arguments or fights at home or outside the home. Males and females reveal similar levels of risk taking on national surveys, but married men and women reflect much lower levels than those who are divorced.

9 How does marriage affect healthy behaviors? It provides individuals—especially men—with someone who monitors their health and health-related behaviors and encourages them to drink and smoke less, eat a healthier diet, get enough sleep, and generally take care of their health. In addition, husbands and wives offer each other moral support that helps in dealing with stressful situations. Married men especially seem to be motivated to avoid risky behaviors and take care of their health by the sense of meaning that marriage gives to their lives and the sense of obligation to others that it brings.

10 **Mortality.** Married men and women appear to live healthier lives. Perhaps as a result, they face lower risks of dying at any point than those who never have married or whose previous marriage has ended.

11 How does marriage reduce the risk of dying and lengthen life? First, it appears to reduce risky and unhealthy behaviors. Second, it increases material well-being—income, assets, and wealth. These can be used to purchase better medical care, a healthier diet, and safer surroundings, all of which lengthen life. This material improvement seems to be especially important for women. Third, marriage provides individuals with a network of help and support, with others who rely on them and on whom they can rely. This seems to be especially important for men. Marriage also provides adults with an on-site, readily available sex partner.

12 **Sexual satisfaction.** In 1991, a national survey research organization conducted the National Health and Social Life Survey on a probability sample of 3,432 adults. It asked, among other things, how often they had sex with a partner. Married respondents reported levels of sexual activity about twice as high as singles. Married men cited a mean frequency of sexual activity of 6.8 times and single men 3.6 times per month over the last year. Married women indicated a mean of 6.1 times and single women 3.2

times per month over the last year. Cohabiting men and women also reported higher rates of sexual activity—7.4 and 7.2 times per month, respectively, over the past year—suggesting that, as far as sexual activity, cohabitation surpasses marriage in its benefits to the individuals involved.

13 In addition to reporting more active sex lives than singles, married men and women say they are more emotionally satisfied with their sex lives than do those who are single or cohabiting. Although cohabitors report levels of sexual activity slightly higher than married people, both cohabiting men and women cite lower levels of satisfaction with their sex lives. In all comparisons where there is a difference, the married are more satisfied than the unmarried.

14 How does marriage improve one's sex life? Marriage and cohabitation provide individuals with a readily available sexual partner with whom they have an established, ongoing sexual relationship. Since married couples expect to carry on their sex lives for many years, and since most married couples are monogamous, husbands and wives have strong incentives to learn what pleases their partner in bed and to become good at it. Then, sex with a partner who knows what one likes and how to provide it becomes more satisfying than sex with a partner who lacks such skills. The emotional ties that exist in marriage increase sexual activity and satisfaction with it as well.

15 **Assets and wealth.** In addition to having more sex, married couples have more money. Household wealth—one comprehensive measure of financial well-being—includes pension plans and Social Security, real and financial assets, and the value of the primary residence. According to RAND economist James Smith, married men and women age 51–60 had median wealth in 1992 of about $66,000, compared to $42,000 for the widowed, $35,000 for those who never had married, $34,000 among those who were divorced, and $7,600 for those who were separated. Although married couples have higher incomes than others, this fact accounts for just about a quarter of their greater wealth.

16 **Children's well-being.** To this point, we have focused on the consequences of marriage for adults—the men and women who choose to marry (and stay married) or not—but these choices have consequences for the children borne by these adults as well. Sociologists Sara McLanahan and Gary Sandefur compared children raised in intact, two-parent families with those raised in

one-parent families, resulting either from disruption of a marriage or from unmarried childbearing. They found that approximately twice as many teenagers raised in one-parent families drop out of high school without finishing. Children raised in one-parent families are more likely to become mothers or fathers while teenagers and to be "idle"—both out of school and out of the labor force—as young adults.

17 Youngsters living outside an intact marriage are more likely to be poor. McLanahan and Sandefur calculated poverty rates for children in two-parent families—including stepfamilies—and for single-parent families. They found very high rates of poverty for single-parent families, especially among blacks. Donald Hernandez, chief of marriage and family statistics at the Census Bureau, estimates that the rise in mother-only families since 1959 is an important cause of increases in poverty among children. Clearly, poverty, in and of itself, is a bad outcome for kids.

18 Single-parent families and stepfamilies move much more frequently than two-parent families. These moves are extremely difficult for kids, both academically and socially. Finally, individuals who spent part of their childhood in a single-parent family, either because they were born to an unmarried mother or because their parents divorced, report substantially lower-quality relationships with their parents as adults and have less frequent contact with them, according to University of Washington demographer Diane Lye.

19 **Labor force and career.** Wharton School economist Kermit Daniel has examined the difference in the wages of young men and women who are single, cohabiting, and married, once one takes into account other characteristics that might affect salaries, and labels the remaining difference a "wage premium" for marriage. He finds that both black and white men receive a wage premium if they are married: 4.5% for blacks and 6.3% for whites. Black women receive a marriage premium of almost three percent. White women, however, pay a marriage penalty, in hourly wages, of more than four percent. Men appear to receive some of the benefit of marriage if they cohabitate, but women do not.

20 For women, Daniel finds that marriage and presence of children together seem to affect wages, and the effects depend on the woman's race. Childless black women earn substantially more money if they are married, but the marriage premium drops with each kid they have. Among white women, just the childless

receive a marriage premium. Once white women become mothers, marriage decreases their earnings compared to remaining single (without children), with very large negative effects of marriage on females' earnings for those with two offspring or more. White married women often choose to reduce hours of work when they have children. They make less per hour than either unmarried mothers or childless wives.

21 Why should being married increase men's wages? Some researchers think that it makes men more productive at work, leading to higher wages. Wives may assist husbands directly with their work, offer advice or support, or take over household tasks, freeing their spouses' time and energy for work. As mentioned earlier, being married reduces drinking, substance abuse, and other unhealthy behaviors that may affect men's job performance. Finally, marriage increases men's incentives to perform well at work, so as to meet obligations to family members.

22 To this point, all the consequences of marriage for the individuals involved have been unambiguously positive—better health, longer life, more sex and more satisfaction with it, more wealth, and higher earnings. However, the effects of marriage and children on white women's wages are mixed, at best. Marriage and cohabitation increase women's time spent on housework; married motherhood reduces their time in the labor force and lowers their wages. Although the family as a whole might be better off with this allocation of females' time, women generally share their husbands' market earnings only while they are married. Financial well-being declines dramatically for women and their offspring after divorce or widowhood. Women whose marriages have ended often are quite disadvantaged financially by their investment in their husbands and children, rather than in their own earning power. Recent changes in law that make divorce easier seem to have exacerbated this situation, even while increases in women's education and work experience have moderated it.

23 **Is marriage responsible?** The obvious question, when one looks at all these benefits of marriage, is whether marriage is responsible for the differences. If all, or almost all, arise because those who enjoy better health, live longer lives, or earn higher wages anyway are more likely to marry, then marriage is not "causing" any changes in these outcomes. Social scientists vigorously and often acrimoniously debate the extent to which marriage is responsible for these better outcomes.

24 Social scientists have a responsibility to measure the evidence on the consequences of social behaviors in the same way as medical researchers evaluate the evidence on the consequences of, say, cigarette smoking or exercise. As evidence accumulates and is communicated to the public, some people will change their behavior as a result. Some will make different choices than they otherwise would have because of their understanding of the costs and benefits, to them, of the options involved.

25 If, as I have argued, marriage as a social institution produces individuals who drink, smoke, and abuse substances less, live longer, earn more, are wealthier, and have children who do better, society needs to give more thought and effort to supporting marriage through public policies.

Marriage: The State of the Union

Mike Anton. **Los Angeles Times**. Los Angeles, Calif.: Mar 31, 2004. pg. E.1

Throughout most of human history, a man married a woman out of desire — for her father's goats, perhaps. Marriage was a business arrangement. The bride was a commodity, her dowry a deal sweetener. And the groom was likely to be an unwitting pawn in an economic alliance between two families.

2 A church may or may not have been involved. Government was out of the loop. There was no paperwork, no possibility of divorce, and — more often than not — no romance. But there was work to be done: procreation, the rearing of children and the enforcement of a contract that allowed for the orderly transfer of wealth and the cycle of arranged matrimony to continue.

3 In the debate over same-sex marriage, each side offers competing ideals that they claim hark back to the historical essence of matrimony.

4 In calling for a constitutional amendment banning homosexual marriage, President [George W.] Bush has described contemporary heterosexual marriage as "the most fundamental institution of civilization," forged during "millennia of human experience."

Thousands of gays and lesbians who have married in defiance of state law in San Francisco and elsewhere maintain they possess what has always mattered most in a relationship: Love.

5 But marriage, it turns out, has never been that simple. For much of its history, matrimony has been a matter of cold economic calculation, a condition to be endured rather than celebrated. Notions of marriage taken for granted today — its voluntary nature, the legal equality of partners, even the pursuit of happiness — required centuries to evolve.

6 **A 'malleable' institution.** Marriage as Americans know it today didn't exist 2,000 years ago, or even 200 years ago. Rather than an unbending pillar of society, marriage has been an extraordinarily elastic institution, constantly adapting to religious, political and economic shifts and pliable in the face of sexual revolutions, civil rights movements and changing cultural norms.

7 "It's extremely malleable," said Thomas Laqueur, a history professor at UC Berkeley who has studied marriage and sexuality. "Historically, anthropologically, the word 'marriage' needs to be placed in quotation marks." One reason that marriage seems so unchanging is that it has evolved glacially, inching forward on many paths at once.

8 In Greek mythology, Zeus created Pandora, the first woman. Then he made her the first bride and gave her as a gift to the Titan Epimetheus. The union ended poorly when Pandora opened the wedding gift she came with, unleashing from the box all of the evils of mankind.

9 And some newlyweds today complain when they get a toaster.

10 Like Zeus, Greek fathers considered their daughters property and essentially bartered them for the purpose of cementing an economic or political alliance.

11 The Romans codified marriage, introducing the idea of consent and setting the minimum age of grooms at 14, brides at 12. There were three types of union, and which one you got depended on your social class. The rich got a confarreatio, which included a big celebration, a special cake, maybe an animal sacrifice. The masses simply shacked up, and after a time they were considered married. A woman in a coemptio was essentially sold to her husband and had the same status as a child.

12 Arranged marriages remained common in Western societies into the 19th century. It is still the rule in parts of central Asia,

Africa and the Middle East. It's a practice replete with abuse, from female infanticide by parents fearful of having to pay for a marriage someday to "bride burnings" of women whose families provide an insufficient dowry.

13 The Romans promoted monogamy at a time when polygamy was common throughout the pre-Christian world. The ancient Chinese had their concubines, and from David to Abraham, the Hebrew scriptures read like Utah in the mid-19th century, full of men who had dozens, even hundreds, of wives.

14 **Polygamy more common.** In fact, polygamy has been more common than monogamy over the full sweep of human history. The Roman Catholic Church would take up the push for monogamy, and through the centuries it overtook polygamy as the standard worldwide.

15 But polygamy is stubborn. Though the U.S. Supreme Court outlawed it in 1879, polygamy survives in the shadows of the Mormon West. And, while waning, it is still practiced in the Muslim world and illegally in Israel by some ultra-orthodox Jews, among other places. Polyandry, marriages involving one woman and more than one man, have cropped up among Eskimos and, even today, in Tibet.

16 Even where there have been clear rules about marriage, there have been more loopholes than there are in the U.S. Tax Code.

17 King Henry VIII famously broke from Catholicism and started his own church largely so he could divorce and marry again — and again. European commoners who couldn't legally divorce sold their wives.

18 The Muslim tradition of a temporary "pleasure" union, which dates to the days of Muhammad, is still used to legalize sex under Islamic law.

19 Its Western counterpart: the Vegas quickie wedding, sometimes sanctified at a drive-through chapel or presided over by an Elvis impersonator. Impassioned couples began to flock to Nevada in the 1920s, after California imposed a three-day waiting period in an attempt to keep drunken lovers from the altar.

20 What constitutes a marriage is so fluid that many anthropologists sidestep the word altogether, preferring "unions" or "alliances," said Roger Lancaster, a professor of anthropology and cultural studies at George Mason University in Virginia. Other scholars refer to same-sex unions throughout history — in cultures as varied as ancient Greece, tribal Africa and native North America — as marriages.

21 **No single, timeless thing.** "The strong conclusion that anthropologists have arrived at is that marriage isn't a single, timeless, unchanging thing," Lancaster said. "People are inventive and creative about the ways they've forged ties to one another."

22 If there is a constant in the fluid history of marriage it is that economics has shaped the institution.

23 Some historians believe marriage evolved during the shift from nomadic cultures to settled agrarian societies. When you're roaming the desert with your possessions on a camel's back, property and inheritance rights aren't as complicated as when land and buildings are involved.

24 With increasing urbanization, children once seen as economic assets, as a source of labor, became an expense. Women were no longer property.

25 The social upheavals spawned by industrialization — transient populations, mass education, the women's rights movement and the creation of leisure time — redefined marriage just as the plow once did.

26 "Inventions like the bicycle, the telephone and the car all played a role," said Bernard Murstein, a professor emeritus of psychology at Connecticut College who wrote a book on the history of marriage. "These things gave kids a chance to get together on their own." Shakespeare was, of course, way ahead of the curve when he had Juliet dismiss her parents' plan for an arranged patriarchal marriage and hook up with a young hottie instead.

27 In the 1500s, this was forward-thinking stuff. But by 1905, the idea that love should be the paramount reason for marriage was mainstream enough for the *Ladies' Home Journal*.

28 "No high-minded girl and no girl with refined feeling," a woman writer noted, "ever admits the advisability of marriage without love." Ever so slowly, marriage had become about compatibility, not how many goats the prospective in-laws had. Some believe that the modern institution of marriage didn't emerge until the early 19th century.

29 "It's a 200-year-old story: the slow, haphazard but ultimately triumphal ascension of individual human happiness as the primary reason for marriage," Hartog said. "It's a huge change, and unprecedented. Love has always existed. But the idea that love should exist in marriage is a historic novelty."

30 **Latest debate about gays.** Today, in the debate over same-sex marriage, both sides claim history is on their side. Advocates for

gay marriage say it's the natural evolution of an institution that's no longer tied exclusively to procreation.

31 "Is there some reason a heterosexual couple without children should have the rights and responsibilities of civil marriage but a lesbian couple with biological children from both mothers should not?" writer Andrew Sullivan, who is gay, said in a 2000 essay.

32 Opponents say legalizing same-sex marriage would undo all of the progress that has perfected marriage as we know it today: a union between one man and one woman. In their view, placing gay marriage on the same legal and cultural footing as heterosexual marriage would further undermine the nuclear family and would be tantamount to endorsing homosexuality.

33 In the battle over same-sex marriage, the lessons that history might provide are like everything else: a point of disagreement.

34 "It's hard to predict where marriage will go in the future," said Marilyn Yalom, a senior scholar at Stanford University's Institute for Research on Women and Gender. "The only thing that I can predict is that there will always be something in us that calls for another to complement ourselves, someone to be a soulmate and to witness our lives."

EXERCISES

1. In "Here Come the Brides" why do Sarah and Kristin want to get married? What to they hope to get from the marriage? To what extent and in what way are their feelings of marriage tied to the ceremony and celebration of the wedding day?

2. Don Wasserman's cartoon lays out what he sees of the basic conflict between gay men and women and some modern politicians. State the two positions in your own words. What is the source of humor in the cartoon?

3. How important do you think the wedding ceremony is and do you have special plans for your own?

4. Interview two people you know who are planning to be married or have married recently about their feelings about marriage and about the wedding ceremony.

5. Linda Waite in "The Importance of Marriage is Being Overlooked" presents a number of ways in which marriage helps people. List and explain each of the ways she presents. Do you agree with her? Why or why not?

6. Do you think there are advantages for people to live together without being married or is it always best for them to get married as soon as possible? Why?

7. How, according to "Marriage: The State of the Union" has marriage changed across history? What to you has been the most surprising change? Are any of the arrangements described here not really marriage to you? Why not?

8. What do you think are the current economic benefits for marriage? How could it be made more economically beneficial?

9. Do you think marriage between people of the same sex will be of benefit to the people marrying? Will the benefits be the same as in marriage between people of opposite sex? Will marriage between people of the same sex be of benefit to all of society or will it hurt society? Do you think marriage should be allowed between people of the same sex?

Casebook Writing Assignments

1. Why do advertisers of a wide range of commercial items draw on love and romance to sell their products? Write a paragraph or two to explain your answer.

2. Among the many new applications of technology to love and romance, computer dating services have grown very popular for today's single people. Check the website of an on-line dating service to see what the service offers. Then write a short essay on why you think these services are popular. What problems do you see with such services?

3. Write a brief essay on how you would define "good men" and "bad men" or "good women" and "bad women."

4. Write a letter of advice to young teenagers on what you think is the best and worst ways to find a suitable partner.

5. Write a paragraph or two to explain how you think marriage will change over the next century—if you think it will change. If you don't think it will change, explain why.

6. In the last several years the issue of gay marriage has dominated the news and has served as the basis of heated discussion by politicians, religious leaders, and ordinary citizens. Write a letter to the editor of your college (or a local) newspaper to explain why you think that gay marriage has become such a "hot" topic.

SELF-TEST Answer Key

CHAPTER 1

1. met
2. crystal clear
3. basic principle; rule
4. forbidden acts
5. adding details to
6. periods of time
7. leaders of organized religions
8. dark; gloomy
9. go over again
10. insignificant
11. strong and extreme
12. wandering people
13. not given to action
14. unfriendly
15. coax
16. supporter, advocate
17. beaten up; injured badly
18. announced call
19. gave
20. quick and brilliant

CHAPTER 2

	Word parts	Meaning
1. malaise	mal/aise	b
2. indescribable	in/de/scrib/able	h
3. interethnic	inter/ethn/ic	i
4. distended	dis/tended	e
5. prefabricate	pre/fab/ric/ate or pre/fabric/ate	c
6. circumspection	circum/spec/tion	j
7. inequality	in/equal/ity	d
8. fieldwork	field/work	f
9. deportation	de/port/ation	g
10. truehearted	true/hearted	a

CHAPTER 3

1. nidi
2. from the Middle English for an added name
3. New Testament, New Year, Nickname

4. Circle *nickel, niche, nick*
5. a tie, link
6. Latin
7. ignorant
8. newsboy, newsgirl, newsblast, newspaper, newsreel, etc.
9. *Niceness* is the quality of being *nice.* Knowing that the suffix *ness* turns the word into a noun describing a quality helps us to know the meaning.
10. Possible answers include aviator, avidity, avocado, avocation, avocet.

CHAPTER 4

1. six
2. Finding Information
3. Unit One
4. Chapter 11
5. Chapter 16
6. four
7. Freewriting
8. subsection 10c(2)
9. 365
10. Jean Folkerts and Stephen Lacy
11. "Climates in the United States and Canada"
12. The subject index lists the various topics covered in the book. The author index lists who wrote the selections.
13. 96–100
14. 65, 328–336
15. first paragraphs, first sentences, inferences from, main ideas in, stated and implied main ideas, time order, place order, order of importance, summarizing, topic sentences, topics, patterns
16. major details; minor details
17. 291
18. 450
19. 382–392
20. four

CHAPTER 5

1. How Darwin came to his theory of evolution
2. a. Summarize ideas influencing Darwin.
   b. Identify Darwin's key observations.
   c. Describe two points of theory.
3. a. evolution
   b. adaptation
   c. descent with modification
   d. natural selection
4. They appear in bold print in the main text, where they are defined.

5. a. ideas from Darwin's time
   b. the voyage of the Beagle
   c. the publication of the theory
   d. Darwin's main points
6. A map of Darwin's journey on the Beagle
7. a. animals and plants
   b. They provide evidence and examples for Darwin's theory.
8. a. Organisms change over generations.
   b. Changes are determined by natural selection.

CHAPTER 6

1. By thinking about a subject, you prepare your mind to accept new information.
2. (a) making a list; (b) making a word map; (c) brainstorming; (d) freewriting.
3. They are not important; don't worry about them.
4. Follow the ideas that come to mind about the subject of the reading.
5. c
6. a
7. d

CHAPTER 7

1. A
2. across the top and left-hand borders and at the bottom
3. provides links, is the navigation bar
4. Click "Education" in the left-hand column.
5. Click "Detailed Tables" at the top.
6. Click "Data Sources" at the top.
7. Click "International comparisons" on list on left of A.
8. Click pie slice in page A or at bottom of others.
9. Click "Feedback" on left of A or bottom of others or "Contacts" at bottom of others
10. 72.9 million, from page B
11. increase
12. white
13. decrease
14. Asian and Hispanic
15. between 15 and 18 percent
16. Female-householder families have over twice the poverty rate.
17. Married couple families with children are less than half as likely to be poor as all families with children.
18. about 85 to 90 percent
19. Hispanic, with graduation rates ranging from 58 to 65 percent
20. They have improved from well below the overall rate to being almost the same.

CHAPTER 8

1. c
2. b
3. c
4. a
5. d
6. d
7. a
8. c
9. b
10. b
11. d
12. b
13. c
14. b
15. c
16. b
17. b
18. a
19. c
20. d

CHAPTER 9

1. c
2. b
3. a
4. a
5. b
6. d
7. d
8. c
9. a
10. d
11. b
12. c

CHAPTER 10

1. He was a Harvard economist.
2. minor
3. the "affluent society"
4. major
5. more than ten times—from $5.7 billion in 1945 to $58 billion in 1961
6. to the Sunbelt
7. Houston, Phoenix, Los Angeles, San Diego, Dallas, and Miami
8. Florida, Nevada, and Alaska
9. 39 percent
10. 1963
11. agribusiness, aerospace, oil, real-estate development, recreation, and defense
12. oil tax breaks, military base sitings, and defense and aerospace contracts
13. 1970
14. 1930
15. House builders operated on a massive scale.
16. In 1947, the construction of Levittown, New York, began; Levittowns also arose in New Jersey and Pennsylvania.
17. Congress authorized construction of a national chain of highways.
18. Highways made high-speed trucking possible.
19. time order
20. order of importance

CHAPTER 11

1. (a) survey; (b) question; (c) read; (d) recite; (e) review
2. (a) sentences that introduce; (b) main headings and subheadings; (c) illustrations and photographs; (d) checklist at beginning and questions at end

3. You ask questions about the information that might be contained in the reading, based on the headings.
4. (a) How is (are)? (b) How do (did)? (c) When did? (d) Why (or What) did? (e) What is (are)?
5. (a) Look for answers to your questions. (b) Read short segments, from one heading to the next.
6. the answers to your questions
7. Try to answer each question.
8. Reread only the material under the heading that will answer the question.

CHAPTER 12

1. Place a check mark beside a, b, d, e, f.
2. a. F
   b. O
   c. O
   d. F
   e. O
   f. O
3. a. W
   b. T
   c. T
   d. W
   e. T

CHAPTER 13

1. d	6. d	11. c	16. c	21. b
2. b	7. c	12. a	17. b	22. c
3. b	8. d	13. d	18. a	23. a
4. a	9. c	14. b	19. d	24. d
5. b	10. a	15. b	20. c	25. d

CHAPTER 14

1. Author
   meaning: Is the person who wrote the piece identified?
   importance: If no one takes responsibility for the information, it cannot be trusted.
2. Expertise
   meaning: Does the author know much about the topic?
   importance: Someone who knows and has experienced more on the topic, as well as being more respected, is more to be believed and trusted.
3. Quality
   meaning: Does the publication have standards for the quality of material it publishes?
   importance: Information and ideas from publications having high standards are more likely to be credible.

4. Evidence
   meaning: Does the author have facts to back up the ideas and claims?
   importance: If a claim has strong evidence, it is more believable.
5. Accuracy
   meaning: Is the author careful in getting the facts right?
   importance: If the facts are not precisely right, either the author is careless or is trying to shade the truth. In either case, the author is to be trusted less.
6. Comprehensiveness
   meaning: Is the author aware of the full range of facts and ideas on the subject?
   importance: An author who shows knowledge of more of the facts and ideas is likely to take more into account and is also likely to have thought through alternative views.
7. Reasoning
   meaning: Is the argument and reasoning logically presented?
   importance: You need to be able to follow and accept an author's reasoning in order to accept his or her conclusions. Lack of logic should make you suspect the ideas.
8. Bias
   meaning: Does the author seem to favor one perspective over all others?
   importance: If the author has a one-sided view, he or she may not be representing other views and facts fairly that do not support the favored view.
9. Worldview
   meaning: Does the author have a view of life that predetermines his or her view on the subject?
   importance: If the author has a predetermined view on the subject, he or she may not be considering all the facts and ideas fairly and equally.

CHAPTER 15

Listing

Student responses may vary, but the following are important statements that should be listed:

- Seven- to ten-year-olds tease each other all the time.
- Children will focus teasing on a child who seems vulnerable or embarrassed.
- Teasing is a deliberate attempt to create tension in someone else.
- Insults cut a child deeply because the child can't defend him- or herself.
- Good-natured teasing helps children learn and develop.
- Teasing is normal for seven- to ten-year-olds because they want to fit in, and teasing unifies the teasers.
- Teasing is a form of competition.
- Teasing is part of learning to observe, describe, and add value in language.
- Teasing offers the fun of social control.
- Parents can help a teased child learn from the experience by listening sympathetically to the stories of teasing incidents.
- Parents should not lecture; instead, they should encourage the child.

- If they can, parents should help the child change what he or she is being teased about.
- Parents should help the child develop a strategy to deal with the teasing.
- Ignoring the tease doesn't always work.
- The child should take action without being confrontational.
- Parents should not make a big issue of teasing.

Summarizing

Student responses may vary, but the following sample summary contains most of the important ideas.

> Seven- to ten-year-olds tease each other all the time, and they will focus their attention on any child who seems particularly vulnerable or embarrassed. Teasing is a deliberate attempt to create tension in someone else and can hurt a child deeply because the child doesn't have the maturity or confidence to defend him- or herself. Nonetheless, good-natured teasing can help a child learn and develop, and teasing is normal for seven- to ten-year-olds.
>
> Children tease for many reasons. They want to fit, and teasing others unifies the teasers. Teasing is a form of competition. Teasing is part of learning to observe, describe, and add value to language. Finally, teasing is just fun, as the teaser enjoys the pleasure of social control.
>
> Parents can help a teased child cope with and learn from the experience in several ways. By listening sympathetically to the stories of teasing incidents, parents can help the child get beyond just being a victim. By encouraging the child, rather than lecturing, you can help the child see an active role. You can sometimes help a child fix a superficial thing that is attracting the teasing. Parents can help the child develop a strategy to take action without being confrontational. Finally, by not making a big issue of teasing, parents can help the child not feel so upset and vulnerable.

CHAPTER 16

Student responses will vary.

TEST SCORE
Summary

Record your chapter test scores below for a ready progress reference in the *Basic Reading Skills Handbook*.

Unit One: Building Vocabulary	**Score**
1. Recognizing Word Meanings	________
2. Using Word Part Clues	________
3. Using a Dictionary	________
Unit Two: Using Aids to Reading	
4. Previewing the Parts of a Book	________
5. Previewing Individual Selections	________
6. Using Prereading Warm-Ups	________
7. Using Visual Aids	________
Unit Three: Understanding Main Ideas	
8. Reading for the Main Idea	________
9. Main Ideas in Long Selections	________
Unit Four: Finding Information	
10. Reading for Information	________
11. Using SQ3R	________
Unit Five: Interpreting What You Read	
12. Interpreting Fact and Opinion	________
13. Using Inference	________
14. Critical Reading	________
Unit Six: Writing to Read	
15. Underlining, Listing, and Summarizing	________
16. Keeping a Reading Journal	________

Acknowledgments

Text Credits

From *Prentice Hall World Cultures: A Global Mosaic* by Iftikhar Ahmad, Herbert Brodsky, Marylee Susan Crofts © 2005 by Pearson Education, Inc., publishing as Pearson Prentice Hall. Used by permission.

"What Causes Earthquakes," from *Investigating the Earth* by the American Geological Institute. Reprinted by permission of Houghton Mifflin Company.

"Marriage: The State of the Union" by Mike Anton. Copyright © March 31, 2004 Los Angeles Times. Reprinted by permission of TMS Reprints.

"3-foot alligator caught in New York City." Copyright © 1995 Associated Press. Reprinted by permission of Valeo Intellectual Property.

"Two Arizona Scientists Discover New Moons Circling Saturn" Copyright © 1995 Associated Press. Reprinted by permission of Valeo Intellectual Property.

From *Prentice Hall World Geography: Building a Global Perspective* by Thomas Baerwald and Celeste Fraser © 2005 by Pearson Education, Inc., publishing as Pearson Prentice Hall. Used by permission.

"Punishment in Historical Perspective" from *Fundamentals of Criminal Justice* by Steven E. Barkan and George Bryjak. Published by Allyn and Bacon, Boston, MA. Copyright © 2004 by Pearson Education. Reprinted by permission of the publisher.

"Here Come the Brides" by Jon Barrett. Copyright © February 2004 *Glamour* Magazine. Reprinted with permission of the author.

"Choices for Anger Diagram." Reprinted by permission of the authors, Judith K. Beebe and Sandra Nowakowski.

From Berko, Wolvin & Wolvin *Communicating,* 7th Edition. Copyright © 1998 by Houghton Mifflin Company. All Rights Reserved. Used with permission.

"A Second Feminist Wave," from *The Enduring Vision*, Concise Third Edition by Paul S. Boyer et al. Copyright © 1998 by Houghton Mifflin Company. Reprinted by permission.

William Boyes and Michael Melvin, *Economics,* Copyright © 1991 by Houghton Mifflin company. Reprinted with permission.

"Bad Men Can Be Transformed by Women's Love and Bad Men are Dangerous to The Women Who Love Them" from *Gender: Psychological Perspectives*, 3rd Edition by Linda Brannon. Published by Allyn and Bacon, Boston, MA. Copyright © 2002 by Pearson Education. Reprinted by permission of the publisher.

From *Biology: Exploring Life* by Neil A. Campbell, Brad Williamson, Robin J. Heyden © 2004 by Pearson Education, Inc., published as Pearson Prentice Hall. Used by permission.

"The Burden of a Happy Childhood," by Mary Cantwell. Reprinted by permission of the author.

Excerpts from Betty J. Brown and John E. Clow, *Our Business and Economic World*. Copyright by Houghton Mifflin Company. Reprinted by permission.

"1138 Reasons Marriage is Cool" by John Cloud. Copyright © March 8, 2004 Time Inc. Reprinted by permission.

"Teaching About Teasing" by Martha S. Connors. Copyright © June 1998 *Parents Magazine*. Reprinted by permission of the author.

"Mathematical Skills" from *Child Development: Principles and Perspectives*, 1st Edition by Joan Littlefield Cook and Greg Cook. Published by Allyn and Bacon, Boston, MA. Copyright © 2005 by Pearson Education. Reprinted by permission of the publisher.

"Intelligence and Academic Skills" from *Child Development: Principles and Perspectives*, 1st Edition by Joan Cook and Greg Cook. Published by Allyn and Bacon, Boston, MA. Copyright © 2005 by Pearson Education. Reprinted by permission of the publisher.

"Cupid Academy: Matchmaking" by Lisa Takeuchi Cullen. Copyright © February 16, 2004 Time Inc. Reprinted by permission.

"Toughlove—Parents in Crisis," by Dann Denny. Copyright © 1986, *Sunday Herald Times*. Used by permission.

Excerpt from "Should I Have Left an Hour Earlier?" by Judith H. Dobrzynski. Copyright © 1995 by The New York Times Co. Reprinted by permission. \

"Scholarship Scams" from the Federal Trade Commission website.

Child Statistics from The Federal Intergency Forum on Child and Family. Used by permission.

"The Commercialization and Globalization of Rap" from *The Media In Your Life: An Introduction to Mass Communication*, 3rd Edition, by Jean Folkerts and Stephen Lacy. Published by Allyn and Bacon, Boston, MA. Copyright © 2002 by Pearson Education. Reprinted by permission of the publisher.

"MTV" from *The Media In Your Life: An Introduction to Mass Communication*, 3rd Edition, by Jean Folkerts and Stephen Lacy. Published by Allyn and Bacon, Boston, MA. Copyright © 2002 by Pearson Education. Reprinted by permission of the publisher.

"Rock 'n' Roll" from *The Media In Your Life: An Introduction to Mass Communication*, 3rd Edition, by Jean Folkerts and Stephen Lacy. Published by Allyn and Bacon, Boston, MA. Copyright © 2002 by Pearson Education. Reprinted by permission of the publisher.

The Table of Contents page from *The Media In Your Life: An Introduction to Mass Communication*, 3rd Edition, by Jean Folkerts and Stephen Lacy. Published by Allyn and Bacon, Boston, MA. Copyright © 2002 by Pearson Education. Reprinted by permission of the publisher.

"Step by Step, Cutting a Chicken," by Pierre Franey. Copyright © 1986 by The New York Times Co. Reprinted by permission.

Eugene Garcia, "The Extent of Cultural Diversity Among U.S. Students Today," from *Understanding and Meeting the Challenge of Student Cultural Diversity*, 1st Edition. Copyright © 1994 by Houghton Mifflin Company. Used by permission.

Excerpts from *Health* by Bud Getchell, Rusty Pippin, and Jill Varnes. Reprinted by permission of Houghton Mifflin Company.

"Gunfire at Night" by Paul Gordon. Copyright © 1991 *Los Angeles Times*.

From *America the Glorious Republic* by Henry F. Graff. Copyright © 1995 by Houghton Mifflin Company. All rights reserved. Reprinted by permission of McDougal Littell, a division of Houghton Mifflin Company.

"Nonhuman Culture" from *Cultural Anthropology*, 6th Edition by Marvin Harris and Orna Johnson. Published by Allyn and Bacon, Boston, MA. Copyright © 2003 by Pearson Education. Reprinted by permission of the publisher.

Excerpts from *The New Wellness Encyclopedia*, © 1995 by Health Letter Associates. Reprinted by Permission of Houghton Mifflin Company. All rights reserved.

Preface from *Careers as a Rock Musician* by Del and Margaret Hopkins. Copyright © 1993 by Rosen Publishing Group. Reprinted courtesy of the Rosen Publishing Group, 29 East 21st Street, New York, NY 10010.

"How To Spell" by John Irving. Copyright © 1997 The Turnbull Agency, as agent for Garp Enterprises Ltd.

"The 2005 XK—Style, Exhilaration and Performance." Advertisement from www.jaguarusa.com © 2004 Jaguar. Reprinted with permission from Jaguar.

"Predriving Checks" from *Tomorrow's Drivers* by Duane R. Johnson and Don W. Maryott. Copyright © 1986 by Houghton Mifflin Company. Reprinted by permission.

Excerpt from "Building a Powerful Memory" from *The Confident Student*, Second Edition, by Carol Kanar. Copyright © 1995 Houghton Mifflin Company. Reprinted by permission.

"The Good Doctor" by Richard Lacayo © July 3, 1995 Time Inc. Reprinted by permission.

Material from *Psychology* by James D. Laird and Nicholas S. Thompson. Copyright © 1992 by Houghton Mifflin Company. Reprinted by permission.

From *Environmental Science* by Andrew Lapinski, Robert Schoch and Anne Tweed. Copyright © 2002 by Pearson Education, Inc., publishing as Pearson Prentice-Hall. Used by Permission.

"Angry Fathers" by Mel Lazarus. Copyright © 1995, Mell Lazarus. Reprinted by permission.

Excerpt from, "The Lying Game" by Michael Lewis. Copyright © 1995 by The New York Times Co. Reprinted by permission.

"Holding the 911 Line," by Tracy Lorenzano. From *Newsweek*, June 20 © 1994 Newsweek, Inc. All rights reserved. Reprinted by permission.

"Study Techniques" from Richard Marius and Harvey S. Wiener, *The McGraw-Hill College Handbook*, Second Edition. Copyright © 1988 McGraw-Hill Publishing Company.

From *Spaceship Earth: Life Science* by James E. McLaren, John H. Stasik, and Dale F. Levering. © 1981 by Houghton Mifflin Company. All rights reserved. Reprinted by permission of McDougal Littell Inc.

The Table of Contents page from *Racial and Ethnic Relations in America*, 6th edition by S. Dale McLemore, Harriett D. Romo and Susan Gonzalez Baker. Published by Allyn and Bacon, Boston, MA. Copyright © 2001 by Pearson Education. Reprinted by permission of the publisher.

"Eating, Sleeping" from *Cultural Anthropology*, 2nd Edition by Barbara D. Miller. Published by Allyn and Bacon, Boston, MA. Copyright © 2001 by Pearson Education. Reprinted by permission of the publisher.

From *New American Webster's Handy College Dictionary* by Philip D. Morehead and Andrew T. Morehead. Copyright © 1951 (renewed), © 1955, 1956, 1957, 1961 by Albert H. Morehead, 1972, 1981, 1985, 1995 by Philip D. Morehead and Andrew T. Morehead. Used by permission of Dutton Signet, a division of Penguin Group (USA) Inc.

Excerpt from *My first Summer* in the Sierra by John Muir. (Boston: Houghton Mifflin, 1979).

"New Report Sheds Light on Trends and Patterns in Marriage, Divorce, and Cohabitation" from National Center for Health Statistics, Center for Disease Control. Copyright © August 2, 2004.

"Popular Information" from the National Highway Traffic Safety Administration: United States Department of Transportation website.

Excerpt from Mary Beth Norton et. Al., *A People and a Nation*, 5th Edition. Copyright © 1998 by Houghton Mifflin Co. Reprinted by permission.

Index page from *Studying For History* by David Pace, Sharon L. Pugh and Brenda D. Smith. Copyright © 1996 Pearson Education. Reprinted by permission of Pearson Education, Inc.

Excerpts from *History of The World* by Perry et al. Copyright © 1988 by Houghton Mifflin Company. Reprinted with permission of Houghton Mifflin Company.

"Search For A Soul Mate or Love The One You're With?" by Karen S. Peterson. Copyright © May 9, 2003 *USA Today.*

Excerpt from *Pride*, Hughes, Kapor, *Business*, Fourth Edition. Copyright © 1993 by Houghton Mifflin Company. Used with permission.

William M. Pride and O. C. Ferrell, Marketing: *Concepts and Strategies*, Ninth Edition. Copyright © 1995 by Houghton Mifflin Company. Reprinted with permission.

"Paul Newman: It's an Epidemic," by Michael Satchell. Copyright © 1985 by Parade Publications, Inc. Used by permission of the author and the publisher.

"My World Now," by Anna Mae Halgrim Seaver. From *Newsweek*, June 27, 1994. Copyright © 1994 by Anna Mae Halgrim Seaver. Reprinted by permission from Richard Seaver.

"In Praise of the F Word," by Mary Sherry. Copyright © 1991 by Mary Sherry. Appeared in *Newsweek*, May 6, 1991. Used by permission of the author.

From *Shopping Smart* by John Stossel. © 1989 by John Stossel. Used by permission of G.P. Putnam's Sons, a Division of Penguin Group (USA) Inc.

"Zero to Romance in Three Minutes Flat" by Sora Song. Copyright © March 24, 2003 Time Inc. Reprinted by permission.

"How Did They Do That?" by Caroline Sutton © 1984 by Hilltown Books. Reprinted by permission of HarperCollins Publishers Inc.

"State and County Quick Facts" from the U.S. Census Bureau website.

Illustration, "Estimated Number of Aliens" (US Census Bureau) as appeared in *USA Today*, 10/17/86.

"The Importance of Marriage is Being Overlooked" by Linda J. Waite. Copyright © January 1999 *USA Today*. Reprinted by permission.

Excerpt from *The People's Almanac* by Irving Wallace and David Wallenchinsky. Copyright © 1978 by Irving Wallace and David Wallenchinsky. William Morrow and Company.

"Improving Your Academic Performance," from *Manage Your Life* by Robert Williams and James Long. Copyright © 1978 by Stephanie Winston. Reprinted by permission of W. W. Norton & Company.

"Please Straighten Out My Life," by Stephanie Winston. From the book, *Getting Organized*, WW Norton, Publisher. Copyright © 1978 by Stephanie Winston. Reprinted by permission of the author and her literary agent, Susan Ann Protter.

Art and Photo Credits

Page 76: Michael S. Yamashita/CORBIS; **77TR:** The Granger Collection, New York; **77L:** Portrait of Charles Robert Darwin by George Richmond, 1840. Science Source/Photo Researchers, Inc.; **77R:** The Granger Collection, New York; **78L:** Joe McDonald/CORBIS; **78R:** L. Rue/CORBIS; **196:** Laura Dwight; **247:** Tim Kiusalaas/Masterfile Corporation; **248:** Bob Daemmrich Photography, Inc.; **249:** Eric Millette/Index Stock Imagery, Inc.; **250:** Michael Zide; **257:** Michael Nichols/National Geographic Image Collection; **259:** Miles Barton/Nature Picture Library; **282:** Jean-Claude Lejeune; **288:** Courtesy of CIGNA. Photography by Norris McNamara/ibid.; **293:** Public Service Announcements provided courtesy of the Partnership for a Drug-Free America®; **317(both):** Michael Zide; **356:** Garry D. McMichael/Photo Researchers, Inc.; **357:** Garry Black/Masterfile Corporation; **415:** Frank Driggs Collection/Hulton Archive Photos/Getty Images; **478:** Fair Street Pictures; **479:** Courtesy of Diamond Trading Company; **480:** Kevin Fleming/CORBIS.

Author Index

Subject Index